Bloom's Modern Critical Interpretations

Bloom's Modern Critical Interpretations

Walt Whitman's
SONG OF MYSELF

Edited and with an introduction by
Harold Bloom
Sterling Professor of the Humanities
Yale University

CHELSEA HOUSE
PUBLISHERS
A Haights Cross Communications ◆ Company

Philadelphia

©2003 by Chelsea House Publishers, a subsidiary of
Haights Cross Communications.

A Haights Cross Communications ✈ Company

Introduction © 2003 by Harold Bloom.

Printed and bound in the United States of America

10 9 8 7 6 5 4 3 2 1

Library of Congress Cataloging-in-Publication Data

Song of Myself / edited and with an introduction by Harold Bloom.
      p. cm. — (Bloom's modern critical interpretations)
  ISBN 0-7910-7047-6
 1. Whitman, Walt, 1819–1892. Song of Myself. 2. Self in literature.
I. Bloom, Harold. II. Series.
  PS3222.S63 S66 2002
  811'.3—dc21   2002013721

Chelsea House Publishers
1974 Sproul Road, Suite 400
Broomall, PA 19008-0914

http://www.chelseahouse.com

Contributing editor: Janyce Marson

Cover design by Terry Mallon

Layout by EJB Publishing Services

Contents

Editor's Note

My Introduction maps the imagistic and figurative design of *Song of Myself.*

Robert J. Scholnick traces the uses of chemical and evolutionary science, as mediated by Edward Youmans, in Whitman's poem, after which William E. McMahon suggests that "grass" in *Song of Myself* is the husband of "air."

Zong-qi Cai finds Hegelian phenomenology in Whitman's structure, while Mark Bauerlein (to me unpersuasively) sees Whitman as defeated because: "The self is inaccessible."

In two essays, Herbert J. Levine considers the politics of Union in *Song of Myself*, and then meditates upon the poem as Whitman's "American Bible."

Whitman's rhetoric is analyzed by Mark DeLancey as the poet's attempt to achieve interpretive control over his own text, after which Gayle L. Smith finds *Song of Myself* to progress to a conclusion where the reader assumes the role of the poet.

To William Birmingham, the poem invites a spiritual reading, of possibilities for the American self, while Dana Phillips gives us a Bakhtinian reading of *Song of Myself.*

The composition of a New American Bible, by Whitman, returns as a theme in an essay by W.C. Harris, after which Michael D. Sowder reflects upon Whitman's efforts to convert his reader to "the birth of a new American personality."

In this volume's final essay, Bill Hardwig shows Whitman's gradual emancipation from the political doctrine of the Democratic party in favor of his own doctrine of the "open road."

Introduction

Wordsworth celebrated the continuities of hearing, and dreaded the discontinuities of seeing. Emerson, in the defensive discontinuities of seeing, found a path to a more drastic, immediate, and total Sublime than European tradition wished or needed to discover. His greatest disciple, Whitman, an American bard at last, illustrates better than his master, the seer, both the splendor and the disaster of so aboriginal a repression.

My proof-text in Whitman is inevitably *Song of Myself*, but of its fifty-two sections I will concentrate only upon some Sublime centers, though I want to give a mapping-out of the revisionary pattern of the entire poem, for Whitman's romance of the self does follow essentially the model of the British Romantic crisis-poem, though with revealing, Emersonian, further distortions of the model. Employing my own shorthand, this is the pattern of ratios in *Song of Myself*:

Sections:	1–6	*Clinamen*, irony of presence and absence
	7–27	*Tessera*, synecdoche of part for whole
	28–30	*Kenosis*, metonymy of emptying out
	31–38	*Daemonization*, hyperbole of high and low
	39–49	*Askesis*, metaphor of inside vs. outside
	50–52	*Apophrades*, metalepsis reversing early and late

To adumbrate this pattern fully would take too long, but the principal contours can be sketched. The opening six sections are overtly a celebration, and what they celebrate presumably is a return of the repressed, an ecstatic union of soul and self, of primary and antithetical, or, more simply, they celebrate the American Sublime of influx, of Emersonian self-recognition

---

Originally published in *Poetry and Repression: Revisionism from Blake to Stevens*. © 1976 by Yale University Press.

and consequent self-reliance. What ought to be overwhelmingly present in the first six sections is what Whitman, criticizing Keats, referred to as the great poet's "powerful press of himself." But in these opening sections, the reader confronts instead images of absence rather than of presence; indeed, the reader is led inevitably to the bewildered observation that the poet's absence is so sacred a void that his presence never could hope to fill it. Defensively, Whitman opens with a reaction-formation against his precursor Emerson, which rhetorically becomes not the digressiveness or "permanent parabasis" of German Romantic irony, but the sharper, simpler irony of saying one thing while meaning another. Whitman says "I celebrate" and he cunningly means: "I contract and withdraw while asserting that I expand." Thus in section 2, he evades being intoxicated by all outward fragrance, narcissistically preferring "the smoke of my own breath." This characteristic and beautiful evasiveness intensifies in section 4, where the true self, "the Me myself," takes up a stance in total contradiction to the embracings and urgings that the poet only ostensibly celebrates:

> Apart from the pulling and hauling stands what I am,
> Stands amused, complacent, compassionating, idle, unitary,
> Looks down, is erect, or bends an arm on an impalpable certain rest,
> Looking with side-curved head curious what will come next,
> Both in and out of the game and watching and wondering at it.

If this dialectical evasion is a *clinamen* away from Emerson, then precisely what sort of guilt of indebtedness does it seek to void? Is there a crucial enough difference between the Emersonian and Whitmanian versions of an American Sublime so as to allow Whitman enough breathing-space? I need to digress again, upon antithetical theory and the American Sublime, if I am to answer this question and thus be able to get back to mapping *Song of Myself*. What I want to be able to explain is why Whitman, in section 5, resorts to the image of transparency when he describes the embrace between his self and his soul, and why in section 6 he writes so firmly within the materialist tradition of Epicurus and Lucretius. Epicurus said: "The what is unknowable," and Whitman says he cannot answer the child's question: *What is the grass?* Poetically, he does answer, in a magnificent series of tropes, much admired by the hesitant Hopkins, and progressing from the Homeric: "And now it seems to me the beautiful uncut hair of graves" until we are given the astonishing and very American: "This grass is very dark to be from the white heads of old mothers."

In the 1856, Second Edition of *Leaves of Grass*, Whitman addressed Emerson directly, acknowledging that "it is yours to have been the original true Captain who put to sea, intuitive, positive, rendering the first report, to be told less by any report, and more by the mariners of a thousand bays, in each tack of their arriving and departing, many years after this." But Whitman aspired after strength, and so could not abide in this perfectly accurate tribute. In 1863, in a private notation, full of veneration for the precursor, he subtly described Emerson, perhaps better than even Nietzsche was to describe him:

> America in the future, in her long train of poets and writers, while knowing more vehement and luxurious ones, will, I think, acknowledge nothing nearer [than] this man, the actual beginner of the whole procession—and certainly nothing purer, cleaner, sweeter, more canny, none, after all, more thoroughly her own and native. The most exquisite taste and caution are in him, always saving his feet from passing beyond the limits, for he is transcendental of limits, and you see underneath the rest a secret proclivity, American maybe, to dare and violate and make escapades.

By the time he wrote *Specimen Days* (1882), the consequences of misprision had triumphed in Whitman. Emerson was then condemned as having only a gentleman's admiration of power, and as having been an influence upon Whitman just "for a month or so." Five years later, Whitman lied outright, saying: "It is of no importance whether I had read Emerson before starting *L. of G.* or not. The fact happens to be positively that I had *not*." Rather desperately, Whitman went on to say: "*L of G.*'s word is *the body, including all*, including the intellect and soul; E's word is mind (or intellect or soul)." Though I will return to this last remark of Whitman's later, in studying his opening swerve away from Emerson, I wish to end these citations from Whitman-on-Emerson by quoting the truest of them, again from *Specimen Days*:

> The best part of Emersonianism is, it breeds the giant that destroys itself. Who wants to be any man's mere follower? lurks behind every page. No teacher ever taught, that has so provided for his pupil's setting up independently—no truer evolutionist.

Here, Whitman has provided antithetical theory with the inevitable trope for Emersonianism or the American Sublime: "it breeds the giant that destroys itself." We need not be surprised to discover that the trope was, however, Emerson's own invention, crucial in the essay *Self-Reliance* (which Whitman certainly *had* read before he wrote *Song of Myself*):

> I affect to be intoxicated with sights and suggestions, but I am not intoxicated. My giant goes with me wherever I go.

(...)

I return finally to the opening six sections of *Song of Myself*, with their defensive swerve away from Emerson, even as they appear to celebrate an Emersonian realization of the self. Whitman, not a poet-of-ideas like Emerson, but more traditionally a poet (however odd that sounds), seems to have known implicitly that a poetic representation of a desire tends to be stronger (that is, less limiting) than a poetic representation of an act. *Song of Myself*, in its beginnings, therefore substitutes the desires for union between split parts of the self, and between self and soul, for the acts of union proper, whatever those might be. Whitman wishes to originate his own mode, but he cannot do so without some discontinuity with Emerson, a prophet of discontinuity, and how do you cast off an influence that itself denounces all influence? Emersonianism urges itself to breed a giant that will destroy itself, but this most gigantic of its giants painfully found himself anticipated in nearly every trope, and in every movement of the spirit, a pain that Whitman shared with Thoreau.

It is evident, both from the opening emphases in *Song of Myself* and from Whitman's comments in *Specimen Days*, on the rival words of precursor and ephebe, that Whitman's intended swerve from Emerson is to deny Emerson's distinction between the Soul and Nature, in which Nature includes all of the NOT ME, "both nature and art, all other men and my own body." Whitman's ME must include his own body, or so he would persuade us. He writes what in 1881 he would title at last *Song of Myself*, and not *Song of the Soul* or even *Song of My Soul*. But the embrace between his soul and his self in section 5, which makes the axis of things appear not opaque but transparent, oddly makes "you my soul" the active partner, and the self, "the other I am," wholly passive in this courtship. If we translate soul as "character" and self as "personality," then we would find it difficult to identify so passive a personality with "Walt Whitman, a kosmos, of Manhattan the son, / Turbulent, fleshy, sensual, eating, drinking and breeding" of section 24. Clearly, there is a division in Whitman between two elements in the self, as well as between self and soul, and it is the first of these divisions that matters, humanly and poetically. Indeed, it was from the first of these divisions that I believe Emerson initially rescued Whitman, thus making it possible for Whitman to become a poet. The "real me" or "me myself" in Whitman could not bear to be touched, ever, except by the maternal trinity of night, death, and the sea, while Walt Whitman, one of the roughs, learned from Emerson to cry: "Contact!" There is a sublime pathos in Whitman making his Epicurean *clinamen* away from Emerson by overproclaiming the body. Emerson had nothing to say about two subjects and two subjects only, sex and death, because he was too healthy-minded to believe that there was much to say about either. Emerson had no sexual problems, and was a Stoic about death.

I return to mapping *Song of Myself*, with its implicit contrast that Whitman, gloriously and plangently, always had much too much to say about sex and death, being in this the ancestor not only of Hart Crane and, perhaps surprisingly, of Wallace Stevens and, these days, of Ammons and Ashbery, but also of such prose obfuscators of sex and death as Hemingway and his egregious ephebe, Norman Mailer. Whitman, surpassing all his descendants, makes of a linked sex-and-death a noble synecdoche for all of existence, which is the figurative design of sections 7–27 of *Song of Myself*. A universalizing flood tide of reversals-into-the-opposite reaches a great climax in section 24, which is an antithetical completion of the self without rival in American poetry, astonishing both for its dignity and its pathos, and transcending any other modern poet's attempt to think and represent by synecdoche. The reader cannot know whether to admire this proclamation more for its power or for its precision:

> Unscrew the locks from the doors!
> Unscrew the doors themselves from their jambs!
>
> Whoever degrades another degrades me,
> And whatever is done or said returns at last to me.
>
> Through me the afflatus surging and surging, through me the
>   current and index.
>
> I speak the pass-word primeval, I give the sign of democracy,
> By God! I will accept nothing which all cannot have their
>   counterpart of on the same terms.

Through me many long dumb voices,
Voices of the interminable generations of prisoners and slaves,
Voices of the diseas'd and despairing and of thieves and
        dwarfs,
Voices of the threads that connect the stars, and of wombs
        and of the father-stuff,
And of the rights of them the others are down upon,
Of the deform'd, trivial, flat, foolish, despised,
Fog in the air, beetles rolling balls of dung.

We can say of this astonishing chant that as completing synecdoche it verges on emptying-out metonymy, reminding us of the instability of all tropes and of all psychic defenses. Primarily, Whitman's defense in this passage is a fantasy reversal, in which his own fear of contact with other selves is so turned that no outward overthrow of his separateness is possible. It is as though he were denying denial, negating negation, by absorbing every outward self, every outcast of society, history, and even of nature. To say that one will accept nothing which all cannot have their counterpart of on the same terms is indeed to say that one will accept no overthrow from outside oneself, no negation or denial. Whitman, with the genius of his enormous drive towards antithetical completion, can be judged to end the *tessera* phase of his poem in the remarkable triad of sections 25–27. For in section 25, nature strikes back against the poet, yet he is strong enough to sustain himself, but in 26–27 hie exhaustedly begins to undergo a kind of passive slide-down of spirit that precludes the fierce *kenosis* or emptying-out of his poethood in sections 28–30. At the end of 27, Whitman confesses: "To touch my person to some one else's is about as much as I can stand." The Whitmanian *kenosis*, in 28–30, appears to make of masturbation a metonymic reduction of the self, where touch substitutes for the whole being, and a pathetic salvation is sought through an exaltation of the earth that the poet has moistened:

A minute and a drop of me settle my brain,
I believe the soggy clods shall become lovers and lamps,
And a compend of compends is the meat of a man or woman,
And a summit and flower there is the feeling they have for
        each other,
And they are to branch boundlessly out of that lesson
        until it becomes omnific,
And until one and all shall delight us, and we them.

This is the prelude to the most awesome repression in our literature, the greatest instance yet of the American Sublime, sections 31–38. Rather than map the glories of this Sublime, I will examine instead the violent descent into the abyss that culminates it in section 38. Having merged both the fathering force and the universal brotherhood into himself, with terrifying eloquence ("I am the man, I suffer'd, I was there"; and "Agonies are one of my changes of garments"), Whitman pays the fearful price of Emersonian Compensation. Nothing indeed is gotten for nothing:

> Enough! enough! enough!
> Somehow I have been stunn'd. Stand back!
> Give me a little time beyond my cuff'd head, slumbers, dreams, gaping,
> I discover myself on the verge of a usual mistake.
> That I could forget the mockers and insults!
> That I could forget the trickling tears and the blows of the bludgeons and hammers!
> That I could look with a separate look on my own crucifixion and bloody crossing.
>
> I remember now,
> I resume the overstaid fraction,
> The grave of rock multiplies what has been confided to it, or to any graves,
> Corpses rise, gashes heal, fastenings roll from me.

Emerson had prophesied a Central Man who would reverse the "great Defeat" of Christ, insisting that "we demand Victory." Whitman, more audacious even than his precursor, dares to present himself both as a repetition of the great Defeat and as the Victory of a Resurrection: "I troop forth replenish'd with supreme power, one of an average unending procession." What are we to do with a hyperbolical Sublime this outrageous? Whitman too is saying: "*I and the Abyss*," despite the self-deception of that "average unending procession." But Whitman's repression is greater, as it has to be, since a crucial part of its anteriority is a primal fixation upon Emerson, a fixation that I want to explore in the conclusion of this chapter once I have concluded my sketchy mapping of the later ratios in *Song of Myself*.

Sections 39–49 are an attempt at a sublimating consolidation of the self, in which Whitman presents us with his version of the most characteristic of High Romantic metaphors, his self as inside reciprocally addressing the natural world as a supposedly answering outside. The final or reductive form of this perspectivizing is summed up in an appropriately entitled poem of Wallace Stevens, *The American Sublime*:

> But how does one feel?
> One grows used to the weather,
>
> The landscape and that;
> And the sublime comes down
> To the spirit itself,
>
> The spirit and space,
> The empty spirit
> In vacant space.

That is to say: the Sublime comes down to the Abyss in me inhabiting the Abyss of space. Whitman's version of this coming down completes his great *askesis*, in section 49:

> I hear you whispering there O stars of heaven,
> O suns—O grass of graves—O perpetual transfers and promotions,
> If you do not say any thing how can I say any thing?
> . . . .
> Of the turbid pool that lies in the autumn forest,
> Of the moon that descends the steeps of the soughing twilight,
> Toss, sparkles of day and dusk—toss on the black stems that
>   decay in the muck,
> Toss to the moaning gibberish of the dry limbs.
>
> I ascend from the moon, I ascend from the night,
> I perceive that the ghastly glimmer is noonday sunbeams reflected,
> And debouch to the steady and central from the offspring
>   great or small.

The steadiness of the central is reached here only through the rhetorical equivalent of sublimation, which is metaphor, the metaphor of two lights, sun and moon, with the sun necessarily dominating, and taking as its tenor the Emersonian "steady and central." I return to the formula for poetic sublimation ventured earlier in this discourse. The sublimating ratio is a limitation because what it concentrates is being evaded, that is, is remembered only in order not to be presented, with something else substituted in the presentation. Whitman does not present what he is remembering, his dream of divination, of being a dazzling sunrise greater than the merely natural sun. Instead of this autonomous splendor, he accepts now a perspectivizing, a balancing of "sparkles of day and dusk." His restitution For this *askesis* comes in his great poem's close, in sections 50–52, which form a miraculous transumption of all that has gone before. Yet the Whitmanian metaleptic reversal differs crucially from the Wordsworthian–Tennysonian model, in that it places the burden upon the reader, rather than upon the poet. It is the reader, and not the poet, who is challenged directly to make his belatedness into an earliness. Whitman was to perfect this challenge in *Crossing Brooklyn Ferry*, appropriately called *Sun-Down Poem* when it first appeared in the second *Leaves of Grass*, in 1856. Here, in *Song of Myself*, the challenge is made explicit at the close of section 51: "Will you speak before I am gone? will you prove already too late?" Nowhere in Emerson (and I concede to no reader in my fanatical love of Emerson) is there so strong a representation of the Central Man who is coming as there is in Whitman's self-presentation in section 52. I would select this as the greatest of Emerson's prophecies of the Central Man, from the journals, April 1846:

> He or That which in despair of naming aright, some have called the *Newness*,—as the Hebrews did not like to pronounce the word,—he lurks, he hides, he who is success, reality, joy, power,—that which constitutes Heaven, which reconciles impossibilities, atones for shortcomings, expiates sins or makes them virtues, buries in oblivion the crowded historical past, sinks religions, philosophies, nations, persons to legends; reverses the scale of opinion, of fame; reduces sciences to opinion, and makes the thought of the moment the key to the universe, and the egg of history to come.
>
> ... 'Tis all alike,—astronomy, metaphysics, sword, spade, pencil, or instruments and arts yet to be invented,—this is the inventor, the worth-giver, the worth. This is He that shall come; or, if He come not, nothing comes: He that disappears in the moment when we go to celebrate Him. If we go to burn those that blame our celebration, He appears in them. The Divine Newness. Hoe and spade, sword and pen, cities, pictures,

gardens, laws, bibles, are prized only because they were means he sometimes used. So with astronomy, music, arithmetic, castes, feudalism,—we kiss with devotion these hems of his garment,— we mistake them for Him; they crumble to ashes on our lips.

The Newness is Influx, or fresh repression, lurking and hiding, imaged in depth, in burying and in sinking. This daemonic force then projects the past and introjects the future, and yet *not now*, but only in the realm of what *shall come*: "He ... disappears in the moment when we go to celebrate Him," and more than his garment would crumble to ashes on our lips. Whitman, as this Newness, is even more splendidly elusive:

> The spotted hawk swoops by and accuses me, he complains of
> 　　my gab and my loitering.
>
> I too am not a bit tamed, I too am untranslatable,
> I sound my barbaric yawp over the roofs of the world.
>
> The last scud of day holds back for me,
> It flings my likeness after the rest and true as any on the
> 　　shadow'd wilds,
> It coaxes me to the vapor and the dusk.
>
> I depart as air, I shake my white locks at the runaway sun,
> I effuse my flesh in eddies, and drift it in lacy jags.
>
> I bequeath myself to the dirt to grow from the grass I love,
> If you want me again look for me under your boot-soles.
>
> You will hardly know who I am or what I mean,
> But I shall be good health to you nevertheless,
> And filter and fibre your blood.
>
> Failing to fetch me at first keep encouraged,
> Missing me one place search another,
> I stop somewhere waiting for you.

The hawk accuses Whitman of belatedness, of "loitering," but the poet is one with the hawk, "untranslatable" in that his desire is perpetual, always transcending act. There, in the twilight, Whitman arrests the lateness of the day, dissolving the presentness of the present, and effusing his own presence until it is air and earth. As the atmosphere we are to breathe, the ground we are to walk, the poet introjects our future, and is somewhere up ahead, waiting for us to catch up. So far ahead is he on our mutual quest, that he can afford to stop, though he will not tell us precisely where. His dominant trope remains the grass, but this trope is now transumptive, for it is grass not yet grown but "to grow." Implicit in such a trope is the more-than-Emersonian promise that this Central Man will not disappear "in the moment when we go to celebrate him."

I end by returning to Whitman's American Sublime of sections 31–38, with specific reference to the grand march of section 33, where the poet says: "I am afoot with my vision." Here is a part of this audacious mounting into the Sublime:

> Solitary at midnight in my back yard, my thoughts gone from
>   me a long while,
> Walking the old hills of Judaea with the beautiful, gentle God
>   by my side,
> Speeding through space, speeding through heaven and the
>   stars,
> Speeding amid the seven satellites and the broad ring, and the
>   diameter of eighty thousands miles,
> Speeding with tail'd meteors, throwing fire-balls like the rest,
> Carrying the crescent child that carries its own full mother in
>   its belly,
>
> Storming, enjoying, planning, loving, cautioning,
> Backing and filling, appearing and disappearing,
> I tread day and night such roads.
>
> I visit the orchards of spheres and look at the product,
> And look at quintillions ripen'd and look at quintillions green.
>
> I fly those flights of a fluid and swallowing soul,
> My course runs below the soundings of plummets.
>
> I help myself to material and immaterial,
> No guard can shut me off, no law prevent me.

As an hyperbolical progression, this sequence is matched only by its misprision or sublime parody, the flight of the Canon Aspirin in *Notes toward a Supreme Fiction*. Whitman's angelic flight breaks down the distinction between material and immaterial, because his soul, as he precisely says, is "fluid and swallowing." Similarly, the Canon's angelic flight breaks down the limits between fact and thought, but the Canon's soul being more limited, the later angelic flight fails exactly where Whitman's cannot fail. The Canon imposes orders upon reality, but Whitman discovers or uncovers orders, because he is discovering himself (even though he does not uncover himself, despite his constant assertions that he is about to do so). I vary an earlier question in order to conclude this discourse. Why is Whitman's American Sublime larger and stronger than either the Sublime of his precursor, Emerson, or the Sublime of his ephebe, Stevens? In the language of misprision, this means: why and how is Whitman's poetic repression greater and more forceful than that of the other major figures in his own tradition?

Whitman's ego, in his most Sublime transformations, wholly absorbs and thus pragmatically forgets the fathering force, and presents instead the force of the son, of his own self or, in Whitman's case, perhaps we should say of his own selves. Where Emerson *urges* forgetfulness of anteriority, Whitman more strenuously *does* forget it, though at a considerable cost. Emerson says: "*I and the Abyss*"; Whitman says: "*The Abyss of Myself.*" The second statement is necessarily more Sublime and, alas, even more American.

ROBERT J. SCHOLNICK

"The Password Primeval": Whitman's Use of Science in "Song of Myself"

Seemingly reversing Shelley's dictum that "poets are the unacknowledged legislators of the world," Walt Whitman, in the preface to the 1855 edition of *Leaves of Grass*, asserted that scientists are "the lawgivers of poets and their construction underlies the structure of every perfect poem." Rejecting the image of antagonism usually thought to characterize their relationship, Whitman used sexual imagery to depict a harmonious and productive coming together of poet and scientist: "No matter what rises or is uttered," the scientists "sent the seed of the conception of it ... of them and by them stand visible proofs of souls..... always of their fatherstuff must be begotten the sinewy races of bards. If there shall be love and content between the father and the son and if the greatness of the son is the exuding of the greatness of the father there shall be love between the poet and the man of demonstrable science. In the beauty of poems are the tuft and final applause of science."[1] Typically, the Whitman persona characterizes himself as a virile impregnator of women, but here the poet gives that function to the scientist, who stands first in the order of conception. Out of his "fatherstuff" are born the "sinewy races of bards." The conceptions of the scientist provide the poet with the originating ideas or "seed" of poetic ideas. Still, the poet completes the process; his art transmutes scientific conceptions so that in the aesthetic realm of poetry they have their most complete realization, their "tuft and final applause."

From *Studies in the American Renaissance* (1986). © 1986 by Robert J. Scholnick.

As if to declare that he had remained true to this conception of poetry throughout his career, Whitman, in one of his last poems, "L. of G.'s Purport" (1891), defined in cosmological terms the essential purpose of his life's work, "Begun in ripen'd youth and steadily pursued":

> Haughty this song, its words and scope,
> To span vast realms of space and time,
> Evolution—the cumulative—growths and generations. (pp. 652–53)

Here Whitman identifies evolution as the central idea in his poetry. The theory of evolution—or the development hypothesis as it was known in the years before Darwin—touched on fundamental questions of the origins of the chemical elements that make up the earth, the nature of man, and the relationship of both to a universe whose unimaginable dimensions, its "vast realms of space and time," were just being realized through the work of such scientists as Lyell in geology and the two Herschells in astronomy. While evolution was central to Whitman, his poetry, as Joseph Beaver has shown, demonstrates a remarkable knowledge of the full range of contemporary scientific ideas, particularly of astronomy.[2] And in *Walt Whitman and the Body Beautiful*, Harold Aspiz has shown how Whitman drew from a wide variety of scientific and psuedo-scientific medical sources in creating his powerful poetic persona.[3] Yet, although he used them extensively, scientific ideas do not obtrude in Whitman's poetry, but form an integral part of a unified poetic vision. His friend and early critic John Burroughs appropriately praised his "thorough assimilation of the modern sciences, transmuting them into strong poetic nutriment."[4] Sharing in the wonder occasioned by the revolutionary discoveries of the day—in astronomy, geology, biology, physiology, energetics, and other fields—Whitman made use of scientific ideas to support his extraordinary conception of the scope and power of the poet. "Great is the faith of the flush of knowledge and of the investigation of the depths of qualities and things," he wrote in the 1855 preface. "Cleaving and circling here swells the soul of the poet yet is president of itself always" (p. 15). Despite Whitman's numerous testimonies to their centrality, many scholars have discounted the importance of scientific ideas in his work. For instance, in his thorough review of Whitman's sources, *The Foreground of Leaves of Grass*, Floyd Stovall concludes that "there is no evidence in the poems of the 1855 edition that anything more than the romance of science had interested him seriously."[5] Here I will proceed from the opposite assumption and take the poet at his word. In asserting that science provided the "seed of the conception" of poetic ideas, Whitman established an essential context for understanding his work. To expand our knowledge of the broad range of scientific ideas available to Whitman, I will consider his relationship with Edward Livingston Youmans (1821–87), who came to be recognized as the preeminent expositor of science during the thirty-year period beginning in the mid–1850s. My purpose will be to investigate some of the ways that Whitman in "Song of Myself" was able to make use of the leading scientific concepts which Youmans expounded and with which he came to be identified.

Near the end of his life, in conversation with Horace Traubel, the mention of Youmans' name brought from Whitman a fine appreciation of the scientific habit of mind: "I like the scientific spirit—the holding off, the being sure but not too sure, the willingness to surrender ideas when the evidence is against them: this is ultimately fine—it always keeps the way beyond open—always gives life, thought, affection, the whole man, a chance to try over again after a mistake—after a wrong guess."[6] It may be surprising to us that Whitman found in the scientific spirit a life-enhancing quality, but clearly he was stimulated by its experimental, pragmatic, and non-judgmental method. And it is significant that he associated the scientific method with Youmans. So far as I know, the only scholar to suggest the possibility that Youmans may have served as a source for Whitman is Roger Asselineau. In discussing the sources for Whitman's scientific ideas, Asselineau speculates that "Whitman might also have read the works of Edward Livingston Youmans whom he met several times."[7]

Now evidence has come to light establishing Youmans as an important source for Whitman's understanding of his most important scientific idea, evolution. Edmund Clarence Stedman, the New York poet and critic, makes this claim in the course of a previously unpublished 1907 letter to Bliss Perry, the author of the first objective biography of Whitman. In discussing a subject of some contemporary concern, Whitman's alleged defalcation in 1857 on a loan of $200 from the biographer James Parton, Stedman wrote: "I only knew that Prof. Youmans, who lodged on the same floor with Whitman in Centre Street, and inspired Whitman's eloquent passages on Evolution, told me of the Parton episode, and of various other things, when I was beginning my [November 1880 *Scribner's Monthly*] article [on Whitman]; that I made the journey to Newburyport, visited Parton and his young wife, and that Parton told me at full length, and with much display of feeling, the whole story. Either Youmans or Parton, and probably both, told me that there were two notes and that finally Parton brought suit and was unable to find any property worth attaching."[8] In its mention of "two notes," Stedman's letter adds a new twist to a tangled, unhappy story. But of far greater significance is his unequivocal assertion that Youmans "inspired Whitman's eloquent passages on Evolution."

Of course, we can never know with absolute certainty precisely what ideas—scientific or otherwise—Whitman may have learned from Youmans or, for that matter, Youmans from Whitman. By their very nature, all studies of sources and influences are imprecise. Nevertheless, a review of Youmans' early writings and lectures does provide us with a much fuller understanding of the scientific ideas available to Whitman than we currently have. This, in turn, will enable us better to comprehend the poetic flowering which came from the scientific "fatherstuff" which, by his own admission, meant so much to the poet. In "Song of Myself" he made use of many of the scientific concepts lucidly and vigorously expounded by Youmans, including a categorical rejection of the Cartesian dualism or the mind-body separation; an enthusiastic affirmation of evolution as a process at work throughout the cosmos; an exposition of the power of the subconscious mind, which he identified as a source of the most far-reaching works of artistic creation, and a fervent celebration of the principles of the conservation and correlation of energy. Also, our knowledge of Youmans' own sources—particularly in evolutionary theory—will be helpful to us in identifying other likely sources for Whitman.

I. WHITMAN AND YOUMANS

Whitman first came to know Youmans early in 1842 when both lived for a time at the boarding house operated by a Mrs. Chipman on Centre Street in New York.[9] Only twenty-three, Whitman was the dashing editor of a New York daily, the *Aurora*. The impoverished Youmans had come to the city from his home in Saratoga County near Albany to seek treatment for an eye disease which caused him long periods of sightlessness and threatened to blind him permanently. In an *Aurora* leader dated 19 March 1842, "New York Boarding Houses," Whitman mentions "Y.... from Saratoga Springs" as one of the boarders who regularly gathered around the breakfast table of "Mrs. C."[10] Youmans' biographer, John Fiske, reports that Whitman engaged Youmans to supply a column of "Saratoga Correspondence" for the *Aurora*.[11]

There is a remarkable similarity in the careers of these two writers. Almost exact contemporaries, both were comparatively poor young men who came to the city from rural areas of New York State and found there the resources for extraordinary intellectual growth. Even while supporting himself through such jobs as writing for the *Aurora*, Youmans continued the heroic process of self-education which he had begun at home. Despite his blindness, he conducted chemical experiments with the aid of his sister, Eliza

Ann, and of course, "read"—or was read to—constantly. In 1846, despite periods of blindness, he had largely completed a history of progress in discovery and invention, a project he did not complete because the publisher George Putnam released a similar volume, *The World's Progress*, before he could complete his.[12] It is likely that Whitman had Youmans in mind in writing "A Few Words to the Young Men of Brooklyn," published in the *Daily Eagle* on 17 December 1846: "The biographies of men of science present accounts of people born and nurtured amid the deepest poverty and toil, with hardly money enough to buy a sheet of paper...who yet...acquired learning far beyond others who were living in comfort and enjoying all the advantages of schools.... And more than this: not only have poverty and suffering and weakness been overcome by those bent on advancing, but even blindness and deafness which seem to present unsurmountable obstacles, have not been able to stop the exertions of the knowledge-seeking spirit."[13] And so Whitman urged the young men to seek knowledge and avoid the evils of gambling and drink.

In 1851, with the sight of one eye at last partially restored, Youmans published a surprisingly successful text, *The Class-Book of Chemistry*, which emphasized the importance of the experimental method.[14] At this time he began his career as a lyceum lecturer, which would take him throughout the country. Fiske used procreative imagery similar to that of Whitman's 1855 preface to describe Youmans' work as lecturer: "I believe it is safe to say that few things were done in all those years of more vital and lasting benefit to the American people than this broadcast sowing of the seeds of scientific thought."[15]

Not an original investigator, Youmans nevertheless possessed a true genius for synthesizing the work of leading scientists and cogently presenting their leading ideas to the public at large. Fiske credited him with the ability to move

> on a plane so near to that of the originators that he seized at once upon the grand scheme of thought as it was developed, made it his own, and brought to its interpretation and diffusion such a happy combination of qualities as one seldom meets with.... Youmans ... [could] grasp the newest scientific thought so surely and firmly that he seemed to have entered into the innermost mind of its author [and] speak to the general public in a convincing and stimulating way that had no parallel. This was the secret of his power, and there can be no question that his influence in educating the American people to receive the doctrine of evolution was great and widespread.[16]

A prolific writer, Youmans published such works as *Alcohol and the Constitution of Man* (1854), *Chemical Atlas* (1854), *Chemical Chart* (1855), *The Hand-book of Household Science* (1857), *The Correlation and Conservation of Forces* (edited, 1864), and *The Culture Demanded by Modern Life* (edited, 1867). He conceived and edited for the Appletons the successful International Scientific Library, a series of commissioned volumes by distinguished scientists explaining their work to the layman. He founded *Popular Science Monthly* in 1872, and edited the magazine until his death in 1887. Both as editor and regular essayist, he developed the magazine into a major instrument in the "crusade for scientific autonomy and respectability" that he led in those years.[17] In large part through his efforts, the Appleton firm became the country's leading publisher of scientific works.

A free-thinker religiously, Youmans sought to liberate Americans from the imprisoning theological orthodoxies of the time. But while separating himself from conventional religious worship, he celebrated science almost as a new revelation, giving rise to a force capable at once of improving man's lot on earth through the application of rational principles in such areas as agriculture, education, industry, and mental illness, and expanding his appreciation of the sublime workings of the Creator by opening to him stupendous insights into the orderly working of the cosmos. In his tireless campaign for educational reform, he was conscious of speaking for a new class of intellectual leaders, men who did not have the benefit of formal higher education with its rigid classical curriculum: "The numerous instances of self-made men, who, with no external assistance, have risen to intellectual eminence ... testify to the power of the spontaneous and self-determining tendencies of human character."[18] Whitman had made a similar point in his *Daily Eagle* leader in urging the young men of Brooklyn to continue their studies, even if they did not have the advantages of formal schooling. Whitman too was such a "self-made" and self-educated man and on one level "Song of Myself" may be read as a testimony to the "spontaneous and self-determing tendencies of human character."

Yet, early in the 1860s Youmans became the chief American disciple of Herbert Spencer, whose work he brought to the Appletons. There can be little doubt that, as he devoted himself to promoting Spencer's rigid, allembracing system, he was less willing to trust the "spontaneous and self-determining tendencies" of his own character.[19] Eventually, the careers of the two writers took different directions: Professor Youmans, as the responsible editor of *Popular Science Monthly* and editorial advisor to the prosperous Appleton publishing firm, moved toward conservative respectability. Whitman, of course, refused to repudiate anything, but, as in "Song of Myself," proclaimed his willingness to "beat the gong of revolt, and stop with fugitives and them that plot and conspire" (p. 50).

As might be expected, at some point the two parted company, and with a great deal of bitterness on Youmans' part. Fiske wrote that "in later years Youmans always maintained that Walt was an arrant humbug, and that his 'barbaric yawp' and obtrusive filthiness were assumed purely for pelf, after he had found that polite writing would not pay his bills."[20] No doubt in referring to Whitman's "inability to pay his bills," Fiske had in mind the unfortunate Parton affair. But Whitman's alleged defalcation would occur in 1857, some fifteen years after the two first became acquainted at Mrs. Chipman's establishment, and in the small, heady world of New York writers and reformers of the 1840s and 1850s there would have been ample opportunity for the two to come together and share ideas.

Both, for instance, were active in the temperance movement. Youmans' first book, *The Scientific Basis of Prohibition*, appeared in 1846, the same year that Whitman reprinted *Franklin Evans*, his temperance novel of 1842, in the *Daily Eagle*, where he wrote: "We consider temperance one of the grand regenerators of the age; and that all who, in truth of heart, labor in its promulgation, deserve well of heaven and men."[21] Youmans' 1854 temperance pamphlet, *Alcohol and the Constitution of Man*, was published by the phrenological firm of Fowler and Wells, which distributed *Leaves of Grass* the next year. Youmans, like Whitman, would come to disavow his commitment to temperance, but like Whitman, he continued to advocate the principles of sound nutrition and physical hygiene, and he lectured and wrote on these subjects.

The involvement of both writers in such reforms as temperance and diet should be seen in the context of the extraordinary social optimism of those pre-Civil War years in New York. It was a time when, to use the title of an 1854 address by George Bancroft. "The Necessity, the Reality, and the Promise of the Progress of the Human Race" was widely believed in.[22] Observing the manifold benefits of free institutions, many Americans, as Russel Nye has written, were convinced that the "whole force of history...pointed toward the United States as the climax of a divinely-ordained march toward human betterment."[23]

In this environment the questions to be debated centered on how best to arrange social institutions and realize other reforms so as to accelerate the grand march of progress. Youmans participated in these discussions, attending meetings in Brooklyn "where the subject of the reorganization of society was a leading topic of conversation. At these gatherings questions of reform were presented in a broader light and involved more fundamental changes than the antislavery and temperance discussions to which Edward was accustomed.... [He formed lasting] friendships...in those enthusiastic days when the immediate and indefinite educability of everybody, mentally and morally, was believed in without reserve—when generous zeal believed that a new heaven and a new earth were at hand."[24] Surprisingly for one who would become the chief American disciple of Spencer, Youmans was for a time attracted to the socialism of Fourier, becoming a member of a commune, the North American Phalanx, founded on the principles of Fourier. Whitman apparently remained unconvinced by Fourierism, writing of it critically in the *New Orleans Daily Crescent*.[25] However, as Gay Wilson Allen has written, "in basic ideas and imagery," the "democratic idealism" of Whitman resembles the "social optimism" of *The Social Destiny of Man* (1840) by Albert Brisbane, the leading American advocate of Fourier.[26]

In this visionary atmosphere Youmans came to see science as the means for realizing that "new heaven and ... new earth" thought to be "at hand." One student of his career has written that his "glowing enthusiasm for science is understandable only by setting it against a period wherein science progressed by leaps and bounds. Youmans fought for the dissemination of scientific ideas, constanly directed people's consciousness towards them, battled tooth-and-nail with older cultural traditions of theologians and conservatives, and shared the mystic belief that science would lead to eventual perfection. A channel through which science was diffused to the common man was Edward Livingston Youmans, rationalizer of the new order."[27] Similarly, Whitman created a poetic persona who could directly communicate to the reader a visionary faith in man's creative power. It is likely that Whitman, who sought to keep abreast of the astounding developments in science, followed closely the career of his once-blind former associate on the *Aurora* as he courageously set out to reveal the new science to the people.

In fact, one scholar, Joseph Jay Rubin, has speculated that Whitman is the author of a letter published in the *New York Times* on 23 February 1853, praising Youmans' lectures and urging that he be brought to Brooklyn to speak. In these lectures, one on "Chemistry of Vegetable Growth" and one on "Chemistry of Foods and Digestion," Youmans "talked of ideas from the recently translated *Kosmos* of Baron von Humboldt."[28] While there is no conclusive proof that the letter to the *Times*, which was signed "W" and sent from Brooklyn, was written by Whitman, its enthusiastic style and largeness of vision might well be described as "Whitmanesque," as this excerpt suggests: "It is difficult to comprehend how the least cultivated mind can be made acquainted with the beautiful harmonies that pervade every department of nature without being excited to the highest degree of wonder and admiration. There is so much in those divine laws by which Omniscience governs the universe, so much to the arrest the attention, fix the thoughts, and incite to the profoundest adoration all thinking minds, that it is a wonder there can be one rational being indifferent to the revelations of science."[29]

For the author of this letter—as for Youmans—the "revelations" of the new science led naturally to a sublime and spiritual wonder at the scientific principles, the "divine laws," by which the Creator "governs the universe." There could be no conflict between science and religion. As Youmans wrote, "For the view long held as religious [the Mosaic account of creation] science has substituted a view that is more eminently religious [evolution].... And may it not be that the constructors of the philosophy of evolution are entitled to a leading place among the evangelists of our time?"[30] Since evolution assumed such a large place in the work of both writers, it will be useful, before treating Youmans' career as lecturer and writer, to investigate his immediate sources for evolution.

II. EVOLUTIONARY THEORY

Fiske has written that well before the publication of Darwin's *Origin of the Species* in 1859 evolution burst upon this generation as

> an idea of the first magnitude ... the greatest thought of science. By showing Nature to be a family it gave to classification genetic relationship as its true basis. To education it indicated a new way and the best. It made it possible to write Nature's history backward to the primitive chaos—as wonderful in all its dormant possibilities as the cosmos it contained. It made the universe one in a new sense, for it bound together, in a single web of causation worlds, continents, life, mind. To have lived when this prodigious truth was advanced, debated, established, was a privilege rare in the centuries. The inspiration of seeing the old isolating mists dissolve and reveal the convergence of all branches of knowledge is something that can hardly be known to men of a later generation, inheritors of what this age has won.[31]

For a generation that experienced the loss of traditional religious faith, evolutionary theory came with the force of a new revelation, one which brought startling unity to the universe, for it "bound together" the physical world and "mind."

Unmistakably, the work that first brought a coherent theory of evolution to Youmans' attention was Robert Chambers' *Vestiges of the Natural History of Creation*, published anonymously in London in 1844. We know that not long after its publication it was read to the blind Youmans at home in Saratoga Springs and "was much talked of in the family."[32] Written by an amateur in science (Chambers was an Edinburgh publisher and writer),

Vestiges contained many superficial errors, making it an inviting target for orthodox experts in science and theology. The fortunate result was that evolution became a subject of public controversy in England and America.

In the fall of 1847 the subject was very much on the minds of the general public when the distinguished Harvard naturalist Louis Agassiz came to New York to deliver a series of lectures. Agassiz was expected to offer the decisive word on this vexing question. At last in the sixth lecture, Fiske wrote, "he felt constrained to turn aside from his systematic exposition" and scornfully attacked *Vestiges* as "entirely unworthy of notice by any serious scientific man." Then Agassiz proceeded to "illustrate his favorite conception of the truths of science as the thoughts of God." Youmans was so rapt up in the proceedings that he not only attended the lectures but also requested that the full transcript, as published in the *Tribune*, be read—and re-read—to him. The thinness of Agassiz's attack and the patent weakness of his arguments for direct divine intervention at successive stages of the process of creation confirmed in Youmans' mind the truth of the development hypothesis.[33]

If, then, Youmans did inspire Whitman's treatment of evolution, it is likely that it was the interpretation suggested by Chambers. And there is independent evidence—both internal and external—for recognizing Chambers importance for Whitman. His involvement in the controversy is indicated by his clipping of several articles dealing with Hugh Miller, whose *The Foot-Prints of the Creator* (1849) attacked Chambers.[34] And as one scholar has written, "by *Vestiges*—and, for some fifteen years, by *Vestiges* alone—evolution was kept for the Victorian reader 'in the air.'"[35] In view of Whitman's strong interest in science, he would have been familiar with certain of Chambers' concepts, particularly in astronomy. But in *Vestiges* he would have found something he could have found nowhere else: integration of the separate fields of inquiry around the concept that came to mean most to him, evolution.

Chambers' great achievement was precisely one of integration and synthesis. As Loren Eiseley has written, he put together the "separate pieces of the lost [evolutionary] chart" of previous scientists and "came up with the idea that organic as well as cosmic evolution was a reality."[36] Similarly, one of the distinguishing features of Whitman's treatment of the concept is his ability to bring together evidence from the separate sciences and present an integrated vision of startling force, one which demonstrates the indivisibility of the cosmic and terrestrial processes. Wrong as Chambers certainly was in many of the details of his theory, he was brilliantly right in its essentials. Youmans may well have discussed *Vestiges* with Whitman and helped him separate the sound from the absurd in the book. Also, the highly charged controversy in the periodicals exposed many of Chambers' faulty arguments.

The essential point is that in its broad outline and essential features "Song of Myself" is entirely consistent with *Vestiges*.

A summary of Chambers at this point may be useful. *Vestiges* begins with two chapters devoted to proving that evolution is a cosmic process. After explaining such weighty matters as the great age of our solar system, its position within the Milky Way, the movement of the heavenly bodies, and Laplace's nebular hypothesis, Chambers reached the conclusion that creation is a dynamic and on-going process throughout the cosmos: "The formation of bodies in space is *still and at present in progress*. We live at a time when many have been formed, and many are still forming."[37]

Chambers then argued for the unity of the cosmic and terrestrial realms. After explaining the composition of the earth out of the fifty-four or fifty-five chemical elements then known to exist, he exclaimed, "How infinitely is the knowledge increased in interest, when we consider the probability of such being the materials of the whole of the bodies of space, and the laws under which these everywhere combine, subject only to local and accidental variations!"[38] The ease with which the Whitman persona moves between the earth and the furthest reaches of heaven is one consequence of the discovery of the chemical unity of the two realms. Such ideas led Chambers to speculate on the probable existence of intelligent life in other solar systems. Neither man nor the earth should be seen as unique.

After explaining the geological processes by which the earth was formed, Chambers developed his major argument for evolution: the "vestiges of creation," the fossils of the species that had been found in sedimentary rocks, display a progressive complexity that corresponds to the age of the strata. He pointed out that the fossils from the earliest strata were confirmed to have come from extinct species. He then related the process of developing complexity to the evolution of all living creatures, with man at the top of an unbroken chain which rises from the most elementary organism: "The tendency of all these illustrations is to make us look to *development* as the principle which has been immediately concerned in the peopling of this globe, a process extending over a vast space of time, but which is nevertheless connected in character with the briefer process by which an individual being is evoked from a simple germ."[39] Chambers cited the most recent work in embryology, of Meckel, Tiedemann, and others, to give added proof to his theory: "It is only in recent times that physiologists have observed that each animal passes, in the course of its germinal history, through a series of changes resembling the *permanent forms* of the various orders of animals inferior to it in the scale."[40] In other words, ontogeny resembles phylogeny; through the development of his embryo the individual recapitulates the entire evolutionary process of the species. The challenge which Whitman, as the poet of evolution, accepted was to recall that evolutionary process from deep in his subconscious and find the "voice" to express it.

Chambers' interpretation of the evolutionary process was decidedly optimistic. Since atmospheric conditions for life on the planet were gradually becoming more favorable, he expected to see continuing progress in the development of the human species, with the gradual emergence of more complex beings, "a nobler type of humanity, which shall complete the zoological circle on this planet, and realize some of the dreams of the purest spirits of the present race."[41] Conceding that his theory was fundamentally opposed to the Mosaic account, Chambers emphatically proclaimed his belief that the concept of organic evolution, the gradual emergence of intelligent life out of matter, with each species giving rise to the next higher, was not inconsistent with the wise workings of the Creator: "I contemplate the whole phenomena as having been in the first place arranged in the counsels of Divine Wisdom, to take place, not only upon this sphere, but upon all the others in space, under necessary modifications, and as being carried on ... here and elsewhere, under immediate favour of the creative will or energy."[42] Chambers conceded that he had no certain theory to explain the mechanism actually responsible for evolutionary development, although he cited the work of Quetelet on the application of statistical theory to human behavior as allowing for the gradual appearance of small changes in a large number of instances. And he referred as well to the work of Babbage on computational theory to explain the possibility that God had "programmed" minute changes into the pattern of the universe. By no means was Chambers' the purposeless universe sometimes erroneously associated with Darwin.

At the same time Chambers "argued quite openly that man's character did not stem from a spiritual quality marking him off from the animals, but was a direct extension of faculties that had been developing throughout the evolutionary process."[43] To explain man's superior intelligence Chambers discussed the evolution of the brain as an organ of the mind. He was influenced by phrenology, and although he submerged it, there is a definite phrenological cast in Chambers' concluding chapters, especially where he attempts to account for differences in development between individuals and races. No doubt this dimension of the *Vestiges of Creation* was intriguing to Whitman, whose interest in phrenology is well-known.

For the young Whitman the controversy over *Vestiges* in the years 1846 and 1847 could not have come at a more opportune time. Chambers opened for his readers a seemingly limitless vista, of man's place in an expanding cosmos. In the notebooks dating from these years, in which Whitman experimented with ideas that he would later develop in *Leaves of Grass*, he expressed a vast cosmic yearning, a desire to identify his life with the timeless life of the cosmos. As Gay Wilson Allen has written, what the young Whitman "wanted most in his life of the imagination was to immerse, to bathe, to float (these were to become key images in his poems) in the eternal stream of existence. Having attained these mystical insights and intellectual concepts, Whitman was emotionally and mentally equipped to write the great book he had been dreaming of since his 'Sundown Papers' from his schoolmaster's desk."[44]

In one entry he wrote "I think the soul will never stop, or attain to any growth beyond which it shall not go.—When I walked at night by the seashore and looked up at the countless stars, I asked of my soul whether it would be filled and satisfied when it should become god enfolding all these, and open to the life and delight and knowledge of everything in them or of them; and the answer was plain to me ... No, when I reach there, I shall want to go further still."[45] Evolutionary theory as presented by Chambers could help the poet take such feelings and give them structure and direction within a dynamic theory of the universe. And it enabled Whitman to confront the two problems which, as Asselineau has written, deeply troubled him at this time: death and sin.[46] There are more than "vestiges" of Chambers' book to be found in "Song of Myself"; the concept of cosmic evolution pervades Whitman's epic. But in showing the extensive use which Whitman made of this book, it might be well to begin with the persona's discovery, in Section 31, that the "vestiges" of creation have become an inescapable part of his being, a clear and direct reference to Chambers:

I find I incorporate gneiss and coal and long-threaded moss and fruits and
    grains and esculent roots,
And am stucco'd with quadrupeds and birds all over,
And have distanced what is behind me for good reasons,
And call any thing close again when I desire it.

In vain the speeding or shyness,
In vain the plutonic rocks send their old heat against my approach,
In vain the mastodon retreats beneath its own powdered bones,
In vain objects stand leagues off and assume manifold shapes,
In vain the ocean settling in hollows and the great monsters lying low....

                                             (p. 57)

In asserting that he "incorporates" extinct species, such as the mastodon, later stages of the creation, such as quadrupeds and birds, and such inanimate matter as "gneiss, coal, long-threaded moss," the speaker explicitly defines man as a being who has evolved by passing through these stages and forms. Employing his remarkable powers of language, the speaker uses the development hypothesis to "call anything close again" and make real the intimate connection between the human and that from which it evolved. It is now impossible for the prehistoric forms to escape close inspection, by scientist or poet. Whitman playfully and comically awakens those longslumbering vestiges, and shows the role they have played in determining human identity. And it was precisely here, in arguing that man is a creature whose identity has been formed through the natural process of evolution, not through the direct intervention of the Creator, that Chambers and Whitman were so disturbing to the orthodox thought of the day. It would no longer be possible to think of man as a purely spiritual being, fashioned by the Creator in His image, but as an animal whose superior attributes had been developed gradually, in the course of the evolutionary process. Whitman wisely approaches a subject of bitter controversy with a gentle, ironic humor. His persona admits to descent from quadrupeds and birds.

Whitman's most consistent and fully worked-out exposition of Chambers appears in Section 44, which is a creation story told from the perspective of cosmic evolution. It celebrates the emergence of man, but along the way accounts for the creation of the cosmos itself. The story is exciting, the poet describing the perilous escape of his embryo from the lurking dangers of "fœtid carbon" and dramatizing the work of "monstrous sauroids" in protecting it. Yet, wonderful, miraculous as the story is, its true heroes are not supernatural but natural: the established physical laws of the universe which nevertheless operate with transcendent cosmic power.

Appropriately, the section begins with a formal announcement:

> It is time to explain myself.... let us stand up.
> What is known I strip away.... I launch all men and women forward with
>   me into the unknown.
>
> (p. 79)

The speaker asserts that he will explain both the mystery of his own existence and the even more fundamental question of human existence in space and time. The "unknown" into which the reader is launched is the cosmos itself, treated from the perspective of the unfathomable dimensions of time as revealed by the new astronomy and geology:

The clock indicates the moment.... but what does eternity indicate?

Eternity lies in bottomless reservoirs.... its buckets are rising forever
        and ever,
They pour and they pour and they exhale away.

We have thus far exhausted trillions of winters and summers;
There are trillions ahead, and trillions ahead of them.
(p. 79)

Such is the great age of the earth—and the promise of the future—that time may be said to be infinite, as revealed through the brilliant metaphor of "bottomless reservoirs." Whitman then linked this perception of time, of the great age of the universe and of the infinite expanse of the future, to the development hypothesis. Out of the endless years will come new forms: "Births have brought us richness and variety, / And other births will bring us richness and variety" (p. 79). The evolutionary process is on-going; as did Chambers, Whitman here looks ahead to the continual emergence of yet higher forms of life. Whitman's vision, like that of Chambers, is of a dynamic, constantly changing, open-ended universe.

Even while looking ahead to the development of more complex forms of life, the poet is careful to insist on the principle of equality: "I do not call one greater and one smaller, / That which fills its period and place is equal to any" (p. 79). It may seem to the reader that Whitman is simply imposing his preference for political democracy and social equality on the material universe. But Chambers took a similarly egalitarian approach to the physical universe in *Vestiges*. In responding by implication to accounts of creation that placed the earth in a unique position, Chambers argued for an equality among heavenly bodies: "There is nothing at all singular or special in the astronomical situation of the earth.... It is strikingly—if I may use such an expression—a member of a democracy. Hence, we cannot suppose that there is any peculiarity about it which does not probably attach to multitudes of other bodies—in fact, to all that are analogous to it in respect of cosmical arrangements."[47] Chambers supported this assertion by nothing also that the chemical elements making up the earth are to be found throughout the universe. Thus, Chambers' interpretation of fundamental principles of chemistry and astronomy supports the egalitarianism which Whitman everywhere advocates.

At this point the poet interrupts his account of evolutionary development to draw some moral conclusions. He concedes the existence of evil, remarking that some have indeed found "mankind murderous or jealous." But, he protests, that has not been his experience:

> I am sorry for you.... they are not murderous or jealous upon me;
> All has been gentle with me.... I keep no account with lamentation;
> What have I to do with lamentation?
>
> (p. 79)

In effect the poet repudiates the Christian concept of Original Sin associated with the Fall of Adam and Eve and the mortal sins of Cain and his descendants, which the reference to murder and jealousy calls to the mind of the reader. Nothing in Chambers' progressive evolutionary perspective requires a myth accounting for man's sinful nature, nor does the poet's own experience, which, he claims, has been "gentle," require it. For Whitman the aesthetic significance is clear: he refuses to take up the mode of "lamentation," but signifies instead his desire to continue to celebrate—both himself and the entire creation, the note on which he had begun.

For in the context of Chambers' exposition of the development hypothesis, such celebration is entirely warranted. As the representative man, the poet occupies the highest point in the continuing process of evolutionary development: "I am an acme of things accomplished, and I an encloser of things to be" (p. 79). Just as each man contains within himself the full history of evolutionary development, so does he possess or "enclose" the spermatic fluid out of which future growth will come. To picture that growth, the speaker instantaneously transforms himself, becoming that which, in the long evolutionary perspective, man will become:

> My feet strike an apex of the apices of the stairs,
> On every step bunches of ages, and larger bunches between the steps,
> All below duly traveled—and still I mount and mount.
>
> (p. 79)

The image of climbing cosmic stairs brilliantly combines—and compresses—the interrelated concepts of distance and time. As the new theory of evolution opened to Whitman a perception of the great age of the universe, so it suggested the immense ages to come. The poet's effortless mounting of the cosmic stairs serves to project the human presence forward into those extraordinary reaches of time. The sexual associations of "mounting" are appropriate to the process of generation and development. This arresting image is also reassuring in that it implies a kind of cosmic immortality, for both the species and the individual.

Remarkably the concept of evolution enables the poet to move both forward and backward in cosmic time. In the next passage he reverses the process, and travels back, to recreate the origins of the universe:

> Rise after rise bow the phantoms behind me,
> Afar down I see the huge first Nothing, the vapor from the nostrils of death,
> I know I was even there.... I waited unseen and always,
> And slept while God carried me through the lethargic mist,
> And took my time.... and took no hurt from the fœtid carbon.
>
> (pp. 79–80)

The referrences to the "vapor from the nostrils of death," the "lethargic mist," and "foetid carbon" are to the carbonic gas said by Chambers in the sixth chapter to have so dominated the earth in its early stages that it was incapable of supporting life in land animals. The gradual dissipation of this gas, in Chambers' explanation, made possible the emergence of simple forms of organic life. Here Whitman introduces the concept of God, of a Divine presence which has so directed the process from the outset that human life has been allowed to emerge. Yet, this is not a God who intervenes directly in the creation; rather, He operates entirely through impersonal natural laws. The references in this passage to the "rings" of stars and their "influences" are to Newtonian laws of gravitation. Although those laws are impersonal, Whitman presents them as operating with a wise—even maternal—presence. The speaker's embryo has long been "hugged close" and protected by "faithful and friendly...arms," and his "cradle" has been protected by "cycles" which are likened to "cheerful boatmen" (p. 80). Whitman treats evolution as a warm, nutritive mother.

In the concluding stanzas of this section Whitman brings together his earlier references to the separate sciences and shows how, working together, the manifold "forces" of the universe, have contributed to the creation of the speaker himself:

> Before I was born out of my mother generations guided me,
> My embryo has never been torpid.... nothing could overlay it;
> For it the nebula cohered to an orb.... the long slow strata piled to rest it
>   on.... vast vegetables gave it sustenance,
> Monstrous sauroids transported it in their mouths and deposited it with care.
>
> All forces have been steadily employed to complete and delight me,
> Now I stand on this spot with my soul.
>
> (p. 80)

For the 1881 edition Whitman added the adjective "robust" to modify "soul" in the last line. But this adjective is hardly necessary. The dynamic energy of the speaker's soul is contained within the matter out of which he emerged, a process that had been set in motion by an interconnected series of natural laws or "forces." Through an imaginative use of the concept of the embryo, Whitman recapitulates the entire process. The "embryonic" development of the speaker took place both inside his mother and during the immense expanse of time since the "huge first Nothing." The assertion that his "embryo has never been torpid" is a reference to the idea that ontogeny recapitulates phylogeny, an idea that Whitman almost certainly learned from Chambers.[48] Whitman's imaginative use of the idea of recapitulation enables him to dramatize the broad evolutionary process. In this sublime, yet compressed and wonderfully comic creation story, the poet effortlessly activates and animates vast movements and forces. Even extinct sauroids have been given a job to do in transporting the speaker's endangered embryo, and they work in harmony with the early strata and "vast vegetables." Appropriately, the culminating event is the birth of the poet, who is able to step onto the cosmic stage and through language take his place as a conscious participant in the grand evolutionary process. As promised, he has "stood up" and "explained himself" as a product of the evolutionary process. The section, a summary of the essential features of *Vestiges*, is a brilliant verbal recapitulation of the immense stages of human development. Whitman has transformed the "seed" of Chambers' scientific conception, and created a myth which offers ample reason for celebration.

III. "The Links Uniting the Realms of Matter and Mind"

Evolutionary theory, in binding together, in Fiske's words, "in a single web of causation worlds, continents, life, mind," would seem to offer the poet a most useful new cosmology.[49] But it also raised some difficult questions. Precisely how could these diverse realms be bound together? And how is mind to be understood? If man is not the handiwork of a God who created him in His own image, then how did he develop those qualities which seemed to set him apart from the other animals? Could he still be said to possess a soul? If man's superior intelligence is a function of increased brain size, then how is brain to be understood in physiological terms? Were the explanations of phrenology, which seemed, for a time, so attractive to Chambers, Whitman, and many others, adequate? Just how are mind and body related?

In his pre-1855 notebooks, Whitman wrestled with many of these questions, particularly that of the nature of the soul and its relationship to the material realm. In one of the first entries in the earliest surviving notebook (dating, most likely, from the years 1846 or 1847), he begins with the concept of soul, asserting that "The soul or spirit transmits itself into all matter—into rocks, and can live the life of a rock—into the sea, and can feel itself the sea—into the oak ... into an animal, and feel itself a horse, a fish, or bird—into the earth—into the motions of the suns and stars—"[50] Here the "soul or spirit" is an entity which exists apart from the material world and is in some senses superior to it, because it can penetrate any aspect of the material world and live its life at will. Similarly, a little later, he cautioned himself to "speak of the soul" only in the highest terms, "as intrinsically great," and to use adjectives which "always testify greatness and immortality and purity." Soul, then, would seem to have an independent and superior existence. But in the next entry he qualifies this notion of the autonomy of the soul by asserting that its "effusion or corporation ... is always under the beautiful laws of physiology—I guess the soul itself can never be anything but great and pure and immortal; but it makes itself visible only through matter."[51] From this perspective we can appreciate the crucial importance to Whitman of physical health, for "a perfect head, and bowels and bones to match is the easy gate through which it [the soul] comes from its embowered garden." Conversely, the imperfect body ("twisted skull, and blood watery or rotten by ancestry or gluttony, or rum or bad disorders") is the "darkness toward which the plant will not grow."[52] We can understand, then, why Whitman sought so assiduously to comprehend the principles of good health, a subject of Youmans' early lectures and writings.

In a later diary entry Whitman wrote of having been taught "that mind is greater than matter," but rejects this notion: "I cannot separate them, and call one superior and the other inferior, any more than I can say my sight is greater than my eyes." Since he admitted to himself that "I cannot understand the mystery" of the relationship of body and soul, he resolved to consider them as equal, and to make the question of their relationship a subject of his poetry.[53] Among the first trial lines for "Song of Myself" are the following: "I am the poet of the body / And I am the poet of the soul."[54] In the 1855 Preface he spoke of the rightful expectation of readers that the true poet would "indicate more than the beauty and dignity which always attach to dumb real objects.... they expect him to indicate the path between reality and their souls" (p. 10). Here, the poet takes as his starting point the world of matter and sets for himself the challenge of so penetrating it as to find in it the "soul." Gay Wilson Allen has commented on this passage that "whatever the soul was, Whitman's most serious ambition was to show the 'path' to it."[55]

Similarly, Youmans came back repeatedly to this basic question, observing that science, in considering the "singular properties of matter, opens the doorway to the temple of mind, and unfolds to us the most august contemplation that can engage the powers of human thought." For, he asked, "what facts of our nature are so grand and awful, as those which concern the alliance of the spiritual and material?"[56] Reflecting this search, we know that early in his career as scientific lecturer he "gave a series on the sunbeam, explaining the varied influences of the solar ray, with an analysis of its forces; the relation of the sun to life on our planet; the chemistry of the sun and the stars; the links uniting the realms of matter and mind."[57]

This description may remind us of the passage in Section 24 of "Song of Myself" in which the speaker through his poetic voice becomes a link joining man to the stars, among other dimensions of the universe:

> Through me the afflatus surging and surging....through me the current and
>   index.
>
> I speak the password primeval.... I give the sign of democracy;
> By God! I will accept nothing which all cannot have their counterpart of on
>   the same terms.
>
> Through me many long dumb voices,
> Voices of the interminable generations of slaves,
> Voices of prostitutes and deformed persons,
> Voices of the diseased and despairing, and of thieves and dwarfs,
> Voices of cycles of preparation and accretion,
> And of the threads that connect the stars—and of wombs, and of the
>   fatherstuff,
> And of the rights of them the others are down upon....
>
>   (p. 50)

Here the poet himself becomes a connecting link between diverse realms of matter and mind. He is an "intelligent terminal," to use a contemporary phrase, in a most complex network, one which extends back to the origins of time, outward to the furthest dimensions of space, and laterally to other human beings, particularly the dispossessed, all those who have been denied a voice of their own. He also gives voice to the process of cosmic evolution through his ability to articulate "voices of preparation and accretion," a reference to Laplace's nebular hypothesis, which, as we have seen, Whitman accepted.

The poet's ability to serve as a vehicle for these "many long dumb voices" is predicted upon his own dynamic participation in the material realm. He describes two forces "surging and surging" through him, the "afflatus," which refers denotatively to physical breath and connotatively to poetic inspiration, and the "current," electricity. The speaker becomes an "index" or instrument which registers the movement of these forces through his body. Harold Aspiz, who has explicated the sources behind Whitman's use of "the body electric" metaphor, has observed that "some of the most dazzling imagery in *Leaves of Grass* derives from the new science of electricity, which many of Whitman's contemporaries believed would unlock the secrets of the universe and bridge the chasm between materialism and the idealistic faith."[58] One of Whitman's contemporaries, D. H. Jacques, described electricity as the "subtle fluid [which] seems to form the connecting link between the soul and the body, and to be the instrument by means of which the former builds, rebuilds, or shapes the latter."[59] Some contemporary theorists held that electricity was a vital energy inhering in the sperm, while others, such as Samuel Warren, in an 1849 essay, "Electricity the Great Acting Part of Nature," concentrated on the function of this "subtle fluid" as generative force in the cosmos at large.[60] Of the passage quoted above, Aspiz observes that "the electric and spermatic 'threads' connecting the stars seem to be a projection of the persona's sexual and visionary powers. Just as the 'fatherstuff' represents the electrical source of human life, so the stars represent the electrical sources of universal life."[61] The masculine poet, then, feels himself joined to the cosmos through the electrical energy of the "fatherstuff," and since electricity may be thought of as a "vital fluid" connecting mind and body, the poet is able to bring to his mind electrical impulses from throughout the cosmos and then translate those impulses into poetic speech and give them "voice."

I have not found anything in Youmans' writing that would support such an understanding of electricity. He repeatedly insisted upon the importance in science of rigorous experimental methods, and, needless to say, not all of Whitman's likely sources for his suggestive treatment of the body and cosmos electric waited for the confirmation of experiment before propounding their theories. Yet Youmans, who approached science almost as a new revelation, could wax rather speculative and metaphorical himself, and he may have served as a source for Whitman's treatment of the other force "surging" in the poet's body, the "afflatus."

In the *Chemical Atlas* (1854), in which he evidently treated at length the topics of his lectures on the sunbeam, he explained in detail the chemical intricacies of the complementary production of oxygen and carbon dioxide by plants and animals. He then grew rapturous in describing the agency of the sun in controlling the earth's atmosphere and insuring a life-promoting balance of gases: "It has been stated that the two worlds of organization [plant and animal] are condensed from the intangible gases with which our planet is enshrouded. If thus all living beings are derived from these fleeting airs, which are so rare and ethereal that they seem almost designed to connect the worlds of matter and spirit, it is fit that the forces which control such changes should have a celestial origin."[62] Youmans' prose can be described as scientific in its description of physical processes, aesthetic in its celebration of the beauty and harmony of those processes, and spiritual, as when, a little later, he refers to the sunbeam as the "divinest effluence of the stars," the "force of antagonization by which all life and beauty and glory upon the earth are perpetually called into being."[63] In reading such passages or listening to the inspired Youmans speak them, Whitman would be justified in assuming, for the purposes of his poetry, that the "fleeting airs" did indeed "connect the worlds of matter and spirit." Concerned with discovering the metaphoric possibilities of scientific concepts, Whitman would have found Youmans' language suggestive. From this perspective, the physical breath "surging and surging" through the speaker could be thought of as connecting the "worlds of matter and spirit," and so become the traditional poetic afflatus.

Paradoxically, then, Whitman's use of the latest scientific concepts restores to him the most ancient power of poetry, that of "the password primeval," giving him entry into a world that had been barred and restricted. In basing his art firmly in the body, the poet is able to uncover and possess the hidden dimensions of the physical world, and through the concepts of science, discover the links joining the material world to mind. He can then speak the "password primeval," use language with original force. In one of his first notebook entries Whitman wrote that "in the earliest times ... everything written at all was poetry."[64] Paradoxically, the new science enabled the poet to recover the original power of poetry. For this reason Whitman could write in the 1855 Preface that "exact science and its practical movements are no checks on the greatest poet but always his encouragement and support" (p. 15). In learning how to use the concepts and vocabulary of the new science metaphorically, Whitman turned to his advantage the threat to poetry which modern science, with its positivism, seemed to present.

The poet who possesses "the password primeval" can interpret the pulses surging within his own body and give voice to the things and people of the external world and find their true meaning. For Whitman, as had been true for Chambers, that meaning has a democratic dimension. Immediately after speaking the "password primeval," the poet gives the "sign of democracy." He gladly becomes the voice of those who have not been able to articulate their own meaning: slaves, prostitutes, the diseased, thieves, and the deformed. For all share with the poet "on the same terms" in the dynamic currents of the material world, and that gives the poet access to them. The poet is demonstrating that their existence also is worthy of being celebrated. Aware of the many connections uniting mind and matter, body and soul, the speaker makes use of physical concepts to become himself an articulate, intelligent link in a most complex and wondrous network.

On the other hand, some readers may recall the passage in Section 23 in which the speaker, rather than using science as a "password," seems instead to place a barrier between himself and the scientists: "Gentlemen I receive you, and attach and clasp hands with you, / The facts are useful and real....they are not my dwelling.... I enter by them to an area of the dwelling" (p. 49). The passage has been interpreted as a polite, but firm rejection of science; the poet and scientist, it seems to say, go their separate ways. Certainly the speaker asserts that his method is not that of "positive science" and "exact demonstration." He does not employ the experimental method to test hypotheses, something that Youmans insisted was the essential condition of science. Since science is not his "dwelling," he does not feel obligated to emulate the methods of the scientist in working with the natural world. Nevertheless, the passage explicitly testifies to the importance of the work of the scientist for the poet. For the "facts" discovered by the scientist make it possible for the poet to "enter" his "area of the dwelling." Figuratively, the two—poet and scientist—are housed under the same roof.

The poet's starting point—and the first line of Section 23—is "A word of reality.... materialism first and last imbueing" (49). The speaker accepts the challenge of finding in the real world, both as he has experienced it and as it is revealed to him by the "facts" (and concepts) of the scientist, the "password" which will enable him to "enter" his "area of the dwelling." As Emerson wrote in "The Poet," the facts become "vehicular and transitive," "good ... for conveyance."[65] Whitman here asserts that the poet employs the "facts" of the scientist so that they become a vehicle which enables him to enter his portion of the "dwelling," to enter the imaginative realm. In "Song of Myself" Whitman uses those facts so that the persona becomes the link, a force, connecting the realm of material fact with that of imaginative realization: "I am less the reminder of property or qualities, and more the reminder of life" (p. 49). Where the scientist uses the "facts" of the material world so that he can develop abstract theories about its "properties or qualities," the poet employs those facts for their own sake and suggests their living significance, particularly through connecting mind and matter. Paradoxically, while pointing out that the poet does not use the methods of "exact demonstration," Whitman has written a remarkably precise statement of the differing procedures of poet and scientist, one which reveals just how crucially important the "facts" of the scientist are in enabling the poet to "enter his area of the dwelling." Although they live in different parts of the "dwelling," they certainly inhabit the same universe of discourse.

IV. THE POETRY OF THE BODY, OR MAN AS A "VORTEX OF FORCES"

The area of Whitmans' artistic "dwelling" that Youmans ruled out of bounds was that where the poet treated human sexuality. Implicitly he denied the poet's claim that he had "clarified and transfigured" the "voices of sexes and lusts," the "voices indecent," which are heard in his work (p. 50). Youmans himself seems not to have dealt directly with human sexuality in his own work. But at the same time Youmans was one of the leaders in the 1850s in urging that human identity be defined in material, not spiritual terms. Youmans argued forcefully that as a product of evolution, man is a physiological being whose essential nature is to be found not in some remote abstraction called spirit, but in his organic capacities. He saw human growth and development as a function of the organism's dynamic interaction with the material world. Throughout his writings he, like Whitman, called for "A word of reality.... materialism first and last imbueing."

In his *Chemical Atlas*, for instance, he asserted that even the most exalted and rarified activities of man—his triumphant achievements in the creative arts and in science—are grounded in matter, both as subject and as medium of expression. Like the agricultural worker, the mechanic and other laborers, the "cultivators of art, though their pursuit be deemed 'divine,'" are "chained to matter by the invincible necessities of [their] vocation." Youmans explicitly challenged the common assumption that the high creative endeavors are valuable because they lift man out of a corrupt world of matter to the spiritual realm. On the contrary, the process of creation, the process by which the most valuable visions are realized, consists in a "circle ... of explorations into the several departments of matter."[66]

In this book he defined man as a "vortex of forces" in constant and dynamic interaction with the external world:

> It is the destiny of man that the life-period of his being shall be passed in a world of *matter*. Not only is he born *into* a material universe, but he is born *of* it; not only is it to be his time-residence, but he is part and parcel of its fabric, created of its elements, and participating in its constitution. But the simple fact that man's body is composed of matter, by no means indicates the intimacy or extent of his alliance with material nature.... The

system of man is less a mere physical body of a certain bulk and weight, than it is a vortex of forces, of which matter in a rapid state of transition is but the means of manifestation.... So vital is the relationship which subsists between the living man and the world of physical nature, that he cannot cease the introduction of surrounding matter into his system, even for a few moments, except upon the penalty of death.[67]

In this volume Youmans lucidly explained just how the chemical elements interact to sustain life. Since chemical reactions are not visible to the naked eye, he made use of color-coded drawings so that their intricate wonder could be visualized by the non-scientist. Youmans' purpose in this volume is to depict from a chemical perspective, the full range of man's interaction with the material universe.

Whitman also presented man as a "vortex of forces," although his image of him is more sensual and decidedly less tidy than that presented by Youmans. "One of the roughs, a kosmos," the speaker of "Song of Myself" is "fleshy and sensual.... eating drinking and breeding" (p. 50). Throughout the poem he explores the interaction of his body with the forces of the external world, speaking of "the smoke of my own breath," and his "respiration and inspiration.... the beating of my heart.... the passing of blood and air through my lungs" (p. 27). Like Youmans, Whitman warned of the imminent danger to man if he should cease the introduction of surrounding matter into his system: "Dazzling and tremendous how quick the sunrise would kill me, / If I could not now and always send sunrise out of me" (p. 52).

Metaphorically, the "sunrise" that the speaker returns to the external world is his poetic vision, but the image has its basis in physiological fact. It is another metaphoric description of the poetic process which has its origin in the life of the body. In *Chemical Atlas* Youmans described the many ways in which the sun is essential to the continuation of life on this planet, and, as we have seen, came to speak metaphorically in describing the sunbeam as "the divinest effluence of the stars." During his early lectures on the solar ray, Youmans explained "the links uniting the realms of matter and mind."

While recognizing the fact that man "possesses an intelligent and immortal spirit" as the "grandest fact" of his existence, Youmans argued that man's soul can have no development or even existence apart from "the material universe" which is its "sphere of ... evolution and education." He piled phrase upon phrase to demonstrate the dynamic process of man's growth through his sensory interaction with the physical world: man's spirit "comes into being as a thought-germ planted in the soil of matter; that by an exquisite apparatus of material senses, it is put into connection—brought as it were into universal contact—with the physical world; that it grows and expands by impressions poured in from the outward universe through the channels of sense; and that power is thus acquired by which the developed soul reacts upon external nature."[68] Youmans here divides man's growth into two stages. The first, the stage of childhood, is a process of absorption; the individual is receptive to the rich sensory life around him. While outwardly passive, the individual, in receiving impressions from the external world, is active. For, through the process of absorption, the individual develops the "power" which enables him to enter the second stage in which he acts "upon external nature."

"Song of Myself" describes an analogous process. Particularly in the first half of the poem the speaker is remarkably receptive to the full range of sense impressions poured in upon him from the external world. Almost exactly half-way through the poem, in Section 25, immediately after the speaker mentions his need to "send sunrise out of me," he celebrates the creative power which he is now conscious of possessing:

> My voice goes after what my eyes cannot reach,
> With the twirl of my tongue I encompass worlds and volumes of worlds.
>
> Speech is the twin of my vision.... it is unequal to measure itself.
>
> It provokes me forever,
> It says sarcastically, Walt, you understand enough.... why don't you let it
> out then?
>
> (pp. 52–53)

In later editions, Whitman would alter the last line to read, "*Walt you contain enough, why don't you let it out then.*" The verb "contain" implies a process of filling up, of receiving. "Understand" implies a process of intellectual comprehension. Together, the lines suggest that through a process of receiving impressions from the external world and of comprehending those impressions, the poet has completed an action. He has developed "power," and now is prepared for the second stage. He is now prepared to act upon the external world, to "let out" or express the creative power which he has developed through his absorption of sensory impressions. For the poet, that new "power" is the imagination, which enables him to capture even that which he cannot see; through his art, the "twirl of my tongue," he has the power to encompass "worlds and volumes of worlds."

Perhaps the most important consequence of Youmans' attempt to understand man in physiological terms, as a product of the evolutionary process, was his exploration of the brain as an organ of mind. In an essay published in *The Culture Demanded by Modern Life* (1867), he condemned the Cartesian dualism, which resulted in the denigration of the body at the expense of mind, as presenting the greatest possible obstacle to a true understanding of man:

> The method of regarding man which tradition has transmitted to us from the earliest ages, is, at the outset, to cleave him asunder, and substitute the idea of two beings for the reality of one. Having thus introduced the notion of his double nature—mind and body as separate, independent existences—there grew up a series of moral contrasts between the disjointed products. The mind was ranked as the higher, or spiritual nature, the body as the lower, or material nature. The mind was said to be pure, aspiring, immaterial; the body gross, corrupt, and perishable; and thus the feelings became enlisted to widen the breach and perpetuate the antagonism. Having divided him into two alien entities, and sought all terms of applause to celebrate the one, while exhausting the ocabulary of reproach upon the other, the fragments were given over to two parties—the body to the doctors of medicine, and the spirit to the doctors of philosophy, who seem to have agreed in but one thing, that the partition shall be eternal, and that neither shall ever intrude into the domain of the other.[69]

Both Youmans and Whitman devoted themselves—but in different ways—to healing this destructive "breach" and "antagonism" between two realms of man's being, which were universally believed to be discrete. Both writers insisted on "intruding" from one realm into the other and back again. Whitman's persona asserts simply, "I believe in you my soul.... the other I am must not abase itself to you, / And you must not be abased to the other." And in the ecstatic experience of Section 5, he captures the "peace and joy and knowledge that pass all the art and argument of the earth" when body and soul come together and are blissfully experienced as one (p. 30).

Youmans was also forceful in his efforts to heal the destructive division in man's understanding of mind. He summarized for his readers recent advances in neurophysiology. Noting particularly the work of English physicians, he explained how science now "proceeds at the outset to reunite the disserved fragments of humanity, and reconstitute the individual in thought as he is in life, a concrete unit—the living, thinking, acting being which we encounter in daily experience."[70] Youmans wrote of his hopes for a radical change in the methods of treating the mentally ill and feeble-minded. If their afflictions were understood organically and not as a sign of spiritual infirmity, then they would receive the respect and dignity that all human beings deserve. And only then could medical science proceed to discover cures for the underlying physical problems. Youmans' was an enlightened voice in an area which, because of problems within his own family—four of his six siblings were afflicted with various mental illnesses—was a sensitive one to Whitman. And Youmans argued forcefully for a complete revision of educational methods at all levels. He rejected the rote learning then practiced and called for an experimental and experiential approach, one which was based on a recognition that the organic capacity of the individual at different stages of his development conditioned his ability to learn. Abstract learning should be introduced only gradually. For instance, he observed that "the whole plastic power" of the brain of the child is "devoted to the storing up of perceptions, while the vigour of cerebral growth insures the highest intensity of mental adhesiveness." He recognized the educational value of natural childhood experiences, writing that as the child observes and absorbs "the aspects, properties, and simple relations of the surrounding objects of Nature," then the "scenes of childish pleasure and exuberant activity furnish the objects of thought."[71] Youmans' comments on the value of such learning may be read as a gloss on Whitman's great poem of childhood development, "There Was a Child Went Forth." In education, too, Youmans' was a voice for enlightened reform.

Further, Youmans' investigation of the physiology of the brain led him to a recognition of the existence of the subconscious mind. Again he drew heavily on the work of English researchers, particularly Thomas Laycock, who was one of the "first to apply the theory of evolution to the development of the nervous centres in the animal kingdom and in man."[72] Recognizing that "consciousness and mind are far from being one and the same thing," Youmans focused on those dimensions of mental activity of which man is only partially aware. What happens when ideas or feelings pass out of consciousness?

Science affirms an organ of mind, and demands an explanation, in terms of its action. As the thought passes from consciousness, something remains in the cerebral substratum, call it what you will,—trace, impression, residue. What the precise character of these *residua* may be, is perhaps questionable, but it is impossible to deny their existence in some form consistent with the nature of cerebral structure and activity. All thoughts, feelings, and impressions, when disappearing from consciousness, leave behind them in the nerve substance, their effects or residua, and in this state they constitute what may be termed latent or statical mind. They are brought into consciousness by the laws of association, and there is much probability that, in this unconscious state, they are still capable of acting and reacting, and of working out true intellectual results.[73]

Youmans credited a physiological mechanism in the brain with the ability to store both ideas and feelings. Potentially, none of the individual's prior experience is lost to him, for under the "laws of association" even long-forgotten experiences may be brought back into consciousness and be responsible for "true intellectual results."

Youmans recognized the significance of this insight for scientific and artistic creation. In fact, he asserted that the subconscious is the source of the very greatest artistic achievements: "It is said of eminent poets, painters, and musicians, that they are born, and not made; that is, their genius is an endowment of nature,—a gifted organism which spontaneously utters itself in high achievements, and they often present cases of remarkable automatism."[74] He cited the testimony of Mozart among others on the wisdom for the artist of allowing the work to shape itself.

If he had not been so troubled by Whitman's "obtrusive filthiness," Youmans might have recognized that in such works as "The Sleepers," "Out of the Cradle Endlessly Rocking," and "Song of Myself" his contemporary had created poems which are excellent examples of the shaping power of the subconscious mind, the expressions of "a gifted organism which spontaneously utters itself in high achievements." Clearly Youmans was not prepared to face the fact that the subconscious may also be the repository of powerful sexual emotions which, as in Whitman's "Spontaneous Me," may become the shaping force of art. Yet, Youmans' insight into the subconscious took him to the doorstep of such insights.

Obviously, I am not suggesting that Whitman's courageous exploration of the subconscious was made possible by Youmans' intellectual discovery of its existence. Whitman's work demonstrates that he, like poets before him, found his own way to explore the subconscious. Also, I do not know just when Youmans arrived at his theory; I have quoted from an essay that was published in 1867. Nevertheless, his discussion of the artistic process in the context of the subconscious does display a sensitivity and understanding which may have been helpful to Whitman. Perhaps, in ways that he was not prepared to admit even to himself, Youmans was influenced by his friendship with the poet. But leaving aside the question of influence, it is remarkable that these two writers, though working in different ways, were pioneers in America in uncovering the subconscious and revealing its shaping power.

Even while approaching the brain physiologically, as an organ of mind, Youmans came to express an unbounded, even spiritual appreciation of its creative power. He described the brain as "that most sacred of the things of time, the organism of the soul!" The paradoxical phrase "organism of the soul" implies that the brain itself serves as a link between the realms of mind and matter. Further, the brain of man, despite its size, is more wondrous even than the immense reaches of the universe: "We speak of the glories of the stellar universe; but is not the miniature duplicate of that universe in the living brain a more transcendent marvel?" For the brain of man, although a material product of the evolutionary process, is capable of comprehending the vast reaches of the universe in space and time: "Geological revelations carry us back through durations so boundless, that imagination is bewildered, and reason reels under the grandeur of the demonstration; but through the measureless series of advancing periods, we discover a stupendous plan. Infinite Power, working through infinite time, converges the mighty lines of causality to the fulfillment of an eternal design,—the birth of an intellectual and moral era through the development of the brain of man, which thus appears as the final term of an unfolding world."[75] The point of convergence of "Infinite Power" and "infinite time," the mind of man takes on heroic stature. A "miniature duplicate" of the universe, it participates in its creative power. If we substitute for "brain" the term "imagination," we can see how serviceable for a cosmic poet like Whitman such an understanding of mind might be. It enables the poet to bring together in his imagination "infinite time" and "infinite power." Since his imagination contains in small the larger workings of the universe, the poet is able to explore his intimate connections with the created universe, and he may be said to possess the originative, creative power to conceive of new worlds. For Whitman the manifestation of that "infinite power" is "voice," which, as we have seen, "goes after what my eyes cannot reach, / With the twirl of my tongue I encompass worlds and volumes of worlds" (p. 52). Contemporary science, as interpreted by Youmans, was capable of opening to the poet with Whitman's cosmic reach the astounding dimensions—in space and time—of the universe. In its heroic concept of mind as an "organism of the soul," it provided him with a link between the material and spiritual realms, a link which enabled him to write a poetry firmly grounded in the body and the material realm, even while capturing the largest possible meanings of the converging of "Infinite Power" and "infinite time" in the mind.

V. The Correlation and Conservation of Forces

Two complementary physical principles—at once ancient and modern—came to have great importance for both Whitman and Youmans in explaining the fundamental principles of the natural world: the "laws" of correlation of force and conservation of matter. These principles, which in their modern guise Youmans introduced into America, fully supported the implications of evolutionary theory. The law of conservation of matter held that the basic elements of the universe could not be destroyed. In the introduction to *Correlation and Conservation of Forces* (1864), his edited collection of essays on the new physical principles by such distinguished European scientists as Helmholtz, Grove, and Liebig, Youmans cited the development of the chemical balance by Lavoisier as providing empirical evidence for this astounding law. Lavoisier's experiments demonstrated that "never an atom is created or destroyed; that though matter changes form with protean facility, traversing a thousand cycles of change, vanishing and reappearing incessantly, yet it never wears out or lapses into nothing."[76] Here was an idea, established by Lavoisier and then confirmed independently by a number of scientists, which could replace the traditional concepts of immortality. Man was part and parcel of a deathless universe. As I shall demonstrate, this idea figures prominently in "Song of Myself."

The second principle, "correlation of forces" or interconversion of energy, is implicit in the idea of conservation. The new science revealed a world where nothing is lost, but where all is in a constant state of change, motion, and transformation: "Heat, light, electricity, and magnetism are now no longer regarded as substantive and independent existences—subtile fluids with peculiar properties, but simply as modes of motion in ordinary matter; forms of energy which are capable of mutual conversion. Heat is a mode of energy manifested by certain effects. It may be transformed into electricity, which is another form of force producing different effects. Or the process may be reversed."[77] Living in a universe of constant motion and change, man could no longer think in static or material terms. He must adjust to a dynamic, active universe, one of forces constantly interacting with—transforming, and being transformed by—other forces. In responding to those who charged that science was bent on substituting an entirely materialistic view of the universe for the spiritual concepts of religion, Youmans responded that science had demonstrated that a "pure principle forms the immaterial foundation of the universe." In comprehending the "universal immaterial force," science had revealed "a truth of the spiritual world, of so exalted an order that it has been said 'to connect the mind of man with the Spirit of God.'"[78]

Here was a point where ancient and modern theories of nature seemed to converge. For the new principles of conservation of matter seemed to confirm the concept of Democritus that since the atoms which make up matter "are indestructible and unalterable, no change of any sort can occur in their shape, size, weight or internal nature, either spontaneously or from their collisions with one another." Democritus held the idea "that matter is indestructible and unalterable, both in quantity and quality."[79] As has been recognized by the historian of science George Sarton, the ancient Greek concept of the indestructibility of atoms may be considered "as an adumbration of the principle of conservation of matter."[80]

It is likely that Whitman was familiar with the Greek concept from his reading of Frances Wright's *A Few Days in Athens* (1822), a semi-fictional exposition of the ideas of Epicurus, one of the transmitters of Democritus' concepts. As Whitman told Traubel, Wright's "book about Epicurus was daily food to me: I kept it about me for years."[81] Wright's instrument for explaining Greek notions of the atomic theory is the character of Metrodorus, who teaches the idea that "everything is eternal," a notion which, as Gay Wilson Allen has written, is "very important" in *Leaves of Grass*.[82] Accepting the principle of permanence in the universe, Wright followed Democritus and Epicurus in recognizing another fundamental idea: the universality of change. Metrodorus explained that it is "the different disposition of these eternal and unchangeable atoms that produces all the varieties in the substances constituting the great material whole, of which we form a part. Those particles, whose peculiar agglomeration or arrangement, we call a vegetable to-day, pass into, and form part of, an animal to-morrow; and that animal again, by the falling asunder of its constituent atoms...is transformed into some other substance presenting a new assemblage of qualities."[83] Needless to say, the fact that this ancient theory of change within a deathless universe was confirmed by the rigorous methods of modern science seemed to lend it particular authenticity.

Fiske reports that at the start of his lecture career in the early 1850s, Youmans gave two talks setting forth "the debt due by chemist and astronomer to alchemist and astrologer; and here he took occasion to point out how the guesses of Democritus and Lucretius [whose *De Rerum Natura* is built on Democritus' ideas] had been barren, not withstanding their shrewdness, from their not having married experiment to speculation."[84] Although Fiske does not identify the particular "guesses" of the ancients that Youmans discussed, it is clear from the context that he treated Democritus' atomic theory. For in his next lectures Youmans focused on the modern versions of this idea. In "The Masquerade of the Elements" he "presented in glowing outline the phenomena of protean chemical transformation." And the related lecture, "New Philosophy of Forces," was "the first popular exposition of the correlation of forces given in America."[85] Unfortunately, Fiske does not report the exact dates of these lectures. Were they delivered before 1855? Did Whitman, as is entirely possible, discuss these ideas with Youmans in the years before 1855? Were there other sources? I doubt that we shall ever know with any certainty. But especially striking is the similarity of Youmans' interpretation of the significance of these ideas with Whitman's treatment of them.

For, as Youmans described them, these ideas served to reveal yet another link joining the realms of mind and matter. The law of conservation and correlation of force, he asserted, could be found in operation throughout the cosmos, binding together all orders of existence, from the mind of man to the outermost reaches of the cosmos. It is the

> highest law of all science—the most far-reaching principle that adventuring reason has discovered in the universe. Its stupendous reach spans all orders of existence. Not only does it govern the movements of the heavenly bodies, but it presides over the genesis of the constellations; not only does it control those radiant floods of power which fill the eternal spaces ... but it rules the actions and relations of men, and regulates the march of terrestrial affairs.... It prevails equally in the world of mind, controlling all the faculties and processes of thought and feeling. The star-suns of the remoter galaxies dart their radiancies across the universe; and although the distances are so profound that hundreds of centuries may have been required to traverse them, the impulses of force enter the eye, and impressing an atomic charge upon the nerve, give origin to the sense of sight. Star and nerve tissue are parts of the same system—stellar and nervous forces are correlated. Nay more; sensation awakens thought and kindles emotion, so that this wondrous dynamic chain binds into living unity the realms of matter and mind through measureless amplitudes of space and time.[86]

This view of the active part played by mind in a dynamic, expanding universe is consistent with other statements by Youmans on the creative power of mind. Again, it places mind at the central point, the intersection, of the uncharted depths of the universe, of space and time. The artist, no less than the scientist, is "charged" with exploring those interconnected realms, and making their meanings manifest. And the law of conservation and correlation of force, combined with the new theory of evolution, seemed to promise unlimited growth and development, and to hold out the promise of underlying order, stability, and purpose beneath the tremendous change and diversity of the universe. In the persona of "Song of Myself" Whitman created a protean being committed to exploring the surpassing universe revealed by science: "To me the converging objects of the universe perpetually flow, / All are written to me, and I must get what the writing means" (pp. 45–46).

VI. "THE TUFT AND FINAL APPLAUSE OF SCIENCE"

As we have seen, Whitman's speaker makes use of the "facts" revealed by the scientist so that he can "enter" his "area of the dwelling," his imaginative realm. One of his most distinguishing characteristics is precisely his ability to move constantly—and seemingly in all directions at once—while absorbing and interpreting all, getting "at what the writing means." "I fly the flight of the fluid and swallowing soul," he tells us; his "course runs below the soundings of plummets." He seems to be both in the air and below the sea at once. In constant motion, "Backing and filling, appearing and disappearing, / I tread day and night such roads" (p. 63). The speaker effortlessly traverses the realms of outer space as well as the familiar—and not so familiar—by-ways of the earth. He escapes the usual limitations of matter and becomes an immaterial force capable of moving through and possessing every dimension of space and time. Youmans spoke of science as, at last, the study not of matter but of forces: "Indeed, as we know nothing of matter, except through its manifestation of forces, it is obvious that the study of matter itself is at last resolved into the study of forces."[87] The new science provided Whitman with a model of immaterial force capable of moving through every dimension of space and time.

And the principle of correlation of force, through which, as Youmans asserted, the material of the universe "changes form with protean facility, traversing a thousand cycles of change, vanishing and reappearing incessantly," provides a scientific basis for the equally protean character of the persona.[88] Throughout the poem the speaker takes on new and diverse identities; he is "of old and young, of the foolish as much as the wise ... maternal as well as paternal, a child as well as a man." He acquires identities characteristic of the diverse regions of the America, and "not merely of the New World but of Africa Europe or Asia.... a wandering savage." He can take up any occupation, including "farmer, mechanic, or artist"; in fact, he admits that "I resist anything better than my own diversity" (pp. 42–43). The new scientific laws opened a world not of rigid fixity, but of change and transformation, and the Whitman persona, recognizing a similar flexibility and diversity in his own character, is encouraged to explore the fluidity of his own identity. The exploratory "flight of the fluid and swallowing soul" of the persona is as much into the psychological depths of the mind as it is into the vast expanse of the universe.

As the new scientific concepts provided the means of locomotion for the poet, so they also provided the conceptual building blocks for his imaginative "dwelling." Throughout "Song of Myself" the speaker testifies to the operation of profound natural laws. In Section 14, for instance, he mentions "the same old law" which unites him with the natural world (p. 38). In Section 43, responding to "doubters and sullen mopers," he identifies an omnipresent force which brings reassuring purpose, even to those who have lost and suffered the most:

> It cannot fail the young man who died and was buried,
> Nor the young woman who died and was put by his side,
> Nor the little child that peeped in at the door and then drew back and was
>   never seen again.
> Nor the old man who has lived without purpose, and feels it with bitterness
>   worse than gall,
> Nor him in the poorhouse tubercled by rum and the bad disorder,
> Nor the numberless slaughtered and wrecked.... nor the brutish koboo,
>   called the ordure of humanity,
> Nor the sacs merely floating with open mouths for food to slip in,
> Nor any thing in the earth, or down in the oldest graves of the earth,
> Nor any thing in the myriads of spheres, nor one of the myriads of myriads
>   that inhabit them,
> Nor the present, nor the least wisp that is known.

(p. 78)

The speaker concedes that the power of prediction eludes him, that he does "not know what is untried and afterward." Still, he can speak of the future in such a way that it takes on the qualities of a natural force which is "sure and alive, and sufficient" (p. 78). It is a natural law universal in scope, extending back in time to all the dead, including even those who have brought failure upon themselves, and going forward to the immensities of space. It applies as well to the life on other solar systems, the "myriads of myriads" who inhabit the spheres. (Chambers, as we have seen, spoke of the high probability of life on other planets.) This law comes to have the force of a predictable and reassuring principle governing and ordering the cosmos.

The poet speaks again regarding the operation of a universal law in

Section 50. Although he is unable to define its essence completely, he can describe certain of its attributes. It is present in him as a creative force, but cannot be located in any of the usual sources:

> There is that in me.... I do not know what it is.... but I know it is in me.
>
> Wrenched and sweaty.... calm and cool then my body becomes;
> I sleep.... I sleep long.
>
> I do not know it.... it is without name.... it is a word unsaid,
> It is not in any dictionary or utterance or symbol.
>
> (p. 86)

This nameless presence within the speaker would seem to defy all attempts at definition; he does "not know what it is." It cannot be denominated with any of the conventional signs of human speech. Intensely personal, it is an experience which comes to the speaker much as a difficult birth, leaving him at last "calm and cool." It has the attributes of an ineffable mystic experience, which at best can be suggested, but not defined. Intensely personal, even ineffable, it is an experience which seems to elude the capabilities of language, to say nothing of the categories of science, entirely.

Yet, in the final lines of this section the speaker is able to find some words to describe it:

> Something it swings on more than the earth I swing on,
> To it the creation is the friend whose embracing awakes me.
>
> Perhaps I might tell more.... Outlines! I plead for my brothers and sisters.
>
> Do you see O my brothers and sisters?
> It is not chaos or death.... it is form and union and plan.... it is eternal
>   life.... it is happiness.
>
> (pp. 86–87)

Here the speaker generalizes and applies what in the first six lines had been an esentially private experience to others, his "brothers and sisters." He has discovered something that gives order and life—not chaos and death—to the universe. He is able to find in his intensely personal experience a larger principle, one which speaks reassuringly of "eternal life" and the existence of "form, and union, and plan" in the universe. The reference to "outlines" suggests that even if there is no definitive external source, then it may at least be found in a sketchy reference elsewhere. While the speaker does not identify the source, he has asserted the presence in both man and the universe of a deathless creative principle which brings order and promises "eternal life" and "happiness." The section suggests that the intuitive, intensely personal knowledge of the first part of the section finds its confirmation in ordering principles of the creation.

In the great law of conservation of force Youmans found such a natural cosmic principle, something "more than the earth I swing on," to use Whitman's language. In discussing this law in the introduction to *The Correlation and Conservation of Forces*, he too grew rapturous, speaking of the "persistence of force" as the "highest law in physical science," one which has been confirmed by the most rigorous experimental methods. He described a deathless universe, one of evolutionary development and expansion, a world where a "wondrous dynamic chain binds into living unity the realms of matter and mind through measureless amplitude of time." Like the world pictured by Whitman, it is ordered and reassuring, a world in which the creative mind of man is intimately involved in a sublime unfolding plan. The contemplation of its laws led Youmans to write rapturously of the "solemn and mysterious worship" he felt at coming into the presence of that "Unknown and Infinite Cause."[89] The speaker suggests, then, that the nameless presence which he had discovered within himself intuitively was somehow connected to the principles or "outlines" which give order to the cosmos, principles which can be known through the investigations of science. In this sense, Whitman could write in the 1855 preface that "exact science and its practical movements are no checks on the greatest poet but always his greatest encouragement and support" (p. 15).

Throughout "Song of Myself" the speaker treats the theme of immortality and ties it closely to the concepts of evolution and conservation of force. Raising the question of the status of the dead in Section 6, he writes confidently that

> They are alive and well somewhere;
> The smallest sprout shows there is really no death,
> And if ever there was it led forward life, and does not wait at the end to ar-
>   rest it,
> And ceased the moment life appeared.
> All goes onward and outward.... and nothing collapses,
> And to die is different from what anyone supposed, and luckier.
>
> (p. 32)

The evidence of the "smallest sprout" shows that the dead have been transformed—"correlated" in Youmans' term—into other elements. The speaker denies the possibility of death in a world in which such transformations and correlations are the rule, a world of evolutionary growth and development. The world of "Song of Myself" is one where "nothing collapses," or, to use Youmans' phrase, where "matter is indestructible." In this universe, "all goes onward and outward." The poet, then, can assert that death is "different" from what has been "supposed" and "luckier." Such an assertion does not demand the intervention of a deity, but may be made on the basis of the natural and predictable processes of the physical world.

The speaker's awareness of such laws makes it possible for him to affirm his own immortality. In Section 20 he emulates their supreme confidence:

> And I know I am deathless,
> I know this orbit of mine cannot be swept by a carpenter's compass,
> I know I shall not pass like a child's carlacue cut with a burnt stick at night.
>
> I know I am august,
> I do not trouble my spirit to vindicate itself or be understood,
> I see that the elementary laws never apologize,
> I reckon I behave no prouder than the level I plant my house by after all.
>
> ....
>
> One world is aware, and by far the largest to me, and that is myself,
> And whether I come to my own today or in ten thousand or ten million years,
> I can cheerfully take it now, or with equal cheerfulness I can wait.
>
> My foothold is tenoned and mortised in granite,
> I laugh at what you call dissolution,
> And I know the amplitude of time.
>
>   (p. 46)

The mention of "elementary laws" leads directly to the speaker's placing of the self in the context of evolution. Confident of the sure process of development, he is prepared to wait even "ten million years." His knowledge of the physical universe enables him to "laugh at ... dissolution." Part of the humor of the passage comes from the ironic reliance on something as insubstantial as granite—when, that is, granite is seen from the perspective of the "amplitude of time."

In the concluding section, the speaker asserts that such is his diversity that he cannot be held to a fixed spot in the material world. He becomes, at last, a force in constant motion. Youmans remarked that "though matter changes form with protean facility, traversing a thousand cycles of change, vanishing and reappearing incessantly, yet it never wears out or lapses into nothing."[90] In the last vision we have of him, Whitman's speaker has become just such a vanishing and reappearing natural force:

> I depart as air.... I shake my white locks at the runaway sun,
> I effuse my flesh in eddies and drift it in lacy jags.
>
> I bequeath myself to the dirt to grow from the grass I love,
> If you want me again look for me under your bootsoles.
>
> You will hardly know who I am or what I mean,
> But I shall be good health to you nevertheless,
> And filter and fibre your blood.
>
> Failing to fetch me at first keep encouraged,
> Missing me one place search another,
> I stop some where waiting for you

(p. 88)

VII. Conclusion

This paper has been built on the assumption that Whitman, in asserting that scientists "are the lawgivers of poets and their construction underlies the structure of every perfect poem," was providing the reader with an important clue to the meaning and structural principles of his own work. It has identified E. L. Youmans as a scientist and writer who was in an ideal position to introduce Whitman to contemporary scientific thought. Fellow borders at Mrs. Chipman's in New York and associates on the *Aurora*, the two knew each other well and would have had ample opportunity to come together and exchange ideas. Even after the sharp rupture in their personal relationship, Whitman witnessed Youmans' emergence as the most important expositor of scientific ideas in America.

In his early lectures and books, Youmans developed scientific ideas which figure prominently in Whitman's poetry. The assertion of Edmund Clarence Stedman that "Professor Youmans inspired Whitman's eloquent passages on Evolution" provides external evidence that Youmans was an important source for Whitman. However, recognizing the imprecision inherent in source studies, this paper has proceeded cautiously, and has avoided categorical claims for Youmans as a source of particular ideas. It is likely that Whitman drew from Youmans, but he was by no means an exclusive source.

Certainly an understanding of Youmans' work expands our knowledge of the range of scientific ideas available to Whitman. By retracing Youmans' own steps toward evolution in the late 1840s, we identified Chambers' *Vestiges of Creation* as an essential source for Whitman. Youmans was encouraged by evolutionary theory to understand man in physical terms, as a "vortex of forces," in constant and dynamic interaction with the material universe. Although he could not abide the "obtrusive filthiness" of Whitman's poetry, in most respects his treatment of man as a being whose identity comes from his body was both consistent with and supportive of this well-known feature of Whitman's poetry. Speaking out against the destructiveness of the Cartesian dualism, Youmans expounded a theory of the enormous power of the subconscious mind, which may well have encouraged Whitman in the development of a poetic persona with such remarkable powers. And it is probable that Youmans, in introducing the conservation theories into America, provided Whitman with two ideas which figure prominently in "Song of Myself." These ideas provide scientific justification for Whitman's protean, deathless persona, capable of moving effortlessly throughout the cosmos.

Youmans sought to uncover the links uniting mind and matter. A fundamental premise of his work is that man is a unified being and that thought is an organic function. One mark of Whitman's genius as a poet is that he recognized the extraordinary implications for poetry in this approach. For in becoming an "index" for the forces "surging and surging" through him, the Whitman persona discovers a firm basis for his art in the natural world. Most importantly Whitman found a "voice" which enabled him to establish the links uniting him with the unsuspected dimensions of the world, including the "threads" connecting the stars, the "cycles of preparation and accretion," and the dispossessed. Paradoxically, then, while grounding his art in the latest principles revealed by "exact science" and its "practical movements," Whitman was able to discover—or rediscover—the magical properties of poetry, and so speak "the password primeval." In this sense, "Song of Myself" succeeds brilliantly in bringing together man's ancient belief in the mythic power of the word along with the results of the latest experimental science. Whatever the personal disagreements between Walt Whitman and Edward Youmans may have been, "Song of Myself" does demonstrate a "love between the poet and the man of demonstrable science," for the poet makes remarkable use of the "seed" of scientific conceptions. And in "the beauty and tuft" of Whitman's poem we may find "the tuft and final applause of [contemporary] science."

NOTES

1. Walt Whitman, *Complete Poetry and Collected Prose*, ed. Justin Kaplan (New York: Library of America, 1982), p. 15. All quotations from Whitman's collected works will be taken from this edition and given in the text.

2. Joseph Beaver, *Walt Whitman: Poet of Science* (Morningside Heights, N.Y.: King's Crown Press, 1951).

3. Harold Aspiz, *Walt Whitman and the Body Beautiful* (Urbana: University of Illinois Press, 1980).

4. John Burroughs, *Birds and Poets with Other Papers* (Boston: Houghton, Mifflin, 1904), p. 241.

5. Floyd Stovall, *The Foreground of* Leaves of Grass (Charlottesville: University Press of Virginia, 1974), p. 153.

6. Horace Traubel, *With Walt Whitman in Camden (March 28–July 14, 1888)* (Boston: Small, Maynard, 1906), p. 101.

7. Roger Asselineau, *The Evolution of Walt Whitman: The Creation of a Book* (Cambridge: Harvard University Press, 1962), p. 289n107. In her pioneering study, "Whitman's Indebtedness to the Scientific Thought of His Day," Alice Lovelace Cooke mentions Youmans as an acquaintance of Whitman's, but is not aware of their friendship in the years before 1855. She writes, "We have no record of an acquaintance with any man particularly interested in science during his formative period" (*Studies in English* [University of Texas], 14 [1934]: 91).

8. Edmund Clarence Stedman to Bliss Perry, 15 March 1907, MH; quoted with permission.

9. John Fiske, *Edward Livingston Youmans* (New York: D. Appleton, 1894), p. 46.

10. *Walt Whitman of the New York* Aurora, ed. Joseph Jay Rubin and Charles H. Brown (State College, Penn.: Bald Eagle Press, 1950), p. 23.

11. Fiske, *Youmans*, p. 46.

12. Fiske, *Youmans*, p. 59.

13. *The Uncollected Poetry and Prose of Walt Whitman*, ed. Emory Holloway, 2 vols. (Garden City, N.Y.: Doubleday, Page, 1921), 1:148.

14. Youmans, *A Class-Book of Chemistry* (New York: D. Appleton, 1851).

15. Fiske, *Youmans*, p. 74.

16. Fiske, *Youmans*, pp. 75–76.

17. William Levrette, "E. L. Youmans' Crusade for Scientific Autonomy and Respectability." *American Quarterly*, 17 (Spring 1965): 12–32.

18. Youmans, "On the Scientific Study of Human Nature," in *The Culture Demanded by Modern Life*, ed. Youmans (New York: D. Appleton, 1867), p. 407.

19. Youmans, "On the Scientific Study of Human Nature," p. 407.

20. Fiske, *Youmans*, p. 46.

21. Quoted in Gay Wilson Allen, *The Solitary Singer* (New York: New York University Press, 1967), p. 58.

22. Quoted in Russel Nye, *Society and Culture in America* (New York: Harper and Row, 1974), p. 30.

23. Nye, *Society and Culture in America*, p. 28.

24. Fiske, *Youmans*, p. 47.

25. *Uncollected Poetry and Prose*, 1:229.

26. Allen, *The Solitary Singer*, p. 30.

27. Charles M. Haar, "E. L. Youmans: A Chapter in the Diffusion of Science in America," *Journal of the History of Ideas*, 9 (April 1948): 195.

28. Joseph Jay Rubin, *The Historic Whitman* (University Park: Pennsylvania State University Press, 1973), p. 287.

29. *New York Times*, 23 February 1853, p. 2, col. 4.

30. "The Religious Work of Science," in Fiske, *Youmans*, p. 501.

31. Fiske, *Youmans*, p. 35.

32. Fiske, *Youmans*, p. 42.

33. Fiske, *Youmans*, pp. 56–58.

34. *Complete Writings of Walt Whitman*, ed. Richard Maurice Bucke et al., 10 vols. (New York: Putnams, 1902), 10:69.

35. Milton Millhauser, *Just Before Darwin* (Middletown, Conn.: Wesleyan University Press, 1963), p. 85.

36. Loren Eisely, *Darwin's Century* (Garden City, N.Y.: Doubleday, 1958), p. 136.

37. Chambers, *Vestiges of the Natural History of Creation*, ed. Gavin DeBeer (New York: Humanities Press, 1969), p. 21.

38. Chambers, *Vestiges*, pp. 35–36.

39. Chambers, *Vestiges*, pp. 202–203.

40. Chambers, *Vestiges*, p. 198.

41. Chambers, *Vestiges*, p. 276.

42. Chambers, *Vestiges*, pp. 203–204.

43. Peter J. Bowler, *Evolution: The History of an Idea* (Berkeley: University of California Press, 1984), p. 138.

44. Allen, *The Solitary Singer*, p. 144.

45. *Uncollected Poetry and Prose*, 2:66.

46. Asselineau discusses these two concerns in *The Evolution of Walt Whitman*, pp. 52–77.

47. Chambers, *Vestiges*, pp. 42–43.

48. Milton Millhauser, "The Literary Impact of 'Vestiges of Creation,'" *Modern Language Quarterly*, 17 (September 1956): 221.

49. Fiske, *Youmans*, p. 75.

50. *Uncollected Poetry and Prose*, 2:64.

51. *Uncollected Poetry and Prose*, 2:65.

52. *Uncollected Poetry and Prose*, 2:65.

53. *Uncollected Poetry and Prose*, 2:66.

54. *Uncollected Poetry and Prose*, 2:69.

55. Allen, *The New Walt Whitman Handbook* (New York: New York University Press, 1975), p. 192.

56. "The Masquerade of the Elements," *Lectures of the American Institute of Instruction* (Boston: Ticknor and Fields, 1861), p. 106.

57. Fiske, *Youmans*, pp. 72–73.

58. Aspiz, *Whitman*, p. 143.

59. D. H. Jacques, *Hints Toward Physical Perfection* (New York: Fowler and Wells, 1859), p. 56–57; quoted in Aspiz, *Whitman*, p. 143.

60. Samuel Warren, "Electricity the Great Acting Part of Nature," *American Phrenological Journal*, 11 (1849): 151; quoted in Aspiz, *Whitman*, p. 148.

61. Aspiz, *Whitman*, p. 149.

62. Youmans, *Chemical Atlas* (New York: D. Appleton, 1854), p. 104.

63. *Chemical Atlas*, p. 104.

64. *Uncollected Poetry and Prose*, 2:76.

65. *The Collected Works of Ralph Waldo Emerson*, ed. Alfred R. Ferguson, Joseph Slater, et al., 3 vols. to date (Cambridge: Harvard University Press, 1971–), vol. 3, *Essays: Second Series*, ed. Slater (1981), p. 20.

66. *Chemical Atlas*, p. 11.

67. *Chemical Atlas*, pp. 10–11.

68. *Chemical Atlas*, pp. 11–12.

69. "On the Scientific Study of Human Nature," p. 375.

70. "On the Scientific Study of Human Nature," p. 377.

71. Youmans, "Mental Discipline in Education," in *The Culture Demanded by Modern Life*, ed. Youmans, p. 26.

72. T[homas]. S[ecombe]., "Laycock, Thomas," *DNB*, 32:302–303.

73. "On the Scientific Study of Human Nature," p. 384.

74. "On the Scientific Study of Human Nature," p. 382.

75. "On the Scientific Study of Human Nature," p. 404.

76. *Correlation and Conservation of Forces*, ed. Youmans (New York: D. Appleton, 1864), p. xii.

77. *Correlation and Conservation*, ed. Youmans, pp. xii–xiii.

78. *Correlation and Conservation*, ed. Youmans, pp. xii.

79. Benjamin A. G. Fuller, *History of Greek Philosophy* (1923; rpt. Westport, Conn.: Greenwood, 1968), pp. 236, 250.

80. George Sarton, *A History of Science* (Cambridge: Harvard University Press, 1952), p. 253.

81. Horace Traubel, *With Walt Whitman in Camden (July 16, 1888–October 31, 1888)* (New York: Mitchell Kennerley, 1915), p. 445.

82. Allen, *The Solitary Singer*, p. 139.

83. Frances Wright, *A Few Days in Athens* (1822; rpt. Salem, N.H.: M. H. Ayer, 1972), pp. 177–78.

84. Fiske, *Youmans*, p. 73.

85. Fiske, *Youmans*, p. 73.

86. *Correlation and Conservation*, ed. Youmans, p. xli.

87. *Correlation and Conservation*, ed. Youmans, p. xxxi.

88. *Correlation and Conservation*, ed. Youmans, p. xii.

89. *Correlation and Conservation*, ed. Youmans, p. xliii.

90. *Correlation and Conservation*, ed. Youmans, p. xlii.

WILLIAM E. McMAHON

Grass and Its Mate in "Song of Myself"

T he deepest component to the formal coherence of "Song of Myself" may well be the fact that the grass is not a bachelor. It has a spouse. The polarity of this male/female pair probably constitutes the strongest of all the symbolic bondings in the poem. Before the woman is identified, it should be noted that many interpreters of Whitman's masterpiece have recognized the crucial role of polarity. A few examples will suggest not only the tendency toward polar interpretations, but also the theoretical impact of recognizing a polar bonding between grass and its feminine counterpart.

In 1957 James E. Miller, Jr., analyzing "Song of Myself" as inverted mysticism, concluded that Whitman subverts the orthodox mode by celebrating body and sensory experience, and by rejecting the concept of sin. Construing Whitman's central postulate to be that "man's sense of sin is his greatest sin" (16), Miller, while emphasizing Whitman's reconciliation of polar opposites such as seen and unseen, body and soul, man and woman, and so on, did not suggest connecting the polarities to a master symbol of grass and its mate. In 1959 in his preface to the Viking edition of *Leaves of Grass*, Malcolm Cowley (assuming that "Song of Myself" lacks formal unity but enjoys psychological coherence) looked to the East and postulated an affinity between Whitman and Hinduism, and he briefly mentioned Taoism, which is steeped in male/female polarity. In 1964 V. K. Chari emphasized the

From *South Atlantic Review* 51, no. 1 (January 1986): 41-55. © 1986 by William E. McMahon.

sharply Vedantic flavor of Whitman's mysticism in that, like Hindu sages, Whitman accepts the phenomenological reality of the physical world, yet does not assign it the absolute reality of the spiritual world. If this thesis were accepted, and if grass is physical and its mate spiritual and unseen, then the interpretation of Chari gains validity. However, I will argue that Hinduism is not as close as Taoism to Whitman's stance.

In 1966 Howard J. Waskow presented a polar explication of Whitman's world, suggesting a bipolar set to Whitman's mind: "The touchstone of fusion, the blending of two extremes, is applied to almost every area about which Whitman records an opinion" (28). Waskow also noted, shrewdly, that sometimes the opposites are not reconciled (30), and that Whitman (not merging time into a fluid drift) maintains sharp linear differentiations between past, present, and future (69). Although Waskow did not relate Whitman's bipolar mode to grass and its consort, such an espousal would obviously enrich his analysis. In 1968 Edwin Haviland Miller stressed the erotic content of "Song of Myself" along with the phallic import of grass. While he did not juxtapose the grass to any female counterpart, his sexual centrism would benefit from the presence of such a pair.

From the seventies three examples may be mentioned. William E. White, both affirming and denying polarity as the key to Whitman's poetry, concluded that all of Whitman's polar opposites (marshalled under a unifying love and procreation dynamism) merge in a manner revealing that they are not opposites at all, but "dual aspects of the same thing." Thus "there is no duality or paradox or ambiguity" because "there are no opposites" (350, 360). In White's opinion Whitman recognizes both male and female components in his personality, worries deeply about the feminine aspect, and solves the problem by moving to an acceptance of "the mystical bisexual nature of his own personality, which is for him like a blade of grass, a microcosm of the benevolent intricacy" (357). White did not suggest that the grass enjoys any logical mate. He did quote Whitman's words, "Out of the dimness opposite equals advance." It seems more plausible to accept Whitman's phrasing and construe the polar opposites as genuine opposites genuinely equal. White's paradigm requires that we see body and soul as the same thing, and good and evil as the same thing. While Whitman does declare that he is beyond good and evil, this does not entail their sameness. However, White's model of negated dualism makes possible this claim about Whitman: "His message is not intellectual; it is anti-intellectual. It is not moral; it flows beyond and beneath morality into a beautiful and loving amorality" (353).

E. Fred Carlisle in 1973 (aligning himself with poststructuralist assaults upon the self) claimed that the core of the poem resides in the transmutation of an improperly isolated unitary self into a more wholesome fluid and dialogic self, ambiguously positioned partly in non-self and in others.[1] Carlisle could have made use of the fluidity of that thing which is the mate of the grass. A different analysis came from Diane Kepner, who in 1979 argued that Whitman displays a coherent theory of reality in which atoms and their composites allow cosmic change because of their powers to recombine, yet also reify cosmic permanence because the atoms and their combinations are saturated with divine purpose. Since Whitman obviously chants of divine purpose in "Song of Myself" and obviously celebrates physical objects as well, Kepner's ideas are plausible and important. If Whitman does project a kind of spiritually centered atomism (a kind of bardic American hylozoism) then this deepest polar ontology would accord well with a master symbolic pairing between grass and some invisible and more spiritual opposite.

While other examples of polar assumptions in analyses of "Song of Myself" could be mentioned, these suffice to demonstrate that a major interpretive tradition exists. With polarity, then, everywhere in the poem, it would be surprising if that major symbol, the grass, did not have a suitable companion, one establishing a dual thrust similar in cosmic scope to the attraction and repulsion of Heraclitus or the tiger and lamb of Blake.

Certainly the opening sections of "Song of Myself" manipulate polarities. In the first section Whitman declares a unity between the self and others: "For every atom belonging to me as good belongs to you." The third section speaks of youth and age, of heaven and hell, of seen and unseen, and of the equal sweetness of body and soul—and Whitman, here at the start, lays down firmly the principle of polar balance:

Urge and urge and urge,
Always the procreant urge of the world
Out of the dimness opposite equals advance,
    always substance and increase, always sex.

Section five, after describing a sexual meeting between the body and the soul, asserts the bond of equality between God and man.

Section six, of course, gives the famous catalogue of the values symbolized by the grass: the sign of optimism, the sign of Godhead, the sign of childhood, the sign of democratic equality, and the sign of immortality. However, if the symbolic grass has some exactly right, some inevitable spiritual mate, we would expect to meet the bride at the start of the poem; furthermore, if the polar female equals the grass, we should find her all through the poem, and should expect an especially strong glimpse of her in Whitman's ending, paired with the grass.

The one spiritual presence that everywhere embraces grass is atmosphere. Grass penetrates the air in exactly the male and female pattern called for by other imagery of the poem. Grass is first mentioned by Whitman in line five of the first section. Note carefully what occurs next in lines six and seven:

> My tongue, every atom of my blood, formed
>   from this soil, this air,
> Born here of parents born here from parents the
>   same, and their parents the same.

After calling attention to grass and soil and air, and to father and mother, next, at the start of section two, Whitman rejects artificial perfumed air. And then he makes a crucial remark:

> The atmosphere is not a perfume, it has no taste
>   of the distillation, it is odorless,
> It is for my mouth forever, I am in love with it.

However, if the air is a genuine complement to the grass, the signs must appear in places other than the opening sections. In section seven Whitman reiterates his copular metaphor: "I am the mate and companion of people." In section ten Whitman says, "I saw the marriage of the trapper in the open air in the far west." Section thirteen contains important lines. Whitman calls himself a caresser of life who flows backwards and forwards and penetrates every niche and does not miss a single person or single object. The one force on earth that can literally do this is the invisible atmosphere. It caresses all objects whether they know it or not, supplying an image of Whitman's ghostly spirit. When Whitman next mentions ducks and their "wing'd purposes," the atmosphere allows the turn upward toward transcendence. In section fourteen the poet asserts, "What is commonest, cheapest, nearest, easiest, is Me"—and these attributes that associate clearly with the grass belong just as conclusively to the air.

The symbol of air emerges strongly in section sixteen—"I resist any thing better than my own diversity, / Breathe the air but leave plenty after me." While amorously courting the night in section twenty-one, Whitman mentions that the darkness contains south winds. In the next section, courting the ocean, Whitman calls the waves the breathing of the sea. In section forty-seven he says he will translate himself only in the open air. Such details, stressing the potency of the atmosphere, could be further multiplied. And then of course there is the obvious fact that all human experience, dominated by sight, depends on the atmosphere, as Whitman suggests in section thirty-three when he imagines the splendors of the arctic ocean: "Through the clear atmosphere I stretch around on the wonderful beauty."

Whitman's passion for opera and oratory, feeding his dream of bardic honor, suggests another aspect of his interest in the air. The mechanism of voice is stressed by the poet in section twenty-five. He writes:

> My voice goes after what my eyes cannot reach,
> With the twirl of my tongue I encompass worlds
>   and volumes of worlds.

In section twenty-six Whitman shows his sexual pairing by praising a great tenor and a great soprano, and the tenor's breath fills the poet "fresh as the creation." Also, in section forty, Whitman, connecting his own voice to the atmosphere, addresses people who might otherwise be defeated: "I dilate you with tremendous breath, I buoy you up, / Every room of the house do I fill with an armed force."

Finally, in his last section, the poet brings together the atmosphere and the grass so openly that readers cannot escape the intention:

> I depart as air, I shake my white locks
>   at the runaway sun,
> I effuse my flesh in eddies, and drift it in
>   lacy jags.
> I bequeath myself to the dirt to grow from
>   the grass I love.
> If you want me again look for me under
>   your boot-soles.

Thus Whitman gives many clues indicating that in "Song of Myself" the grass (of the earth, physical, masculine, cheap, near at hand) enjoys a copular bond with an appropriate spouse (spiritual, feminine, distributed everywhere, also cheap, also near at hand).[2]

For some readers, two kinds of philosophic taint accompany these metaphors of the equality of polar opposites in Whitman's poem. The first taint, declaimed by D. H. Lawrence, is that Whitman's passion to merge opposites into a unity is unwholesome. In Lawrence's vision of the sexual world, the polar opposites do not merge; their individuation endures. The second possible taint upon Whitman's pairings is that the powerful sexual impulse, in Whitman's hymn to energy unchecked, explodes the categories of good and evil. Whitman declares many times in "Song of Myself" his disinterest in condemning any modes of human conduct. His mated symbols of grass and air effectively convey his indiscriminate levelling of values—in contrast to Poe's universe of gradation and to the elitist and Platonic iconography of Hart Crane, Wallace Stevens, and T. S. Eliot.[3] However, since Whitman at times reveals a sharply moralistic side, it is by no means clear that the charge of amorality should be accepted. If Whitman, or anyone, does reject the categories of good and evil, this should be seen as a weakness in view of the general consensus of philosophers that moral neutrality cannot be a serious human attitude.[4]

Whether Whitman was wise or foolish, however, new readings of the poem should weigh the probability that the controlling symbol of "Song of Myself" becomes not the grass alone, but the polarity uniting grass with its mate, the atmosphere arching over all the affairs of earth, unseen, spiritual, transcendental. This claim might need one correction if Walt himself is a kind of symbol as a cosmic male impregnator for whom all objects, creatures, forces of nature, and people supply the beloved counterpart. However, Whitman's presence takes nothing away from the profound integration of the thematics of the poem through the symbolic marriage of grass and atmosphere.

If the grass/air espousal has the importance suggested, interpreters of Whitman's greatest poem should consider an analogy to oriental Yin-Yang design. It was Emerson, not Thoreau, who brought Whitman to a boil, and Lin Yutang asserts that "Emerson's two essays, 'Circles' and 'The Over-soul,' are completely Taoist, and one appreciates them better after reading Laotse" (14). If the Taoist analogy has justice, then the feminine element in Whitman and in the symbolic atmosphere can certainly be given a classically metaphysical and normatively psychological grounding. The metaphysical realm is limned in Max Kaltenmark's description of Taoist polarity:

> This heavenly or natural order, often called simply Tao, was held in classical thinking to be primarily observable in the regular alternation of the seasons and of night and day. This cycle of hot and cold, light and darkness, was said to reflect the alternating influence of two sexual principles, the Yin and the Yang, which governed the behavior of all creatures. The Yin, principle of darkness, cold, and femininity, invited withdrawal, rest, passivity; the Yang, principle of light, heat, and masculinity, incited expansion, activity, even aggression (24).

While not thinking of Whitman, Alan Watts explains Taoism in a manner that illuminates Whitman's central intent. Watts observes that "The *yin-yang* principle is not, therefore, what we would ordinarily call a dualism, but rather an explicit duality expressing an implicit unity" (26). In discussing being and non-being as polar opposites, Watts's remark about western man helps explain why Whitman found the air so suitable: "We ignore space just because it is uniform, as water to fish and air to birds" (24). The metaphor Watts chooses to explain Taoist polarity applies to Whitman's plan: "the different, but inseparable, sides of the same coin" (23).

An analogy to Taoism, then, helps clarify the structure and intent in "Song of Myself." Whitman's polarities become an ordered set grouped under a conceptual treatment of the physical and spiritual universes as harmonizing opposites, and also grouped under the master symbols of grass and atmosphere, symbols that, like Hart Crane's bridge, actualize a spanning and cross-fertilization between the seen and unseen.[5] On the basis of such a unifying symbolic polarity, can one construct some Riffaterrian hypogram for "Song of Myself"? Perhaps we can say this: selfhood explored for its total significance in a dualistic seen and unseen cosmos harmonized by polarity and deity, and for its relevance to a patriotic expansion of American democracy into a levelling spiritual democracy, all this ordered by the pervasive symbolic presence of both Walt himself and the copular bonding of grass and atmosphere. This formula may need adjustments, but any poem with unity of thought should sustain a hypogramatic compression.[6]

If it is true that the luminous atmosphere becomes iconic sign for the spiritual element in matter, in selfhood, and in spiritual democracy (regions more everlasting even if not more valuable than their physical counterparts), then we should not be surprised if Whitman, at the end of "Song of Myself," accords a kind of victory to atmosphere and eternity. While he does bequeath himself to earth and grass, he also says, "I depart as air, I shake my white locks at the runaway sun." These ending lines set a final seal upon the over-arching symbolic mating of grass and air. I have so far avoided mention of section seventeen, which is unusually brief and highly significant, consisting of the following six lines:

> These are really the thoughts of all men in all
> ags and lands, and they are not original with me,
> If they are not yours as much as mine they are
> nothing, or next to nothing.
> If they are not the riddle and the untying of the
> riddle they are nothing.
> If they are not just as close as they are distant
> they are nothing.
>
> This is the grass that grows wherever the land is
> and the water is.
> This the common air that bathes the globe.

The pattern of a marriage between grass and atmosphere might illuminate a reading of Whitman's poem in four ways: (1) local polarities in the different sections take on new cosmic significance, (2) larger structural coherences are brought to light, (3) the poem as a whole can be more firmly placed in the continuing debate about monism and dualism, and (4) the relationship of Whitman's poem to other American poetry can become more clear.

The local polarities which are affected come in an unending chain throughout the poem. In section two Whitman asks us to stop with him one day and one night. Often in other sections a day and night pairing emerges, daytime scenes being more sharp and particularized and nocturnal scenes more fluid and mystical. This pattern acquires new ambience when related to the physical and spiritual thrust of grass and air symbolism. Section three mentions seen and unseen; section thirteen mentions backward and forward motion; section fifteen contains a girl at a spinning machine who advances and retreats, and also an alternation from day to night and life to death; section sixteen calls attention to palpable and impalpable, and section twenty to solid and deathless; section twenty-three stresses matter and time and section twenty-four asserts that the earth and sky stand each other off in their perpetual conjunction; section twenty-five stresses visible and invisible.

These suggestive pairings continue to the end of the poem. Section twenty-nine mentions parting and later recompense, and also connects sprouts (suggesting grass) to physical sexual touch, and also to vertical masculine landscape forms; section thirty-two celebrates Whitman's ride on a magnificent stallion and ends with the hint of a larger ride, not restricted to the physical plane of reality; section thirty-three emphasizes space and time, an extremely important parallel to grass and air, pointing to the larger symbolic meanings of both. In section thirty-three Whitman says, "I help myself to material and immaterial;" a daytime massacre in section thirty-four is followed by a nighttime carnage in section thirty-five. Section forty relates breath to immortality and the defeat of the grave, and also moves from day to night. In section forty-two Whitman says he will leap beyond but also bring nearer, and section forty-three stresses the tried and the untried (that is the materialized past and the immaterial future), giving Whitman's promise that neither will fail. Section forty-seven finds Whitman swearing that he will never again mention love or death inside a house, but only in the open air.

These catalogues that I have presented demonstrate the frequency with which the bonding of grass and air illuminates local material in the various parts of "Song of Myself." Of similar benefit is a new alertness to larger structural patterns. For instance, how many times does Whitman move from birth to death and from day to night? Why is it that in the crucial section six Whitman starts with a child, moves on to the grave, and ends with an onward and outward immortality motif? Why is it that in his catalogues he covers the north and south of America, the east and west, the lands and waters, the small and large? Finally, why is it that from section thirty-eight to the last section, fifty-two, Whitman presents a sustained flood of optimism about immortality and divinity and the defeat of death and doubt? The answer to this last question suggests the answer to the others. Whitman's poem typically ranges from seen to unseen, from physical to mystical, from grass to air. A progression from time to eternity marks the poem. While the domain of grass, matter, and temporality cannot be set lower in ultimate value, Whitman wishes to give a victory and a climax to atmosphere and eternity.

In addition to these insights into the internal structure of "Song of Myself," the grass/air polarity encourages the reader to ponder Whitman's poem as a document in the great Western and Eastern debate over monism and dualism. At present, this ancient dispute focuses in the efforts of logicians and philosophers of science to wield Occam's razor and reduce reality to a single plane of materialism describable in some uniform canonical language of symbolic logic. When Whitman insists that matter and spirit are both basic and both ultimate, he opposes this modern variety of monism, taking his stand with the older traditions of idealism that celebrate mind and soul. Whitman does this, however, in a most radical and most important way when he insists that the material world is equal to the occult world in truth and value. The new monistic materialism faces quite a number of logical difficulties that cannot be developed here.[7] One of these is the improbability that brain events can be reduced to machine events. Aristotle thought a monism would not be logical because reality demands at least three primary components: a physical substratum along with an energizing force of a polar sort such as attraction and repulsion. Furthermore, modern science is not sufficiently developed to give anyone grounds for confidence that a simple materialism will suffice as an explanatory paradigm. As long as there is a difference between nonliving and living cells, and as long as mental states such as wanting and fearing do indeed cause physical changes, and as long as intelligent men and women remain in a religious condition, Whitman's version of a wedding between matter and spirit should be treated with respect.

A materialistic monism faces other problems. As Aristotle explained, the root concepts in any discipline or any discourse community (concepts such as cause, force, form, architectural unity, organic unity, aporia, equality, justice, simple, composite, and so on) are themselves derived by rational intuition, a function of mind. Husserl takes delight in reminding scientists that there can be no valid concept of world or matter until the mind first of all questions and validates the theoretical possibility that there might be a class of objects whose essence lies in substance. Cognitions always come first. Heidegger and Sartre are often invoked to support a materialistic monism. However, Heidegger's program to let Being undercut metaphysics is itself undercut because "Being" is a metaphysical concept. Sartrian material flux is said to discredit the categories of mind and soul. And yet, to encapsulate the matter, it is impossible for existence to precede essence because "existence" is itself an immaterial category of essence. From a different direction, a Whitman dualism of matter and spirit receives support in that apparently neither science nor legal theory can operate unless abstract universals such as causation and negligence enjoy epistemological status as existing, immaterial, and transcending things.

Therefore a reader of "Song of Myself" stands on solid ground if he judges that dualisms showing a transcendental component cannot be defeated by any conclusive philosophic arguments, and that Whitman's dualism should not be something about which a modern mind would have to suspend its disbelief. I have suggested a Yin-Yang pattern to Whitman's logic. In Chinese thought the male Yang is equal in cosmic status to the female Yin, yet there is a kind of privilege to the Yin since the absolute is more clearly reflected in female voids and valleys than in male stones or mountains. Whitman's idealism, I have tried to show, analogously gives a kind of privilege to air, eternity, and immortality, while it fiercely demands the cosmic equality of grass, time, and substance. Whitman's copulation bond between grass and air means that seen and unseen are ontologically interdependent. Perhaps Whitman, as well as Blake, influenced Yeats's symbolic vision of the stallion of eternity mounting the mare of time, and also Yeats's strikingly Whitmanesque male/female interpenetration of his symbolic interlocking cones. Most dualisms (such as those of Plato, Plotinus, and Hinduism) do not exalt the physical as do Whitman and the Taoists, and Whitman carries to the extreme the championing of physicality. Hinduism (to argue against Chari) cannot be as close as Taoism because of the Hindu belief that human selves are illusions, and that God is the only actor on stage. Whitman sharply opposes this view, which inclines toward spiritual monism.

Whitman's carnalized spirituality has various possible antecedents: In pre-Christian fertility religions; in Aristotle's theory that form and matter are of equal age; in Aquinas's refusal to reject creation from eternity rather than in time; in Aquinas's concept of the unity of body and soul; in Plotinus's theory that matter is divine in essence as an emanation from God; in neo-Platonic and Renaissance adorations of physical beauty; in scientific materialism; in Quaker and Methodist levelling tendencies and love theology; and in much more. Even the incarnational aspect of Christian orthodoxy, with its marriage of word and flesh, of time and eternity, gives some fuel to Whitman's vision of cosmic polarity. One crucial item separating Whitman from Christian assumptions is the poet's insistence that no people living at any period in time can have an advantage in the feast of life, along with his insistence that the physical component is equal in value to the spiritual. At both of these points Whitman draws close to Taoism.

The reading of "Song of Myself" in terms of a cosmic marriage of seen and unseen accords especially well with the dualism suggested by Kepner. Her paradigm of atoms wedded to invisible laws reinforces my interpretation, and Whitman's interest in a scientific foundation for his dualism is to his credit. If we today see space and time as interrelated, Whitman's dualism has anticipated us. It remains to be seen whether or not recent offerings in speculative physics and scientific cosmology will enhance a more spiritual and Platonic view of matter itself.[8]

These various comments on monism and dualism are intended to do no more than suggest the important ideational context into which "Song of Myself" should be fitted as we work out the implications of Whitman's symbolic pairings. Whitman makes a unique and logically acceptable contribution to an ancient and on-going debate that is second to none in importance. In Whitman's view (mediated through the grass/air linkage) the fundamental forces, energies, and substances of reality and life are grounded in polar oppositions with these traits: they bridge physical and spiritual, past and future; they contain divine intentionality; they are genuinely opposite; they are genuinely equal; they are equally valuable; they interpenetrate; they make all men and all ages equally rich; and they allow a larger destiny to the spiritual mode.

Finally, the comprehension of the role of grass and its mate causes Whitman's readers to see more clearly the relation between Whitman and other American writers.[9] While Poe's *Eureka* shows affinities with Whitman's version of cosmic harmony, Poe's poems and tales describe horrors of both body and soul that Whitman's optimism could not accommodate. *Moby Dick* and *The Scarlet Letter*, so deeply stained with fierce physicality and deep metaphysics, suggest how suitable Whitman's themes are to the American climate. Emerson's love for Plotinus appears as a strong bond to Whitman. Emily Dickinson's bold plunges into the erotic and the eternal seem much closer to Whitman. *Walden*, that hymn to the wild and also to higher laws, appears in a new light, because the situation in Thoreau's masterpiece sharply parallels "Song of Myself." Many readers consider the physical pond to be Thoreau's chief symbol. But the pond consorts with a spiritual counterpart, a force weaving throughout the whole work. For

Thoreau it is the dawn, a great phase of atmosphere, and no one can understand *Walden* until he ponders the pervasive worship of Aurora. Also, Whitman's erotic Platonism, Whitman's transcendence of space and time, Whitman's backward and forward moving, Whitman's male/female images, Whitman's climacterics of resurrection and eternity, these motifs gleam everywhere in Hart Crane's *The Bridge*. Whitman's model contrasts sharply with Eliot's logos dualism; Eliot's acceptance of incarnation at one point in time is irreconcilable to Whitman's equalizing of divinity in all times. However both poets share a religious conception of reality. The dualism of Wallace Stevens is as unique as Whitman's, but more secular. However the dualism of Stevens is not limited to such purely humanistic polarities as reality and fiction, reason and imagination, green substance and blue intellection, order and disorder. Stevens moves beyond these regions, drawing as close as he dares to the religiosity of Whitman and Eliot when he constructs the figure of major man, a quasi-deific superman whose total wisdom (the wisdom of past and future) creates a sharp, transcendental, polar opposition to the merely human domain of typical modern humanisms.

Whitman's polarities make common cause with the greatest American writers because of the American instinct for transcendentalism. Only rarely has America produced, in its major writers, a materialistic monist (such as Dreiser with his conception of man as an atomic chemism—a Dreiser whose characters seem wooden and gross in comparison to the free intelligences of James). Frost likes the earthbound state, but his remote stars and remote mountain springs point to God as clearly as Whitman's symbols. While Faulkner's ghost-haunted and conscience-stricken people embody his own version of spirituality, his dualism, partly sublime and partly horrific, tilts away from Whitman toward Eliot, Poe, Hawthorne, and Hart Crane. Perhaps the analysis of Whitman's master symbols and their ramifications justifies this conclusion: the American psyche does not really feel at home except in a polar harmonizing of matter and spirit.

NOTES

1. The idea of an independent rational and moral self can be attacked in various ways: blurred into the web of cultural belief, dissolved in the semiotic field, merged in the ocean of others, liquified by the flux of experience, given over to Heiddeger's Being or to maya, riddled by paradox and dialectic, or swallowed by the communal state. In spite of the pummeling that the idea of selfhood is taking, it will almost certainly prove to be one of

those concepts that (whether fact or necessary fiction) we simply will refuse to give up—along with the belief in external objects and the successful power of words to refer to them. Just to assert that referring terms and selfhood can be questioned is not at all to produce a logically convincing argument. Anything can be questioned. Riffaterre asserts that the essential aim of poetry is to refer to things and represent reality, and that "[i]t is immaterial whether or not this relationship is a delusion of those who speak the language or of readers. What matters is that the text multiplies details and continually shifts its focus to achieve an accepted likeness to reality..." (2). Pearce warns about the dangers involved when recent critics try to eliminate the subject-object distinction at the heart of Western metaphysics (121). There are many strong arguments for autonomous selfhood in the history of philosophy, in speculations of Husserl and Piaget and Kohlberg, in common sense, in the uniqueness of each person's DNA and cell structures, in legal theory, and in other persuasive directions. It is only fair to note that Whitman's generally unambiguous references to external objects and to selfhood in "Song of Myself" place his assumptions closer to common sense realism than to modern or post-modern problematics.

2. James Miller did connect grass to air on the basis of their common state but not of their polar bonding. Consequently, he did not give the air a major symbolic role (15).

3. In "The Noble Rider and the Sound of Words" Stevens presents an especially important essay about the elitist nobility which poets must discover in the materials of modernity—the same position taken by Crane.

4. Literary scholarship should be more discerning about the scope of ethicality. Since decisions about how to spend time are moral decisions, not one minute of our waking life goes without moral direction. For artists, the choice of subject belongs to morality; for critics, the choice of method and tone; for scientists, the choice of experiment. Whitman contradicts himself if he rejects value judgments and then values unchecked freedom above moral restraints. For recent insights into the *a priori* ethical basis of all interpretive theories see Armstrong's discussion.

5. I agree with Hirsch that the author's intent takes center stage, and since I present my reading of Whitman as probably correct, I also endorse Hirsch's probability model for the discovery of literary intentionality. Probability theory offers remarkable virtues in being able to accommodate ambiguities and alternatives, yet still escape the anarchy of critical pluralism. Even if certainties seem too much to hope for, extremely high probabilities will serve very well. A high probability means a weak skepticism. For one of Hirsch's latest comments on the primacy of authorial intent, see *Aims* 90.

6. Riffaterre's poetic theory stresses both intent and unity of thought in

poems, a stance long overdue because poetic devices find their essential role as they enrich some ideational core. If such devices do not put themselves at the service of the meanings in poems, they glitter pointlessly. Riffaterre assumes that the poem itself indicates one proper and privileged reading, and he offers a wholesome corrective to the deconstruction view that a good reading can only be a strong misreading. Mailloux reinforces Riffaterre when he observes that the poststructuralists cannot function at all without relying upon interpretive conventions, those "communal procedures for making intelligible the world," procedures which inexorably produce a centering (149, 154).

7. The long debate in philosophy journals over the body-mind identity problem has been inconclusive, with no victory going to materialists or idealists, and with functionalism offering a temporary compromise, a functionalism agreeing to refer to mental states as causative agents. For a treatment of the way in which many schools of twentieth century philosophy tend to slide back into Kantian idealism, see Jones's very valuable survey of recent philosophy in *The Great Ideas Today*. Jones notes (122) that Wilfrid Sellars carries forward the tradition of metaphysical realism by insisting (like Aristotle) that we can "obtain a view of the world that is true of the world, not merely relative to some conceptual scheme or other...." This is the kind of confidence that lies behind Whitman's concept of polar opposites, a confidence that separates much modernism and structuralism from deconstruction theory.

8. In his recent study, Trefil suggests that if quarks are found to rest on unknown underlying particles, then any hope for locating the basic unifying cosmic theories will depend largely on mind itself, not on empirical proof (217–18). This means a long and healthy life for a mind/matter dualism. Near the end of his recent book on cosmology Lovell shows a probable long life for Pythagorean-Platonic sublimities of numericity in the harmonics of the universe. He says that the existence of both persons and cosmos "is critically contingent on the value of a few physical constants and...these constants on the atomic and cosmical scales exhibit unique large-number relationships" (197). Revealing one way in which a reductive use of Occam's razor might be opposed, Lovell quotes Kepler's rule of logic (188) that "When there is a choice between different things which are not completely compatible with each other, preference must be given to the one which has the higher status...."

9. Among English poets, Hopkins offers an interesting contrast to Whitman. Hopkins also wanted a symbol that is spiritual, ubiquitous, and supportive of all life; but thematically all is changed, since Hopkins produced his ode "The Blessed Virgin Compared to the Air We Breathe." He might have been influenced by Whitman.

WORKS CITED

Armstrong, Paul B. "The Conflict of Interpretations and the Limits of Pluralism." *PMLA* 98 (1983): 341–52.

Carlisle, E. Fred. *The Uncertain Self: Whitman's Drama of Identity*. East Lansing: Michigan State UP, 1973.

Chari, V. K. *Whitman in the Light of Vedantic Mysticism*. Lincoln: U of Nebraska P, 1964.

Hirsch, E. D. *The Aims of Interpretation*. Chicago: U of Chicago P, 1976.

Jones, W. T. "The Widening Gyre: Philosophy in the Twentieth Century." *The Great Ideas Today: 1973*. Ed. Robert M. Hutchins and others. Chicago: Encyclopedia Britannica, 1973.

Kaltenmark, Max. *Lao Tzu and Taoism*. Trans. Roger Greaves. Stanford: Stanford UP, 1969.

Kepner, Diane. "From Spears to Leaves: Walt Whitman's Theory of Nature in 'Song of Myself.'" *American Literature* 51 (1979): 179–204.

Lawrence, D. H. *Studies in Classic American Literature*. New York: Viking, 1964.

Lovell, Bernard. *Emerging Cosmology*. New York: Columbia UP, 1981.

Mailloux, Steven. *Interpretive Conventions*. Ithaca: Cornell UP, 1982.

Miller, Edwin Haviland. *Walt Whitman's Poetry*. New York: New York UP, 1968.

Miller, James E., Jr. *A Critical Guide to Leaves of Grass*. Chicago: U of Chicago P, 1957.

Pearce, Roy Harvey. "Poetry and Progress, Criticism and Culmination: A Cautionary Tale." *The Motive for Metaphor: Essays on Modern Poetry*. Ed. Francis C. Blessington and Guy Rotella. Boston: Northeastern UP, 1983.

Riffaterre, Michael. *Semiotics of Poetry*. Bloomington: Indiana UP, 1978.

Trefil, James S. *From Atoms to Quarks*. New York: Scribners, 1980.

Waskow, Howard J. *Whitman: Explorations in Form*. Chicago: U of Chicago P, 1966.

Watts, Alan. *Tao: The Watercourse Way*. New York: Pantheon, 1975.

White, William M. "Dynamics of Whitman's Poetry." *Sewanee Review* 80 (1972): 345–360.

Whitman, Walt. *Leaves of Grass*. Ed. Malcolm Cowley. New York: Viking, 1959.

Yutang, Lin. *The Wisdom of Laotse*. Westport, CT: Greenwood P, 1979.

ZONG-QI CAI

Hegel's Phenomenological Dialectic and the Structure Of Whitman's "Song of Myself"

In studies of Walt Whitman's fifty-two-section poem "Song of Myself," part of the seminal *Leaves of Grass* published in 1855, probably no subject has attracted more critical attention than the poem's structure. The poem has been criticized as structurally flawed,[1] but most critics see a structure from numerous perspectives: religious,[2] existential,[3] numerical,[4] liturgical,[5] that of motif-analysis,[6] and that of reader's response.[7] Paradoxically, these critics often conclude their intertextual analyses by superimposing a traditional beginning-middle-end sequence. For instance, after an achronological study of sex-death motifs, Michael Orth envisages a typically chronological order of conception-youth-maturity-resurrection that unifies the diffuse details of the poem. Similar impositions of chronological sequence may be observed in James Miller, Malcolm Cowley, and Afred S. Reid. To overcome this paradox, Ronald Beck contends that one should not examine the poem "in terms of traditional poetic structure," but must come to terms with it's a chronology as an appropriate structural adaptation to the central theme of the phenomenological interchange of the one and the many. Only by so doing, he believes, can we recognize and give full credit to the poem's "satisfactory structure" and "rationale of selection."[8] However, Beck does not define nor describe the internal structure he has intuited because he does not see the phenomenological laws of the Myself's *kairos* experiences. The Myself, already transcendentally realized, must transcend the *chronos* and

From *CLIO*, vol. 16, no. 4 (Summer 1987). © 1988 by Henry Kozicki.

pursue its course in sustained *kairos*, a Greek word which means "occasion" literally and often refers to the heightened situations of transcendence in critical contexts. Thus this process reveals phenomenological significance quite different from that found in the typical Romantic *kairos* as represented by Wordsworthian "spots of time" or the Emersonian "perfect exhilaration," which indicate the momentary, one-way intuitive expansion of the ego over the non-ego. By contrast, the Myself's *kairos* betokens an ever-progressive, two-way interchange of subject and object. The former *kairos* has been ascribed to Schellingian absolute unity achieved through the innudation of the external world by the ego.[9] The latter *kairos* can be best explained as Hegelian interchange of subject and object within the self-perfecting movement of the Absolute Spirit.[10]

In his "Preface" to the *Phenomenology*, Hegel highlights his phenomenological system with the following passage:

> That the True is actual only as system, or that Substance is essentially Subject, is expressed in the representation of the Absolute as *Spirit*—the most sublime Notion and the one which belongs to the modern age and its religion. The spiritual alone is the *actual*; it is essence, or that which has *being in itself*; it is that which *relates itself to itself* and is *determinate*, it is *other-being* and *being-for-self*, and in this determinateness, or in its self-externality, abides within itself; in other words, it is *in and for itself*.—But thisbeing-in-and being-in-and-for-itself is at first only for us, or *in itself*, it is spiritual *Substance*. It must also be this *for itself*, it must be the knowledge of the spiritual, and the knowledge of itself as Spirit, i.e., it must be an *object* to itself, but just as immediately a sublated subject, reflected into itself.[11]

Here, Hegel has set out both the foundation and the laws of his phenomenological system: (1) "the True" or absolute reality is "essentially Subject" and must be spoken of as Spirit or the pure Notion; (2) the pure Notion must be construed as a system of phenomenological evolutions; (3) the phenomenological evolution operates through a self-moving dialectic of negativity, which drives the pure Notion through the unceasing spiraling cycles of thesis (being-in-itself), antithesis (being-for-itself), and synthesis or new thesis (being-in-and-for-itself), until its ultimate self-recognition of its complete determinations.

Measured against these philosophical postulates, "Song of Myself" strikes us as a poetic version of Hegel's dialectic phenomenology: a celebration of the growth of the Myself as a cosmic subject identical with Hegel's pure Notion or Absolute Spirit. The Myself first transmigrates itself (being-in-itself) into the external plenitude (being-for-itself), and then reflects the multifarious phenomena into itself. As in Hegel's dialectic, these antithetical processes do not become reconciled in a *static* unity, but result in a *kinetic* becoming. The transformed Myself (being-in-and-for-itself) in turn initiates a new, higher cycle of generative and reflective processes. By means of this dialectic of negativity, the Myself evolves through the individual self (poet-persona), the general self (America-persona), to the cosmic self (cosmos-persona) which, while representing "an acme of things accomplish'd," will unceasingly "tramp a perpetual journey."[12] Notably, the Myself's phenomenological evolutions mark five distinct movements in "Song of Myself": (1) Sections 1–5: the dissolution of the individual self into cosmic elements; (2) Sections 6–15: the reflection of the American landscape into the general self; (3) Sections 16–25: the tran-substantiation of the general self into broader cosmic scenes; (4) Sections 26–40: the reflection of the cosmic scenes into the cosmic self; and (5) Sections 40–52: the dissolution of the cosmic self into cosmic elements.

The first movement of the poem witnesses the initial stage of the Hegelian phenomenological evolutions—the liberation of the individual self from its existence in a single determinate form. "The single individual," observes Hegel, "is incomplete Spirit, a concrete shape in whose whole existence one determinateness predominates, the others being present only in blurred outline" (*Phenomenology*, 16). The individual must disembody itself from its single determinate form in order to elevate itself into a general self. In this regard, Hegel contends that "the life of Spirit is not the life that shrinks from death and keeps itself untouched by devastation, but rather the life that endures it and maintains itself in it. It wins its truth only when in utter dismemberment, it finds itself" (*Phenomenology*, 19). This spiritual rebirth through self-dismemberment is exactly what the Myself goes through in the first movement, Sections 1–2 in particular. Immediately after claiming to "celebrate myself, and sing myself" (1), the Myself proceeds to dissolve itself and revitalize myriad creatures hitherto "present in blurred outline" in itself. First, the Myself interfuses with other individual selves represented by "you" the universal reader: "And what I assume you shall assume, / For every atom belonging to me as good belongs to you" (2–3). Then, it transposes itself into cosmic elements that make up the phenomenal multitude:

My tongue, every atom of my blood, form'd from this
        soil, this air...
The smoke of my own breath,
Echoes, ripples, buzz'd whispers, love-root, silk-thread,
        crotch, and vine...
The sniff of green leaves and dry leaves...
The sound of the belch'd words of my voice loos'd to the
        eddies of the wind...
... the song of me rising from bed and meeting the sun.

                                                    (6, 21–29)

Having gone through these disembodiments, the Myself appreciates its new spiritual identity: the possession of "the origin of all poems" (33) and "the good of the earth and sun" (34). In Sections 3–5, the emancipated Myself exalts its deliverance from temporality into the eternal now (38–43), its participation in the dialectic of phenomenologic evolutions (46–48), its capacity to free itself from external fixities (66–74). Now, standing on a higher spiritual level, the Myself proudly sees backward, to "my own days where I sweated through fog with linguists and contenders" (80). Significantly, this recalls Hegel's description in the "Preface" of an elevated individual self: "In a Spirit that is more advanced than another, the lower concrete existence has been reduced to an inconspicuous moment; what used to be the important thing is now but a trace; its pattern is shrouded to become a mere shadowy outline" (*Phenomenology*, 16). Of course, in Hegel's phenomenology, this elevated state is achieved only after the individual self has passed "through the formative stages of universal Spirit so far as their content is concerned, but as shapes which Spirit has already left behind, as stages on a way that has been made level with toil" (*Phenomenology*, 16). That is to say, before rising to the level of general self, the individual self must reflect into itself determinate forms already comprehended by other individuals.

This Hegelian self-reflection is retrogressively described in the second movement of the poem. As if to indicate the onset of a counter movement and to set a reflective tone for it, Section 6 begins with a phenomenological question: "*What is the grass?*" This immediately launches the Myself into a sustained reflection seeking to comprehend exterior plurality as its own outward manifestations. The Myself first discerns in the grass the transfigurations of all human and vegetational forms: "I guess it must be the flag of my disposition ... the produced babe of vegetation ... uniform hieroglyphic ... Growing among black folks as among white ... from old people, or from offspring... And ceas'd the moment life appear'd" (101–28). Having discovered its kindred linkage with creatures transfigured in the grass, the Myself proceeds to meditate things in their untransfigured forms. It identifies itself with general human types ("new-wash'd babe," "boys," "sweet-heart's," "the old maid," "begetters of children") in Section 7; and in Sections 8–13 caresses particular individuals in "life where moving, backward as well as forward sluing"[13]: "absorbing all to myself and for this song" (232–34). In Sections 13–14, the Myself relates to itself the animal world ("wild gander," "tortoise," "sharp-hoof'd moose," "Turkey-hen," etc.), claiming that "what is commonest, cheapest, nearest, easiest, is *Me*" (259). In Section 15, the Myself assimilates into itself American people in every walk of life (from the ordained deacon to the pike-fisher), in every social stratum (from the President to the prostitute), and in every corner of the country (from the Yankee factory girl to the Tennessee coonseeker). "These tend inward to me," the Myself sums up, "and I tend outward to them ... of these one and all I weave the song of myself" (327–29).

Having gone through self-dismemberment and self-reflection in the first two movements, the Myself completes what Hegel calls the education of the individual self, and now rises to a general self. In Hegel's phenomenological dialectic, the general spirit will undertake the education of its own toward fuller self-consciousness. Comparing these two educational stages of human spirit, Hegel observes:

> In this respect formative education, regarded from the side of the individual, consists in his acquiring what thus lies at hand, devouring his inorganic nature, and taking possession of it for himself. But, regarded from the side of universal Spirit as substance, this is nothing but its own acquisition of self-consciousness, the bringing-about of its own becoming and reflection into itself. (*Phenomenology*, 16–17)

Hegel believes that the general spirit undergoes more advanced education because it *actively* pursues its transmutation and self-reflection rather than *passively* acquiring "what thus lies at hand." This higher level of spiritual education aptly characterizes the Myself's growth in the next cycle of phenomenological evolution. In the third movement the Myself *self-consciously* sublates itself into cosmic externality whereas its previous metamorphosis was more by inner necessity than by will. To begin with, the Myself celebrates its acquisition of "what thus lies at hand":

I am of old and young, of the foolish
            as much as the wise...
Maternal as well as paternal, a child
            as well as a man...
A Southerner soon as a Northerner...
A learner with the simplest, a teacher of
            the thoughtfullest...
Of every hue and caste, of every rank and religion...
Prisoner, fancy-man, rowdy, lawyer, physician, priest.

                                                        (330–48)

Then, the Myself candidly acknowledges that all these are
phenomenologically "really thoughts of all men in all ages and all lands, they
are not original with me" (355), echoing the Hegelian concept of a general
self emerging from an acquisition of "what thus lies at hand." Now, as the
American spirit, the Myself begins "the bringing about of its own becoming"
by factorizing its consciousness into the phenomena of cosmic magnitude in
Sections 20–25:

In all people I see myself, none more and not on barley-
corn less.   (401)
To me the converging objects of the universe perpetually flow,
All are written to me, and I must get with what the writing
            means.   (404–5)
The pleasures of heaven are with me and the pains of hell
            are with me.   (423)
Smile O voluptious cool-breath'd earth!...
Sea of stretch'd ground-swells...
I am integral with you, I too am of one phase and of all
            phases.
Partaker of influx and efflux I, extoller of hate and
            conciliation...   (438–459)
Walt Whitman, a kosmos, of Manhattan the son.   (497)
Through me the afflatus surging and surging, through me the
            current and index.   (505)
With the twirl of my tongue I encompass worlds and volumes
            of worlds.   (565)

The transmutation described here is remarkably different from that of the
individual self in two ways. First, it is more dynamic and all-encompassing
because now the Myself transfigures itself not in fixed landscape but in

elemental forces that pursue their course throughout the entire cosmos (heaven, hell, earth, sea, etc.). For instance, earth is depicted not as solid soil on which the poet reclines (5–6), but as flowing cosmic force here in lines 438–45. Similarly, wind and human breath are observed not as common natural phenomena (14–29), but as a surging cosmic breath here in lines 505, 564–65. Second, this process of becoming is more consciously manipulated because the Myself virtually gives commands to elemental forces (438–60) and exercises control over its own metamorphosis: "Whether I come to my own to-day or in ten thousand or ten million years, / I can cheerfully take it now, or with equal cheerfulness I can wait" (417–18). Interestingly, this sense of self-control is also reflected by the reversals of some images' syntactic positions. Compare, for example, "my tongue [is] form'd from this soil, this air" (6) with "with the twirl of my tongue, I encompass worlds and volumes of worlds" (565); and "the belch'd words of my voice loos'd to the eddies of wind" (25) with "through me the afflatus surging and surging, through me the current and index" (505).

The fourth movement begins with the Myself once more shifting to self-reflection: "Now I will do nothing but listen, / To accrue what I hear into this song" (582–3). Having just dissolved itself into the entire cosmos, the Myself must now sublimate back into itself not only familiar American scenes but the "quintilions ripened" (799). Hencefore, the Myself draws into itself, along with two extensive catalogues of American scenes (584–610; 717–88), "old hills of Judaca ... heaven and stars ... the seven satellites ... tail'd meteors ... orchards of spheres" (789–98). By the same token, the human world that the Myself reflects into itself broadens from the individual experiences to general human existence, aptly represented by historical incidents of the San Francisco rescue, the Goliard Massacre, and the famous sea fight with the British. "All this I swallow," concludes the Myself, "it tastes good, I like it well, it becomes mine" (831). In the course of this self-reflection, the Myself demonstrates a greater degree of self-consciousness than in the second movement. Soon after he begins his self-reflection, he *consciously* tries to figure out a phenomenological mystery:

> To be in any form, what is that?
> (Round and round we go, all of us, and ever come back thither,)
> If nothing lay more develop'd the quahaug in its callous
>   shell were enough.
> Mine is no callous shell,
> I have instant conductors all over me whether I pass or stop,
> They seize every object and lead it harmlessly through me. (611–16)

The physical objects' electric responses reassure the Myself of the external plenitude's spiritual origin with itself, thus "quivering me to a new identity" (619). He recognizes his essential self as the "instant conductors" that send divine life through all objects, as a "compend of compends" that unifies all determinate forms of existence (648–62). Consequently, the Myself finds itself something of Hegelian Absolute Spirit to which all things owe their existence:

> I find I incorporate gneiss, coal, long threaded moss,
> fruits, grains, esculent roots,
> And am stucco'd with quadrupeds and birds all over,
> And have distanced what is behind me for good reason,
> But call any thing back when I desire it.   (670–73)

This passage indicates that the Myself has by now recapitulated in abbreviated form what "the World Spirit itself, has had the patience to pass through ... over the long passage of time" (*Phenomenology*, 17), and grown into a cosmic self in vigorous progress. This transformation of the Myself reminds us of Hegel's definition of the world spirit as the outgrowth of national spirits.[14] Indeed, if we compare Hegel's definition with the Myself's self-proclamations, we can hardly doubt the Myself's new identity as the world spirit. Speaking of the world spirit in his own time, Hegel says:

> ... it is not difficult to see that ours is a birth-time and a period of transition to a new era. Spirit has broken with the world it has hitherto inhabited and imagined, and is of a mind to submerge it in the past and in the labour of its own transformation. Spirit is indeed never at rest but always engaged in moving forward (*Phenomenology*, 6).

Hegel distinguishes the world-spirit from the preceding lower stages of consciousness (e.g. the individual self, and the general self) by stressing (1) its complete self-knowledge of the world of "hitherto inhabited and imagined," and (2) its everprogressing motion toward the unknown. These two distinctive features of the Hegelian world spirit are exactly what the Myself exclusively celebrates in the final movement: its mastery of the past and present, and its progression into the future:

> I am an acme of things accomplish'd, and I an encloser of
> things to be.
> My feet strike an apex of the apices of the stairs,

On every step bunches of ages, and larger bunches between
    the steps,
All below duly travel'd, and still I mount and mount.
Rise after rise bow the phantoms behind me,
Afar down I see the huge first Nothing, I know I was even there,
I waited unseen and always, and slept through the lethargic mist,
And took my time, and took no hurt from the fetid carbon.

                                               (1148–55)

The past and present wilt—I have fill'd them, emptied them,
And proceed to fill my next fold of the future.   (1319–20)

Apart from making these general pronouncements, the Myself elaborates on its new identity as the cosmic self. To demonstrate itself fully as "an acme of things accomplish'd," it assumes a possessive relationship with both the physical and human worlds. It addresses the sun and the earth as its inferiors (987–90, 1299–1308), and summons to itself all people as his beneficiaries (1011–22), his household members (1056–59), its "duplicates" (1075–85), its lovers and worshipers (1172–78), and its athletic pupils (1234–46). Furthermore, the Myself declares as its own diverse world religions and mythologies (1026–53, 1096–110)—Hebraic (Jehovah), Greek (Kronos, Zeus, Hercules), Egyptian (Osiris, Isis), Babylonian (Belus), Hindu (Brahma), Buddhist (Buddha), American Indian (Manito), Islamic (Allah), Norse (Odin), and Aztec (Mexitli)—which consummate all knowledge of the cosmos and human experience at different times and places.[15]

To prove itself "an encloser of things to be," the Myself sets out how it will pursue its future course. It frankly admits that its future mode of existence will not be *entirely* atemporal, or temporal, or non-apodeitical:

I know I have the best of time and space, and was never
    measured and never will be measured.   (1201)
My rendezvous is appointed, it is certain,
The Lord will be there and wait till I come on perfect terms.

                                             (1198–99)

The Myself will *not* be completely *atemporal* because it must take existence in the "best of time and space." Thus the Myself has to concede that "I do not know what is untried and afterward" (1121) and that "There is that in me—I do not know what it is" (1309). Nevertheless, the Myself's future becoming will *not* be definitively *temporal* because it "was never, nor will be measured" by time. For this reason, the Myself can boldly chide "the bitter bug of mortality" by calling life "leavings of many deaths," and declares "I have died myself ten thousand times before" (1297–98). These statements pinpoint the Hegelian dialectic between the Absolute Spirit and the time and space: "...the determinations of self-conscious mind are infinitely more substantial, more concrete, than the abstract determinations of juxtaposition and succession. Mind, as embodied, is indeed in a definite place and in a definite time; but for all that it is exalted over them" (*Philosophy*, 38). Exalted over time and space, the Myself cannot possibly be *non-apodeitical*. Its phenomenological evolution itself is the unfolding of God and it will become one with God as "I come on perfect terms." Here we are reminded how the process of phenomenological evolution is identified with the living God by Hegel: "...we apply it [God] to the world, we have nature as mean and the existent spirit as a way of return for nature: when the return is made, this is the absolute Spirit. This living process, this separation and unifying of differences, is the living God."[16] On account of such an inherent relationship with God, the Myself claims to "hear and behold God in every object ... each hour of the twenty-four, and each moment then ... see God, and in my own face in the glass ... find letters from God dropt in the street" (1281–86).

No sooner has the Myself celebrated its emergence as the cosmic self than it embarks on its divine journey along an unbeaten track. It dissolves itself into cosmic elements—,"air," "eddies of wind," "dirt," "grass" (1336–40), just as it has done in the very beginning of the poem. However, in contrast to the individual self trying to catch up with the general consciousness, here the cosmic self blazes a new trail, launching "all men and women forward with me into the Unknown" (1136). So far ahead, it often looks back, beckoning to them:

> Failing to fetch me at first keep encouraged,
> Missing me one place search another,
> I stop somewhere waiting for you.   (1344–46)

Whitman once outlined the three phases of the Myself with these three phrases: "Walt Whitman, an American, Cosmos."[17] Critics seem to interpret these phrases too literally when they search for a chronological order in the poem. The complete lack of *chronos* and the scarcity of biographical details indicate that the poem is anything but a Romantic epic of an individual's spiritual growth. We are thus left to take these three phrases as indicating three distinctive stages of the awakening Absolute Spirit. From this perspective we have divined in the poem well-structured phenomenological evolutions, which demonstrate consistent correspondences with Hegel's phenomenological system. First, the Myself's sublation into and out of externality bear out the uniquely Hegelian conception of subject and object as equal, interchanging manifestations of the evolving Absolute Spirit. Second, the three phases of the Myself's growth correspond with three of the diverse "form[s] of the *relation of the consciousness to the object*"[18] explored by Hegel in *Phenomenology of Spirit*. The individual self represents the Hegelian immediate *consciousness* because the poet-persona "by the negation of its corporeity, raises itself to purely ideal self-identity, becomes *consciousness*, becomes 'I', is for itself over against its Other" (*Philosophy*, 27). The general self typifies the Hegelian national spirit, a fairly developed form of *self-consciousness* that supersedes the immediate *consciousness* insofar as it has reflected into itself, in addition to physical nature, other consciousnesses as its beings-for-itself (but through sympathetic identification rather than the Hegelian master-slave struggles).[19] The cosmic self identifies with the Hegelian world spirit, an even higher form of *self-consciousness* insofar as it has sublimated into itself not only "cosmoscape" but the world's major religions that Hegel regards as the quintessence of national spirits.[20] Third, the presentation of the Myself betrays the typical Hegelian historiography in the sense that actual social and cultural references have been interpreted as traces of phenomenological evolution of the Absolute Spirit. Indeed, even when conjuring up its future journey, the Myself speaks in terms of social history: "Shoulder your duds dear son, and I will mine, and let us hasten forth, / Wonderful cities and free nations we shall fetch as we go" (1215–16). Another aspect of the Hegelian historiography is mirrored by the author's ardent nationalism: here America is taken as the culmination of varied national spirits and hence the world spirit, just as the Prussia was upheld in Hegel's historiography as the world soul. Fourth, the Myself's contradictory claims about its spirituality and materiality spell out the Hegelian dialectic of negativity. By constantly contradicting its previous state, the Myself vigorously goes through the spiraling cycles of phenomenological evolutions toward its final complete self-realization. The Myself seems to consciously exalt this dialectic of negativity or contradiction when he concludes, "Do I contradict myself? / Very well then I contradict myself" (1324–25). In view of all these consistent correspondences, we have every reason to argue that, whether or not Whitman was inspired by actual reading of Hegel's phenomenology, the Hegelian phenomenological dialectic may be taken as the poem's internal structure, which coheres all the achronological *kairos* situations and stylistically unifies the image patterns, shifting subthemes, and poetic persona.

NOTES

1. George Santayana, *Interpretation of Poetry and Religion* (New York: Scribner, 1900), 177–87. Gay Wilson Allen, *The Solitary Singer* (New York: Macmillan, 1955), 164. See also *Walt Whitman Handbook* (Chicago: Packard, 1949), 114–23.

2. Carl F. Strauch, "The Structure of Walt Whitman's 'Song of Myself," *English Journal* (College Edition) 27 (1938):597–607. Afred S. Reid, "The Structure of 'Song of Myself' Reconsidered," *Southern Humanities Review* 7 (1973): 507–14.

3. James E. Miller, Jr. "'Song of Myself' as Inverted Mystical Experience," *PMLA* 70 (1955):636–61; and *A Critical Guide to Leaves of Grass* (Chicago: U of Chicago P, 1957), 6–35. Malcolm Cowley, "Introduction," *Walt Whitman's Leaves of Grass: The First (1855) Edition* (New York: Viking, 1959). Roy Harvey Pearce, "Song of Myself" in *The Continuity of American Poetry* (Princeton: Princeton UP, 1961), 69–83.

4. Elizabeth Philips, "'Song of Myself': The Numbers of the Poem in Relation to Its Form," *Walt Whitman Review* 16 (1970): 67–81.

5. Ida Fasel, "'Song of Myself' as Prayer," *Walt Whitman Review* 17 (1971): 19–22.

6. Michael Orth, "Walt Whitman, Metaphysical Teapot: The Structure of 'Song of Myself'," *Walt Whitman Review* 14 (1968): 16–24.

7. George Y. Trail, "'Song of Myself': Event in the Microstructure," *Walt Whitman Review* 25 (1979): 106–13.

8. Ronald Beck, "The Structure of 'Song of Myself' and the Critics," *Walt Whitman Review* 15 (1969): 32–38.

9. A. C. Bradley notes the obvious correspondences between Wordsworth's poetry and the German Romatic philosophy: *Oxford Lectures on Poetry* (London: Macmillan, 1909), 129. J. W. Beach suggests that the Germans might have influenced Wordsworth, *The Concept of Nature in the Nineteenth Century English Poetry* (New York: Macmillan, 1936), 101. See also E. D. Hirsch, *Wordsworth & Schelling: A Typological Study of Romanticism* (New Haven: Yale UP, 1960). Emerson's debt to Schelling's metaphysics has been acknowledged by many critics. See, for instance, Henry David Gray, *Emerson* (New York: Ungar, 1965), 30–32.

10. Critics acknowledge numerous parallels in Whitman's and Hegel's conceptions of a spirit ever-evolving toward a divine end, although they hold conflicting views as to whether these parallels should be taken as conclusive evidence of Hegel's influence on Whitman. For instance, R. F. Falk, who questions the degree of direct influence, nonetheless assumes that "in the case of Hegel, Whitman certainly buttressed, and possibly largely derived,

his evolutionary conception of a universe, exhibiting conflict and struggle, yet tending toward a vague divine culmination in the return of the individual souls to the Absolute": "Whitman and German Thought," *Journal of English and Germanic Philology* 40 (1941): 329. Nonetheless, critics only examine how Hegel's particular concepts get mentioned or paraphrased in Whitman's works, but seldom consider how a Hegelian phenomenological system may be the structural basis for the portrayal of the ever-evolving human spirit in "Song of Myself." See M. C. Boatright, "Whitman and Hegel," *University of Texas Studies in English* 9 (1929): 134–50; and W. B. Fulghum, "Whitman's Debt to Joseph Gostwick," *American Literature* 12 (1941): 491–96. For an opposing viewpoint, see Olive W. Parsons, "Whitman the Non-Hegelian," *PMLA* 58 (1943): 1073–93.

11. G. W. F. Hegel, "Preface: On Scientific Cognition," *Phenomenology of Spirit*, trans. A. V. Miller (Oxford: Clarendon, 1977), 14.

12. Walt Whitman, *Leaves of Grass*, eds. Sculley Bradley, et al. (New York: New York UP, 1980), 1:71, 74: lines 1148, 1202. Henceforth, this edition will be cited by line numbers in parentheses in my text.

13. These two aspects of life are indicated respectively by the remembered scenes of the trapper and the run-away; and by the on-going scenes of the suicide, 28 pairs of bathers, butcher-boy, and the negro-drivers.

14. The following passage is Hegel's exposition of the relationship between national minds and the world spirit: "As the mind of a special nation is actual and its liberty is under natural conditions ... it passes into universal world-history the events of which exhibit the dialectic of the several national minds,—the judgment of the world.

This movement is the path of liberation for the spiritual substance, the deed by which the absolute final aim of the world is realized in it, and the merely implicit mind achieves consciousness and self-consciousness. It is thus the revelation and actuality of its essential and completed essence, whereby it becomes to the outward eye a universal spirit—a world-mind." *Philosophy of Mind*, trans. William Wallace (Oxford: Clarendon, 1971), 277.

15. This summary list is taken from a footnote to "Song of Myself," in *The American Traditions in Literature*, eds. Sculley Bradley, et al. (New York: Norton, 1967), 2:73.

16. G. W. F. Hegel, *Lectures on the History of Philosophy*, trans. E. S. Haldane and F. H. Simson (London: Routledge & Paul, 1963), 2:77.

17. Quoted without specific documentation of source by John Knaird, "The Paradox of An American 'Identity'," *Partisan Review*, 25 (1958): 390.

18. Quoted from Hegel's summary of *Phenomenology of Spirit*: "In the *Phenomenology of Spirit* I have exhibited consciousness in its movement onwards from the first immediate opposition of itself and the object to

absolute knowing. The path of this movement goes through every form of the *relation of consciousness to the object* and has the Concept of science for its result." *Science of Logic*, trans. A. V. Miller (London: George Allen & Unwin, 1969), 48.

19. Just as the general Myself is distinguished from the individual Myself by its conscious fusion with other individual selves, the Hegelian *self-consciousness* is differentiated from the immediate *consciousness* by its conscious unity with the other consciousnesses. "'I' that is 'We' and 'We' that is 'I'. It is in self-consciousness, in the Notion of Spirit, that consciousness first finds its turning-point, where it leaves behind it the colourful show of the sensous here-and-now and the nightlike void of the supersensible beyond, and steps out into the spiritual daylight of the present": *The Phenomenology of Spirit*, 110–11.

20. Cf. the following remarks by Hegel: "It is evident and apparent from what has preceded that moral life is the state retracted into its inner heart and substance, while the state is the organization and actualization of moral life; that religion is the very substance of the moral life itself and of the state. At this rate, the state rests on the ethical sentiment, and that on the religious. If religion then is the consciousness of *'absolute' truth*, then whatever is to rank as right and justice, as law and duty, i.e., *true* in the world of free will, can be so esteemed only as it is participant of that truth, as it is subsumed under it and is its sequel ... the body of religious truth, as the pure self-subsisting and therefore supreme truth, exercises a sanction over the moral life which lies in empirical actuality. Thus for self-conscious religion is the 'basis' of moral life and of the state" *Philosophy of Mind*, 283–84.

MARK BAUERLEIN

Whitman's Language of the Self

This was a feeling or ambition to articulate and faithfully express
in literary or poetic form, and uncompromisingly, my town
physical, emotional, moral, intellectual, and aesthetic Personality,
in the midst of, and tallying, the momentous spirit and facts of its
immediate days, and of current America—and to exploit that
Personality, identified with place and date, in a far more candid
and comprehensive sense than any hitherto poem or book.

Whitman, "A Backward Glance O'er Travel'd Roads"

To express a self. To display a "Personality" "uncompromisingly" with a
limpid style, a transparent form that ardently renders an identity in all its
plenitude and immediacy. This is the "special desire and conviction" that
incite Whitman to write "Song of Myself," a personal epic in which, with
sustained narcissism, Whitman freely explores his ego in an original style, in
a structureless narrative, in free verse form, in brazen play and naked
confession. As Richard Poirier would put it (though not in direct reference
to Whitman), "not that style should mediate between the self and society but
that it should emanate from the self as a leaf from a tree, expanding itself
naturally to nourish, color, and become the world."[1] Whitman's expansive,
egotistical poetic style fits Poirier's description: founded on a person, it
grows into a "Kosmos." An active repudiation of European models, of Old

From *American Imago*, vol. 44, no. 2 (Summer 1987). © 1988 by Mark Bauerlein.

World ideas and pentameter lines, cleared the way for a genuine revelatory expression as unique and original as its provenance. The obstacles lay in obsolete meters and ossified diction, in styles inadequate for the liberal exuberance of young America. Only a "Personality" as copious and juvenile as the New World could envision and graft a "self-reflecting" poem onto "The United States ... the greatest poem." To present an original self both uncorrupted by an artificial, opaque style and equal to its abundant surroundings, to celebrate the self's continued presence and authority, becomes Whitman's taskwork, his calling. It is the project attempted in *Leaves of Grass*.

But, together with Whitman's glorification of the paramount self, one also finds a series of rhetorical gestures that obscure and even censure the self. Some of Whitman's self-amplifications actually undermine the centrality of his identity. For instance, Whitman often interrupts his self-presentation to insist on the universality of his particular identity—"I am of old and young..." (1.330)[2]; "These are the thoughts of all men in all ages and lands, they are not original with me..." (1.355)—assertions that abstract the self out of its discrete singularity. To affirm one's presence as eternally everywhere is to disintegrate one's individuality and historicity, precisely what Whitman wanted to preserve. When Whitman dilates himself into grandiose, cosmic proportions, what becomes of plain old "Walt...one of the roughs"?

Also, Whitman diffuses his identity into various poses or characters, creating both distancing perspectives on himself—"Who goes there! hankering, gross, mystical, nude?" (1.389)—and new identities that contrast with the poet—"I am the hounded slave..." (1.838); "I am the mashed fireman..." (1.847). Whitman's posing, his empathetic (nearly messianic) assumption of other identities, disperses his authority in a way that contravenes his stated intention. Even more than presenting a coherent "Personality," "Song of Myself" dramatizes a cast of personae, tropic versions of Whitman, none of which evince the concentered self the masks proceed from. Despite the brevity of these characterizations, they are just as vivid and realized as the episodic renderings of Whitman "himself." Alternating randomly between pride and humility, knowledge and ignorance, guilt and complacency, Whitman's "Personality" fractures into an unpredictable succession of moods, one just as typifying as another. By "contain[ing] multitudes," Whitman frustrates any interpretive choice that singles out one attitude as the "true" Whitman. With the multiplicity of characters and personae, a central self informing the others becomes, at most, a tentative inference. Even the direct self-references Whitman makes only beg the question of whether this Whitman is yet another role-playing persona.

At one point, Whitman does mention a self devoid of intermediary masks: the "Me myself" of Section 4. One presumes that this epithet signifies the real Whitman, his core of identity; to be insincere in naming himself would compromise the forthright intercourse Whitman desires to have with his readers. But this essential self remains withheld from contact with others (perhaps because it is an essence), at least in ordinary social discourse— "Apart from the pulling and hauling stands what I am/ Stands amused, complacent, com- passionating, idle, unitary..." (11.75–76). And even though Whitman insists that his relation to the reader is one not of casual exchange, but an intimate communion surpassing conventional social barriers, his characterization of the "Me myself" imports ironic observation, not welcome sensitivity. The synecdoches which follow his initial naming only underscore the disjunction between reader and Whitman.

> Looks down, is erect, bends an arm on an impalable
>   certain rest,
> Looks with its sidecurved head curious what will come
>   next,
> Both in and out of the game, watching and wondering
>   at it.
>
>   (11.77–79)

This personification of the "Me myself" emphasizes its disinterestedness and stability; "out of the game" of rhetorical play, the "Me myself" is beyond signification, is complete. Whitman can denote the "Me myself", but when he begins to describe it he gives us an image of it, a posturing facade. So, do these lines figure forth the central self or do they mark a turn away from it? That Whitman must resort to a superficial figuration when delineating his self suggests that a problem with self-expression may lie at the linguistic level rather than the social level. If Whitman requires figurative language in order to speak or to write the self, even when aiming explicitly to unveil the self and not to clothe it in tropes, one wonders whether sheer self-expression of the kind Whitman prefigures is possible. If figurative language is the seminal ingredient of poetry, can Whitman compose a poem matching his self? Could he discover a pure language of the self, a language which, though thetorical, would have a new rhetoric based on the directions and idiosyncrasies of Whitman's desires, Whitman would create a poem unparalleled in its evocation of self. A language whose rhetorical patterns are based on a literary past slips too easily into a hackneyed, impersonal style and traditionalizes the original self. Two questions pose themselves: 1) Does Whitman's style constitute an original, self-made language? and, if so, 2) can this, or any language embody the "Me myself"? This is Whitman's temporary hope—temporary because a few years later he realizes its unattainability and relinquishes it (as I will show).

Since Whitman's own circle of admirers began writing about him, Whitman scholars have characterized his obsession with self-expression along these lines, but usually underscoring the affirmation of self, even when focussing on the death poems. Skepticism about self-expression has often been analyzed as a problem with literary tradition or with Whitman's upbringing, rarely as a fundamentally linguistic problem. American critics, such as Roy Harvey Pearce and James E. Miller, Jr.,[3] have studied Whitman's egotism as a peculiarly American issue and have placed him at a focal point in the American canon. That is, they claim that the overriding flowering and periodic trepidation of Whitman's Bardic self reflect a cultural crisis in America's pre-war literary identity. Their preconceptions of Whitman's poetic undertaking presuppose a style, a native language, that does allow a true expression of an American self. With truth conceived of as a correspondence between private motive, desire, and experience, and public forms of expression, inherited styles pervert the self, force it to conform to a preordained syntax and decorum that distorts the ego and thereby alienates it from its own manifestations. But the proper "home-grown," "self-made" style, as idiosyncratic as its source, will becomingly unfold the self and liberate it from its privacy. A style measuring up to Whitman's indigenous dynamism and fulfilling his ambition to display a devoted self charged with emotive power demands a special mode: "Such a poem can only be epic in scope ... its form must be self-transcending, as must its heroes" (Pearce, p. 71). It is only when self-transcendence threatens individual integrity, when "expansiveness lose[s] touch with personal identity"[4] and becomes so broadly representative, that Whitman severs contact with the American people and wavers in his self-proclamations.

But, however much canonical studies have charted out the formation and progress of American literature (and Whitman's foremost role in it), criticism of self-expression requires a more intimate, individualizing practice. A biographical approach could explain the alternative self-expression and self-disguise in psychological terms, a method that reveals the psychic turmoil that engenders and perhaps constrains self-expression better than sweeping historicist methods of canonical studies of American literature do. This is precisely what Edwin Miller and Stephan Black have done.[5] They ground Whitman's equivocations in childhood traumas and sexual ambivalences caused by a brutal, withdrawn father and an ignorant, clinging mother and by latent homo-sexuality. That Whitman never resolved his contradictory feelings for his parents (he virtually left home at age 12 when he became an apprentice printer) and that he regarded his homosexuality with alarm (as shown in his reaction to Symonds' imputations) is borne out by his poems, which, Miller and Black claim, are partial disclosures of infantile conflicts. The poems covertly betray a self craving realization but fearing exposure. The furtiveness stems from, as Black says, "His impulse to express sexuality *versus* his fear of punishment for such expressions" (p. 44), a fear originating in a forceful oedipal conflict. Black's reading of Whitman's early writings (puerile and trite as they are) convincingly explains how Whitman translated repressed oedipal feelings, and his consequent fear and guilt, into literary forms that provided momentary catharsis without direct confrontation. However, as Black notes (p. 48), catharsis can offer only temporary appeasement of anxiety, luring one into a false sense of reconciliation and integration; that is, they address a symptom without revealing the underlying problem. This accounts for Whitman's sense, as in "As I Ebb'd with the Ocean of Life," that his poems have somehow betrayed him. Black's commentary on "As I Ebb'd" transforms Miller's interpretation (pp. 44–47), as Whitman's return to and acknowledgment of his infantile relationship with his parents, into Whitman's own commentary on how his poems express occasional attitudes and feelings, but fail to uncover his repressed desires. Whitman's poems, essentially cathartic experiences, undoubtedly sprang from, among other things, opposing feelings towards his parents. But "the repeated failure to get the secret, the clue, the word [the assimilation through language of oedipal desires into the conscious ego], makes the poems 'insolent,' mere 'blab whose echoes recoil upon' him" (Black, p. 59). In "Song of Myself," Whitman never descends to such self-deprecating bitterness simply because he had no poetic "failures" to recall when writing it. The tragic irony for Whitman lies in the modern judgment of Whitman's failures as his greatest successes.

That sense of failure, that feeling of inadequacy in the face of unlimited opportunity for expression, emerges rarely in Whitman's work, but when it does, it carries the power of an oft-repressed sentiment.[6] Whether viewed from a psychological or from a nationalistic perspective, this failure revolves around a fear that poetic expression will never adequately render a self, a "Personality," to the extent Whitman desperately requires. In adding a new interpretation to Whitman's desire for and performance of self-expression, I do not wish to confute other critics' positions. To me, given their respective theoretical premises, their contentions are just and the principles founding their strategies complement one another. Indeed, Whitman invites antithetical readings of his poetry, though he remains confident that no explanation can exhaust the mystery of his creations. Fruitful and complex as the poetry is, it allows opposing interpretations. I only wish to supplement prior readings by taking a philosophical approach to a problem where others have taken a historiconationalistic or psycho-biographical approach. For, notwithstanding the acute analyses, valuable to both students and teachers of Whitman, by Pearce, Black, *et al*, something has been missing from their arguments—namely, the role language plays in frustrating (as opposed to facilitating) self-expression. That is, along with the problem of overcoming inherited styles to express a distinctively American self, and the problem of allowing a repressed unconscious identity to emerge in a way that exceeds euphoric but short-lived catharsis, Whitman also faces the dilemma of wielding an intractable, objectifying form—language—to represent a vigorous, transient person—a subject.

The obvious way to obviate the alienating separation between a subject and the words it uses to manifest itself is to assert a mystical connection between the two. When, in his prose disquisitions, Whitman ascribes an occult bond between self and word, he assigns to language spiritual qualities rather than bringing the self down to rhetorical or empirical levels. In the first Preface, Whitman writes "...the expression of the American poet is to be transcendent..." In *An American Primer*, notes written in the 1850s for a proposed lecture, he says "—All words are spiritual—nothing is more spiritual than words...Words follow character—nativity, independence, individuality."[7] That words could materialize "character" while still partaking in its "spiritual" nature Whitman believed all his life. This faith exemplified his carefree habit of leaping imaginatively from one metaphysical realm to another without bothering to note or to mind the fallaciousness involved. But, just as he flagrantly breached conventional morality, Whitman coveted logical scandals, for without contradiction Whitman could not assert the paradoxical unity of the spiritual self and the material word, nor could he coalesce his own conflicting desires into a unified identity.

The psychic motives compelling the linguistic objectification of an inner self may be explained by Jacques Lacan's notion of the "discourse of the Other" which develops out of the "mirror stage" of infancy.[8] In the mirror stage, the child's ego evolves as he acknowledges his corporeal unity by recognizing the unity of his own mirror image. In identifying with this Other which appears complete in itself, the child gradually infers a corresponding completeness and discreteness in itself. In other words, seeing a quality of isolated and independent being in an external object resembling it, the child begins to become consciously aware of its own quality of independent being. To comprehend the Other and assimilate it into its own ego, to achieve the desired identification, the child resorts to language. That is, the initial discovery (or, more precisely, constitution) of self takes the form of a discourse between self and Other; there is no self before the dialogue takes place. Language allows the self to voice the desires that declare its separation from the Other, to articulate the desires it directs at the Other and that it hopes the Other will respond to.

But, a reliance on the Other for selfhood and fulfillment breeds anxiety in the self; a lack of control over its own genesis fills the self with a dread of annihilation. The fact that the self owes its existence to the Other leads the self to ignore the Other's otherness, to struggle against the Other's autonomy. Because the self needs the mediation of the Other to establish itself as a self, it seeks to repress its dependence in order to live in the gratifying illusion of mastery and permanence. And so, identity endures as a misinterpretation of difference. Lacan revises the Hegelian formulation (through the filters of Freud and Kojeve[9]) that self-consciousness begins as a fundamental misconstruction of the in-itself as a for-another—a misapprehension the self eventually transcends by recognizing its previously unrealized agency in the misapprehension—by claiming that what Hegel considers transcendence is actually repression. The Other is not transcended or overcome; it can only be repressed or accepted in all its threatening otherness. Neurosis results when the desire for the Other remains concealed and disallowed, when the self finds the freedom to experience its desires intolerable. Consciously or unconsciously, the desires will persist even though the Other masterfully refuses to end the self's longings by giving up its otherness—hence the Other's status as lost, the self's status as forsaken. If the child, for whatever reasons, cannot outgrow the appeal of the Other, he then continues his search for the Other to validate his self, to relieve him of his ontological insecurity by filling the painful absence the lost Other plagues him with.

In Whitman's case, this search takes the form of writing poems that he hopes will embody his own tentative and incomplete self and constitute an identifiable Other. The more his words impress an Other, the more Whitman will solidify his existential durability. And the more Whitman's poems fabricate a familiar Other, the easier it is to absorb it into his own ego. As the meeting place of self and Other, composition rests upon the incarnating power of the word, the capacity of words to manufacture an Other and to manifest a self and then to melt them together in a primal embrace abolishing self-Other distinctions altogether. But what words most accurately publicize, without misrepresentation, these inner motives and desires (levelled at the Other) that make up the self? And what words form an Other foreign enough to provide the mediation necessary for selfhood, yet intimate enough to overcome alienation? Whitman's first decision is to prefer spoken words to written words.

How does writing threaten the contiguity of self and word? Put simply, writing distances the self from its expression, its exteriorized self, the self it constructs with and in language. Writing can never satisfy Whitman's desire to soothe his psychic insecurity, for in re-reading his poems for signs of self-acquaintance, he can only find an alienated, lost, impoverished version of himself. As William Carlos Williams says at the beginning of *The Great American Novel*, "Now I am not what I was when the word was forming to say what I am." Writing stabilizes and spatializes an unstable, temporal subject. It consolidates desire or intention into a stasis, preservable and lifeless, severed from the identity that tried to replicate itself, to create a form in its own imageless image. Writing aggravates the differentiation, the figural death, which takes place when expression (understood as an attempt at self-recognition through objectification) divides the self into an external representation of the self and an internal self living temporally, changing from moment to moment. But speech is as evanescent as the shifting psyche it socializes; it vanishes as it is uttered, just as desires and thoughts vanish in a succession of sensations. Because spoken words dissolve as they are realized, they can never cause self-estrangement. There is less opportunity for self-confrontation in speech than there is in print; speech appears indistinguishable from the self it presents. However, while unrecorded speech avoids an alienating embodiment of self by remaining proximate to and ephemeral with desire, it also prevents the reification of a redeeming Other. Self-confrontation, self-recognition, requires the mediation of the Other, but speech, at least in the way Whitman ideally conceives of it, precludes any mediation whatsoever. Only writing, then, offers the hope of encountering the Other, and hence the self.

This hope, unfulfilled as it must be, leads only to despair. Writing appears as a false tempter holding out the pathetic, unsatisfied faith in self-completion. Even the very act of writing frustrates Whitman's pathological search for gratifying self-expression. While the actions of speech immediately mimic (an oxymoron, but one Whitman would condone) the actions of thought without the mechanical intervention of script, writing retards the spontaneity of natural pronunciation. It robs expression of all the human accompaniments of heartfelt communication—physical gesture, tonal modulation, tactile exhilaration—leaving only the meager remainder of black signs on white paper, what Whitman would call "the spectres in books" ("Song of Myself," 1.35). And so Whitman summons his readers to hearken to "the belch'd words of [his] voice" (1.25), to appreciate his impulsive utterances as gushing forth from the natural well-springs of his emotive ebbs and flows.

Recent criticism of Whitman has followed him in his emphasis on voice, not only by pointing out the explicit antiwriting motif in "Song of Myself" and other poems and criticism, but also by borrowing concepts and arguments from phonocentric discourses to analyze the oracular qualities of Whitman's poetry. C. Carroll Hollis has studied *Leaves of Grass* along the lines of speech act theory, singling out Whitman's poetic style for its illocutionary force.[10] Calvin Bedient also stresses the "Orality and Power" of "Song of Myself," basing his orality-literacy categories on Walter Ong's work, which in turn summarizes anthropological studies of pre-literate cultures.[11] And Mitchell Robert Breitweiser, in "Who Speaks in Whitman's Poems?", writes of the pronoun "I" in Whitman's canon using Emile Benveniste's structural linguistics (though Breitweiser notes that "Benveniste's ignores the problems that arise when the word *I* is written...").[12] Without doubt, Whitman's style attempts to represent in writing an oracular performance. The declamatory rhetoric, the simple present and imperative verb tenses, the catalogues, the slang diction, all suggest a speaker-audience relation as the context for experiencing the poetry. An oral style issuing directly from the extemporaneously inspired bard carries with it the force of an authoritative personality, a force that becomes mitigated in writing. Whitman's oracular statements, democratic and coercive in their appeal, foster the illusion of an unmediated presentation of self with an assertiveness and intimacy hard to reject. Whitman intensifies his confidential allure when he insinuates (without actually enunciating) an occult word or mystical sound into his language, a sound whose semantic import exceeds ordinary categories of sense and whose aural magnetism will merge Whitman and his readers in a shared inspiration.

> Not words, not music or rhyme I want.... not custom
>   or lecture, not even the best,
> Only the lull I like, the hum of your valved voice.
> (11.85–86)

> I chant a new chant of dilation or pride ...
> (1.428)

> And mine a word of the modern.... a word en masse.
> (1.478)

> I speak the password primeval ...
> (1.506)

But the ensuing sonic embrace gives place to an even more intimate and affective kind of contact than the communal "chant," although both forms of discourse render the printed poem a provisional marker for a higher communion of souls and bodies. The spiritual communication Whitman envisions transcends both written and spoken words and sounds and so he opts for a meaningful silence, a significant "hush" endowed with value by Whitman's expressive physiognomy. The arresting power of a silent look emerges often in "Song of Myself":

Backward I see in my own days where I sweated
        through fogs with linguists and contenders,
I have no mockings or arguments.... I witness and
        wait.

(11.80–81)

I think I will do nothing for a long time but listen...
(1.582)

Oxen that rattle the yoke or halt in the shade, what is
        it that you express in your eyes?
It seems to me more than all the print I have read in
        my life.

(11.235–36)

Writing and talk do not prove me,
I carry the plenum of proof and every thing else in
        my face,
With the hush of my lips I confound the topmost
        skeptic.

(11.579–81)

John Irwin calls these instances of declared quietude "hieroglyphic gestures"[13]; they figure forth a corporeal text whose meaning will be self-evident. Whitman takes literally Emerson's statement that "men have a pictorial or representative quality" (*Representative Men*). A reliance on pictographic/ physiognomic signs grounded in Whitman's own body (as in the frontispiece of *Leaves of Grass*, 1855) as evidence of identity is less fraught with the possibility of misinterpretation than is a reliance on spoken or written words. Speech vanishes with the moment of utterance and so it imitates the movement of consciousness and desire, a replication comforting to one who yearns for a faithful correspondence of thought and word. But in vanishing, speech thwarts the continued recognition and the preservation of self which motivated Whitman to speak in the first place. The spoken self must then endlessly voice its identity to provide a sense of coherence and centrality, an activity that degenerates into irksome reiteration. A written self can be preserved, but only by succumbing to the desires and misappropriations of whoever should pick up the book. Future readers, unswayed by Whitman's written (and hence attenuated) authorial presence, may either shun the written self in disdain (*a la* Whittier) or pervert the written self through an idiosyncratic interpretation that compromises Whitman's intentions. And who fretted more over future representations of himself than Whitman did?

Whitman's body, however, is both preservable *and* owned—pure, "untranslatable," a pleasurable text responding naturally and spontaneously to his own desires, without the mediation of the Other. As a self-reflexive text whose meaning and value preced linguistic formulation, as a corporeal identity in disregard of linguistic difference, the body affords auto-telic, auto-erotic self-expression. Whitman can expose himself publicly without loss or threat or estrangement through the arrogation of the Other. Although his literal expositions take place in seclusion, still, the Other, which is usually the "woods" or "the sea," he resigns himself to, observes his self-presentation without preempting Whitman's integrity. Nature will approvingly recognize Whitman's bodily identity and the willful desire emanating from it and through it. It is only when Whitman transgresses or falls short of his own ideal of self-expression that nature challenges him.

> The spotted hawk swoops by and accuses me.... he
>   complains of my gab and my loitering.
> (1.1331)

> Dazzling and tremendous how quick the sunrise would
>   kill me,
> If I could not now and always send sunrise out of me.
> (11.560–61)

> To me the converging objects of the universe
>   perpetually flow,
> All are written to me, and I must get what the writing
>   means.
> (11.404–05)

The press of my foot to the earth springs a hundred
    affections,
They scorn the best I can do to relate them.

                        (11.253–54)

In comparing his actual expressions to the ideal expression exemplified by the mute face of nature and verified by its affective power, Whitman downgrades, with varying degrees of self-deprecation, his poems to "gab." Nature becomes an antagonist, an archetypal author and expression (a "discipline," to use Emerson's term) whose peremptory wholeness only reminds Whitman of his deficiency. Had not Whitman sensed a lack, an absence, with the concomitant desire, he would have felt no urge to write. Language would have been merely supplemental and the pitfalls of self-enunciation could have been avoided. With his own body evincing plainly his being to others (to gain their recognition) and comforting him in his self-propriety, Whitman could remain secure in his purity, his integration with *and* segregation from beings knowing that he participated in and did not merely duplicate the expressions (or semiosis) of nature.

But, of course, Whitman must use words. The placid exterior of nature (or the geographical energy of America) may constitute a poem for Whitman, but he cannot rewrite it or use it as a paradigm of creation without the supervention of language. Even when he idealizes non-verbal communication or when he assumes a laconic attitude ("I myself but write one or two indicative words for the future..."—"Poets to Come"), Whitman requires grandiloquent, overflowing lines. And just as the serene exterior of nature is imposed upon by the language, so is the dynamic interior of the self compromised by language. His belief in the potential existence of a fulfilling language of the self, an optimism which sustains Whitman's quickening productivity of 1854–56, fades with the passage of time, despite enthusiastic responses, as language soon proves inadequate to satisfy the pent-up desire for identity that Whitman feels within.

Nowhere is Whitman's consciousness of the failure of language more concentrated and poignant than in Section 2 of "As I Ebb'd With the Ocean of Life." Harold Bloom has characterized this passage as "Whitman undoing the Whitmanian bardic self of *Song of Myself*,"[14] but this is not quite the case, especially if Bloom associates the "bardic self" with the "real Me" of the poem. Since the "real Me" remains supremely intact—indeed, profoundly imperturbable—Whitman does not "undo" it. Instead, he mystifies it by setting it beyond signification. If the "bardic self" is not the "real Me" but rather the process whereby the "real Me" manifests itself in inspired language, then the "bardic self" is still not condemned. The attack is not so much on the agent, the "bardic self," as it is on the means the "bardic self" must necessarily use to represent the "real Me." To become the "outsetting bard," to reify the "real Me" and to prove its authority, Whitman must resort to the word. But the word refuses to dissolve in the face of a self struggling for immediate recognition; the word insistently announces its ubiquitous presence and thus jealously absents or veils the "Me" it stands for.

As the word is not the point Whitman wishes his poems to settle on, he can only lament his inevitable mistake and disdain his life's work.

> O baffled, balk'd, bent to the very earth,
> Oppress'd with myself that I have dared to open my
>   mouth,
> Aware now that amid all that blab whose echoes recoil
>   upon me I have not once had the least idea who or
>   what I am ...

Because of one fateful, ill-conceived decision—he "dared to open [his] mouth"—Whitman now indulges in a brutal self-criticism. The violent verbs ("baffled, balk'd, bent," "Oppress'd," "recoil") exaggerate the bitter regret he feels at having attempted to write poetry, to celebrate himself in language. While he intended his poems to exalt his individuality, they now "recoil upon" him and certify his ignorance of self. What began as a journey of self-discovery and self-elaboration in "Song of Myself," now ends with Whitman lost "amid all that blab," divorced from the subjective truth concealed behind an impenetrable wall of signs. The poems that make up this wall Whitman lumps together with the indiscriminate adjective "all," suggesting that the problem lay not in this or that poem but with poetic language itself, a language alien to the self.

> But that before all my arrogant poems the real Me
>   stands yet untouch'd, untold, altogether unreach'd,
> Withdrawn far, mocking me with mock-congratulatory
>   signs and bows,
> With peals of distant ironical laughter at every word I
>   have written,
> Pointing in silence to these songs, and then to the sand
>   beneath.

That Whitman ever though he could achieve the hopeless goal of embodying a self in words makes his poems "arrogant." With unanswerable superiority, the "real Me" ridicules Whitman's pitifully inadequate "songs" with non-verbal derision. The taunts assume the form of either "mock-congratulatory signs and bows," "distant ironical laughter," or an incontrovertible "Pointing in silence," in each case a non-linguistic action. How is Whitman to respond to an imperially reductive comparison between his own poems and grains of sand? He accepts the comparison with typical Whitmanian abandon and even involves himself as well as his poems. Since Whitman's poems were frank extensions of his own identity, he must share their fate.

> I too but signify at the utmost a little wash'd-up drift,
> A few sands and dead leaves to gather...

Leaves of Grass have become "dead leaves," the poems have fallen short of their transcendent purpose, the Romantic dream of the self is over. And so, in his resentment, Whitman repudiates altogether any knowledge or understanding to be derived from poetry.

> I perceive I have not really understood any thing not a
>   single object, and that no man ever can,
> Nature here in sight of the sea taking advantage of me
>   to dart upon me and sting me,
> Because I have dared to open my mouth to sing at all.

Because the words could not contain the desire which occasioned them, Whitman's initial unlimited optimism collapses into an all-encompassing skepticism. He feels "tak[en] advantage of," exposed as insignificant, revealed in all his trivial facticity by a recondite force surpassing the comprehensive verbal powers of the proud poet. Nature exercises its retribution on him like an unseen, irritating insect—"to dart upon me and sting me"—torturing Whitman for his unfounded superiority, his pretentions that he, above all others, could translate the meanings of nature (e.g., the bird's song in "Out of the Cradle Endlessly Rocking") without subjugating or impoverishing nature with his own exiguous meanings and defective words. His failure to express the inexpressible compels Whitman to take refuge in a blank denial of any expression, especially that which would point to a transcendent origin, be it "Nature" or the "real Me." He can "perceive" only the meagre limits of his understanding (that is, what his language makes available to him). A comfortless and unredemptive knowledge of ignorance offers him no consolation, leaving Whitman with a hapless impotence.

Whitman's assumption of a regressive ignorance is accompanied in the rest of the poem by a symbolic return, as Miller says, to an infantile relationship with his parents: "Paumanok," his father, and the "ocean of life," his mother. Only in Section 2 does Whitman condemn his poetry. But despite the brevity and intermittance of Whitman's despairing reflections on his own poems, both in "As I Ebb'd" and across the entire canon, they still indicate the sole reason for his self-deprecating attitude. Whitman offers no autobiographical explanation for his cynicism. "As I Ebb'd" precedes the wartime horrors Whitman experienced firsthand; despite the poet's claims to the contrary, the first two editions of *Leaves of Grass* successfully established Whitman as a major, if notorious, poet in America and, soon after, in Europe; no concrete evidence exists for a failed love affair or a personal tragededy; the death of his father in 1855 did not interfere with the output of 1856.[15] It is not his life but rather his poetry that disheartens him. Even if the poetry functions as a disguised meditation on or sublimation of his repressed sexuality or his troubled childhood, only through the poetic disguise can he come to terms with his life. In fact, from the war onward, Whitman would shape his life and character around the mythical persona of "the good, gray poet." He even went so far as to insist that biographers send him their manuscripts so he could "authenticate" them, always sacrificing verity for wish-fulfillment. As Whitman was surrounding himself with reverential disciples, and fostering a mythical persona at the expense of his actual experiences and memories (his "real Me"?), his creative talents declined. Of the poems written after the war, only a handful are of any lasting value; his later work amounts to little more than adding to and revising (usually for the worse) *Leaves of Grass*. Not only the printed poems but also much of the prose, letters, documents Whitman either destroyed or scrupulously fitted to his fictional self-image in the last decade of his life to the extent that, as Justin Kaplan says, "By the time he died scarcely a period in his life had not been 'revised' in one way or another."[16]

And yet his attempts to subsume his life and his self into a poetic fiction became such an obsession that they supplanted the historical "Personality" Whitman claimed was to occupy the center of his poetry. While Whitman longed to exteriorize his self, to signify his desires in a transparent medium that would preserve the ego's primacy and integrity, the opposite occurred. Instead of Whitman structuring his poetry along the lines of his free, transcendent identity, the poetry structured Whitman's identity along the lines of its figurative conventions. This is why Whitman singles out his poems as his own worst enemy. At first, an open poetic sytle seemed to provide an adequately expressive means of publicizing the self; but actually publication spells the death of the self. Writing divides the self, turns the self away from itself, versifies it beyond recognition. Though speech or gesture may produce self-estrangement less radically than writing, still, in poetry, aural or pictographic signs can only be indicated through the letter. Whitman entreats us to ignore that fact—"The words of my book nothing, the drift of it everything" ("Shut Not Your Doors")—but nevertheless the printed word relentlessly interposes itself between not only the reader and the "drift" of Whitman's poetry but also between Whitman and the "drift" of Whitman's poetry. As a reader of his own poetry, Whitman finds himself implicated in an interpretive process, an act grounded on and frustrated by mediation. Feeling estranged from his own words, having little intuitive understanding of what should have been self-evincing language, Whitman, just like any other reader, must identify the personality behind the words in order to experience the initial inspiration. This necessary reconstruction marks the distance between him and his expressions. Having to recognize his own willfully objectified, printed personality, Whitman realizes the impracticality of his poetic project, a realization upsetting enough to oblige him to reduce the central shaping event of his life (save for, perhaps, the war) to "only a language experiment."

Such a conclusion may surprise causal readers of Whitman accustomed to the sanguine poems glorifying the self, democracy, the Union, America, humanity, and so on. Whitman's ambition to embrace and be embraced by his culture carried him through several triumphant inspirational poems (as well as some embarrassingly bathetic poems); his mood is usually confidently optimistic, making the moments of bitter despair seem anomalous. But, in fact these pessimistic moments are indissolubly linked to Whitman's exultant hopes. His periodic descents into despondence issue from a sudden awareness of the futility of his hopes. Because of the alienating consequences of self-expression, the differential relation between self and language, Whitman's overriding desire for a fully self-presenting language is doomed to remain unsatisfied. And unsatisfied desires eventually turn on the ego. Whitman's target is his own ego-centered poetry, that which was to manifest his ego. But, it was also the only means of freeing his ego, leaving Whitman in a tragic double-bind. Desire may demand a language that will allow it a mature fulfillment, but no language will sufficiently articulate and preserve Whitman's desires. To express a self and its desires is a prerequisite of being human, but to maintain the purity and transcendence of the self in the expressive process is, at best, a solacing illusion. The self is inaccessible.

NOTES

1. Richard Poirier, *A World Elsewhere* (New York: Oxford University Press, 1966), 6.

2. All quotations of Whitman's poetry are from *Leaves of Grass: A Textual Variorum of the Printed Poems*, 3 vols. Edited by Sculley Bradley *et al* (New York: New York University Press, 1980). I have quoted the earliest version of "Song of Myself" and the last versions of all other poems, except when otherwise indicated.

3. Roy Harvey Pearce. *The Continuity of American Poetry* (Princeton, NJ: Princeton University Press, 1961); James E. Miller, Jr. *The American Quest for the Supreme Fiction* (Chicago: University of Chicago Press, 1979).

4. Albert Gelpi, *The Tenth Muse, The Psyche of the American Poet* (Cambridge, MA; Harvard University Press, 1975), 186.

5. Edwin Miller. *Walt Whitman's Poetry: A Psychological Journey* (New York: New York University Press, 1968); Stephen Black. *Whitman's Journey into Chaos, A Psychoanalytic Study of the Creative Process* (Princeton, NJ: Princeton University Press, 1975).

6. For example, in *Democratic Vistas*, Whitman writes "Never was anything more wanted than, to-day, and here in the States, the poet of the modern is wanted, or the great literatus of the modern" (p. 365). Whitman then goes on to assert the primary influence literature has on all other aspects of culture. The implication is that Whitman's national epic has failed and that America has no indigenous cultural identity. See *Prose Works*, v. II. Edited by Floyd Stovall (New York: New York University Press, 1964).

7. The phrase from the Preface appears on page 712 of *Leaves of Grass, Comprehensive Reader's Edition*. Edited by Harold W. Blodgett and Sculley Bradley (New York: New York University Press, 1965). *An American Primer* was edited and issued as a separate book by Horace Traubel in 1904 (Cambridge, MA: The University Press). The quotation appears on pages 1–2.

8. See "The mirror stage as formative of the function of the I," in *Ecrits, A Selection*. Translated by Alan Sheridan (New York: W.W. Norton & Co., 1977).

9. Like most Parisian intellectuals of his generation. Lacan was introduced to Hegel by Alexandre Kojeve's celebrated lectures on the *Phenomenology*. Kojeve's lectures were published as *Introduction to the Reading of Hegel*. Assembled by Rayond Queneau, edited by Allan Bloom, translated by James II. Nichols, Jr. (New York: Basic Books, Inc., 1969).

10. C. Carroll Hollis, *Language and Style in "Leaves of Grass"* (Baton Rouge, LA: Louisiana State University Press, 1983).

11. Calvin Bedient, "Orality and Power (Whitman's 'Song of Myself')," *Delta: Revue de Centre d'Etudes et de Recherche sur les Ecrivains du Sud aux Etats-Unis*, 16 (May, 1983), 79–94.

12. Mitchell Robert Breitweiser, "Who Speaks in Whitman's Poems?" *Bucknell Review*, v. XXVIII, no. 1 (1983), 121–43.

13. John Irwin, *American Hieroglyphics* (New Haven, CN: Yale University Press, 1980), 98.

14. Harold Bloom, *A Map of Misreading* (New York: Oxford University Press, 1985), 180. If Bloom uses the term "undoing" in its psychoanalytic sense, then his summary of "As I Ebb'd with the Ocean of Life" is closer to Whitman's purpose, but still misleading. In their *Language of Psychoanalysis* (N.Y.: Norton, 1973), J. Laplanche and J.-B. Pontalis define "undoing" as "an attempt to cause past thoughts, words, gestures or actions not to have occurred..." (p. 477). Lady Macbeth's handwashing is a clear example of pathological denial and undoing that "is directed at the [prior] act's very reality," and the aim is to suppress it absolutely, "as though time were reversible" (p.478). But Whitman's retraction does not deny the "reality" of his earlier attitude—instead it laments the very irreversibility of his earlier attitude.

15. Gay Wilson Allen scrupulously documents this period in *The Solitary Singer, A Critical Biography of Walt Whitman* (New York: New York University Press, 1955). See Chapters VI and VII.

16. Justin Kaplan, *Walt Whitman, A Life* (New York: Simon & Schuster, Inc., 1980), 19.

HERBERT J. LEVINE

Union and Disunion in "Song of Myself"

In 1850, when California sought to enter the Union as a non-slaveholding
state, the Southern states threatened to secede unless compromises extended
slavery to other territory conquered in the Mexican war. During the
acrimonious debate, the leading disunionist, John C. Calhoun, pointed out
the insufficiency of political rhetoric to prop up the American Union: "It
cannot be saved by eulogies on the Union, however splendid or numerous.
The cry of 'Union, Union, the glorious Union!' can no more prevent
disunion than the cry of 'Health, health, glorious health!' on the part of the
physician can save a patient."[1]

During the 1840s, Walt Whitman had offered such eulogies, but in his
anger at the Compromise of 1850, he stopped praising so he could
administer physic to a sick Union. In a group of satiric poems, he railed
against the Congressional betrayers of freedom, the very principle for which
the Union had been founded. One recent study has argued that the
escalating crisis of the Union allowed Whitman to discover the healing role
so central to "Song of Myself."[2] Another has argued that the economic
downturn of 1854, which put Whitman out of as celebrator of the artisan,
who was rapidly being displaced by entrepreneurs and managers of capital.[3]
Such studies have made obsolete the widespread view that in the 1850s
Whitman detached himself from practical politics in order to advocate a

From *American Literature*, vol. 59, no. 4 (December 1987). © 1987 by Duke University Press.

purely spiritual democracy. This essay seeks to anchor Whitman's first great poem, the 1855 "Song of Myself," in the political discourse of the 1850s. Part I surveys that discourse in order to illuminate two important early prose statements by Whitman: the manuscript, "Slavery—the Slaveholders," and the preface to the 1855 poems. Part II demonstrates that Whitman reflected contemporary political concerns in the figurative language of "Song of Myself," where we find figures of union counterpoised by figures of disunion. Finally, Part III proposes a three-part plot for "Song of Myself," a structure of Union, Disunion, and Reunion, which anticipates the painful trajectory of American destiny in the era of the Civil War.

I

Disunionist rhetoric, as old as anti-Federalist resistance to the Constitution, reappeared periodically through the first half of the nineteenth century. New Englanders resorted to it at the Hartford Convention after the War of 1812; Southerners took it up at the time of the Missouri Compromise (1820), again during the South Carolina nullification crisis (1833), and during each of the great legislative battles over the extension of slavery in the 1840s and 1850s, all won by Southern interests, in part, at least, because Northerners so feared the disunion that Southerners threatened. When John Quincy Adams was prevented from presenting to Congress an abolitionist petition in 1842, calls for disunion rose in the North and soon became an article of faith for Garrisonian abolitionists. Northern radicals kept talk of disunion alive after every defeat for anti-slavery: the failure of the Wilmot Proviso (1847), which was to have banned slavery from the Mexican territories; the Compromise of 1850, and especially its new Fugitive Slave Law, enforceable by Federal authority; the Kansas-Nebraska Act (1854), which repealed the Missouri Compromise that had kept slavery out of most of the Louisiana Purchase territory.

While this sort of disunionism was fuel for Northern abolitionists and Southern "fire-eaters," it was anathema to Walter Whitman, journalist and ardent nationalist. "This Union dissolved?" he wrote in 1847. "Why the very words are murky with their own most monstrous portent! And yet these words are flippantly turned over and over in the mouths of men, at the present time.... Thinking, as we do, that hardly any evil which could be inflicted on the people of this hemisphere, and the cause of freedom all over the world, would be so great as the disunion of these States—their parting in bitterness and ill-blood—we believe it incumbent on every Democrat always to bear testimony in the same spirit, and the same words, as one now in heaven—the *Union!* it must and shall be preserved!"[4] Nor did he adopt the rhetoric of disunion in breaking from the Democratic Party and taking up with the Free Soilers and the Free Democrats in the elections of 1848 and 1852. One of that party's leaders proposed in 1851 that it adopt the time-honored motto of Daniel Webster, "Liberty and Union," to impress upon the electorate *both* its essential goals.[5]

Whitman preserved these goals even as political rhetoric became increasingly divisive and more and more Americans "came to think of themselves as forming not one but two distinct peoples."[6] His own Senator, William H. Seward, who had vaunted the inevitable continuance of the Union in 1850 had become by 1854 during the Kansas-Nebraska debates a sectional tactician, appealing to the North to preserve its interests, not the Union's, against a growing Southern conspiracy to extend its slaveholding empire.[7] Whitman, by contrast, spoke on behalf of "all Freemen north and south ... the whole population of the 31 states who have no human property." In a little-known prose manuscript that he entitled "Slavery—the Slaveholders—The Constitution—the true America and Americans, the laboring persons," Whitman addresses the slaveholders from a Unionist point of view. "Our territory of Nebraska and Kansas is wanted for our Children.... If you or your children choose to come, of course you have the same right to come that we have, and on the same terms.—This vast tract is *ours*—ours, the people's of the whole 31 states, north and south...." To an anti-slavery advocate like Seward, the struggle over Kansas was between two systems of labor, one moral and the other immoral. To Whitman, that moral struggle was subordinated to a more pressing political question: whether the Territories, which the Constitution mandated to the whole Union, would continue to belong to the millions of free workingmen or to the few "hundreds" of slave-owners.[8]

The slave-owners were representative for Whitman of the capitalist class that threatened his egalitarian vision of the Union. Democracy and riches, he understood, were opposed. "For this circling Confederacy, standing together with interlinked hands, ample, equal, each one with his grip of love wedged in life or in death to all the rest, we must share and share alike.... If there be any of good dish, and not enough of it to go completely round, it shall not be brought on at all" (*NUPM*, VI, 2178–79). Opposed to this ideal was the reality of exclusive self-interest that Whitman saw everywhere around him, North and South. "Is the whole land becoming one vast model plantation, whose inhabitants suppose the ultimate and best ends of man attained when he drives a profitable business, no matter how abject the terms—and when he has enough to wear and is not bothered for pork?" (*NUPM*, VI, 2190).

Whitman's concern for the Union is also evident in his anger at Federal

enforcement of the Fugitive Slave Law, which the Constitution had left up
to the discretion of the States. The same week that the Kansas-Nebraska Act
was passed by Congress, a fugitive slave named Anthony Burns was arrested
in Boston by Federal marshals.[9] Whitman's acerbic poem on the subject,
included in the first *Leaves of Grass* (later titled "A Boston Ballad"), berates
the people of Boston for letting themselves be trampled by a tyrannical
authority that reminds him of George III. In the prose piece, he enters into
the political principle at stake, the Constitutional theory of states' rights that
should limit the powers of the Union. Tell the Union, he exhorts an
imagined audience, "that having delegated to it certain important functions,
and having entered into certain important engagements with our brother
states, we like all the rest, have reserved more important functions,
embodying our primary rights, exclusively to ourselves" (*NUPM*, VI, 2189).
Whitman thus combined an egalitarian vision of Union with a fiercely
individualistic view of states' rights, a balancing of the one and the many that
would prove crucial in his poetic reworking of the political problems facing
the American Union.

Both "Slavery—the Slaveholders" and "A Boston Ballad" are fueled by
Whitman's anger, which he chose to bury in order to become the healer of
the nation in *Leaves of Grass*. In what appear to be the first notebook lines that
he drafted for "Song of Myself," Whitman adopts an equalizing perspective
that was inconceivable for any contemporary politician:

> I am the poet of slaves and of the masters of slaves
> . . . .
> I go with the slaves of the earth equally with the
>   masters
> And I will stand between the masters and the slaves,
> Entering into both so that both shall understand me
>   alike. (*NUPM*, I, 67)

The poet, Whitman says in his 1855 preface, "supplies what wants supplying
and checks what wants checking,"[10] such as checking the angry divisiveness
of contemporary politics, including his own anger at the betrayals of
democratic ideals, whether on the part of slaveholders, Congressmen, or
Presidents.

Anger erupts occasionally into both the preface and "Song of Myself,"
where he is ironic at the expense of slave-catchers, greedy capitalists, and
self-serving politicians who refuse to come into the democratic feast he has
prepared. But, given the background we have been examining, it is
remarkable how serene Whitman is about the contentious political issues of

his day, almost as if he deliberately reset his clock to a time when most of the country believed disunion an utter impossibility. "The union" he describes as "always surrounded by blatherers and always calm and impregnable" (p. 7). As to slavery, he put his faith in the inexorable unfolding of progressive historical laws. The American poet will therefore allow to enter into him both "slavery and the tremulous spreading of hands to protect it, and the stern opposition to it which shall never cease till it ceases or the speaking of tongues and the moving of lips cease" (p. 8). Whitman's reference to anti-slavery speech is but the final item in a long list of all that the American poet is to "enclose," including what were for him the primary bonds of Union, the geographical, natural, and human history of his vast land.[11]

Enclosing America, the poet unites its diversity in himself so that he comes to embody the Union. Like the Union, the poet makes an equal place in his poetic microcosm for all "strata" and "interests," for western and eastern, nothern and southern states (p. 14). And like the Union, too, the poet recognizes individual differences, beginning with those qualities distinguishing him from others, making him "a great master" (p. 15), "complete in himself" (p. 9), his soul, "president of itself always" (p. 14). As a new kind of egalitarian master, balancing "sympathy" and "pride" (p. 12), this poet has the conviction that he can perfect the work that the people of the United States started in their Constitution, namely, "to form a more perfect Union."

II

"Poetry situates itself," the poet-critic Allen Grossman has said, "where other instruments of mind find impossibility."[12] Where political rhetoric was failing to preserve the Union, poetry, Whitman saw, could attempt an alternative discourse of union based on the unity of a representative American self. With respect to such a unified self, the experience of his own body and soul, his land, its animals, people, occupations and history, the earth, its evolutionary past and cosmic future—all was to be portrayed as a vast seamless web, within which differences could be accommodated without dismembering the whole.

But when we begin to take apart Whitman's style, we can see the seams. Two very different personal and verbal styles, as the warp and the woof of the carpet, are woven into his seemingly unified poetic practice. The one is based on connection and inclusion, the other on disconnection and exclusion. I call them styles of union and disunion, diverging orientations to the relationship of self and world, which Whitman offers to reconcile the democratic paradox of the many individuals and States affirming their own separate identities under the banner of Union, *e pluribus unum*.

In Whitman's style of union, the figure most closely associated with the speaker's political self-presentation is a serial synecdoche, a list of parts democratically representing a whole that includes them all.[13] If we separate out the parts of one of Whitman's lists, they seem to stand on their own, as a Kentuckian, a Hoosier, a Badger, a Buckeye (Sec. 16).[14] Yet, just as in classical synecdoche, the sail that stands for the ship cannot function apart from it, so too in Whitman's series, individuals (and their states) are dependent on the Union that gives them both individual and collective identity. Whitman spells this out in a line describing American Federalism. The speaker *is*, he says, "one of the great nations, the nation of many nations—the smallest the same and the largest the same." Having provided the allegorical key to his synecdochic catalogue, he goes on to counteract both sectionalism and nativism, two of the greatest dangers to the Union in the 1850s. He is therefore "a southerner soon as a northerner," and "not merely of the New World but of Africa Europe or Asia," in short, a true American. As he explains in the preface, in America "a bard is to be commensurate with a people" (p. 6).

Another characteristic device in Whitman's style of union is what we might call redundant metonymy, a trope so nearly transparent that it hardly seems a deliberate figure. Where in classical metonymy an idea is evoked by the *substitution* of some closely associated term, Whitman generally supplies both the idea *and* the association, the occupation *and* the instrument or sign by which it is known.[15] Instead of substituting a thing for a person, as in the classical metonymy of arms for soldier, Whitman multiplies the terms by which any one person is represented. Thus, in the serial line, "The heavy omnibus, the driver with his interrogating thumb, the clank of the shod horses on the granite floor" (Sec. 8), the second and third terms could be metonymically substituted for the first term, but have been deliberately added on instead. By extending this principle across many lines, Whitman creates a realistic sense of physical interconnections among the democratic mass. M. Thomas Wynn has suggested that Whitman's catalogues portray all workers as independent artisans rather than as employees in order to displace onto a few mercantile villains his anxiety about the widespread capitalization and consequent alienation of labor (pp. 79–82). I would add that redundant metonymy contributes directly to this compensatory project. Though Whitman cannot make the driver own his means of production, he makes him and every other worker poetically inseparable from the tools of his or her trade.

Whitman uses metonymy figuratively (that is, substituting one term for another) to represent personal, especially erotic, union, which also has political implications for the poet. For instance, his depiction of the soul as a sexual body, "You settled your head athwart my hips and gently turned over upon me" (Sec. 5), uses the metonymy of the container (the body) for the contained (the soul). With his soul and body interpenetrating and becoming indistinguishable from one another, Whitman shows himself to be a non-hierarchical being. Later in the poem, in a moment of ecstatic union with the night and the ocean, Whitman characterizes these with erotic adjectives properly belonging to himself, using the metonymy of transferring an adjective from one subject to a related one: "Press close barebosomed night" (Sec. 20); "You sea!... Dash me with amorous wet" (Sec. 22). Whitman's metonyms, both redundant and figurative, always connect human beings to the material world they inhabit. These figures show a representative American self experiencing life as a union of each and all.

In his style of disunion, by contrast, Whitman allows himself to become disengaged from the vast union he has formed. He relies on the tension in metaphoric expressions that reveals the differences between tenor and vehicle as much as it suggests their similarities.[16] His most characteristic figure of disunion is an extended personification—built up of similes, metaphors, and metonyms—in which an aspect of the world or of the self is evoked by animal or demonic, rather than by human imagery, thus opening a gap between the speaker and the personified agent (e.g., the sun in Section 24, his own sexuality in Section 28). As if to overcome this self-created sense of difference, Whitman interacts with his personifications, struggling with the metamorphosing figures for control of his identity. In these powerful, fictitious scenarios, transitive and intransitive dangerously switch places: orchestral music "throbs" and "sails" the speaker till he loses his hold on reality (Sec. 26); not he but "prurient provokers" external to him are "straining the udder" of his "heart for its withheld drip" (Sec. 28). Rather than uniting self and world or integrating various aspects of the self, such figures act, as Richard Chase has noted, "as a radical individualist conceives society to act. They break down the self."[17] Unlike the synecdoches and metonyms that are spread throughout the poem, Whitman's metaphoric figures of disunion are concentrated in a single sustained crisis section of the poem. They are best understood therefore in terms of the poem's overall plot, to which I now turn.

III

Whitman begins "Song of Myself" by establishing what I call a federated model of personal identity: self and world, soul and body, Whitman and his compatriots, shown as equal parts within a unified whole, which is at once political, religious, and cosmic. He goes on to dramatize a rupture in that federated identity, depicting his several faculties each insisting on their distinctive separateness. Then Whitman represents their reintegration. These three large movements in Whitman's poem—Union, Disunion, and Reunion—dramatize the crisis of the Union in 1855. To Whitman's highly political sensibility, threats of secession by the States showed democratic individualism grown to monstrous proportions, just as Federal enforcement of the Fugitive Slave Law showed national uniformity overcoming individual states' rights and becoming a tyranny. Whitman takes these dangers into his poem and represents them as crises of his own identity. In the phase of Disunion, we see the dismemberment of an identity whose various parts refuse to work together as one. In the phase of Reunion, we witness the tyranny of an egalitarianism that swallows up all individual distinctions before learning to relinquish authoritarian control. The outcome of Whitman's poem was intended to show that it was possible to unify a highly stressed self and, by analogy, an increasingly divided country.

The phase of Union opens with the poet inviting his soul to connect with the leaning body on the grass. He then goes on to attach himself to what lies around him through the permeable membrane of his identity. Such interpenetration of one's outside and inside is bivalent: it can either open the poet and poem to an idealized embrace of self and world, or it can dissolve a stable personal identity altogether, as happens later in the poem. At the start of his self-presentation, in Section 12, Whitman choosses to open the membrane, so as to integrate his body's activities with its environment:[18]

> The smoke of my own breath,
> Echos, ripples, and buzzed whispers.... loveroot, silkthread,
>   crotch and vine,
> My respiration and inspiration.... the beating of my heart
>   .... the passing of blood and air through my lungs,
> The sniff of green leaves and dry leaves, and of the
>   shore and darkcolored sea-rocks, and of hay in the barn

To define a self with permeable boundaries, Whitman needs an assemblage of images whose limits cannot be precisely defined: "echos, ripples, and buzzed whispers." The terms are metonyms, effects of unnamed causes. In naming only perceived effects, the speaker externalizes himself through his senses and internalizes what is sensed as part of the self. The poet cannot easily externalize his sexuality, however, which remains private, even in the boundariless world of Whitman's poetry. So he safely evokes the male genitals by substituting the genus "loveroot" for the species, penis, the material "silkthread" for the pants made of it, the container "crotch" for what it contains, and concludes with the nearby "vine," apparently begotten by the "loveroot." Whitman was wise to use such elliptical metonymies. His more overt treatment of phallic imagery in Section 24 (11. 532, 536, 538) provokes an undesirable self-consciousness, the dangers of which we shall note below.

In the long first movement of the poem, Whitman's bodily awareness is integrated with non-physical aspects of his consciousness, most famously in the marriage of body and soul in Section 5. It is impossible for an observer of the scene to tell that one of the two bodies on the grass is anything other than body. Whitman avoids the traditional hierarchical dualism of body and soul in favor of a complementary notion of identity, the "I" remembering a moment when it felt itself to be an indivisible "we." The "I" is thus represented as a federation of two equal selves, a sort of "We, the people" within a unified body. The poetic gain from this experience is represented in a list that spans the largest principles ("a kelson of the creation is love") and the smallest entities ("mossy scabs of the wormfence, and heaped stones, and elder and mullen and poke-weed"), which grow on the ground where the poet lies.

From these specifically named grasses, it is a small step to the child's question, "What is the grass?," but a much larger one to Whitman's provisional answers. These offer the reader various hermeneutic techniques that unite the simple physical object, grass, with a range of abstract meanings, so that "the unseen is proved by the seen" (Sec. 3). The poet starts Section 6 with personal and impersonal allegory: the grass as the "flag" of his disposition or the emblem of a coy God's designing hand. Qualifying his anthropomorphism, he then suggests a contextual, almost literal reading of the grass as "the produced babe of the vegetation." Focusing on the grass as "a uniform hieroglyphic," Whitman's study of signs becomes a democratic homily, as he actualizes the meaning of the grass, "growing among black folks as among white," by his equal naming of the red, white and black inhabitants of America. Seeing in the grass a traditional icon of mortality, "the beautiful uncut hair of graves,"[19] the exegete transforms the image into its opposite: "The smallest sprout shows there is really no death." Its climactic placement and lengthy exposition show this to be Whitman's preferred interpretation. Why then did he tease us with his series of artificial guesses?

Whitman's political ideal of Union required both liberty and equality, whose aesthetic equivalents were variety and uniformity. Uniformity is represented here by Whitman's democratic homily that the grass has a universal meaning. But in the interest of variety, he makes room for other possible views among his audience or within a pluralized democratic self.

Only after presenting these other interpretations, does he present his preference for a spiritualized reading of physical matter.

After these set-pieces on body-soul union and the varieties of union conceivable to a democratic interpreter, Whitman launches into the meat of his first phase: cataloging the world around him from his unified vantage point on the grass, merging himself in the unity of the seen and the unseen. This procedure continues through the first half of the poem: he and every other self are depicted as being of a piece with the objects and activities with which that self associates. The merging swells to an ecstatic crescendo in Section 24 (11. 530–44), where his sexual euphemisms elaborately conflate self and nature.

In the next moment, however, begins the dismantling of Whitman's enlarged self, the second phase, Disunion, in his plot. In the clear light of dawn, the speaker reports a doubt—"I pause to consider if it really be"— followed by a growing unease, signalled by his alienating shift to a non-human personification: "Something I cannot see puts upward libidinous prongs,/ Seas of bright juice suffuse heaven." "Libidinous prongs" and "seas of bright juice" defamiliarize the sunrise, evoking a nonhuman world of myth and archetypal battle. Whitman identifies the sun's seeming coupling with the earth as a challenge to his own sexual potency. He further admits the precariousness of his boundariless self-definition: "how quick the sunrise would kill me...." The hyperbolic language indicates how much is at stake in this encounter: if Whitman and the sun are not equal, then the egalitarian poetic universe he has so carefully built up crumbles. There can be no union of self and world, when each aggressively asserts its distinctive identity.

Whitman dramatizes the destructiveness of such self-assertion in Sections 24–28. In these crisis sections, the poet's previously unified identity breaks into parts, each seceding in turn. He assumes successively the exclusive viewpoint of vision, speech, hearing, and touch, only to discover that his total identity begins to malfunction, leading to feelings of madness and suffocation, his figures for psychological and physical breakdown. Contemporary politicians, it is worth recalling, described those who would dismember the Union as "madmen" belonging "in an insane hospital."[20] Whitman's seceding senses are similarly those of a madman imprisoned in subjectivity, a feeling the poet expresses through figures that disconnect and exclude him from his previously equalized world.

The first sense to separate from the whole being is vision, threatened by the sun's visual brilliance. The poet seeks figures of speech to reestablish himself as a master equal to the sun. Transferring modifiers appropriate to the sun ("dazzling and tremendous") to himself, he sends sunrise "out of me," so that the threatening external sunrise becomes a self-validating internal one: "We also ascend dazzling and tremendous as the sun, / We found our own my soul in the calm and cool of the daybreak" (Sec. 25). Whitman has switched from "I" to "we," it seems, as a defensive maneuver, reaffirming the pluralized unity of bodily self and soul at this moment of challenge to his identity. Apostrophically, he calls upon "my soul" (clearer in the "O my soul" of later editions) to draw a boundary between himself and the threatening world around him. In a world of inequalities, the poet relies on a figure of poetic self-consciousness for self-protection.[21]

To restore his feeling of mastery, he turns to his all-encompassing voice, but speech becomes the second faculty to secede from Whitman's federated self. Turning on the poet, speech "says sarcastically, Walt, you understand enough.... Why don't you let it out then?" The poet's speech, his essential genius, refuses to be manipulated by one who, sun-like, would ascend above the democratic mass. Whitman wishes he could retreat into silence, though of course carrying out this Quakerish boast would put an end to his poem.[22] Instead, he challenges speech to articulate what cannot be articulated, the sheer physicality of grass: "Do you not know how the buds beneath are folded?"[23] By attempting this quid pro quo of privileging inarticulateness, Whitman ironically stumbles in speech, his agrammatical language mirroring his confusion about how to demarcate public from private identity:

> Waiting in gloom protected by frost,
> The dirt receding before my prophetical screams,
> I underlying causes to balance them at last,
> My knowledge my live parts.... it keeping tally
>   with the meaning of things,
> Happiness.... which whoever hears me let him or her
>   set out in search of this day.

What is the subject of this sentence? First, the grass, then himself, then an ambiguous "it"—for none of these can he provide a predicate to complete an action. So he turns to the silent reader/ listener, seeking from him or her some equivalent act in pursuit of the inalienable right of happiness. Only by bringing those who hear his message into harmony with the founding purposes of the Union can the poet justify the undemocratic role he has taken in separating himself from the democratic mass in order to speak for it.

To become again a representative member of his society, a listener, Whitman turns to his sense of hearing. With the catalogue of "I hear" statements in Section 26, Whitman abandons the alienating self-consciousness of his dialogue with speech filling himself with the sounds of the natural and social worlds: "I hear the bravuras of birds.... the bustle of growing wheat.... gossip of flames ... clack of sticks cooking my meals." When he begins to listen to music, however, he is disconnected from his external environment and propelled inward: "I hear the trained soprano.... she convulses me like the climax of my love grip." The one simile gives rise to a crescendo of metaphors, and as Whitman interacts with the personified music, he experiences the polarities of his imagination—passing from "wider than Uranus flies.... to gulps of the farthest down horror."

In these two kinds of hearing, Whitman offers a parable about both egalitarian and individualist models of identity. On the one hand, the shared, social experience, represented by the uninterpreted listening in the first half of the section, is overwhelmed by the greater vividness of private fantasy. Yet this private identity, discovered by Whitman in his erotic response to the opera, cannot survive the figurative ocean into which it has been plunged. In Whitman's imagined descent into self, his bodily identity is represented as being at risk. He is one moment pleasantly laved and licked, but in the next, his body is defaced and drugged, "cut by bitter and poisoned hail," "steeped amid honeyed morphine"; his windpipe is squeezed as if by the looped coil of a rope, the "fakes" (or also feigning) of death. If one's breath cannot circulate outside the body, life ends; analogously, anyone seceding into a private selfhood, without salutary interchange with the world, is consigned to a death-in-life.

The explosion of figurative language in this section suggests the alienation Whitman experiences by withdrawing into his own finiteness. Too vulnerable to touch another person and to have to relate on another's terms, Whitman touches himself only to become absorbed again in private erotic fantasy. In Section 28, we witness his tragic isolation through an extended allegorical image, which shows him as both animal and human, alternately pitiable and condemnable. Pictured as a pastured animal alone on a headland, he is left defenseless by the other errant members of the herd, his fellow senses, against the incursions of "prurient provokers" and a "red marauder," demonized images of his hands and penis during masturbation. Again, he uses tightness of breath to convey his feeling of entrapment: "my breath is tight in its throat; / Unclench your floodgates! you are too much for me."

The outward thrust of ejaculation, however, offers the poet a safe, external vantage point for viewing the crisis he has just represented allegorically. His sperm becomes metaphoric rain, which produces real growth, and through these compensatory images of natural fecundity, he reconnects to a non-fictive world of his own imagining: "Rich showering rain, and recompense richer afterward. / Sprouts take and accumulate....

stand by the curb prolific and vital, / Landscapes projected masculine fullsized and golden" (Sec. 29).[24] These lines conclude Whitman's representation of Disunion. In them, we see him relearning what he seemed to know at the start of the poem: that to establish an equalized identity with the world he has to turn consciousness into physical presence. The poet can speak of the soul, but only in connection with the equalizing bodily world. In extremity the poet had used the soul-term to differentiate himself from the sun, but henceforth, he must use it also as an equalizer. To do this he must anchor it again in the body.

Commencing the third phase of the poem's plot, Reunion, Whitman embarks on a journey through space and time, taking in American places, people and the wars that founded and expanded the country, demonstrating, as in other catalogue sequences, the myriad connections possible and necessary in a unified democratic land. During this journey, Whitman leaps not only to other historical moments but also beyond earth itself into space. His lived body, which can only exist at one point in space and time, is joined by his embodied soul: "I visit the orchards of God and look at the spheric product, / And look at quintillions ripened and look at quintillions green" (Sec. 33).

In this leap, Whitman delights in presenting himself as a poet of the imagination, seeing orchards among the quintillions of stars, gaily incorporating ingestion, the aerial grace of birds, and the slipperiness of water into a composite metaphor for the imagining soul: "I fly the flight of the fluid and swallowing soul." A few lines later, he anchors his "ship," and sends the messengers of his imagination off to report back to him. Such bird and ship metaphors for the soul could as easily be found in "Alastor" or "Prometheus Unbound."[25] But such images, which traditionally privilege and disconnect the aspirations of the soul from those of the body, do not exhaust Whitman's presentation, which is also anchored in bodily metonyms for the soul. Whitman's man's soul does not simply fly but, as a body, also swallows and swims. This soul does not sail in uncharted metaphoric waters, but rather is stationed by the poet in a very real Arctic sea, where nineteenth-century explorers, painters, and poems did venture.

Whitman brings his body with him when he visits those realms to which only soul has traditionally had access. To be "the poet of the body" and "the poet of the soul" (Sec. 21), Whitman developed figures that could treat body and soul as identical wholes, as in the body-soul coupling of Section 5, and as parts of one whole, as in the body-soul journey of Section 33, which hovers between the difference-making of metaphor and the connection-making of metonymy. For when the body-soul no longer functions as a union of its different parts, but lets any one part separate from the others or dominate them, then the self can no longer function as a coherent entity, as he showed in the crisis of Sections 24–28.

There is another parallel danger faced by Whitman's self, which he has yet to dramatize. Just as the Federal Union could abuse its power over states and individuals, so Whitman's reunited "I" can succumb to the temptation to swallow up everything outside the self and thereby erase the distinction between persons so necessary in a democratic society. It is one thing to keep open a membrane for interchange between self and others, but it is quite another to promote a tyrannical union and claim to *be* other selves. He *is*, he tells us, the suffering survivor of a shipwreck. "All this I swallow and it tastes good.... I like it well, and it becomes mine, / I am the man.... I suffered.... I was there." This totalitarian incorporation (figuratively, ingestion) of the other, is followed by several more illocutionary acts of total identification: "I am the hounded slave.... I wince at the bite of the dogs"; "I am the mashed firearm with breastbone broken"; "I am an old artillerist, and tell of some fort's bombardment.... and am there again" (Sec. 33). These synecdochic statements of identity (the whole subsuming the parts) isolate the speaker in self-glorifying fantasy, just as much as the earlier metaphoric personifications mired him in self-destructive fantasy.

In stating his identity with others through the construction "I am," Whitman was adopting a divine prerogative used by Christ in the Gospel of John and by Krishna in the *Bhagavad Ghita*.[26] In these scriptures, each of them has an *a priori* right of universal identification because he is thought to embody the complete divine presence. Though Whitman called himself "divine" earlier in the poem (Sec. 24, 1.526), in Section 38, he confronts the perplexities of his mortal nature. His images of the grave, paired antithetically with those of Christ's resurrection, show that whatever identity Whitman feels with the resurrected Christ is precisely a function of their shared mortality. While thinking of himself as a god bolsters Whitman's egalitarian refusal to be subservient to other, it also impedes his social intercourse with his fellows. Therefore, he changes his "I am" discourse after this point in the poem (see Sec. 47) to refer only to his wholly human role as teacher, preaching his faith in the united body and soul.

Near the end of the poem, Whitman's chastened, reunited self claims that the essence of his experience "is not in any dictionary or utterance or symbol." Nevertheless, he proceeds to define that essence: "It is not chaos or death.... it is form and union and plan.... it is eternal life ... it is happiness" (Sec. 50). The opposition of chaos and death to form, union, plan, life and happiness could not be clearer. Nor is it an accident that the crucial word "union" comes together with "life" and "happiness" from the Declaration of Independence. Whitman saved "union" for this exegetical moment, for making plain the meanings of what Whitman calls in his preface the new, "indirect" American poetry (p. 8).

The time had passed for Whitman to write another series of ineffectual editorials eulogizing the Union. What Whitman could do for the country, he ambitiously hoped, was to offer a book so governed by principles of natural and harmonious union, so aware of the alternative dangers of both secession and tyranny, that his readers would be persuaded of the analagous political benefits of the Constitutional Union for themselves. We know now that his contemporaries did not possess the literary sophistication necessary to see the indirect figures in his carpet. We also know that even if his few readers had been able to decipher his political message, they were helpless to fend off the economic, social, and political forces leading to disunion and war. Whitman, of course, lacked our hindsight. Instead, he had faith and hope. And out of the extravagance of that hope, he created a poetic blueprint of an ideal America, so that his compatriots might yet retreat from disunion and constitute themselves, in all their conflicting diversity, as one nation.[27]

NOTES

1. Quoted in Paul C. Nagel, *One Nation Indivisible: The Union in American Thought 1776–1861* (New York: Oxford Univ. Press, 1964), p. 248.

2. George B. Hutchinson, *The Ecstatic Whitman: Literary Shamanism and the Crisis of the Union* (Columbus: Ohio State Univ. Press, 1986); on the satiric poems of 1850, see pp. 11–16.

3. M. Thomas Wynn, *The Lunar Light of Whitman's Poetry* (Cambridge: Harvard Univ. Press, 1987).

American Literature, Volume 59, Number 4, December 1987. Copyright © 1987 by the Duke University Press. CCC 0002-9831/87/$1.50.

4. *The Gathering of the Forces*, ed. Cleveland Rodgers and John Black (New York: Putnam's, 1920), 1, 230, 238.

5. Eric Foner, *Free Soil, Free Labor, Free Men: The Ideology of the Republican Party Before the Civil War* (New York: Oxford Univ. Press, 1970), p. 309.

6. David Herbert Donald, *Liberty and Union* (Boston: Little, Brown, 1978), p. 81.

7. Seward's speech of 11 March 1850, on the admission of California, should be compared with that of 17 Feb. 1854, on the Kansas-Nebraska bills: in both, images of geography dominate, but in the first Séward cites the East-West links that unify the country, while in the second, he traces tho-South's attempted takeover and incorporation of the West into its domain. See *The*

Works of William H. Seward, ed. George E. Baker (Boston: Houghton Mifflin, 1884), 1, 57–58, 83–84; IV, 441–42.

8. *Notebooks and Unpublished Prose Manuscripts*, ed. Edward F. Grier (New York: New York Univ. Press. 1984), VI, 2176–77; hereafter cited as *NUPM* within my text. The reference to thirty-one states was later amended to thirty-two, upon the admission of Minnesota in 1858.

9. The order of these events structures Whitman's address, suggesting a clear date for "Slavery—the Slaveholders" in the summer of 1854. Edward Grier, the editor of the manuscript, finds the circumstances of composition uncertain.

10. *Walt Whitman's Leaves of Grass: The First (1855) Edition*, ed. Malcolm Cowley (New York: Viking, 1959), p. 8; further quotations from the preface will be paginated within my text.

11. Whitman's bonds of Union are all included in Seward's speech of 11 March 1850, as is his argument that inexorable historical laws will eliminate slavery (see Seward, 1, 87). In an 1855 letter to Seward, Whitman indicates their political affinity: "I too have at heart Freedom, and the amelioration of the people"; see *The Correspondence*, ed. Edwin H. Miller (New York: New York Univ. Press, 1961), 1, 41–42.

12. "The Poetics of Union in Whitman and Lincoln: An Inquiry toward the Relationship of Art and Policy," in *The American Renaissance Reconsidered*, ed. Walter Benn Michaels and Donald E. Pease, Selected Papers from the English Institutes, NS 9 (Baltimore: Johns Hopkins Univ. Press, 1985), p. 187.

13. On synecdoche and political representation, see Kenneth Burke, *A Grammar of Motives* (New York: Prentice Hall, 1945), p. 508.

14. For ease of reference, quotations from the 1855 "Song of Myself" (ed. Cowley) will be referred to by their later section numbers.

15. Classical definitions of metonymy include these distinct substitutions: cause for effect and vice versa, container for contained, possessor for possessed, sign for office or occupation, instrument for action, the physical for the moral, an adjunct of the subject for the subject itself. Discussions of Whitmanian metonymy have not noted the crucial difference in the poet's use of the figure: see D. S. Mirsky, "Walt Whitman: Poet of American Democracy," trans. B. G. Guerney, *Dialectics: Critics Group*, 1 (1937), 23–24, and C. Carroll Hollis, *Language and Style in "Leaves of Grass"* (Baton Rouge: Louisiana State Univ. Press, 1983), pp. 173–203, esp. pp. 177–78.

16. This view of metaphor is memorably described in Max Black, *Models and Metaphors: Studies in Language and Philosophy* (Ithaca: Cornell Univ. Press, 1962), pp. 25–47.

17. *Walt Whitman Reconsidered* (New York: William Sloane, 1955), p. 69.

18. My commentary on Whitman's consciousness of the body has been informed especially by Michael Fried, "The Beholder in Courbet: His Early Self-Portraits and Their Place in His Art," *Glyph*, 4 (1978), 97–98; and Jean Starobinski, "The Inside and the Outside," *Hudson Review*, 28 (1975), 333–51.

19. Gay W. Allen. *The Solitary Singer: A Critical Biography of Walt Whitman* (New York: Macmillan, 1955), p. 159, cites Homer as the source for Whitman's image; there are also numerous biblical uses of grass as a metaphor for mortality (e.g., Psalm 90:5–6; Isaiah 40:6–8; Matthew 6:30).

20. Comments by Seward and Lewis Cass, quoted in Nagel, p. 268.

21. See Jonathan Culler, "Apostrophe," *Diacritics*, 7 (1977), 59–69.

22. As background to Whitman's ambivalent attitude to speech, see Richard Bauman, "Speaking in the Light: The Role of the Quaker Minister," in *Explorations in the Ethnography of Speaking*, ed. Richard Bauman and Joel Sherzer (Cambridge: Cambridge Univ. Press, 1974), pp. 144–60.

23. I am indebted to Kerry Charles Larson, "Voices in the Grass: Whitman and the Conception of 'Free Growth,'" *Centennial Review*, 26 (1982), 203–04, for his explication of this image.

24. Roy Harvey Pearce, *The Continuity of American Poetry* (Princeton: Princeton Univ. Press, 1961), p. 79, argues similarly that Whitman solves the mystery of being by reconceiving it as the mystery of creativity.

25. Suzanne Nalbantian, *The Symbol of the Soul from Holderlin to Yeats: A Study in Metonymy* (New York: Columbia Univ. Press, 1977), provides a useful compendium of nineteenth-century poetic figures for the soul, though she does not treat Whitman, who cannot fit her neat classification of later nineteenth-century poets preferring dark pessimistic images for the soul.

26. See John 6:35; 8:12; 9:5; 10:7, 11; 11:25; 14:6; 15:1; and J. A. B. Van Buitenen, *The Bhagavadgita in the Maharabata, Text and Translation* (Chicago: Univ. of Chicago Press, 1981), pp. 99, 105, 110–11.

27. I am indebted to the American Council of Learned Societies and the Committee on Grants, Franklin and Marshall College, for funding a year's leave spent at Brandeis University, where a seminar and conversations with Prof. Allen Grossman and Claudia Yukman stimulated this work. I have also benefited from the research assistance of Heather Fitzgerald through the Hackman Scholars Program of Franklin and Marshall College. I want to thank Ellen Frankel, Robert Greenberg, C. Carroll Hollis, and David Leverenz for commenting on earlier drafts.

HERBERT J. LEVINE

"Song of Myself" as Whitman's American Bible

W hile he was working toward a third edition of *Leaves of Grass*, during June 1857, Whitman wrote himself a note that is often quoted but rarely used as a guide to reading his poetry:

The Great Construction of the
New Bible

Not to be diverted from the principal object—the main life work—the Three Hundred & Sixty five—(it ought to be read in 1859.—[1]

This quotation does not record a new discovery but rather reaffirms Whitman's earliest and fundamental ambition: to provide a religious foundation for American democracy foundering on the verge of disunion. Whitman's first attempt to write an American bible was his founding poem, "Song of Myself," as I will show by examining the biblical basis of its generic and narrative patterns. After he had written this scriptural poem, he became his own religious tradition, devoting his first volume and six subsequent editions to exegesis, drawing out its fundamental images and beliefs into new poems.[2]

From *Modern Language Quarterly*, vol. 48, no. 2 (June 1987). © 1987 by Duke University Press.

It has long been recognized that Whitman's poetry, like that of his American Renaissance contemporaries, is steeped in the Bible. The search for biblical allusions, initiated by Gay W. Allen, led to Thomas Edward Crawley's allusion-based study of the Christ symbol in *Leaves of Grass*, in which he claims that Whitman's self-presentation as preacher-healer-messiah provides the structural key to his poetry.[3] More recently, Herbert Schneidau has anchored Whitman's gadfly antinomianism in biblical tradition,[4] while Dennis K. Renner and George B. Hutchinson have pointed to the national crisis of the 1850s as the motivator of Whitman's idealizing, his prophetic exhortations, and his shamanistic imagining of both his own powers and his audience's need for spiritual revitalization.[5]

This wealth of biblically oriented criticism bears out the argument of John E. Becker that the secular literature we value most highly keeps its hold on us precisely because it fulfills the cultural role that the Bible performed for earlier generations.[6] Using the three divisions of the Hebrew Bible—law, prophets, and writings (from the last of which he singles out wisdom literature)—Becker argues that our secular literature performs one of three basic functions: to celebrate the central myths and mores of a culture, as does the narrative in the Five Books of Moses; to challenge the materialistic assumptions of its ruling elites and to inspire their reform, as do the poetic oracles of the Israelite prophets; and finally, to relay the traditions by which that culture deals with the existential problems of life, often in universal terms borrowed from outside its own provincial sphere, as in the case of Job.

Including Whitman under his rubric of celebration, Becker notes that Whitman felt impelled "to celebrate and thereby create the new American man" (p.257). Whitman was indeed a celebrator, but he was also an anti-institutional exhorter and a pedagogue of existential wisdom. To these older biblical functions, I would add those he learned from the three primary divisions of the New Testament: from the Gospels, how to make the story and speech of one divine individual stand for the highest aspirations of an entire culture; from the Epistles, how to reach out to disciples through argument and creed; and from Revelation, how to use a language of earthly images to point to a nonearthly future. We will see all six of these functions operating within "Song of Myself," often with very clear references to the religious genres that Whitman adapted to his own American ends.

Whitman's poetry took these biblical forms because he conceived of his poetic role evangelically. In his analysis of the national crisis, the greatest threat to the union was the failure of democracy on a personal level. Individuals did not believe in their own worth, he felt, but deferred to others of superior wealth, education, and status. Whitman's self-assumed task was to reeducate individuals away from either subservience to others or mastery over them.

In the notebooks where the poet recorded the germinal insights that were to become "Song of Myself," he formulated the religious corollary of his radical democratic egalitarianism: "I never yet knew how it felt to think I stood in the presence of my superior.—*If the presence of* God were made visible immediately before me, I could not abase myself..." (*NUPM*, 1:56). Not to abase oneself to God, to human beings, or even to one's own soul— this is the creed to which Whitman attests through all the editions of *Leaves of Grass*. His first notebook formulations of this creed were in the first person, but soon he was imagining an audience, whom he hoped to persuade: "I am not so anxious to give you the truth. But I am very anxious to have you understand that all truth and power are feeble to you except your own.—Can I beget a child for you?" (*NUPM*, 1:80).

Egalitaranism and individualism were, in Whitman's view, essential American values. In his version of the national myth, the American people had made a solemn covenant in the Declaration of Independence and the Constitution to make equality and liberty the sacred principles of national life. And the rising generation needed to be inspired to rededicate itself to these covenantal values of the nation.[7] "Have you in you," he asked in a notebook entry, "the enthusiasm for the battles of Bunker Hill and Long Island and Washington's retreat?—Have you the heroic feeling..." (*NUPM*, 1:148). His ironic poem "A Boston Ballad" (1854) satirized the people for turning their backs on their revolutionary past in allowing a fugitive slave to be taken by Federal troops. It was clear to him that American democracy needed to have its cardinal principles reformulated on a religious basis. Christianity, he saw, could not be the religion of the republic: its theology was monarchical and its doctrine of the Incarnation, privileging the divinity of one special person, was undemocratic.[8] Therefore, he would

> ...break up this[?] demention that man is the
>   servant of God, or of many gods;
> I say that every man is great to himself and every
>   woman to herself;
> And that to take an inferior place or be humble is
>   unbecoming....   (*NUPM*, 1:165–66)

In his democratic vision, as he explained it in the 1855 preface, the "whole theory of the special and supernatural and all that was twined with it or educed out of it departs as a dream.... It is also not consistent with the reality of the soul to admit that there is anything in the known universe more divine than men and women."[9]

To help promote the divinity of men and women, Whitman celebrated his own divine body and soul. He understood that body and soul had to be equalized before a democratic religion could take over from the religions of the past, which had undermined the individual with their hierarchies of immortal soul and mortal body, infinite God and finite human beings. Because Whitman was both promoting a new religion and breaking up the old ones, he modified past religious discourse to suit his democratic ends. The famous body-soul marriage of "Song of Myself" is a reprise and transvaluation of at least four kinds of biblical writing:

[Creed]

I believe in you my soul.... the other I am must
        not abase itself to you,
And you must not be abased to the other.

[Petition]

Loafe with me on the grass.... loose the stop
        from your throat,
Not words, not music or rhyme I want.... not
        custom or lecture, not even the best,
Only the lull I like, the hum of your valved voice.

[Narrative of Revelation]

I mind how we lay in June, such a transparent summer
        morning;
You settled your head athwart my hips and gently
        turned over upon me,
And parted the shirt from my bosom-bone, and
        plunged your tongue to my barestript heart,
And reached till you felt my beard, and reached till you
        held my feet.

[Wisdom]

Swiftly arose and spread around me the peace and
        joy and knowledge that pass all the art and argument
        of the earth;
And I know that the hand of God is the elderhand of
        my own,

> And I know that the spirit of God is the eldest brother of
>   my own,
> And that all the men ever born are also my brothers
>   .... and the women my sisters and lovers,
> And that a kelson of the creation is love;
> And limitless are leaves stiff or drooping in the fields,
> And brown ants in the little wells beneath them,
> And mossy scabs of the wormfence, and heaped
>   stones, and elder and mullen and pokeweed.[10]

These biblical genres do not comprise all of Whitman's religious models, but their concentration in this one section of his founding poem makes it the scriptural kernel around which the whole poem grows. The forms all recur with slight modifications: there are brief apostrophic petitions to the soul in sections 25 and 33, a creed in 30 and 31, other moments of revelation hinted at in the opening of 33, and wisdom purveyed throughout the poem, especially in passages addressed directly to the reader as newfound disciple.

The immediate context for these inspirational passages is akin to prophetic castigation. Whitman shows his society to be dominated by the same materialism and greed condemned by the Hebrew prophets and by Jesus. His narration of body-soul union arises out of a protest against a world that wants him to "postpone" his "acceptation and realization" (62) and turn instead to ciphering "Exactly the contents of one, and exactly the contents of two, and which is ahead?" (65).[11] "Trippers and askers" (66) surround him, he explains, seeking to possess and manipulate the facts of his life, but "Apart from the pulling and hauling stands what I am" (75), the distinctive "Me myself" (74) that is the soul. If Whitman were to tolerate this separation from his bodily identity, "the other I am," then the democracy he seeks personally to model would crumble into a disunited collection of alienated, atomized selves. Instead, his creedal apostrophe places body and soul in a relationship of direct, reciprocal address, to keep them on an equal plane where they can be united: "I believe in you my soul.... the other I am must not abase itself to you, / And you must not be abased to the other."

As a secularizing writer, Whitman revises the Nicene Creed to produce his own creedal formulation.[12] The object of belief is no longer one God, the Father, and one Lord, Jesus Christ, consubstantial with the Father, but Whitman's own integral selfhood, soul and body consubstantial with one another. No longer is the self divided, as throughout Western intellectual history since Plato, between an external body connected to the world and an internal soul (or, in Cartesian terms, mind) connected to God. Furthermore, Whitman does not grant a privileged status to the aspiration of the soul toward God, as do all previous religions. Instead, he goes on to open body and soul totally to one another and point this integrated self onto the open road, traveling through time and space with all the beings and objects of the world he inhabits.

Having announced his creed, Whitman lovingly petitions the soul to hum into his bodily ear. The nonverbal revelation sought in this prayer is different from biblical revelations, which center around hearing God speak, whether as a "still small voice" (1 Kings 19:12) or as "the voice of many waters" (Rev. 19:6). Allen Grossman comments that for Whitman "the sound of the blood" is "doing the cultural work of God" (p. 195). The subvocal hum of the soul, an internal communication unmediated by language, cannot be codified or argued with, as could a belief that one had heard the voice of God. But as an externalization of an inner state, its reality also cannot be denied.

The experience on the grass is the foundation upon which Whitman bases the entire religio-political gospel of *Leaves of Grass*, because in this "transparent" moment, the "I" first knew itself as a "we," a plurality of equal selves, body and soul, within a unified whole. *E pluribus unum* could thus serve as Whitman's founding motto as well as his country's. Unlike Whitman's other representations of unified body-soul consciousness, described in the poem as ongoing and virtually timeless (e.g., sections 2 and 33), Whitman chose to narrate this one in the past tense, which he usually used to narrate uncomfortable experiences of loss.[13] He relies on it here, conversely, to emphasize this revelation as a story of beginning, a *ovus ordo seclorum*, that can be recalled and reenacted to counteract the "pulling and hauling" of contemporary life. As an ideal promise of what the self can be, it functions within his poetic scripture as do biblical theophanies (e.g., God's promise at the Burning Bush or at the Annunciation), founding events that preceded the formulation of law and creed.

Within the narrative itself, Whitman's "I" refers to the bodily self and the "you" to the soul, but it is important to note that this secularized soul is characterized naturalistically and metonymically entirely in terms of bodily activity ("settled your head," "plunged your tongue"), and the body itself is not even named. Which is which? To an observer of the scene, it is impossible to tell that one of the two bodies joined on the grass is anything other than body. And their crossed position further contributes to our sense of blending, as the cross has long symbolized in Western culture the interpenetration of finite and infinite, human and divine.

The controlling word in Whitman's account is "transparent." Mirroring the transparency of the summer morning, body and soul no longer demarcate an outside from an inside but become totally transparent to one another. The bosom kiss that reaches one's own heart is another instance of such transparence.[14] When lovers become "one flesh," to use the biblical hyperbole, they always know that they remain two separate individuals, striving through love to transcend conflict, but resigned to tragic loss and ultimate separation in death. The kiss of utter penetration through which Whitman comes to know himself implies that there can be *nontragic* otherness *within* identity. He perceives that his heart has been laid bare (contra Baudelaire) in order to overcome once and for all the alienation of body and soul from one another. And if this alienation can be overcome in one individual, then why not in each and between all?

The import of Whitman's revelation is therefore to extend this model of identity in functional, social terms. The wisdom that he formulates as personal knowledge ("to know" being a key verb in biblical wisdom literature) is that the vast sweep and particularity of the world can be known and loved by all. He does not suggest that he has lost his identity in the greater unity of God, as a traditional mystic might represent his experience, but rather that he has gained a sense of reciprocity among himself, God, and the world.[15] When Whitman says, "And I know that the hand of God is the elderhand of my own," he uses the biblical idiom for God's power (e.g., Exod. 3:20) as both model and harbinger of his own representative power. The rest of the wisdom section shows that the function of humanity is to keep alive the knowledge of what the world contains. "The hand of God" and "the spirit of God" are the first items in an equalizing list of "and" clauses that federates the people, objects, and fundamental energy of the world into a "limitless" democracy. In this federation, everything is named, "elder and mullen and pokeweed," alongside human brothers and sisters.

Whitman's next poetic act in "Song of Myself" is to become an exegete of his own religious vision and, in that process, to model for his readers a variety of ways to make their own meanings out of what began as his private religious experience. In section 6 he instructs a hypothetical child (the child within each of us?) in techniques useful for interpreting his sort of poetic scripture, which takes the world itself as sacred text. To the child's innocent question, "What is the grass?" (99), the poet offers interpretations on at least four levels, a strategy comparable to the traditional fourfold method of rabbinic and patristic exegesis: contextual, allegorical, homiletic, and mystical. (In invoking the rabbis and the church fathers, I do not mean to suggest that Whitman was acquainted with these strands of religious tradition, but rather that he treated his own religious vision as would a traditional interpreter of sacred texts.) Contextually, then, "the grass is itself a child.... the produced babe of the vegetation" (105). Allegorically, it is both a personal emblem of the poet's disposition, "out of hopeful green stuff woven" (101), and an impersonal emblem of God's designing hand, "Bearing the owner's name someway in the corners..."(104). Homiletically, the grass teaches a democratic lesson, "Growing among black folks as among white" (108), a lesson the poet then enacts by recording Americans' names regardless of race: "Kanuck, Tuckahoe, Congressman, Cuff, I give them the same, I receive them the same" (109).

The final interpretation, "And now it seems to me the beautiful uncut hair of graves" (110), is the most mysterious and requires fourteen lines of exegesis before the poet points of the mystical doctrine of metempsychosis. Paradoxically, Whitman uses the most physical sort of imagery—grass as tongues, hair, beards, laps, roofs of mouths—to convey an idea that defies materialism: "The smallest sprout shows there is really no death" (126). In the Bible grass is a prominent image of mortality (e.g., Ps. 90:5–6, Isa. 40:6–8, Matt. 6:30), but Whitman has transformed it into material evidence of the immortal continuity of life. When we see immortality in grass, it has become "transparent," like that famous June morning of the poet's revelation. We see *through* it to another order of reality, in which "the unseen is proved by the seen" (53). The figurative interpretation of the grass is thus paradigmatic. It could have been offered about any sort of material evidence, such as the individual details in the catalogues that follow, because for Whitman all such evidence suggests an unseen spiritual realm, now seen.[16]

The biblical prototype for thus reenvisioning the world in the shape of a list are the catalogues of Job 38–41, where the Voice from the Whirlwind offers Job pictures of his mortal reality which Job sees for the first time from the immortal vantage point of divinity. From Whitman's similarly divinized vantage point on the grass, having unified body and soul, mortal and immortal perspectives, he too offers his readers pictures of a world made innocent by virtue of *his* seeing its conflicting diversity as a harmonious union.

In attempting to create an epical poetic scripture that would mirror and unify the diversity of American life, Whitman interwove the fundamental narrative patterns from the two biblical testaments. He fused the ongoing story of a people (the Hebrew Bible) with the story of a completed self (the Gospels).[17] His complaint about the Bible was that Christ does not "merge and make fruitful all the Syrian canticles that preceded him"; Whitman thought to supply "that unquestionable, self-proved, identity" lacking in the Bible (*NUPM*, 5:1877) with the force of his own personality. Thus, the poem tells both the story of Whitman's identity—its apotheosis and its crises—as well as the epic story of the nation: its founding through revolutionary battle (sections 35–36), its wars of expansion (section 34), and its contemporary traumas (the runaway slave of section 10). Only if these national events are internalized by Whitman's readers, can they attain the shaping power of the biblical Exodus, the entry into the Promised Land, and the difficulties the Israelites encountered in living up to that promise. To help his readers, both contemporary and future, accomplish this internalization, Whitman shows himself, as a representative American, assimilating these events directly into his identity.

In this fusion of national and personal motifs, Whitman models his self-presentation on that of Jesus. In the Gospel of John, Jesus defines himself as the typological fulfillment of various symbols from his nation's scriptural past. "Before Abraham was, I am," he asserts (8:58). Thus, the manna that fed the Israelites in the desert is transvalued into an image of Jesus' self: "I am the bread of life: he that cometh to me shall never hunger; and he that believeth on me shall never thirst" (6:35). Where in Isaiah the vineyard is a national image of the household of Israel (5:7), in Jesus' revisionary stance it is "I," he says, that "am the true vine" (15:1). In this pattern of Christian symbolization, the divine Self replaces a prior text and in the process becomes the new sacred text.

When Whitman deliberately presents himself as reminiscent of Jesus,[18] he is the secular antitype that replaces religious texts and deeds: "Behold I do not give lectures or a little charity,/What I give I give out of myself" (994–95), a line improved in later editions to "When I give I give myself." As an American version of Jesus, Whitman is a deliberately naturalized messiah, setting his communion table with the words, "this is the meat and drink for natural hunger" (372). We see him gathering disciples among both "wicked" and "righteous" (373), making a point to invite those spurned by polite society: "The keptwoman and sponger and thief are hereby invited..." (375). We hear him denigrating those who will not come in to his democratic "feast," hucksters and capitalists ("A few idly owning") who take the "wheat" and leave but "chaff" for the workingmen "sweating and ploughing and thrashing" (1073–74). Despite Whitman's notable affection for the figure of Jesus, we see him here inverting language from Jesus' parables; the "wheat" is not the fruit of righteousness (Matt. 13:30) but that of economic inequality and injustice. We find a similar undoing of Christian imagery when Whitman unmiraculously feeds his followers with homely American "biscuits" and "milk" (1226). These are deliberately nontypological images, replacing the wafer and wine of Christian communion with nothing other than themselves.[19]

The Judaic and the Christian patterns in Whitman's narrative come together most prominently in section 33, where Whitman explicitly identifies himself with the sufferings of his fellow Americans, taking into himself both those wounded in the service of the nation and those scarred by its laws: "I am the hounded slave.... I wince at the bite of the dogs" (838); "I am the mashed fireman with breastbone broken" (847); "I am an old artillerist, and tell of some fort's bombardment.... and am there again" (858). In short, he tells us, "I am the man.... I suffered.... I was there" (832). Whitman's repeated "I am" is a naturalistic version of Jesus' symbolic discourse,[20] but unlike Jesus, the democratic Whitman finds this stance of total identification with the sufferers deeply problematic: "I project my hat and sit shamefaced and beg" (958).

The next moment ("Somehow I have been stunned" [960]) marks the apogee of Whitman's self-awareness in the poem, his recognition that in erasing the distinction between persons so necessary in a democratic society he has inappropriately assumed a divine prerogative. He sets out to rectify his "mistake" (962) by resuming "the overstaid fraction" (967) of personal identity.[21] This is the burden of the celebrated crucifixion scene of section 38. Whitman remembers that not just his countrymen, and not just Jesus alone, but he too has suffered "mockers and insults," "trickling tears," blows of "bludgeons and hammers," in short, a "crucifixion and bloody crowning" (963–65). Crucifixion leads directly to resurrection, as the American messiah emerges from the "grave of rock" knowing what has been confided "to any graves" (968). Measured against its biblical prototype, the importance of this last phrase cannot be overestimated. Because of Whitman's deliberate insistence on the lesson to be learned from "any graves," the "whole theory of the special and supernatural" that surrounds the life of Jesus "departs as a dream":

> The grave of rock multiples what has been confided to
>   it.... or to any graves,
> The corpses rise.... the gashes heal.... the
>   fastenings roll away.
>
> I troop forth replenished with supreme power, one of an
>   average unending procession....   (968–70)

This democratic revision of the Crucifixion allows Whitman to throw off the specialness of his prior poetic identity so that he can be reborn as "one of an average unending procession." As a traveler in this mortal procession, Whitman no longer assumes the divine prerogative of total identification with others. After this point in the poem, Whitman refuses to be anyone but himself, a teacher preaching his equal faith in the body and in the soul.

Despite his constant naturalizing of religious experience, and despite anchoring his poetry in bodily sensation, Whitman was committed to imaginatively exploring a transcendental realm. His bridge to the transcendental, however, is through the naturalistic paradigm of scientific evolution, which he offers as his secularized equivalent of biblical apocalypse. His images drawn from biology, geology, and astronomy suggest a vast, temporal trajectory: the "huge first Nothing" (1153), the "Monstrous sauroids" (1167), "the nebula" that "cohered to an orb," "the long slow strata piled" upon it (1164–65), all having progressed and still progressing toward some future orbicular existence. Like biblical apocalypse, Whitman's version of evolution is a faith that promises to resolve the multiple contradictions of the present, whether manifested in personal experience or in the sectional conflict of the union.[22] Evolutionary optimism, then, offered Whitman answers to both current questions of national policy and to traditional concerns of theodicy.

But unlike biblical versions of apocalypse, Whitman does not attach ultimacy to such future reconciliation: "I do not talk of the beginning or the end" (39). A recent critic notes, "Whatever appears at a given moment as a god, a *telos* or *arché*, is always actually hiding something more remote behind it...."[23] When Whitman announces that his spirit will one day enfold the heavenly orbs, his spirit counters, "we level that lift to pass and continue beyond" (1122). Hence the "perpetual journey" (1122) he tramps, the open road for body and soul in this life and for soul alone in the next, a journey through "limitless space" and "limitless time" (1196–97). At that place of "rendezvous," Whitman tells us, "God will be there and wait till we come" (1198). Whitman willingly speaks of God, but reminds us that "there is no object so soft but it makes a hub for the wheeled universe" (1276). In his final sermon, he enjoins us not to be curious about God but instead to follow his democratic, anthropocentric example and be "curious" (in the root sense of the word, to care) about one another (1278–79).

Though Whitman's scriptural message is complete in "Song of Myself," he presents it more directly in the prose preface and eleven other poems of the first edition.[24] In these exegeses, he is both lawgiver and prophet, roles not fully developed in "Song of Myself" which provide further evidence of the biblical character of Whitman's mission in the first *Leaves*.

In his preface, Whitman offered his readers imperatives for action in the world outside the poem. We should not be surprised by the presence of laws in an antinomian poet, for the Hebrew prophets likewise attacked institutions and urged on their listeners the self-evident laws of morality: "what doth the Lord require of thee, but to do justly, and to love mercy, and to walk humbly with thy God?" (Mic. 6:8). The laws of self-reliance, as a student of Emerson's religion has noted, are "delivered by God to the self and received by the self from the God within the self."[25] In such a view of divine law, a lawgiver, whether it be Whitman or Jesus, has authority to command us only in so far as he himself has exemplified these commandments. Whitman first announces this new rule of inner-directed law, and then, in the poems that follow, becomes the exemplar of this redemptive process.

Living according to Whitman's law produces the superior person whom Whitman celebrates in "Song of Myself," a person who could never enslave another or ever be enslaved. That is why Whitman could claim in his preface that the "attitude of great poets is to cheer up slaves and horrify despots" (*LG*, p. 720). A nation of such superior persons could not long tolerate slavery in its midst. "This is what you shall do," he enjoins the reader:

> Love the earth and sun and the animals, despise riches, give alms to every one that asks, stand up for the stupid and crazy, devote your income and labor to others, hate tyrants, argue not concerning God, have patience and indulgence toward the people, take off your hat to nothing known or unknown or to any man or number of men, go freely with powerful uneducated persons and with the young and with the mothers of families, read these leaves in the open air every season of every year of your life, reexamine all you have been told at school or church or in any book, dismiss whatever insults your own soul, and your very flesh shall be a great poem and have the richest fluency not only in its words but in the silent lines of its lips and face and between the lashes of your eyes and in every motion and joint of your body. (pp. 714–15)

Whitman's rededicated person attains a spiritual greatness that results in a changed attitude not only to others, especially to the unfortunate of society, but also to his or her own body. Reorienting contemporary readers to their bodies is a central preoccupation in "I Sing the Body Electric," his poem most directly concerned with slavery. Like the many celebrations of the body in "Song of Myself" (see especially the evocation of the Negro driver's "polish'd and perfect limbs" [229] in section 13), this exegetical poem presumes that the human body is a miracle and that anyone brought face to face with it will acknowledge its functional perfection.

In "I Sing the Body Electric," after praising bodily beauty and perfection ("The male is perfect and that of the female is perfect" [10]), Whitman ironically assumes the role of an auctioneer at a slave market, outdoing the professionals in praising the slaves' perfect bodies.

Contemporary readers, coming to Whitman's poem from the melodramatic accounts of slave selling in *Uncle Tom's Cabin*, might well have been put off by his seemingly irreverrent performance. Whitman's aim, however, like Stowe's, is essentially that of the biblical prophets: to make a whole people confront its moral failings. Whitman places his readers in close proximity to a hypothetical slave's body in order to force them to identify their own bodies with what is on display:

> Examine these limbs, red black or white.... they
> > are very cunning in tendon and nerve;
> They shall be stript that you may see them.
>
> Exquisite senses, lifelit eyes, pluck, volition,
> Flakes of breastmuscle, pliant backbone and neck,
> > flesh not flabby, goodsized arms and legs,
> And wonders within there yet.
>
> Within there runs his blood.... the same old
> > blood.... the same red running blood;
> There swells and jets his heart.... There all passions
> > and desires...all reachings and aspirations:
> Do you think they are not there because they are not
> > expressed in parlors and lecture-rooms?
> > > (104–12)

How can we witness the degradation of another's body without becoming ourselves degraded? Empathy begins, Whitman would have us see, by recognizing the identity of bodies with one another, but it must soon extend to recognizing the identity of human feelings. Whitman's taunting question, like that of an Amos or an Isaiah, is intended to provoke remorse in any of his contemporaries who has ever condoned slavery or denigrated a slave. What kind of repentance could the reader make, except to adopt more democratic attitudes? Without such repentance, the reader incurs Whitman's curse, not outdone by anything in Leviticus or Deuteronomy: "Who degrades or defiles the living human body is cursed, / Who degrades or defiles the body of the dead is not more cursed" (128).

In raising these issues of contemporary morality, Whitman's poetry concerns itself with his audience's spiritual health. I take the view that Whitman had experienced a revelation expanding his consciousness, in which state he identified with all persons living, dead, and yet to be born, as well as with rocks, vegetation, animals, stars, the celestial orbs that his spirit would one day enfold, and finally, with God, the elder brother whom he would one day meet. He could not, of course, provide this subjective religious experience for his readers, but he could encourage them to identify emotionally and intellectually with the whole panoply of persons in American life. Providing an encouraging model of union and reconciliation to a nation on the verge of disunion—what prophetic task could be more important in Whitman's mind?

Feeling himself to be the new national poet called for in Emerson's essays, Whitman wrote an American bible that, like Emerson's teachings, deconstructed the authority of externally defined religion. His was a bible that necessarily called into question its own authority. Whitman preferred to think that the American people would keep producing home-grown scriptures:

> We consider the bibles and religions divine.... I
>   do not say they are not divine,
> I say they have all grown out of you and may grow out
>   of you still,
> It is not they who give the life.... it is you who
>   give the life;
> Leaves are not more shed from the trees or trees
>   from the earth than they are shed out of you.
>   ("A Song for Occupations," 78–81)

Whitman's punning move from lower-case "bibles" to upper-case "Leaves" points, of course, to his own *Leaves*, shed from himself to exemplify and teach naturalized divinity. His faith in individual autonomy and organicism, both evident in this quotation, demanded that his own bible continue to grow with him and with America, sprouting new leaves and shedding old ones. No two editions of *Leaves of Grass* could be the same. The *"New Bible"* that Whitman first wrote in 1855, and then projected for completion in 1859, turned out to be the work of a lifetime.

Notes

*I am indebted to the American Council on Learned Societies and the Committee on Grants, Franklin and Marshall College, for funding a year's leave spent at Brandeis University, where a seminar and conversations with Allen Grossman and Claudia Yukman stimulated this work. I have also benefited from the research assistance of Heather Fitzgerald through the Hackman Scholars Program of Franklin and Marshall College. My thanks to Ellen Frankel and David Leverenz for commenting on drafts of this essay.

1. *Notebooks and Unpublished Prose Manuscripts*, ed. Edward F. Grier, 6 vols. (New York: New York University Press, 1984), 1:353; hereafter cited as *NUPM*.

2. For statements of this view spanning the twentieth century, see Oscar Lovell Triggs, "The Growth of 'Leaves of Grass,'" in *The Complete Writings of Walt Whitman*, ed. Richard Maurice Bucke et. al., 10 vols. (New York: G. P. Putnam's Sons, 1902), 10:101, 113; and Lawrence Lipking, *The Life of the Poet: Beginning and Ending Poetic Careers* (Chicago: University of Chicago Press, 1981), p. 118.

3. Allen, "Biblical Echoes in Whitman's Works," *AL*, 6 (1934): 302–15; Crawley, *The Structure of "Leaves of Grass"* (Austin: University of Texas Press, 1970); pp. 50–79.

4. "The Antinomian Strain: The Bible and American Poetry," in *The Bible and American Arts and Letters*, ed. Giles Gunn (Philadelphia: Fortress, 1983), pp. 11–32.

5. Renner, "Tradition for a Time of Crisis: Whitman's Prophetic Stance," in *Poetic Prophecy in Western Literature*, ed. Jan Wojcik and Raymond-Jean Frontain (Rutherford, N.J.: Fairleigh Dickinson University Press, 1984), pp. 119–30; Hutchinson, *The Ecstatic Whitman: Literary Shamanism and the Crisis of the Union* (Columbus: Ohio State University Press, 1986), pp. xi–xxviii, 1–25.

6. "The Law, the Prophets, and Wisdom: On the Functions of Literature," *CE*, 37 (1975): 254–64; for a more extended discussion that includes New Testament literary functions, see Northrop Frye, *The Great Code: The Bible and Literature* (New York: Harcourt Brace Jovanovich, 1982), pp. 105–38.

7. See *NUPM*, 6:2172–90, esp. 2174–75.

8. Sidney E. Mead, *The Old Religion in the Brave New World: Reflections on the Relation between Christendom and the Republic* (Berkeley: University of California Press, 1977), pp. 76–80, argues that constitutional disestablishment of religion had made competing Christian denominational claims for salvation irrelevant to defining a citizen's responsibility in the new republic. On Whitman as a post-Christian writer, see Renner, pp. 121–22; and Quentin Anderson, "Whitman's New man," in *Walt Whitman: Walt Whitman's Autograph Revision of the Analysis of "Leaves of Grass" (for Dr. R. M. Bucke's "Walt Whitman")*, ed. Stephen Railton (New York: New York University Press, 1974), pp. 19, 22–25.

9. *Leaves of Grass: Comprehensive Reader's Edition*, ed. Harold W. Blodgett and Sculley Bradley (New York: New York University Press, 1965), p. 719; hereafter cited as *LG*.

10. *Leaves of Grass: A Textual Variorum of the Printed Poems*, ed. Sculley Bradley et. al., *The Collected Writings of Walt Whitman*, 1 (New York: New

York University Press, 1980): 5–6, lines 82–98; all quotations from Whitman's poems are from the 1855 texts and, for ease of reference, are cited by the line numbers assigned in this edition.

11. On Whitman's polemic against possessive individualism, see M. Wynn Thomas, *The Lunar Light of Whitman's Poetry* (Cambridge: Harvard University Press, 1987), pp. 40–71.

12. Allen Grossman, "The Poetics of Union in Whitman and Lincoln: An Inquiry toward the Relationship of Art and Policy," in *The American Renaissance Reconsidered*, ed. Walter Benn Michaels and Donald E. Pease, Selected Papers from the English Institute, 1982–83, New Series, 9 (Baltimore: Johns Hopkins University Press, 1985), p. 194.

13. On the past tense, see Howard J. Waskow, *Whitman: Explorations in Form* (Chicago: University of Chicago Press, 1966), pp. 114–15; and Anderson, pp. 25, 35. On the timeless present as used by Whitman and other poets, see George T. Wright, "The Lyric Present: Simple Present Verbs in English Poems," *PMLA*, 89 (1974): 563–79.

14. I have been unable to trace any other bosom kiss in Western art; the nonerotic kiss most closely resembling Whitman's may be found in representations of Christ's entombment, where Mary Magdelena and/or the Apostle John lean over the supine body of the dead Jesus and kiss his cheek and/or hand; see Gertrud Schiller, *Iconography of Christian Art*, trans. Janet Seligman, 2 (Greenwich, Conn.: New York Graphic Society, 1972): illus. 575–79. Divine kisses are always bestowed on the mouth, according to Nicolas James Perella, *The Kiss Sacred and Profane: An Interpretive History of Kiss Symbolism and Related Religio-Erotic Themes* (Berkeley: University of California Press, 1969), pp. 18–19.

15. See James E. Miller, Jr., *A Critical Guide to "Leaves of Grass"* (Chicago: University of Chicago Press, 1957), pp. 8–11, who argues that Whitman inverts traditional mystical experience. On Whitman's deliberate democraticization of mysticism, see David Kuebrich, "Whitman's New Theism," *ESQ*, 24 (1978): 229–41, esp. 235–40; and Ernest Lee Tuveson, *The Avatars of Thrice Great Hermes: An Approach to Romanticism* (Lewisburg: Bucknell University Press, 1982), pp. 241–42.

16. See Diane Kepner, "From Spears to Leaves: Walt Whitman's Theory of Nature in 'Song of Myself,'" *AL*, 51 (1979); 179–204.

17. Sacvan Bercvitch, "The Biblical Basis of the American Myth," distinguishes between the two patterns (Gunn, p. 266).

18. See Crawley, pp. 91–95; Schneidau, pp. 18–19.

19. On Whitman as a secularizer of biblical typology, see Karl Keller, "Alephs, Zahirs, and the Triumph of Ambiguity: Typology in Nineteenth-Century American Literature," in *Literary Uses of Typology from the Late*

Middle Ages to the Present, ed. Earl Miner (Princeton: Princeton University Press, 1977), pp. 274–314, esp. 290–94.

20. See John 8:12, 9:5, 10:7, 10:11, 11:25, 14:6; Schneidau relates this form to both the Johannine Jesus and to the divine "I AM THAT I AM" of Exodus 3:14 (p. 18). The divine "I am" can also be found in *The Bhagavadgita in the Mahabharata*, ed. and trans. J. A. B. van Buitenen (Chicago; University of Chicago Press, 1981), pp. 99, 105, 109.

21. See Sholom J. Kahn, "Whitman's 'Overstaid Fraction' Again," *WWR*, 20 (1974): 67–73.

22. On Whitman's teleological evolutionary paradigm, see David Charles Leonard, "Lamarckian Evolution in Whitman's 'Song of Myself,'" *WWR*, 24 (1978): 21–28.

23. Paul A. Bové, *Destructive Poetics: Heidegger and Modern American Poetry* (New York: Columbia University Press, 1980), p. 173.

24. See Ivan Marki, *The Trial of the Poet: An Interpretation of the First Edition of "Leaves of Grass"* (New York: Columbia University Press, 1976), pp. 231–49; and "The Last Eleven Poems in the 1855 *Leaves of Grass*," *AL*, 54 (1982): 229–39.

25. William A. Clebsch, *American Religious Thought: A History* (Chicago: University of Chicago Press, 1973), p. 109.

MARK DeLANCEY

Texts, Interpretations, and Whitman's "Song of Myself"

Aristotle tells us that the rhetorician must be able to argue both sides of a question.[1] The poets have responded to this demand all along. In the *Odyssey*, the suitors speak for the opposition, as do Satan and his crew in *Paradise Lost*. In Westerns, the opposition wears the black hats. Shorter forms such as the lyric often signify wrongheaded argument with a simple negative. "Thy trivial harp," Emerson complains in the first lines of "Merlin," "will never please / Nor fill my craving ear." Against the harpist, the black-hats, or Satan the author develops his case, and that they merit rebuttal presupposes that their views are forces in the community he addresses. The community to be formed by persuasion is always yet to be, and if the author speaks for the future, the opposition parties speak for conventional experience. The nature of the rhetorician's task demands that he aspire to a modernity beyond the horizon of the familiar. But if the author is committed to the new, we may ask how he escapes the old while compelling the assent of his listeners, who would not need to be persuaded did not the author assume that they were committed to the world he abandons. How does the author propose to achieve modernity?, How does the audience, committed to the old world, gain access to the new? The idea of observing both sides of a question suggests an answer.

From *American Literature* 61, no. 3 (October 1989). © 1989 by Duke University Press.

1. *The Question of Difference*

Experience is many-sided. By observing two sides of a question, an author hopes to arrive at an answer that reconciles different and conflicting experiences. Thus he achieves something new. As Cleanth Brooks suggests, a text dramatizes a conflict of familiar "attitudes."[2] His analysis of Donne's "Canonization," for example, charts the clash and reconciliation of two conventional views of love, Petrarchan and Christian (pp. 10–17). "In a unified poem," he says, "the poet has 'come to terms' with his experience" (p. 189). He comes to terms with an experience of a world constituted by modes of discourse that have solicited or won his assent.

To argue two sides of a question, in this view, is not simply to argue pro and con. It is to deliberate on a question answered differently by two modes of familiar discourse. A difference within experience, and by extension a rift within the community, drives the author to question the community's self-understanding and to affirm a new understanding. He argues both sides of the question to embrace and to bridge the difference that makes change available to him and his community. The coherence of a poem, what Brooks calls its "real meaning," "lies in the unification of attitudes into a hierarchy subordinated to a total and governing attitude" (p. 189). To achieve this unity, which can authentically reconcile two sides of the question, and thus compel the reader's agreement, only if those two sides and their differences are preserved intact, the author must do justice to both. Each side speaks as a half of a new whole. Both belong to the opposition party, and wear the black hats, if they resist change. If they consent to change, both belong to the author's party and wear the white hats. If the community consents to the new understanding affirmed by the author, its understanding of experience changes.

Brooks thus very nearly closes ranks with Deconstruction. To say, as the deconstructers do, that a text emerges from a play of differences in the language system is to say that it emerges from historical difference—from differences among established discourses. Historical difference gives rise to the possibility of the traditional task, shared by the texts of Deconstruction itself, of compelling agreement by arguing both sides of a question. The text "decenters" the historical community, "deconstructs" the edifice of habit and common sense, and defeats opposition to change by observing the differences within familiar experience. Because any reconciling (or "effacing") of differences creates new differences, the decentering of experience is perpetual. Familiar experience and the new experience made available by a given text put one another in question. It then falls to yet another text to resolve the new question.[3]

Though he emphasizes the author's achievement, Brooks would not deny that it relies on a "deconstruction" of familiar experience. Nor would he deny that the decentering of experience is perpetual. The deconstructers, however, are less inclined than Brooks to concede that the author and in turn the audience achieve understanding. J. Hillis Miller insists that

> the critic's attempt to untwist the elements in the texts he interprets only twists them up again in another place and leaves always an element of opacity, or an added opacity, as yet unraveled. The critic is caught in his own version of the interminable repetitions which determine the poet's career. The critic experiences this as his failure to get his poet right in a final decisive formulation which would allow him to have done with that poet, once and for all. Though each poet is different, each contains his own form of undecidability. This might be defined by saying that the critic can never show decisively whether or not the work of the writer is "decidable," whether or not it is capable of being definitively interpreted. The critic cannot unscramble the tangle of lines of meaning, comb its threads out so they shine clearly side by side. He can only retrace the text, set its elements in motion once more, in that experience of the failure of determinable reading which is decisive here.[4]

Meaning is indeterminate because any understanding questions, and is reciprocally questioned by, any understanding already achieved. Caught in "interminable repetitions" of the act of questioning, author and critic alike are condemned to a world whose meanings are always questionable.

This difference between Brooks and Miller is important because it reveals a blind spot in their assumptions. Both assume that an author's characteristic act of questioning consists in, or at least coincides with, a questioning of meaning: having put meaning in question, a text is the place where one tries (successfully or unsuccessfully) to interpret, to understand. Brooks and Miller thus fail to observe a primary difference: one may question a truth affirmed by an author, and one may question an interpreter's understanding of what an author affirms. Just as there is a diversity of answers, and one truth competes with another, there is a diversity of interpretations of a given answer.

The end of rhetoric is agreement in the sphere of truth. Persuasion, that is to say, begins in a difference that puts truth in question. What troubles an author is that the answers affirmed by his community differ: the text emerges from a difference that renders truth questionable and to that extent indeterminate. By observing both sides of the question, the author hopes to reconcile the difference and put the question of truth to rest. Only by affirming and transcending difference can the author determine what he considers to be the truth and secure the agreement of his community. "Truth," in this sense, is not "absolute" truth, though it may appear so if the difference resolved appears to embrace all possible experience. It is a settling of differences between accepted truths. Authors who claim to have nothing to do with "truth" make a negligible exception to the general rule, given this sense of the term. If they do not put the truths of my experience in question, they do not address questions important to me. If they give reasons for denying these truths, or the possibility of truth in general, they give me reason to think they speak the truth. If they give no reasons, I have no reason to listen.

The end of interpretation, by contrast, can only be agreement in the sphere of meaning. Interpretation begins in a difference that puts meaning in question. What troubles the interpreter is that a given text evidently means different things to different interpreters and indeed to himself. Hence to the interpreter, a text emerges from a difference that renders its meanings questionable and indeterminate. By observing both sides of the question, the interpreter hopes to reconcile the difference and put the question of meaning to rest. In this sense, "meaning," like "truth," is a provisional solution to a problem. By transcending difference in the sphere of meaning, the interpreter determines meaning and secures the agreement of his community. But after an interpreter has determined the meaning of a text, and hence too of the truth that it affirms, that meaning and that truth may be put in question by other meanings and other truths.

Brooks and Miller arrive at contradictory conclusions because their premise, which denies the difference between texts and interpretations, is self-contradictory. How the difference reasserts itself in their conclusions is a question I address later, when I explore the reason behind the nearly universal tendency to deny it. But first I want to illustrate the difference by looking at Whitman's rhetoric in "Song of Myself."

II. *Whitman and the Rhetoric of Democracy*

"Song of Myself" opens with the speaker inviting the audience to embrace him:

> I celebrate myself, and sing myself,
> And what I assume you shall assume,
> Every atom belonging to me as good belongs to you.
>
> I loafe and invite my soul,
> I lean and loafe at my ease observing a spear of summer grass.[5]

The "soul" that he invites is also the audience that he addresses as "you." In the embrace of his reader and soul, the words on the page—the poet's "atoms," his body—will awaken to life. Since the soul will then assume the poet's atoms, reader and writer will share one living body and one embodied soul.

The poet thus speaks as a body estranged from its soul. The soul cannot attend to Whitman's ample body—will not read "Leaves of Grass"— because the community, confined to "houses and rooms" and intoxicated by the "perfumes" of "creeds and schools," has its nose stuck in other books. When the reader does come to him, soul and body reunite, and the poet comes to himself. Leaving the library, and becoming "undisguised and naked" at the "bank by the wood," Whitman comes to himself, and literally to his senses, by embracing the pure, unintoxicating "atmosphere" ("I am mad for it to be in contact with me").

On the one side are the "houses and rooms," their shelves crowded with intoxicating books. On the other is the pure "atmosphere" of the out-of-doors. The two sides voice different rhetorical appeals. The library expresses its seductiveness in images of containment. The schools and creeds bring nature indoors by distilling out its essences. This rhetoric of refinement invites the soul to take all of Nature into itself—to become a delirious vessel of Nature's wine, which can then be poured out for other bacchants. The rhetoric of the atmosphere, by contrast, invites all things to lose themselves in its currents. As it speaks through him, the atmosphere drowns the poet's voice ("The smoke of my own breath, / Echoes, ripples, buzz'd whispers") in a sea of voices indistinguishable from his own. In an orgiastic abandonment of identity, he complies with the persuasions of a rhetoric that urges him to identify himself with all that he is not.

Each side lacks what the other claims as its virtue. If the one, for all its intoxicants, stands accused of too much refinement, the other, for all its massive sobriety, stands accused of "buzzing," of saying everything and nothing. But the poet, who has come to the wood from the library, combines them both in himself. As he dissolves in the atmosphere, and then falls asleep, the alienated halves of his experience reunite. The poet awakens revitalized, and the two streams of his experience blend together in a "full-noon trill, the song of me rising from bed and meeting the sun."

This song of mature mid-day does not reveal its central commitment until Section 5, when the poet finally confronts his soul and reader face to face. Pointedly, the poet asks his lover to "loose the stop from your throat," to free his voice from the self-imposed and repressive checks of the schools. He does not want "music" or "lecture," just the "hum" that has been bottled up inside.

The soul accepts the body's renewed invitation, and a memory revives.

> I mind how once we lay such a transparent summer morning,
> How you settled your head athwart my hips and turn'd gently
>   over upon me,
> And parted the shirt from my bosom-bone, and plung'd your
>   tongue to my bare-stript heart,
> And reach'd till you felt my beard, and reach'd till you held
>   my feet.

"Swiftly arose and spread around me," the poet continues, "the peace and knowledge that pass all the argument of the earth." Then, changing to the present tense, he announces what the recollection teaches: "And I know...." Here are the two sides of Whitman's experience and the whole conceived in their embrace: the present of the living soul, which, loosing the stop from its throat, reanimates the past; the past itself, a transparent summer morning in which soul and body once embraced; and the past regained as present truth.

The past recalled by the poet is the dawn of the sense of his immortality, when the soul first embraced the body and its transient world. Borne into the bodily eye by the transient light that rises and spreads across the landscape, the "argument of the earth" is in effect taken up and resolved by the soul, whose light, rising and spreading over the landscape of mortality, immortalizes it as transcendent peace and knowledge. The transient light, the earth in its arms, and the things of day dematerialize in the embrace of the soul's eternal light. "I mind how once we lay such a transparent summer morning." Transparency is their achievement. Each pervading the other, body and soul sing together a poem of early knowledge and rising peace, which dissolves all things in the transparency it creates.

Considered as one side of a controversy in which familiar attitudes are put in question, this moment suggests to me Wordsworth's "Ode," in particular the relation between the "celestial light" and "the light of common day." To Wordsworth—Wordsworth-the-child, that is—"every common sight ... did seem / Apparelled in celestial light, / The glory and the freshness of a dream."[6] The common *seems* celestial. The child's "dream" effectively denies commonplace nature and divorces him from it. The real, however, quickly reasserts itself as this priest of nature watches the light he thought celestial "die away, / And fade into the light of common day." But because the common light, measured against the "vision splendid," must appear demonic, the child in his heaven-born freedom puts himself at strife with his blessedness. He falls into a demonic universe of death until, halted in his flight "like a guilty Thing surprised," the life within his dying embers remembers and gathers him and his faded moments back to its breast.

Just as the light of the soul embraces Whitman and immortalizes the transient report of the senses, an interior light immortalizes Wordsworth's passing moments. The heart's affections and recollections—the "master light of all our seeing"—"make / Our noisy years seem moments in the being / Of the eternal Silence; truths that wake, / To perish never." This inextinguishable light explains why the common at first "seems" celestial and at the same time authorizes (though on different grounds) the dream of nature's priest as a truth. The "immortal sea / Which brought us hither" reclaims all things. "In a moment"—in all moments at once given and taken by eternal, "celestial" life—the soul can "travel thither, / And see the Children sport upon the shore, / And hear the mighty waters rolling evermore."

The *transparency* of Whitman's vision points to a different Wordsworthian experience.

> Five years have past; five summers, with the length
> Of five long winters! and again I hear
> These waters, rolling from their mountain springs
> With a soft inland murmur.—Once again
> Do I behold these steep and lofty cliffs,
> That on a wild secluded scene impress
> Thoughts of more deep seclusion; and connect
> The landscape with the quiet of the sky.
> The day is come when I again repose
> Here, under this dark sycamore, and view
> These plots of cottage-ground, these orchard-tufts
> Which at this season, with their unripe fruits,
> Are clad in one green hue, and lose themselves
> 'Mid groves and copses. Once again I see
> These hedge-rows, hardly hedge-rows, little lines
> Of sportive wood run wild: these pastoral farms
> Green to the very door; and wreaths of smoke
> Sent up, in silence from among the trees!
> With some uncertain notice, as might seem
> Of vagrant dwellers in the houseless woods,
> Or of some Hermit's cave, where by his fire
> The Hermit sits alone.[7]

It is summer, and it is morning. The poet listens to the inland murmur because he cannot yet see. He records what he hears, pauses, and then, as dawn begins to break, beholds the steep and lofty cliffs: "The day is come."

Casting their shadow, with the sun rising behind them, on a secluded scene, the cliffs impress thoughts of yet deeper seclusion. The poet's thoughts are in effect a shadow impressed on the scene by cliffs blocking out the sun. But the shadow bears witness to the light, and thus the cliffs "connect" the landscape with the quiet of the sky. Running wild like the lines of sportive wood, Wordsworth's syntax also permits "I" as the subject of "connect": "Once again do I behold ... and connect." The "I" or self, then, is like the cliff that both blocks out the sun and connects the darkened landscape with the quiet of the sky. The subject and the landscape are one in their power to sever and connect, and this power now begins to "connect" things formerly severed, the subject and his landscape chief among them. In this day and this scene the poet sees what he saw before: past and present merge. Orchard tufts, clad in one green hue, lose themselves amid groves and copses. The lines of hedge-rows run wild, the green threatens to swallow the farmhouses, and the smoke of breakfast fires drifts away into the light.

This act of connecting is a rhetorical gesture. Subject and object are wedded, so to speak, by a copula that urges each, as it flickers in the moment of syntactical distinction, to lose itself in the other. Different things become one being, which speaks through them to identify each with all. This "power that rolls through all things"—a "something far more deeply interfused"—lends them a transient identity that dissolves immediately in a oneness. Though the superficial (i.e., syntactical) differences between them are preserved, all things die into the living whole.

The wreaths of smoke commemorate this death. Carrying a double valency like that of the cliffs, the smoke suggests to Wordsworth the two sides of his own divided experience—the dark seclusion that he shares with the Hermit in his cave and the community with nature, and with one another, that he shares with the vagrants. When he acknowledges, as the sun rises from behind the cliffs and spreads its light across the landscape, the power that rolls through all things, the divided halves of his experience unite, consume themselves in one another, and dissolve like the smoke rising and spreading into the transparency of the sky.

Whitman's coupling of soul and body achieves the same transparency, and achieves it by the same means, as though he were assenting to a Wordsworthian rhetoric of unity. The poet's "body"—everything that belongs to transient sensory experience—dies into, and is immortalized by, the soul's transparent light. Whitman's problem, the primary problem addressed not only by "Song of Myself" but by his poetry as a whole, is that the soul that embraced him on that summer morning has gone on to a new incarnation in the present-day American schools. Its rhetorical program is now one of internalization. The soul now bottles intoxicating perfumes distilled from nature.

Though he reproaches the schools, landing a glancing blow at their effeminacy, for distilling "perfumes" out of life, Whitman says he "likes" their "fragrance" (l. 15). He "likes" the "lull" and "hum" of the schools' "valvéd voice" (l. 86). The experience of the schools is his own present experience, and it moves between an act of (feminine and "feudal") refinement—of bringing the outside inside in the form of intoxicating essences—and an act of pouring out, in drunken song, what has been contained. This new commitment of the soul to self-containment suggests the rhetorical program of Emerson.

"The Supreme Being," Emerson writes in "Nature," "does not build up nature around us, but puts it forth through us, as the life of the tree puts forth new branches and leaves through the pores of the old."[8] Nature is God's word—"a projection of God in the unconscious" (I, 64–65)—and "the present expositor of the divine mind" (I, 65). But since God pours forth his Word through man, and exclusively through him, nature is equally human history and the expositor of man's own divinity:

> Man is the dwarf of himself. Once he was permeated and dissolved by spirit. He filled nature with his overflowing currents. Out of him sprang the sun and moon; from man the sun, from woman the moon. The laws of his mind, the periods of his actions externized themselves into day and night, into the year and the seasons. But, having made for himself this huge shell, his waters retired; he no longer fills the veins and veinlets; he is shrunk to a drop. He sees that the structure still fits him, but fits him colossally. Say, rather, once it fitted him, now it corresponds to him from far and on high. He adores timidly his own work. Now is man the follower of the sun, and woman the follower of the moon. Yet sometimes he starts in his slumber, and wonders at himself and his house, and muses strangely at the resemblance betwixt him and it. He perceives that if his law is still paramount, if still he have elemental power, if his word is sterling yet in nature, it is not conscious power, it is not inferior but superior to his will. It is instinct. (I, 71–72)

The spirit that contained and permeated nature has withdrawn itself, becoming unconscious instinct. Man's creation, a shell now containing his drop of conscious power, lies dead around him as what Emerson calls the "Not Me."

Emerson's rhetoric hopes to persuade his community that what man creates, which is the Not Me because it constitutes a fixed past resisting present power, waits to be drunk in by the spirit that poured it forth. Man "thinks his fate alien," but "the soul contains the event that shall befall it, for the event is only the actualization of its thoughts" (VI, 40). The soul is a vessel and its acts both realize and take the stamp of the nature it contains. Man "shall see that nature is the opposite of the soul, answering to it part for part. One is seal and one is print. Its beauty is the beauty of his own mind. Its laws are the laws of his own mind. Nature then becomes the measure of his own attainments. So much of nature as he is ignorant of, so much of his own mind does he not yet possess" (I, 86–87). Piercing the husk of the world, the spirit abstracts its essence, and the circuit of conscious life expands. The act of comprehending, made available by an influx of unconscious power, lends actuality to that which is comprehended. Thus the fully comprehending spirit—the transparent eyeball of "Nature"—contains, pours out, and is the world that it sees.

When Whitman characterizes the schools' project of absolute self-containment as "intoxicating," he borrows Emerson's vocabulary. The god invoked by Emerson in "Bacchus" is the alienated god within, the capricious god of "instinct." The Not Me is his vineyard, and a draught of wine, "Food which teach and reason can," assimilates the communicant to his own alienated powers, whereupon he "May float at pleasure through all natures" and "unlock / Every crypt of every rock" (IX, 125–26).

Emerson's prayer is thus a prayer to become Bacchus, and then something more than Bacchus, as he reclaims from the Not Me the power to distill and drink in the essence of original godhead that he once yielded to it.

> Pour, Bacchus! the remembering wine;
> Retrieve the loss of me and mine!
> Vine for vine be antidote,
> And the grape requite the lote!
> Haste to cure the old despair,—
> Reason in Nature's lotus drenched,
> The memory of ages quenched. (IX, 127)

Reason sleeps, drenched in the lotus of the Not Me, but when the antidote takes effect, reason reawakens to discover itself in a Nature renewed.

> Let the wine repair what this undid;
> And where the infection slid,
> A dazzling memory revive;
> Refresh the faded tints,

Recut the aged prints,
And write my old adventures with the pen
Which on the first day drew,
Upon the tablets blue,
The dancing Pleiads and eternal men. (IX, 127)

His essence abstracted from the written record of the Not Me, and placed again within the circuit of the spirit, the Man that hardened into the material forms of the Not Me awakens once more as man. His alienated and dormant essence again becomes actual thought, which is to say a thought-in-act, and the spirit writes again its old adventures.

Whitman's complaint, to return to Section 5 of "Song of Myself," is that the soul, in its Emersonian incarnation, abases the body: "I believe in you my soul, the other I am must not abase itself to you,/And you must not be abased to the other." Distilling the thought or essence out of the Not Me, Emersonian intellectuality devalues the body of nature, and the body of nature reciprocates by drenching Reason in the lote. To neutralize their "stupendous antagonism" (VI, 22), as Emerson in "Fate" calls the interplay of spirit and nature, Whitman adopts the Wordsworthian attitude of repose beneath the sycamore and loafs on the grass. In this repose, the transient body merges with the quiet of the sky, and all things, as they sink in the depths of the sea of being, are made one. The problem is that a state in which all things are one, and in which they lose themselves like smoke in the light, cannot be an object of thought, except as Being again materializes in individual beings. Of each single "truth" the whole is predicated. The being that dwells in such peace is everything and nothing—a "huge first Nothing" (l. 1153) as Whitman calls it when he looks back upon the depths out of which he has risen—and can neither think, nor be thought, nor listen, nor speak.

Whitman's solution is to reunite the alienated halves of his experience. Past and present redefine one another. Embraced by the Emersonian soul, the transparent summer morning of Wordsworthian oneness awakens as a memory. The soul unstops its throat, pours back into the past the essences it lacks, and thus transforms Wordsworth's "sea" into a mass of equal but thinkable entities comprehended by the soul. Under the pressure of Wordsworthian unity, the soul in turn is made one with the sea whose parts it embraces as its own knowable form and body.

The rhetorical resources of the Wordsworthian and Emersonian experiences thus speak simultaneously in an emerging Whitmanian modernity:

And I know that the hand of God is the promise of my own,
And I know that the spirit of God is the brother of my own,
And that all the men ever born are also my brothers, and the
women my sisters and lovers,
And that a kelson of the creation is love,
And limitless are leaves stiff or drooping in the fields,
And brown ants in the little wells beneath them,
And mossy scabs of the worm fence, heap'd stones, elder,
        mullein and poke-weed.

This is the rhetoric of Whitmanian democracy. The speaker is one with God, and with the other members of the community, but he *knows* each one, and every blade of grass, as a self-contained part of a whole constituted by the parts that it comprehends. In contrast with Emerson's rhetoric of internalization and Wordsworth's of unity, Whitman's rhetoric is one of harmony. Diverse individuals, the atoms of a spiritual whole, compose a community whose soul, which embraces each member equally, and which therefore communicates the experience of each to all, expresses itself in a harmony of voices.

III. *Argument and Representation*

The achievement of "modernity" begins with the poet's commitment to two contradictory truths. Whitman addresses himself, as the voice and "body" of the Wordsworthian past, to the soul of the Emersonian present. A substitution has occurred. For its conventional or historically established object, the Wordsworthian subject substitutes a new object. Instead of addressing the Wordsworthian soul whose redemptive power identifies each with all, the Wordsworthian subject addresses the Emersonian soul whose similarly redemptive power contains all. We may say that Whitman predicates the Emersonian subject of the Wordsworthian subject. The two subjects, so joined, put one another in question because the proposition is unconventional—the conventional of course corresponding to the discourses of the "past" and "present" (as Whitman understands them). Whitman's questioning of conventional experience is thus founded on a trope, an unconventional combination of conventional elements.

The trope behaves like a complex simile. In the simile "men are [like] birds," what I. A. Richards would call the vehicle ("birds") suggests properties that literally or conventionally belong to the tenor ("men").[9] The nature of this suggestiveness implies that the trope arises from the substitution of an unconventional predicate—"birds," whose own conventional predicates are thus provisionally eclipsed—for the conventional predicates of "men," which are likewise eclipsed. While the trope may suggest any number of predicates, and we recover them only by a kind of guesswork, our conventional understanding of the two terms limits the possibilities. Each suggestion puts all other suggestions in question, and we select from the alternatives only those predicates that common sense or familiar experience tells us can be predicated of "men." Alternatively, from the range of predicates that common sense attaches to "men," we select only those predicates suggested by "birds." My understanding of "birds," involving as it does the idea of flight, suggests to me an idea of spiritual aspiration that is conventionally predicable of "men," and I then assume that this predicate is the one for which "birds" has been substituted. Once I have fixed upon this point of its conventional history, "men" in turn suggests other properties conventionally predicable of "birds"—perhaps that they sometimes soar beyond eye's reach. Thus I reconstruct, as an object of belief made available through a reasoned or commonsense guesswork, the grounds of the substitution that gave rise to the simile.

As the trope leads back to a determinate awareness of the conventional histories of the likened terms, it also leads forward, as does Whitman's unconventional combination of conventional elements, to a vision of something new. After I have chosen from the available alternatives a particular property of the tenor (or a number of its properties), the vehicle ceases to be suggestive (though its suggestiveness may be revived at any time). To me, and in this case, the vehicle "birds" designates the spiritual aspirations that it once only suggested. Properties conventionally belonging to "men" accordingly supplement the conventional definition of "birds."[10] This event of mutual redefinition reconciles what the trope, considered as a *representation*, posits as its own past and present. Because the vehicle re-presents the properties of the tenor, the tenor belongs to a past re-presented and the vehicle to a present that re-presents. The representation that links past and present belongs to an emerging modernity.

The difference that generates the argument is thus a similarity-in-difference, the broadest or most fundamental kind of relation capable of being affirmed. Difference implies relation; nonrelation is indifference. Since to say that two things differ is to say that they are not the same, the relation between them must be such that there might be some possibility of confusing them. I will say that the moon is different from a mandrake only if they might be thought to be the same. If they were not similar, or thought to be similar, the question of their sameness or difference could not arise. As similarity implies difference, difference implies similarity. A text begins in an "understanding-as."

By understanding Emerson's truth and Wordsworth's each as the other,

Whitman commits himself to both. He argues just these two sides of the question because the representation demands that he do justice to only the past and present that it postulates. He thus commits himself to a particular historical sequence. As it distinguishes between a past represented and a present representing, Whitman's trope projects a future born of their mutual redefinition. His representation of the Wordsworthian past in the Emersonian present commits him to a modernity of fixed dimensions.

Familiar experience, conventional common sense, restricts the poet's freedom to affirm the new. In the formation of simile, the availability of an unconventional substitute breaks the bond between a subject and its conventional predicate. The subject becomes the simile's tenor as it captures the substitute, which becomes the vehicle, in the displaceable energies freed by the breaking of the conventional bond. But the energies displaced onto the vehicle "properly" belong elsewhere. The gravity of the familiar draws them back to the conventional predicates for which the vehicle has substituted. The vehicle is suggestive precisely to the extent that the voice of common sense insists on being heard. Freeplay exhausts itself in doing justice to familiar experience. The representation liberates energies from the constraints of orthodoxy while preserving its accomplishment.

A representation of the past in the present is thus the text's constitutive moment, the first cause of the new. Because it liberates the energies and tensions that animate Whitman's world, the trope that joins Wordsworthian and Emersonian discourses awakens Whitman both to his own rhetoric and to the new community it envisions. Any "Whitman" prior to his own rhetoric, a creative spirit or imagination that might be viewed as the maker of the poem, coincides with one or another of the conventional experiences that the poem puts in question. An ego or maker or imagination is in question, in other words, only to the extent that it has been constituted by conventional discourses that are supported by the communal labor—a labor that will be variously defined by the bond in question—of binding a subject to a predicate. Because this labor defines the members of the community as subjects of a certain kind, the availability of an unconventional substitute for the subject's conventional predicates frees the labor consumed in the task of conventional self-definition to a task of redefinition and change. The possibility of "understanding-as," in short, awakens the conventional "I" to new life, and the representation, pulling the subject toward the conventional and unconventional simultaneously, constitutes the imagination's will to reconcile the opposition in a new whole.

Whitman's question is a large one—"What is the truth of things?" Acting as the spokesman of the first, and attributing the second to his alienated soul and reader, he has to do justice to both the Wordsworthian experience and the Emersonian experience because his answer can only be that the truth comprehends both. That the halves of his and his community's experience are substantially one he does not recognize fully until Section 5, when the Emersonian soul, belonging to the living present of his audience, recollects and revives the Wordsworthian past. He sees and asserts the larger truth, which has been eclipsed by the temporality of experience, that the past and present and all their properties make up the predicates of "Life."

This truth figures as the thesis of Whitman's argument. The rhetorical project of the rest of the poem is to defend this truth, and we may suppose that the poet achieves the traditional rhetorical aims by observing the traditional rhetorical means. However we conceive them, they are necessarily enclosed, constituted, and made available by the metaphoricity that grounds his argument and asks the question that he seeks to answer. In particular, the "agreement" that marks the end of persuasion is a resource of simile. Subject and object, author and audience, past and present, each understands itself *as* the other and so comes to recognize itself in the other. Because a vehicle's conventional definition is supplemented by what it suggests about the tenor, the two terms mutually redefine one another and thus resolve their differences. The author agrees with the audience, and the audience, if it understands what the author has said, and if it acknowledges that he has done justice to both sides of the question, agrees with the author. The freedom that a poem makes available to its readers may be a threat to their experience, but by doing justice to its alienated halves, the poem preserves it transfigured in an emerging modernity.

IV. *Representation and Interpretation*

The metaphoricity in which the text begins, and which challenges the author to argue both sides of the question, challenges the interpreter to understand both sides of the question. Metaphoricity embraces the text on two registers. As it posits a difference in the sphere of truth, it also posits a difference in the sphere of meaning. "Song of Myself," for example, posits a difference in the meaning that Emerson and Wordsworth give to the words "life" or "experience." The difference puts meaning in question. Of virtually any word in "Song of Myself," two different accounts, Emersonian and Wordsworthian, can be given. This kind of metaphoricity—metaphoricity in the sphere of meaning—accounts for and justifies the interpreter's inescapable hypothesis that the text's meanings are questionable and indeterminate. The text is opaque because it understands one order of meaning as or in terms of another order of meaning. The text does not insist on just one meaning; it both dissembles and suggests a whole range of meanings.

To settle the question of meaning, the interpreter enters into the text's representation of meaning as meaning. The text speaks suggestively, and the interpreter responds to its suggestions. The vehicle of the representation, speaking within the interpreter's familiar experience, asks him to recall a past that it suggests. Because the tenor of a simile may at any time function as a vehicle—if A is like B, B is like A—this recovered past reciprocally suggests something about the present. These suggestions put in question his initial understanding of the present. The interpreter's corrected or revised or expanded understanding of the present may then suggest a new range of properties that put in question his initial understanding of the past.

The text's suggestiveness thus gives the interpreter access to his own experience, to what he already understands. As it gives access to familiar meanings, the text's suggestiveness exercises a selective surveillance that singles out meanings that are adequate to the clarification of the text. The criterion of adequacy is twofold: a meaning must be suggested by the text, and what is suggested must agree with common sense. The meanings that the interpreter attaches to the text must belong, according to the judgment of common sense, to the familiar experiences, past and present, that the suggestive play of representation makes available to reflection. A suggestion is valid, in other words, if it does not, in the judgment of common sense, contradict other suggestions.

The judgments of common sense make interpretation inseparable from criticism. If the interpreter happens to be the author of the text, these judgments give him the opportunity to revise his interpretation of the arguments that his own argument puts in question. Any revision in the sphere of meaning will of course require him to rework his argument. If he is not the author, the interpreter can justify criticism of the text on the grounds that its author has misinterpreted the arguments that he, as author, questions. The critic then judges that the meanings attached by the author to familiar experience, and thus to the modernity to which the author's representation is committed, cannot stand the test of common sense.

An interpreter of Whitman, for example, might object that Whitman's interpretations of the conventional experiences that he attributes to his community do not agree with his community's interpretations. The criticism, I emphasize, applies not to the author's argument, but to his interpretation of the two sides of the question that he argues (though a criticism of the argument may follow). In his exploration of the question of truth, the author recovers, reconstructs, or "does justice to" two arguments, two rhetorical commitments, which he has already interpreted. By contrast, the interpreter's exploration of the question of meaning recovers and reconstructs a conventional interpretation of the two sides of the question. Because the interpreter's exploration unfailingly presents to reflection alternative interpretations of the two sides, it puts in question the author's interpretation of them. Since an argument can appear to reflection only "inside" an understanding of its two sides, the interpreter's criticism—a criticism specifically of the author's interpretation of the two sides—also applies to what the interpreter will take to be the author's interpretation of his own text.

V. *The Destiny of the Text*

An author must insist that he understands his own argument. Lest he undercut both his own ground and the future that it foresees, the author cannot question his *interpretation* of the arguments that he questions. An argument accordingly represses the possibility of questioning its own self-understanding. No argument can free itself from this dogmatism. The author denies, at least provisionally and until he becomes once again his own interpreter, that meaning is questionable. His text thus tacitly affirms that it grounds itself in certainty and self-evidence. To say that the understanding that grounds the argument is unquestionable is to say that the author understands his argument unquestionably and truly. By declaring that it appears fully in the light of its own self-evidence, the text repudiates its opacity and its status as a representation waiting to be clarified. The text claims to be a locus of meaning.

It is if we grant this claim that we follow Brooks and Miller in collapsing the difference between texts and interpretations. The difference reappears, however, in the conclusions that can be drawn from the hypothesis of the equivalence of texts and interpretations. Brooks, for example, tacitly defines a text as an interpretation. If interpretations achieve meaning, the author, considered as an interpreter, achieves meaning, and the reader or critic, whose role has been usurped by the author, can only hope to appropriate the understanding that the author has already achieved. By contrast, Miller tacitly defines an interpretation as a text. Neither authors nor readers can ever really understand because, whenever they interpret, they author another text whose meanings must be interpreted in yet another text, which likewise remains to be understood. In the one account, a text is the locus of achieved meaning; in the other, a text is the locus of failed meaning.

The act of interpretation, however, always amounts to a practical denial of the text's claim to meaning. One does not interpret that which is already clear. The interpreter enters into the text's representation of meaning as meaning to determine what it suggests. And if a text's meanings, apart from interpretation, are therefore indeterminate, interpretation does not change them. Something indeterminate cannot be changed. By entering into the questioning of meaning repressed by the author, the interpreter makes the text fulfill the destiny anticipated by the metaphoricity of its origins. Interpretation produces a transparent text. The text appears to reflection in the familiar experience made available to us by its suggestiveness, and as the text appears it changes, or its rhetoric seeks to change, our experience of truth. As our experience brings the argument to reflection, the argument, in partnership with our experience, bequeaths not only a past and a present that we are asked to view as our own, but also a modernity that we are yet to live.

I emphasize that a text hopes to reconcile a conflict in *communal* experience. Whitman's community is divided, at least as he understands it, because it urges contradictory claims that constitute the indubitable "truths" of the community's experience. To clarify these truths, and to make the modernity that emerges from them available to reflection, the interpreter must appeal to his own experience: we understand the new in terms of what we already understand. Thus I appealed to my understanding of Emerson and Wordsworth. But the two criteria that an interpretation must meet—that it be suggested by the text and that it agree with common sense—leave room for the widest spectrum of different and equally valid interpretations. A Marxist critic might characterize Whitman's argument differently. Had he met these criteria, however, his interpretation would tend to make available to reflection, though in different terms, the same two sides of the question and the same answer. Meeting these criteria is not easy. The metaphoricity of the text asks the interpreter to question the presuppositions that he brings to it. These presuppositions are determined by experiences that have already been made available to reflection. They constitute his "common sense." If the text, as it appears to reflection, disconfirms the interpreter's "common sense," he usually abandons the text, not his own common sense.

What links all interpreters, regardless of their presuppositions, is a shared, or potentially communicable, historical experience that can be recognized, and which to that extent remains the same, in the different languages that make it available to reflection. The sum of this experience, as it appears to reflection in the sum of the languages of criticism, comprehends the whole of "common sense." Beginning with his allotted portion, the interpreter reconstructs the text's historical ground by listening to its suggestions. By judging according to common sense, he acts in behalf of the community. Hence the final arbiter of the validity of an interpretation is the community, the reservoir of common sense. Ideally, an interpretation should be judged against all possible interpretations of the same text. In practice, we judge it against the available interpretations. Hence, not only is a wide spectrum of competing interpretations inevitable; it is essential to the community's task of self-understanding. A pluralistic community, unsubdued by dogma, has the best chance of knowing what to believe about itself.

Communal assent to an interpretation makes a text's modernity available to communal reflection. The whole process of raising and settling a question of truth then becomes an actual communal resource available to actual communal experience. The question may belong to our past: the moment of change, whatever its place in history, makes itself available to actual experience only through interpretation. But change takes place only if we agree to change. As we reflect upon the text, we ask whether it speaks for us. Is its question our own? Does it, as it observes the two sides of the question, observe a difference within our own experience? In short, does it make possible an authentic transformation of our own experience? We assent to change and arrive at the experience of the new if we decide that the text argues its question of truth in our behalf and argues it fairly. We assent to a change located in our past—to Whitman's vision of Democracy, for example—if we decide that the text argues fairly a question of truth in behalf of the community it addresses. We assent if the text does justice to a difference between moments of our collective past. We then arrive at the experience of a living and changing past different from our own present.

NOTES

1. *Rhetoric*, 1355a. The passage in question runs as follows: "We must be able to employ persuasion, just as strict reasoning can be employed, on opposite sides of a question, not in order that we may in practice employ it in both ways (for we must not make people believe what is wrong), but in order that we may see clearly what the facts are, and that, if another man argues unfairly, we on our part may be able to confute him."

2. *The Well Wrought Urn* (New York: Reynal & Hitchcock, 1947), pp. 186–87. Further references to this volume are indicated in the text by page number.

3. This "decentering" is the primary concern of Jacques Derrida's "White Mythology," *New Literary History*, 6 (1974), 5–74: For a more focussed account of "difference" see his essay "Differance" in *Speech and Phenomenon*, trans. David P. Allison (Evanston: Northwestern Univ. Press, 1973), and Lacan's "The Agency of the Letter in the Unconscious" in *Ecrits*, trans. Alan Sheridan (New York: Norton, 1977).

4. "The Critic as Host," in *Deconstruction and Criticism* (New York: Seabury, 1975), pp. 247–48.

5. *Leaves of Grass*, ed. Harold W. Blodgett and Sculley Bradley (New York: Norton, 1968), p. 28. Further references to "Song of Myself" are from this edition and are indicated in the text by line number.

6. *The Poetical Works of William Wordsworth*, ed. E. de Selincourt (Oxford: Clarendon Press, 1940–1949), IV, 279.

7. Ibid., II, 279–80.

8. *The Complete Works of Ralph Waldo Emerson*, The Centenary Edition, 12 vols. (Boston: Houghton Mifflin, 1903–1904), I, 64. Further references to Emerson's writings are from this edition and are indicated in the text by volume and page number.

9. The *Philosophy of Rhetoric* (London: Oxford Univ. Press, 1936), pp. 95–112. I use the term "simile" where Richards uses the term "metaphor" to distinguish the trope in question from another trope, more properly termed "metaphor," that effectively identifies two things by giving the name of the one to the other.

10. The mutual redefinition of a simile's terms gives rise to what is known technically as a "transfer." For a discussion of "transfer," see William Empson, *The Structure of Complex Words* (London: Chatto & Windus, 1951), pp. 334–36.

GAYLE L. SMITH

Reading "Song of Myself":
Assuming What Whitman Assumes

"D o I contradict myself?" Whitman asks near the end of "Song of Myself" (95). The answer, of course, is the resounding "yes" Whitman would have expected. As casual as he sounds about his contradictions, readers and critics have sought to resolve the intertwined issues of style, intention, and relationship to the reader in Whitman's poetry. Specifically, how are we to reconcile Whitman's dedication to an aesthetics of clarity and simplicity, to being "the channel of thoughts and things" with his insistence that the "transcendant [sic] and new" poetry of America "is to be indirect and not direct or descriptive or epic," especially when both statements appear in his 1855 Preface to *Leaves of Grass* (417, 413)? Furthermore, how do we reconcile Whitman's dedication to clarity with the undeniable difficulties we encounter, even at the level of the grammar of the sentence (or the non-sentence)? What then is the poet's actual relationship with the reader? To what extent does he absorb and project the unheard voices of others? To what degree does he strive to inspire his readers to be their own seers, their own poets, to use this poem to create their very own? Whose song is it anyway?

Two recent articles grapple with these kinds of questions in particularly rewarding ways. Alan D. Hodder sees Whitman using various "strategies of indirection" in order to transcend the usual barriers among writer, reader,

---

From *American Transcendental Quarterly* vol. 6, no. 3 (September 1992). © 1992 University of Rhode Island, Kingston, RI.

and text; these strategies involve the use of paradox and the development of a poetic voice that is deeply personal and musical (124–125). Herbert J. Levine uses Roman Jakobson's range of language functions to trace the shifting balances between Whitman's more lyric and more persuasive styles, between a speaker more concerned to express his own emotion and one more interested in exhorting his listener to action or belief. While Whitman's larger rhetorical structures offer great insights into the aesthetics and dynamics of his poetry, so do his syntactic structures. Before we can assess issues of clarity, we must confront his language at the level of the sentence. Patterns of deletion, fragmentation, and pronoun reference involve readers in definable and important ways, allowing us to explore his relationship to the reader on a new and indispensable level. Whitman's syntactic choices are distinctive, but they do change somewhat through time and, more significantly here, through the poem itself. These changes reveal the poet's evolving relationship with his medium, his subject, and his readers.

Anyone who has spent much time with Whitman's poetry can attest to the fact that reading it can indeed be the "gymnast's struggle" that Whitman says it should be in "Democratic Vistas" (500). Sounding like a twentieth-century reader response critic, he goes on to say that the reader "must himself or herself construct indeed the poem, argument, history, metaphysical essay—the text furnishing the hints, the clue, the start or framework" (500). Few poems so self-consciously demand the efforts at creation that "Song of Myself" does, at least until its final sections. Yet in his 1855 Preface, Whitman had declared, "I will not have in my writing any elegance or effect or originality to hang in the way between me and the rest like curtains.... What I experience or portray shall go from my composition without a shred of my composition. You shall stand by my side and look in the mirror with me" (417–418). We cannot explain the discrepancy between these statements simply by positing a change over time, for the 1855 edition of "Song of Myself" requires many of the heroic efforts he would describe in "Democratic Vistas," published in 1871. In fact, he anticipates the "gymnast" image in the first edition by declaring, "I am the teacher of athletes" and "He most honors my style who learns under it to destroy the teacher" (88).[1]

Robert E. Abrams is correct when he observes that Whitman's style throughout *Leaves of Grass* is far more "marked" and difficult than his Preface would imply (75). Despite what Whitman says about the reader "constructing" the text, however, the reader is not very free in his efforts. "Song of Myself" places great demands on the reader, in large part because of the freedom Whitman takes with word order, his heavy use of deletion or ellipsis, and his strong anaphoric, backward reaching patterns of reference. All of these stylistic devices make the reader active indeed, even puzzled, but scarcely free. What Whitman reorders, the reader must at least imagine in a more normal syntactic pattern; what he leaves out, the reader must supply, not even to interpret the text but merely to make sense of it. As much as his surprising statements, apparently free association of items in long catalogs, and parallel and coordinated constructions suggest an unpremediated, or as Whitman termed it in his notebook *Words*, an "insociant" (sic) style, his style is in fact surprisingly controlling for the reader (*DBN* 3:667). In the second line of the poem, Whitman suggests how aware he is of the degree of control he exerts: "And what I assume you shall assume," he tells the reader (3).

In another of his linguistic notebooks, Whitman distinguishes between artificial, prescriptive systems of rules and the inherent, "real grammar" he sees vitalizing the English language, allowing for maximum flexibility, individuality, and growth. This grammar, he notes with obvious pleasure, has "plenty of room for eccentricities and what are supposed to be gaucheries— and violations" (*DBN* 3:810). More specifically, he celebrates the free order of words in English, words that "stand loose, and ready to go this way or that," allowing users to connect ideas "any way we please" (*DBN* 3:723). When he notes the shortcomings of Lindley Murray's *English Grammar*, he is critiquing all the prescriptive grammarians. As James Perrin Warren notes, Murray's *Grammar*, first published in 1795, became a popular textbook both in England and America, an abridged version of the 1816 edition going through more than one hundred and twenty impressions (2). Therefore, it is appropriate that Whitman writes of Murray's position in the present tense, charging that he "fails to understand those points where the language [is] strongest, and where [the] developments should [be] most encouraged, namely, in being *elliptic* and *idiomatic*" (*DBN* 3:666–667). These are the very qualities he specifically associates with the strength of American English, and for him, they are entwined with the language's unique ability to express "new spirits" (*DBN* 3:810). As a "new spirit" himself, Whitman uses ellipsis in many forms, each of which demands different responses from his readers.

One form of ellipsis occurs frequently in long parallel passages. For example, he begins section 31 with the following declaration:

> I believe a leaf of grass is no less than the journey-work of the stars,
> And the pismire is equally perfect, and a grain of sand, and the egg of
>   the wren,
> And the tree-load is a chef-d'oeuvre for the highest,
> And the running blackberry would adorn the parlors of heaven,
> And the narrowest hinge in my hand puts to scorn all machinery,
> And the cow crunching with depress'd head surpasses any statue,
> And a mouse is miracle enough to stagger sextillions of infidels. (49)

The syntactic parallelism itself serves repeatedly to connect Whitman's utterances with epic and Biblical style, lending a special incantatory authority. Lawrence Buell and James Perrin Warren have devoted considerable attention to the rhetorical, historical, and prosodic implications of this style.[2] However, the parallel constructions that characterize the Psalms, for example, generally repeat entire syntactic units. Here, presumably, the reader simply needs to supply the illocutionary statement "I believe" before each line. Its deletion after the first line presents no obstacle to comprehension, but it does allow the believer's voice to grow more and more oracular; it is easy to forget after a few lines that these are statements about what the poet believes and not necessarily proclamations of general truth.

He bends parallel structure more freely and engages in more creative deletion of repeated phrases as he concludes section 30:

> I believe the soggy clods shall become lovers and lamps,
> And a compend of compends is the meat of a man or woman,
> And a summit and flower there is the feeling they have for each
>   other,
> And they are to branch boundlessly out of that lesson until it becomes
>   omnific,
> And until one and all shall delight us, and we them. (49)

It is easy enough to supply "I believe" before each statement, but the final line requires a good deal more. First the reader must repeat the subject and verb phrase of the previous line ("they are to branch") and then, in the clause that is reduced to nothing more than subject and object pronouns, repeat this construction and fill out the statement to something like, "and [until] we [shall delight] them." The pronoun references and the omissions in the final line prevent us from reading the sentence as a simple list; instead we are sent back through the entire passage to supply more and more gapped material. In the process, we are likely to achieve a degree of belief we might not have if all the elements were there for our full consideration or rejection. By the time we have supplied the missing words, we have invested something in them; we have participated in writing the poem, but it is a carefully programmed participation.

The most common kind of gap Whitman leaves requires the reader to complete a sentence fragment. In the second section appears a nine-line catalog of more than twenty noun phrases:

The smoke of my own breath,
Echoes, ripples, buzz'd whispers, love-root, silk-thread, crotch and vine,
My respiration and inspiration, the beating of my heart, the passing of
   blood and air through my lungs,
The sniff of green leaves and dry leaves, and of the shore and dark-
   color'd sea-rocks, and of hay in the barn
The sound of the belch'd words of my voice loos'd to the eddies of the
   wind.
A few light kisses, a few embraces, a reaching around of arms,
The play of the shine and shade on the trees as the supple boughs wag,
The delight alone or in the rush of the streets, or along the fields and
   hill-sides,
The feeling of health, the full-moon trill, the song of me rising from
   bed and meeting the sun. (5)

In *Words*, he discusses Wilhelm von Humboldt's theory that language "expresses originally objects only, and leaves the understanding to supply the connecting form"; here is a series of objects in need of formal and logical connections (*DBN* 3:721). Since there is no clear introduction to his listing, we must go back through his discussion of the difference between the "perfumes" found indoors and the "atmosphere" that he seeks and surmise that these are the experiences he anticipates when he goes out into nature. We must make the statement and the logical connection. At the very minimum, we need to insert "There is" or "I behold" before the list, as we might do again in the next section with this more dramatic pair of fragments:

Urge and urge and urge,
Always the procreant urge of the world.
Out of the dimness opposite equals advance, always substance and
increase, always sex,
Always a knit of identity, always distinctions, always a breed of life. (5)

As Whitman concludes what Carl Strauch considers the first half of the poem, he creates a large proportion of fragmentary expressions (117). Five passages in sections 24 and 25, accounting for 27% of the lines in these two sections, lack finite verbs. Three need verbs of being to make participles into present progressive tense verbs, as in "Hefts of the moving world at innocent gambols silently rising, freshly exuding, / Scooting obliquely high and low" in which the absence of a verb of being leaves us with a noun phrase,

ultimately static despite the movement suggested by the participles (41). We
must supply *is* again when we read, "Through me the afflatus surging and
surging, through me the current and index," and we must also supply the
predication again at the end of the expression (39). As C. Carroll Hollis
points out, most readers if asked whether Whitman's poetry was dynamic or
static would probably say it was dynamic, despite the fact that grammatically
it is quite stative, owing in part to his use of participles and the simple present
tense rather than the progressive present or other tenses that would set an
action in a particular time frame (216). Nouns, by definition, are also stative,
and as we have already seen, Whitman frequently presents them without any
predication whatsoever. In *Words* he considers the linguistic argument about
the primacy of nouns of verbs and, not surprisingly, says, "I think ... that
nouns begin the matter.—Language may have since been scraped and
drenched down to the completer state, which makes the verbs the centres,
for grammatical purposes; but, in the nature of things, nouns must have been
first, and essentially remain so" (*DBN* 3:715).

A few lines later in section 24 we find two more parallel passages that
in their verblessness help him celebrate his ability to transcend time:

> Through me many long dumb voices,
> Voices of the interminable generations of prisoners and slaves,
>
>   . . . .
>
> Through me forbidden voices,
> Voices of sexes and lusts, voices veil'd and I remove the veil,
> Voices indecent by me clarified and transfigur'd. (39)

To attach a tensed, finite verb to these statements, to write "Through me
[are/there are/speak/sing] many long dumb voices," would be to diminish the
universal power he claims to project past, present, and future. It is significant
that this cluster of "ungrammatical" passages occurs as he declares the special
power of his own words. He opens section 23 with the verbless exclamation,
"Endless unfolding of words of ages! / And mine a word of the modern, the
word En-Masse" (37). He closes the section with an interesting indication of
how he sees his words acting:

> Less the reminders of properties told my words,
> And more the reminders they of life untold, and of freedom and
>   extrication,
> And make short account of neuters and geldings, and favor men and
>   women fully equipt,
> And beat the gong of revolt, and stop with fugitives and them that plot
>   and conspire. (37)

The actions described in the final lines are undercut by the simple present tense that keeps us in a perpetual, suspended present and by the absence of subject actors for those verbs after the *and's*. In the first two lines, the violently inverted word order may eclipse the fact that there is no verb. The simple, stative verb *are* would at least make of his words a unified statement, a proposition about reality, rather than what we actually have here, words as somewhat separate "reminders," hints about reality. If he will not make the connections explicit, the reader must.

When Whitman tacks on surprising but structurally incomplete final statements, he creates a sense of spontaneity, of his own dynamic voice reaching conclusions and sharing them with us before bothering to put everything in prescribed grammatical order. At the same time, he obliges the reader to work through the preceding lines to fill in syntactic gaps he has left, as with the buried subject discussed above. He concludes the first section of the 1892 edition with a rather dramatic example of this structure when he says, "I harbor for good or bad, I permit to speak at every hazard, / Nature without check with original energy" (3). The last three words seem curiously detached from the rest of the sentence until we insert "and I permit Nature to speak" before them. The alternative is for the reader to rearange the phrases into more usual, transitive order, placing *Nature* immediately after *permit*, thereby losing much of the emphasis on the free manner of Nature's and Whitman's speaking.

In the following passage from section 32 in which he explores his relation to animals, the interjected phrase "and with velocity" invites us to slip in before it the subject and finite verb that would support the allusions to movement and transitivity:

> Myself moving forward then and now and forever,
> Gathering and showing more always and with velocity,
> Infinite and omnigenous, and the like of these among them,
> Not too exclusive toward the reachers of my remembrancers,
> Picking out here one that I love, and now go with him on brotherly
> terms. (51)

In the final lines of this section, he articulates his concern for functions, states, and poetic perceptions over the actions and beings that crowd the poem. Here his statements are grammatically complete and independent:

> I but use you a minute, then I resign you, stallion,
> Why do I need your paces when I myself out-gallop them?
> Even as I stand or sit passing faster than you. (51)

Nor is this the only passage in which he seems to dismiss the very
entities and individuals to whom he appeared to be devoting his entire poem.
After several sections in which he describes many individuals, in section 13
he summarizes the teeming variety. The third line below, absent in the 1855
edition, makes us reconsider what has gone before, not merely in order to
complete the clause, but to determine what it means to the poet:

> In me the caresser of life wherever moving, backward as well as
>   forward sluing,
> To niches aside and junior bending, not a person or object missing,
> Absorbing all to myself and for this song. (19)

The final statement of purpose tends to deprive the baby, blacksmith,
"picturesque giant," and all the others of the intrinsic value he seemed to be
affirming. Our attention, and we suspect, his, is now on "this song." More
reductively, in section 15, he follows over 150 lines of specific, active
statements like "The pure contralto sings in the organ loft," "The machinist
rolls up his sleeves," and "The Missourian crosses the plains" with a rather
surprising conclusion:

> And these tend inward to me, and I tend outward to them,
> And such as it is to be of these more or less I am,
> And of these one and all I weave the song of myself. (25)

Again, the final line does not appear in the 1855 edition, in which he seems
to discourse less about the finished work itself. The repeated anaphoric
pronouns send us back through the entire list, from President to prostitute,
living to dead, to create unity of diversity, even chaos. The inclusive pronoun
these, which we do not generally use by itself to refer to people, suggests that
the separate identities he has catalogued have merged. All are reified, become
things, means to the end of creating this poem, as his last metaphor indicates:
we weave with pliant materials, not autonomous individuals.

Whitman seems to have been aware of his attraction to demonstrative
pronouns. In his *Primer of Words* he declares, "All words are spiritual" and
lists "those eluding, fluid, beautiful, fleshless, realities, Mother, Father,
Water, Earth, Me, *This*, Soul, Tongue, House, Fire" (*DBN* 3:730; emphasis
mine). We might have guessed the referential words, but *this*? Whitman's
statement proves that he was as sensitive to the function of words in his
poetry as he was to their associations, as aware of how his words made his
readers organize his text as he was of what they might envision as they read.
The pronouns *this* and *these*, as Whitman characteristically uses them, make

readers retrace and synthesize long stretches of text, accepting because helping to create the essential oneness out of variety. Whitman's usage is important in another way too. It seems odd at first that he should call *this*, a word that typically specifies, makes clear, points to one entity as opposed to another, "eluding" and "fluid," but often what his demonstratives point to is elusive. Unlike Emerson, Whitman rarely gives us a new name for all that went before; instead he leaves it up to the reader to decide who and what the demonstrative can refer to. Even when he does give us a new noun phrase, as he does here in section 3, it does not necessarily make interpretation easier:

> Sure as the most certain sure, plumb in the uprights, well entretied,
>   braced in the beams.
> Stout as a horse, affectionate, haughty, electrical,
> I and this mystery here we stand. (7)

We need to consider at least the previous eleven lines to identify "this mystery," which seems to have something to do with what he sees as a process of eternal procreation and renewal. "This mystery" remains mysterious despite the modifier.

Having declared himself throughout section 16 to be a kind of American Everyman in every place and his place at the same time, when he opens section 17 by saying, "These are really the thoughts of all men in all ages and lands," he makes us reevaluate his statements in a new and broader light (27). A few lines later, however, his use of the demonstrative is more troubling: "This is the grass that grows wherever the land is and the water is, / This the common air that bathes the globe" (27). "These thoughts," plural and abstract, seem to have become singular asnd concrete. After section 18, in which he says that he plays for the dead and defeated, he suggests another meaning of "This is the grass" as he opens section 19 with a new list of demonstrative identifications:

> This is the meal equally set, this the meat for natural hunger,
>
> This is the press of a bashful hand, this the float and odor of hair,
> This the touch of my lips to yours, this the murmur of yearning,
> This the far-off depth and height reflecting my own face,
> This the thoughtful merge of myself, and the outlet again. (29)

Now it is quite clear that *this*, back in section 17 as well as here, refers to the poem itself and the poetry-making process. In the 1855 edition, this is the first such summative statement, equating foregoing experiences, actions, and persons with the poem and the writing process itself. By the 1892 edition, however, this is at least the third time the poem turns out to be self-referring.

Anaphoric references are exceptionally important in the long section 33, in which he describes his panoramic vision. After eighty lines of grammatical suspension through prepositional and participial phrases, comes the main clause of the sentence, "I tread day and night such roads," the phrase *such roads* unifying and redefining the myriad experiences, actions, and emotions catalogued above (57). Again, having claimed to "understand the large hearts of heroes," and having described graphically the women, the infants, and the sick saved from shipwreck by the heroic skipper, he draws back abruptly, abstractly considering his own imaginative process: "All this I swallow, it tastes good, I like it well, it becomes mine, / I am the man, I suffer'd, I was there" (59). Events are reified, first to the plural noun phrase, "such roads," and then to the singular demonstrative pronoun "this." His verb "swallow" indicates the transitory and merely functional nature of all he describes and also suggests a connection with his thoughts about the relationship between language and reality. In *Words* he uses this same verb to describe the relationship he sees: "Language follows events, and swallows them to preserve them.—Conquests, migrations, commerce, &c are fossilized in language" (*DBN* 3:718).

For all his apparent attempts to depict unmediated reality, to allow the reader to see for himself, his practice and occasionally his commentary suggest that he did not really believe this to be possible, that he accepted, refined, and finally celebrated his own altering, shaping, simplifying role as poet. Toward the end of the poem, presumably having won the reader's assent and confidence in the act of creating the poem, his message and style change somewhat. He addresses the reader more and insists upon the reader's necessary separation from him, saying things like "Not I, not any one else can travel that road for you, / You must travel it for yourself" and "You are also asking me questions and I hear you, / I answer that I cannot answer, you must find out for yourself" (87). More radically, he says in the next section, section 7. "He most honors my style who learns under it to destroy the teacher" and "I teach straying from me," although he follows it with the question, "yet who can stray from me?" (89).

His style in the final ten sections or so in fact makes it easier to argue with him, to stray, to be the "bold swimmer" of section 46 who would laughingly dash him with water from his own secure spot in the sea. Section 42 is the last to contain significant passages built on fragments. Thereafter, he is more declaratory and sometimes, as in section 48, emphatically repeats his affirmation: the passage begins in the present perfect tense, "I have said that the soul is not more than the body, / And I have said that the body is not more than the soul," and includes six more indirect statements and a restatement that reminds us that all of these are his personal beliefs and therefore arguable, "And I say to any man or woman, Let your soul stand cool and composed before a million universes" (91). The corresponding line in the 1855 edition, "And any man or woman shall stand cool and supercilious before a million universes," projects the more oracular tone characteristic of the first three-quarters of the poem (90). Lists of participial phrases still occur in the final fifth of the poem, but coming as they do in sections 41 and 43, after independent clauses, they do not suspend or limit the reader's understanding. In fact, they leave the reader free to stop reading, to stop following the poet word for word, virtually any time after the first line of the passage and still grasp a meaningful message.

A parallel change occurs in his voice as the poem draws toward a conclusion. Earlier in the poem he identifies himself with everyone, frequently using the verb *be*. For example, in section 33 after listing the feelings of martyrs, the mother executed as a witch, and the suffering slave, he declares, "All these I feel or am," and then, "I am the hounded slave," and elsewhere in the same key section, "My voice is the wife's voice, the screech by the rail of the stairs, / They fetch my man's body up dripping and drown'd" (59). Having imaginatively completed the act of merging with his subject and with his reader and having emerged again as himself, the poet, toward the end of the poem, still expresses a profound closeness to his listeners, but he no longer presumes to be one with them:

> I do not say these things for a dollar or to fill up time while I
>   wait for a boat,
> (It is you talking as much as myself, I act as the tongue of you,
> Tied in your mouth, in mine it begins to be loosen'd.) (89)

Earlier in the poem, the poet was devouring everything and everyone into his admittedly "omnivorous lines" to fashion the song of himself (77). Now, he has become an instrument of his readers; he does not claim to *be* their voice but, more modestly and more actively, to *act* as their voice. He relinquishes some of his control by asking challenging questions as the song concludes. Questions abound throughout "Song of Myself," signs in themselves of a desire to establish a more intimate relationship with the reader than most poets ever attempt, although many are rhetorical and unanswerable. In section 51, however, he packs seven questions into just twelve lines. "Listener up there! what have you to confide to me?" he asks, and urges confidentially, parenthetically, "(Talk honestly, no one else hears you, and I stay only a minute longer.)" (95). "Who wishes to walk with me?" he asks, implying a relationship of equals, and, "Will you speak before I am gone? will you prove already too late?" (95). Melting away like the daylight and merging with the landscape, he promises to help the listener turned poet, but indirectly. The seeker need not even specifically recognize him or his message: "You will hardly know who I am or what I mean,/ But I shall be good health to you nevertheless" (95).

The drama of "Song of Myself" involves complex, subtly shifting relationships among poet, experience, text, and reader, played out at many linguistic levels. Were it not for these changes, syntactic, stylistic, and rhetorical, the poem might well prove too demanding and overwhelming for most readers. It is almost as if the poet tests his readers through the earlier sections of the poem, demanding a great deal but controlling the nature of the reader's participation. In order to make good sense of the passages characterized by elipsis, anaphoric references, and suspended sentence structures, the reader must follow the poet and follow carefully. What the reader follows is the poet in the process of making the poem out of the variegated stuff of experience, assuming many roles, using and then abandoning that which he seeks to know when it has served his purpose. Like the teacher he says he is, however, the poet comes to afford more and more independence to the reader, stating himself more plainly, more arguably, confessing his purpose to create "this song," and, finally, "bequeathing" himself not merely to the dirt but to the poets of the future. Now we can interpret Whitman's early challenge to the reader, "What I assume you shall assume" in two different ways. The grammar of approximately the first forty sections of the poem demands that we make the same assumptions the poet does, merely to make sense of the poem, line by line. By the end of the poem, however, we are invited to assume the role of the poet.

NOTES

1. In the 1855 edition of *Leaves of Grass*, "Song of Myself" appeared without a title and without numbered sections. This passage opens section 47 in subsequent editions. My references to "Song of Myself" are to the 1892 edition, unless otherwise indicated. All "Song of Myself" references are to James E. Miller, Jr.'s *Whitman's "Song of Myself"—Origin, Growth, Meaning*, which reprints the 1855 and 1892 versions on facing pages for convenient reference.

2. See Lawrence Buell, especially ch. 6, "Catalogue Rhetoric," 166–167, and James Perrin Warren, especially ch. 3, "The 'Real Grammar': Syntactic Parallelism in *Leaves of Grass, 1855–1856*," in which he also relates parallelism to prosody and temporality.

Works Cited

Abrams, Robert E. "Space, Image, and Language in *Leaves of Grass.*" *American Transcendental Quarterly* 41 (1979): 75–83.

Buell, Lawrence, *Literary Transcendentalism: Style and Vision in the American Renaissance* Ithaca: Cornell University Press, 1973.

Hodder, Alan D. "Wonderful Indirections' and Whitman's Rocking Cradle." *ESQ: A Journal of the American Renaissance* 35:2 (1989): 109–146.

Hollis, C. Carroll. *Language and Style in Leaves of Grass*. Baton Rouge: Louisiana State University Press, 1983.

Levine, Herbert J. "The Interplay of Style and Purpose in the First Three Editions of *Leaves of Grass.*" *ESQ: A Journal of the American Renaissance* 37:1 (1991): 35–55.

Strauch, Carl F. "The Structure of Walt Whitman's 'Song of Myself.'" *The English Journal*. College Edition 27 (1938): 597–607. rpt. in *Whitman's "Song of Myself" — Origin, Growth, Meaning*. Ed. James Miller, Jr. New York: Dodd, Mead & Company, 1964, 115–122.

Warren, James Perrin. "The 'Real Grammar': Deverbal Style in 'Song of Myself.'" *American Literature* 56 (1984): 1–16.

—. *Walt Whitman's Language Experiment*. University Park: The Pennsylvania State University Press, 1990.

Whitman, Walt. *Daybooks and Notebooks*. Vol. 3. Ed. William White. New York: New York University Press, 1978 (cited in text as *DBN* 3 plus page number).

—. "Democratic Vistas." *Complete Poetry and Selected Prose*. Ed. James E. Miller, Jr. Boston: Houghton Mifflin Co., 1959. 455–501.

—."Preface to 1855 Edition of *Leaves of Grass.*" *Complete Poetry and Selected Prose*. Ed. James E. Miller, Jr. Boston: Houghton Mifflin Co., 1959. 411–427.

—. "Song of Myself." *Whitman's "Song of Myself" — Origin, Growth, Meaning*. Ed. James E. Miller, Jr. New York: Dodd, Mead & Company, 1964. 3–95.

WILLIAM BIRMINGHAM

Whitman's Song of the Possible American Self

My suggestion is this: religious Americans might profit spiritually from a committed reading of Walt Whitman's "Song of Myself." By a committed reading I mean one in which, having suspended disbelief, readers allow themselves to experience the text as meaningful aesthetic event, bringing to bear only later their critical faith practice.

Whitman, I should warn, was a great poet of experience and the possibilities it contains, but a terrible philosopher. A stanza from the last poem in the first edition (1855) of *Leaves of Grass* only slightly exaggerates how badly he often wrote when a philosophical mood came upon him:

Great is justice;
Justice is not settled by legislators and laws.... it is in the soul,
It cannot be varied by statutes any more than love or pride or the attraction
    of gravity can,
It is immutable .. it does not depend on majorities.... majorities or what
not come at last before the same passionless and exact tribunal. (144)

The ungainly and demotic "what not" instances, however, one of Whitman's great gifts to later poets—license to replace conventionally poetic English with the language and rhythms of common American speech.

From *Cross Currents*, vol. 43, no. 3 (Fall 1993). © 1993 by the Association for Religion and Intellectual Life.

Examples from two minor African-American poets may clarify the effect of this democratization of language. (Other groups and other poets could as easily be used.) Three or four decades before Whitman's birth in 1819, Phyllis Wheatley, doing her best to work in a language foreign both to her African and to her American heritage, writes that her love of freedom springs from having been "snatch'd from *Afric's* happy seat" and concludes, "Such, such my case. And can I then but pray / Others may never feel tyrannic sway?" (Randall, 38). However valid Wheatley's generous sentiment, the language rings untrue. (Its falseness brings to the poem an aura of cultural imperialism that may, paradoxically, enhance its effectiveness.) Three decades after Whitman's death in 1892, the congregation in James Weldon Johnson's "Listen, Lord—A Prayer" prays that the minister "Who breaks the bread of life this morning" be kept "out of the gunshot of the devil":

> Wash him with hyssop inside and out,
> Hang him up and drain him dry of sin.
> Pin his ear to the wisdom post;
> And make his words sledge hammers of truth—
> Beating on the iron heart of sin. (Randall, 41–42)

Johnson is not writing dialect poetry, yet his language rises from within the congregation's experience, capturing the black Baptist sacramentalization of the sermon. He can do so because the tradition Whitman began opened up poetry to the varieties of American language. Literary language no longer reigns. Or, better, every language feeds the poetic imagination.

I cite the African-American tradition because it has been marginalized by our culture as a whole, and Whitman's aesthetic vision—not only of language but of the possible American self—comprehends those relegated to society's edge. In her preface to *Passion*—I continue to draw on the African-American tradition—June Jordan, alluding obliquely to Whitman's homosexuality, speaks of him as "the one white father who shares the systematic disadvantages of his heterogeneous offspring trapped inside a closet that is, in reality, as huge as the continental spread of North and South America" (x) and ultimately asserts that "[a]gainst self-hatred," which is what those at the margins are so often taught, "there is Whitman" (xxiii). At its best, Whitman's poetic vision affirms, against self-hatred, a possible American self that is inclusive rather than exclusive, trusting rather than suspicious, egalitarian rather than hierarchical, relational rather than individualistic.

Whitman's inclusive vision of the possible self will surely appeal to those at home with contextual theology, though it is in other ways disquieting to the religious mind. It discovers the transcendent, if at all, in the immanent—in the spirit (but not the Spirit) with whose grandeur the world is charged. In "Song of Myself," the self experiences the divine not as Other but as merged with the cosmos, with which the self merges as well. Further—and this limitation is secular as well as religious—that cosmos seems closed to evil and to tragedy. There is more here than facile optimism, however; "Song of Myself" offers not an ideal self, realized or to come, but a delineation of what the empirical American self and its world may become if it follows the trajectory of the best in its democratic experience. If taken as optimism from below, this bears a close resemblance to hope.

"Song of Myself" is a single poem that Whitman in editions after the first divided into separate songs. Since the poem works better for me if I ignore the divisions, I shall use the first edition as I attempt to share my experience of the American self that the poem portrays. The poem's hero is "Walt Whitman," whom I will call "Walt." This Walt is no more Walt Whitman than the Dante who "saw the Highest Light [...] raised so far above / the minds of mortals" was Dante Alighieri, supporter of Emperor Henry VII. And no less, unless we take the products of imagination to be unreal.

The opening lines are familiar:

I celebrate myself,
And what I assume you shall assume,
For every atom belonging to me as good belongs to you. (27)

The third line is crucial: as I am, so are you; to celebrate myself is to celebrate you. Of equal importance is a kind of a-telic passivity, with soul here used— much as in African-American speech—to name the integrated self alive in matter and spirit to the present moment:

I loafe and invite my soul,
I lean and loafe at my ease.... observing a spear of summer grass.

There is nothing less or more important than either a blade of grass or the air around us:

The atmosphere is not a perfume.... it has no taste of the distillation....
    it is odorless,
It is for my mouth forever.... I am in love with it,
I will go to the bank by the wood and become undisguised and naked,
I am mad for it to be in contact with me.

Walt's recurrent obsessions with health and nakedness are often, as here, distracting, and sometimes risible. Clothed or not, the self rejoices in the air, the simple air, and the vitality it makes possible:

> The smoke of my own breath,
> Echos, ripples, and buzzed whispers.... loveroot, silkthread, crotch and
>   vine,
> My respiration and inspiration.... the beating of my heart.... the passing
>   of blood and air through my lungs,
> The sniff of green leaves and dry leaves, and of the shore and darkcolored
>   sea-rocks, and of hay in the barn,
> The sound of the belched words of my own voice.... words loosed to the
>   eddies of the wind,
> [...] the song of me rising from bed and meeting the sun.

The self exercises presence, to the common grass and air, to itself. Both presence and the present—"There was never any more inception than there is now [...] Nor any more heaven or hell than there is now"—orient the self toward the future. (Hegel provides the linguistic frame for Walt's insight but is not, as the last sentence indicates, its source.)

> Urge and urge and urge,
> Always the procreant urge of the world.

> Out of the dimness opposite equals advance.... Always substance and
>   increase,
> Always a knit of identity.... always distinction.... always a breed of life.

> To elaborate is no avail.... Learned and unlearned feel that it is so. (28)

"I and this mystery"—the mystery of self, situated in time and place and present to itself—"I and this mystery here I stand":

> Clear and sweet is my soul.... and clear and sweet is all that is not my soul.

> Lack one lacks both.... and the unseen is proved by the seen,
> Till that becomes unseen and receives proof in its turn. (29)

Internal to Walt's soul is all that is not itself; exclusion would empty his soul's existence. "I am satisfied.... I see, dance, laugh, sing; / As God comes a loving bedfellow and sleeps at my side," who, when he departs, "leaves for me baskets [...] bulging the house with their plenty." Walt will not "scream at my eyes" that they should calculate the contents' market value but will continue to gaze "after and down the road" at the one who left "close on the peep of the day."

Walt will not be distracted by questions of the curious, or even

The real or fancied indifference of some man or woman I love,
The sickness of one of my folks—or of myself.... or lack or loss of money
    .... or depressions or exaltations,
These come to me days and nights and go from me again,
But they are not the Me myself. (29–30)

All mockings and arguments are in the past; now, "I witness and wait."

Walt-witnesses, waits, and remembers. He believes, he says, in his soul, experienced though unseen; and "the other I am must not abase itself to you, / And you must not be abased to the other." What he remembers is this: experiencing the union of self and soul, which he expresses through the metaphor of oral intercourse, and the awareness to which that union led. "Loafe with me on the grass.... loose the stop from your throat," he says, "Not words, not music or rhyme I want.... not custom or lecture, not even the best, / Only the lull I like, the hum of your valved voice."

I mind how we lay in June, such a transparent summer morning;
You settled your head athwart my hips and gently turned over upon me,
And parted the shirt from my bosom-bone, and plunged your tongue to my
    barestript heart,
And reached till you felt my beard, and reached till you held my feet.

Swiftly arose and spread around me the peace and joy and knowledge that
    pass all the art and argument of the earth;
And I know that the hand of God is the elderhand of my own [...] (30–31)

It is tempting, in an age when the confessional poetry of Robert Lowell and Sylvia Plath is so greatly admired, to center on autobiographical questions: is this heterosexual? homosexual? is it based on an actual, not an imagined event, with the soul an unnamed lover? I assume that Whitman's imagination is here remembering and re-creating an act of homosexual love, but that is beside the point I wish to make: in an erotic transport, Walt experiences the ensouled self and in peace and joy now perceives

[...] that the hand of God is the elderhand of my own,
And I know that the spirit of God is the eldest brother of my own,
And that all the men ever born are also my brothers.... and the women
    my sisters and lovers
And that a kelson of the creation is love;
And limitless are leaves stiff or drooping in the fields,
And brown ants in the little wells beneath them,
And mossy scabs of the wormfence, and heaped stones, and elder and
    mullen and pokeweed.

Walt's self, now integrated, experiences a divine presence that relates it intimately to humankind and the realization of the binding power of love, which embraces the trees and ants, the moss and weeds—in other words, the cosmos from the immanent God to the disregarded elements of life.

Recurrent throughout the rest of "Song of Myself" are epiphanic images that disclose the mystery—and the incalculable worth—of each element of the cosmos. The common grass is a symbol for them all:

A child said, What is the grass? fetching it to me with full hands.
How could I answer the child.... I do not know what it is any more than he.

Walt guesses. The grass may represent his "disposition, out of hopeful green stuff woven." Or may be "itself a child.... the produced babe of the vegetation." Or—"Growing among black folks as among white, / Kanuck, Tuckahoe, Congressman, Cuff"—it may be "a uniform hieroglyphic" bespeaking the singleness of humankind. It may be all those things, and more; "[...] now it seems to me the beautiful uncut hair of graves," the symbol of unity through time, and of death's meaningfulness:

Tenderly will I use you curling grass,
It may be you transpire from the breasts of young men,
It may be if I had known them I would have loved them,
It may be you are from old people and from women, and from offspring
    taken soon out of their mothers' laps,
And here you are the mother's laps.

This grass, "dark to be from the white heads of old mothers, / Darker than the colorless beards of old men, / Dark to come from under the faint red roofs of mouths," is "so many uttering tongues," (32) speaking what the dead are, what they have become:

They are alive and well somewhere;
The smallest sprout shows there is really no death,
And if there ever was it led forward life [....]

All goes onward and outward.... and nothing collapses,
And to die is different from what any one supposed, and luckier.

Whitman, biographers have pointed out, seems to have feared death mightily. Walt, perhaps because his self has already died once through ensoulment, conceives it as leading forward life; a philosopher distinguishing Walt from Heidegger, might say that he sees the human person as a being-for-life, a life at whose end "nothing collapses" and all is explosively good— not the self, but part of the self:

I pass death with the dying, and birth with the new-washed babe.... and
    am not contained between my hat and my boots,
And peruse manifold objects, no two alike, and every one good,
The earth good, and the stars good, and their adjuncts all good.

As "the mate and companion of people, all just as immortal and fathomless as myself" (33),
    Walt rejects no one:

For me all that have been boys and love women,
For me the man that is proud and knows how it feels to be slighted,
For me the sweetheart and the old maid.... for me mothers and the mothers
    of mothers,
For me lips that have smiled, eyes that have shed tears [....]

When next he asks, "Who need be afraid of the merge?" he has entered treacherous terrain. "Undrape," he cries, ".... you are not guilty to me, nor stale nor discarded [....]" He can "see through the broadcloth and gingham"; he is "[...] acquisitive, tireless.... and can never be shaken away." At this point in the poem, there is no need to dread "the merge"—the process by which others may enter and touch the heart of one's being. Later, Walt himself is its victim. Yet without merging in the sense that Whitman uses it—Buber's I-thou is a possible analogy—the self is closed off. Walt's self is indiscriminate in its embrace:

The little one sleeps in its cradle,
I lift the gauze and look a long time, and silently brush away flies with my
   hand.

The youngster and the redfaced girl turn aside up the bushy hill,
I peeringly view them from the top.

The suicide sprawls on the bloody floor of the bedroom.
It is so.... I witnessed the corpse.... there the pistol had fallen.

Thus begins one of the catalogues, close to random in their order, that fill
Whitman's poetry. Here, Walt recalls in all its wondrous and overwhelming
variety what the open self admits as *thou*. The city:

The blab of the pave.... the tires of carts and sluff of bootsoles and talk of
   promenaders,
The heavy omnibus, the driver with his interrogating thumb, the clank of
   the shod horses on the granite floor,
The carnival of sleighs, the clinking and shouted jokes and pelts of
   snowballs;
The hurrahs for popular favorites.... the fury of roused mobs,
The flap of the curtained litter—the sick man inside [....]
The impassive stones that receive and return so many echoes,
The souls moving along.... are they invisible while the least atom of the
   stones is visible? (33–34)

The country:

The big doors of the country-barn stand open and ready,
The dried grass of the harvest-time loads the slow-drawn wagon,
The clear light plays on the brown gray and green intertinged,
The armfuls are packed to the sagging mow:
I am there.... I help....

Walt encounters a runaway slave, who "came to my house and stopped
outside":

Through the swung half-door of the kitchen I saw him limpsey and weak,
And went where he sat on a log, and led him in and assured him,
And brought water and filled a tub for his sweated body and bruised feet
   [....] (35)

He experiences the gently erotic fantasy of a young woman—"Twentyeight years of womanly life, and all so lonesome" (36)—as she watches from behind the window blinds, young men, one for each of her years, swimming close to the shore. She pictures herself joining them:

> Dancing and laughing along the beach came the twenty-ninth bather,
> The rest did not see her, but she saw them and loved them.

> The beards of the young men glistened with wet, it ran from their long hair,
> Little streams passed all over their bodies.

> An unseen hand also passed over their bodies,
> It descended tremblingly from their temples and ribs.

And the young men "do not know who puffs and declines with pendant and bending arch."

Walt, let me recall, is not Whitman in my reading, but Whitman's possible and often enough realized self. The young woman's fantasy may indeed, as some have suggested, derive ultimately from Whitman's putative desire for anonymous sex. Certainly, Whitman shared prejudices against blacks common among Northern whites of his day (a fact made all the less forgivable by his awareness of how he might regard them, how the self of "Song of Myself"—and, later, "I Sing the Body Electric"—did regard them). Whatever the bare facts, Whitman imagines through Walt possibilities—a woman's erotic moment, a white man's moral opportunity to wash a black man's feet—that bring the future into the present.

Walt turns now to the recollection of workers, He delights in the butcher-boy's street dance, "his shuffle and breakdown," and the rhythmic cooperation of blacksmiths ringing an anvil:

> The lithe sheer of their waists plays even with their massive arms,
> Overhand the hammers roll–overhand so slow–overhand so sure,
> They do not hasten, each man hits in his place. (37)

He admires the mastery of the teamster who "holds firmly the reins of his four horses":

> The negro that drives the huge dray of the stoneyard.... steady and tall he
>   stands poised on one leg on the stringpiece [...]
> His glance is calm and commanding.... he tosses the slouch of his hat
>   away from his forehead,
> The sun falls on his crispy hair and moustache.... falls on the black of his
>   polished and perfect limbs.

Walt's self is "the caresser of life wherever moving:" a team of oxen ("What is that you express in your eyes?"); the wood-drake and wood-duck which, frightened by his tread, "rise together [...] slowly circle around. / .... I believe in those winged purposes [....]"; the wild gander's "Ya-honk!" which "The pert may suppose [is] meaningless, but I listen closer, / I find its purpose and place up there toward the November sky." Meaning animates living creation if the self is present to it, accepts union with it: "What is commonest and cheapest and nearest and easiest is Me." The possible self rejects otherness through opposition.

Whitman's was, to borrow the aesthetic theologian John Dixon's term, a horizontal imagination, polar to the vertical, hierarchical imagination dominant in Western culture. (Dixon notes that the Reformation belief in the priesthood of all believers was the product of the horizontal imagination, but as decades passed, the pulpit rose higher and higher, creating in Protestant church architecture a visual hierarchy that implicitly denied the belief.) The horizontal imagination is democratic; it prizes each reality for what it is, not for the height of the step it occupies on the stairway to the heavens. When Walt proclaims "Every kind for itself and its own [....]" he is not insisting on the superiority of human to beast but stating his primary affinity with the human. In "Song of Myself," we next find a catalog more than three pages long in which Walt through anamnesis summons up in wild disorder epiphanic images, mostly one to a line, of the human: a prostitute "draggles her shawl," the "President holds a cabinet council [...] surrounded by the great secretaries," matrons walk on the piazza arms entwined, the "crew of the fish-smack pack repeated layers of halibut in the hold." No person is better than the others, none worse; all are there—and valued. They "tend inward" to Walt and he outward to them:

> The pure contralto sings in the organ loft,
> The carpenter dresses his plank.... the tongue of his foreplane whistles its
>   wild ascending lisp,
> The married and unmarried children ride home to their thanksgiving dinner,
> The pilot seizes the king-pin, he heaves down with a strong arm [....]
> The spinning-girl retreats and advances to the hum of the big wheel,
> The farmer stops by the bars of a Sunday and looks at the oats and rye,
> The lunatic is carried at last to the asylum a confirmed case,
> He will never sleep any more as he did in the cot in his mother's bedroom
>   [....]
> The deckhands make fast the steamboat, the plank is thrown for the
>   shoregoing passengers,
> The young sister holds out the skein, the elder sister winds it off in a ball
>   and stops now and then for the knots [....]

Patriarchs sit at supper with sons and grandsons and great grandsons
    around them,
In walls of adobe, in canvass tents, rest hunters and trappers after their day's
    sport,
The city sleeps and the country sleeps,
The living sleep for their time...the dead sleep for their time,
The old husband sleeps by his wife and the young husband sleeps by his
    wife;
And these one and all tend inward to me, and I tend outward to them,
And such as it is to be of these more or less I am. (39–42)

The last line offers a useful ambiguity: "to be of these" can mean both "to
belong to these" and "to be made up of these." That ambiguity persists:

I am of old and young, of the foolish as much as the wise,
Regardless of others, ever regardful of others,
Maternal as well as paternal, a child as well as a man [....]

Walt is of "the great nation, the nation of many of many nations" and is

Of every hue and trade and rank, of every caste and religion,
Not merely of the New World but of Africa Europe or Asia.... a wandering
    savage,
A farmer, mechanic, or artist.... a gentleman, sailor, lover or quaker,
A prisoner, fancy-man, rowdy, lawyer, physician or priest. (43)

"I resist anything better than my own diversity [....]" The diversity springs
from the inward and outward movements of the relational self, which is "at
home" with and "comrade of" the human. To this Walt adds the claim,
which might justly have terrified Whitman in later years ("Only Emily
Dickinson was as formidably alone" (143), Paul Zweig says in commenting
on Whitman's lack of literary friendships):

These are the thoughts of all men in all ages and lands, they are not original
    with me,
If they are not yours as much as mine they are nothing or next to nothing
    [....]

    I find—others do not—an undertone of anxiety in the lines that follow;
there is a rush of recapitulation and a braggadocio that betrays unsureness.
These thoughts, Walt says, like the grass and air, are common; they are for
the illiterate and the learned, for the powerful and the powerless, for the

victors and the vanquished, and he feels at one with them all. His thoughts are like a "meal pleasantly set [...] meat and drink for natural hunger" (44), and "like the press of a bashful hand." He is not trying to astonish any more than the daylight does. "Who goes there!" he asks, "hankering, gross, mystical nude?" (45). He does not echo the "snivel" that "life is a suck and a sell." Instead of whimpering, he cocks his hat as he pleases. Shall he pray? There's no need, for he has "found no sweeter fat than sticks" to his own bones. He knows that he is "solid and sound," that he is deathless and— august–"I do not trouble my spirit to vindicate itself or be understood [....]" (46). He does not care whether he is acknowledged today or in a thousand years, since "One world is aware, and by far the largest to me, and that is myself [....]" Walt laughs at "what you call dissolution." And I am convinced that he has been weeping—in loneliness. He reminds me of Teilhard de Chardin, as he searched fruitlessly for permission from his superiors to publish *The Phenomenon of Man*, writing to his brother that "it is here in Rome that we find the Christic pole of the earth" (299). The willfulness is sad.

Now the tone changes, growing peaceful:

I am the poet of the body,
And I am the poet of the soul.

The pleasures of heaven are with me, and the pains of hell are with me,
The first I graft and increase upon myself.... the latter I translate into a
    new tongue.

I am the poet of the woman the same as the man,
And I say it is as great to be a woman as to be a man [...]

No longer frenetic, in the rhythms of irenic eros, Walt now "walks with the tender and growing night":

Press close barebosomed night! Press close magnetic nourishing night!
Night of south winds! Night of the large few stars!
Still nodding night! Mad naked summer night! (47)

He is lover to the earth "of the slumbering and liquid trees [....] of the mountains misty-topt [....] of the vitreous pour of the full moon just tinged with blue!" And to the sea: "Cushion me soft.... rock me in billowy drowse [....] I am integral with you." (48). And they are lovers to him, and any humans who know them.

Walt Whitman, an American, one of the roughts, a kosmos,
Disorderly fleshy and sensual.... eating drinking and breeding,
No sentimentalist.... no stander above men and women or apart from
    them.... no more modest than immodest. (50)

Walt has just praised "materialism" and the "exact demonstration" of positive
science, which discloses facts which "are useful and real." But "they are not
my dwelling.... I enter by them to an area of the dwelling" (49). His is the
materialism of life. As "one of the roughts," he is free from the laws of polite
society which at the time may have been ready to acknowledge scientific facts
about the body but despised its carnality. He is a fleshly "kosmos" who would
speak for all those voices that are dumb—"the interminable generations of
slaves [...] of prostitutes and deformed persons [...] of the diseased and the
despairing [....] of the threads that connect the stars—and of wombs and of
the fatherstuff [...] of the rights of them the others are down upon [...]" (50)

Whoever degrades another degrades me.... and whatever is done or said
    returns at last to me,
And whatever I do or say I also return.

Through Walt, "forbidden voices" will be heard. He moves from the visually
incongruous ideal of keeping "as delicate around the bowels as around the
head and heart" (51) to celebration of his body—"translucent mould of me."
If he worships anything,

Breast that presses against other breasts it shall be you,
My brain it shall be your occult convolutions,
Root of washed sweet-flag, timorous pond-snipe, nest of guarded duplicate
    eggs, it shall be you,
Mixed tussled hair of head and beard and brawn it shall be you [...]
Hands I have taken, face I have kissed, mortal I have ever touched, it shall
    be you.

The last line, in which bodies truly touched become integral to the bodyself
that Walt worships, diminishes the autoeroticism for which this passage has
been praised and blamed.

Walt turns from "the flesh and its appetites" to the "miracles" of
seeing, hearing, and feeling. The tension grows when he comes to hearing:
"Speech is the twin of my vision" and "provokes me forever, / It says
sarcastically, Walt, you understand enough.... why don't you let it out then?"
(53) Not all things can be articulated—buds wait "in gloom protected by

frost," and some of what he knows he must now refuse to speech. "Writing and talking do not prove me,"

> I think I will do nothing for a long time but listen,
> And accrue what I hear into myself ... and let sounds contribute toward me.

And he hears "the bravura of birds.... the bustle of growing wheat.... gossip of flames [....] the recitative of fish-pedlars and fruit-pedlars...the loud laugh of workpeople at their meals [....]" He hears "the violincello or man's hearts' complaint, / And hear the keyed cornet or else the echo of sunset." The opera's music plunges him to "the farthest down horror" and raises him up "again to feel the puzzle of puzzles, / And that we call Being" (55).

And what is being? "If nothing lay more developed," Walt answers, "the quahaug and its callous shell were enough." Unlike the clam,

> I have instant conductors all over me whether I pass or stop,
> They seize every object and lead it harmlessly through me.
> I merely stir, press, feel with my fingers and am happy,
> To touch my person to some one else's is about as much as I can stand.

When Walt for the second time meditates on touch, there is nothing of the unitive touch of that "transparent summer morning." Touch, "quivering me to a new identity," is nightmare:

> My flesh and blood playing out lightning, to strike what is hardly different
>   from myself [...]
> Immodestly sliding the fellow-sense away,
> They bribed to swap off with touch, and go and graze at the edges of me
>   [...]
> Fetching the rest of the herd around to enjoy them awhile,
> Then all uniting to stand on a headland and worry me.
>
> The sentries desert every other part of me,
> They have left me helpless to a red marauder [....]
> I am given up by traitors;
> I talk wildly.... I have lost my wits.... I and nobody else am the greatest
>   traitor,
> I went myself first to the headland [....] (55–56)

Sensitivity to touch permeates Whitman's poetry, as does the desire to "merge"—to accept unity with all that is not himself. The clam with its shell is miracle enough, but evolution has brought the human into being. Walt's open self, with its "instant conductors" develops out of trust in the not-self it allows to become part of it. And, inevitably, that trust will meet betrayal by "prurient provokers [...] / Behaving licentious toward me" (55); touch becomes invasion. Yet:

> All truths wait in all things,
> They neither hasten their own delivery nor resist it,
> They do not need the obstetric forceps of the surgeon,
> The insignificant is as big to me as any,
> What is less or more than a touch? (56)

Through touch Walt may suffer betrayal, but through touch, especially through the images brought forth by memory and imagination, the delight of the cosmos enters the self. And so, he can say,

> I believe a leaf of grass is no less than the journeywork of the stars,
> And the pismire is equally perfect, and a grain of sand and the egg of a wren,
>   [....]
> And the narrowest hinge of my hand puts to scorn all machinery,
> And the cow crunching with depressed head surpasses any statue, [...]
> And I could come every afternoon of my life to look at the farmer's girl
>   boiling her iron tea-kettle and baking shortcake.

Through imagination that seeks all and lets all in, Walt is "afoot with my vision," without "ties and ballasts." He is

> By the city's quadrangular houses.... in log-huts, or camping with
>   lumbermen, [....]
> Where the black bear is searching for roots or honey.... where the beaver
>   pats the mud with his paddle-tail; [...]
> Over the sharp-peaked farmhouse with its scalloped scum and slender
>   shoots from the gutters,
> Over the western persimmon.... over the longleaved corn and the delicate
>   blueflowered flax; [...]
> Where the cheese-cloth hangs in the kitchen, and andirons straddle the
>   heart-slab, and cobwebs fall in festoons from the rafters;
> Where triphammers crash.... where the press is whirling its cylinders; [...]
> Approaching Manhattan, up by the long-stretching island,
> Under Niagara, the cataract falling like a veil [...]
> Through the salt-lick or orange glade.... or under conical firs;

Through the gymnasium.... through the curtained saloon.... through the
    office or public hall [...]
Speeding with tailed meteors.... throwing fire-balls like the rest,
Carrying the crescent child that carries its own full mother in its belly;
Storming enjoying planning loving cautioning,
Backing and filling, appearing and disappearing,
I tread day and night such roads. (59–63)

Walt's identification through imagination extends to the heroic
suffering of "The mother condemned for a witch and burnt with dry wood,
and her children gazing on" (65), "The hounded slave that flags in the race
and leans by the fence, blowing and covered with sweat," "[...] the mashed
fireman with breastbone broken...." He does "not ask the wounded person
how he feels.... I myself become the wounded person." He experiences
through imagination and recounts the story of the wounds and deaths
suffered at the Alamo and during the sea-battle between the British *Serapis*
and John Paul Jones's *Bon Homme Richard*. "I become any presence of
humanity here" (70).

Walt has "heard what was said of the universe"—what was said of
Kronos and Zeus, "of Osiris and Isis and Belus and Brahma and Adonai" (74)
and will limn them all, "In my portfolio placing Manito loose, and Allah on
a leaf, and the crucifix engraved [....]" but discovers "as much or more in a
framer framing a house, / Putting higher claims for him there with his
rolled-up sleeves, driving the mallet and chisel." The Egyptians may have
divinized the bull and held the scarab an ikon of the sun god, but the natural
is of more account than the supernatural, with

The bull and the bug never worshipped half enough,
Dung and dirt more admirable than was dreamed.

Walt's "Magnifying and applying" does not turn the bull and the bug
into gods; by letting them remain themselves in all their complex and
ultimately cosmic significance, he allows their sacred truths to emerge. It is
not a question of despising the supernatural; his faith, Walt says, is the
"greatest of faiths," because it "encloses all worship ancient and modern"
(77), but is also "the least of faiths," because it centers on what is there, the
thing itself in all its interrelationships. Each man and woman, like Walt, can

perceive that "Immense have been the preparations for me, / Faithful and friendly the arms that have helped me. [....] All forces have been steadily employed to complete and delight me, / Now I stand on this spot with my soul" (80).

> I have said that the soul is not more than the body,
> And I have said that the body is not more than the soul,
> And nothing, not God, is greater to one than one's-self is,
> And whoever walks a furlong without sympathy walks to his own funeral,
>   dressed in his shroud,
> And I or you pocketless of a dime may purchase the pick of the earth,
> And to glance with an eye or show a bean in its pod confounds the learning
>   of all time,
> And there is no trade or employment but the young man following it may
>   become a hero,
> And there is no object so soft but it makes a hub for the wheeled universe,
> And any man or woman shall stand cool and supercilious before a million
>   universes. (84–85)

There is no need to be "curious" about God; traces of the divine are everywhere:

> I see something of God each hour of the twenty-four, and each moment then,
> In the faces of men and women I see God, and in my own face in the glass [....]

Death and the "bitter hug of mortality" leave Walt unalarmed for death is another birth:

> And as to you corpse I think you are good manure, but that does not offend me,
> I smell the white roses sweetscented and growing,
> I reach to the leafy lips.... I reach to the polished breasts of melons.(86)

And "There is that in me.... I do not know what it is.... [....] it is without a name.... it is a word unsaid:

> Do you see O my brothers and sisters?
> It is not chaos or death.... it is form and union and plan.... it is eternal
>   life.... it is happiness.(87)

If this seems to contradict what he has said, "Very well then.... I contradict myself; / I am large.... I contain multitudes."

"The last scud of day [...] coaxes me to the vapor and the dusk," Walt says to the reader:

> I bequeath myself to the dirt to grow from the grass I love,
> If you want me again look for me under your bootsoles. [....]
> Failing to fetch me at first keep encouraged,
> Missing me one place search another,
> I stop some where waiting for you.

"Song of Myself" is the story-song of the possible American self, Walt's and own and that of his compatriots. For religious believers, the poem will not be, as it was for Whitman, their foundational story—the sacred vision through which creation is understood. My foundational story—incarnation, teaching and healing, suffering and death, resurrection, communion within God and with God (through community as well as alone) and among the panoply of God's creation—conditions how I have read Whitman's poem and sets limits on the extent to which I can participate in it with willing belief. The same will and should be true for others who bring to Whitman's text their own foundational stories.

Stories do not preclude one another, however Graham Greene's *Brighton Rock*, which performed a mythic role in my life when I was twenty, did not forestall my simultaneously profiting from Jane Austen's wisdom. When I outgrew the nearly manichean dilemma of *Brighton Rock* and, briefly, found Kafka's myth a key to understanding, I had no need to reject Greene. Without lessening my ability to profit from the creation stories of the Seven Days and the Gospel of John, the religious convergence that marks our day has enabled me to discover contrary yet valid meanings in the Rig Veda's Hymn of Creation. Among the more salubrious demands of our age may be its requirement that we participate in sacred stories not our own. Our fundamental stories now remain incomplete unless we confront them with the fundamental stories of others, including the stories of those who like Whitman embrace all religions and the stories of those who embrace none.

Leaves of Grass, more than any of the other seminal works published during the half–decade of 1850–1855, addresses America as a geographical and cultural totality in the process of self-creation. The Union was threatened; Whitman unity present. Greed was manifest; he supposes heroes "pocketless of a dime" and originates delight in the common grass and air. American individualism was raw; he raises egocentricity to impossible heights on the one hand and affirms the inherently relational nature of the self on the other. Democracy was, given the depredations of slavery and the deprivations of women, unrealized; he imagines equality of dignity and respect. He loves and finds hope in both city and countryside.

The angel, however, is in the details, what Zweig calls "the unvarnished, shaggy particulars of the everyday world." Whitman perceives, Zweig says, "a sexual prodding from within life to produce more and better life" (137–137). In "Song of Myself," Walt witnesses the particulars and waits, observing with ear and touch as well as eye—trusting in the inner capacity of each thing to make itself new. One essential element is patience. Those who loiter instead of rushing by see the "butcher-boy [put] off his killing clothes" and dance "his shuffle and breakdown" (36). Another is compassion, which Walt exercises without the pity that reduces sufferers to their pain, whether it is the "child that peeped in at the door and then drew back and was never seen again" or a man "in the poorhouse tubercled by rum" (78). But the most important is trust. To readers, Walt says:

> [...] each man and woman of you 1 lead upon a knoll,
> My left hand hooks you round the waist,
> My right hand points to landscapes of continents, and a plain public road.
>
> Not I, not any one else can travel that road for you,
> You must travel it for yourself. (82)

References

Dixon, John W. "Hierarchy and Laity." *Christian Century*, October 25,1967, 1353–58.

Jordan, June, *Passion: New Poems, 1977–1980*. Boston: Beacon Press, 1980.

Randall, Dudley, ed. *The Black Poets*. New York: Bantam Books, 1971.

Teilhard de Chardin, Pierre. *Letters from a Traveller*. New York: Harper & Brothers, 1962.

Whitman, Walt. *Complete Poetry and Collected Prose*, selected by Justin Kaplan. New York: Library of America, 1982.

Zweig, Paul. *Walt Whitman: The Making of the Poet*. New York: Basic Books, 1984.

DANA PHILLIPS

Whitman and Genre: The Dialogic in "Song of Myself"

I: "FUSION," LITERATURE, AND OTHER DISCOURSES

In the preface to the first edition of *Leaves of Grass*, Whitman attributes to the poet a special character: only the poet possesses all the traits which define Americans as a people. This kind of representative character is also basic to present-day popular culture, which deploys images of the famous as metonymic representations of (all) value: the famous thus seem to enjoy a greater degree of personhood than the rest of us do. They alone are "personalities." That Whitman's 1855 portrait of the bardic personality should seem congruent with the values of contemporary popular culture reveals one of the ironies of his canonization as a great poet: the definition of his work as "literature" obscures the ways in which it aspires to be something other than an object of academic study. Whitman himself thought that his poetry ought to have popular appeal of a sort not unlike that which, since his day, has been enjoyed by—for example—the western and the detective story. These are the kinds of texts likely to have been carried around in the hip pockets of workingmen's jeans, one of the ideal sites in which Whitman would have placed copies of his *Leaves*.

Recently, Whitman's relationship to the popular has been reinterpreted by David S. Reynolds, in whose book on the relationship of the American

From *Arizona Quarterly*, vol. 50, no. 3 (Autumn 1994). © 1994 by the Arizona Board of Regents.

Renaissance to popular culture—*Beneath the American Renaissane*—the poet figures centrally. The new and more socially-inclusive character of Whitman's poetry has often been cited as contributing to his greatness. Inclusiveness is the chief ideological imperative of his aesthetic, as well as one of the necessities of his celebrity, of his being the American bard, which many of Whitman's readers—following the poet's own suggestions—have identified with his very being. Reynolds, however, argues that Whitman's inclusiveness is not simply a matter of personal character and genius: he contends that the poet was indebted to popular culture as a source for much of what critics and scholars have long regarded as a product of Whitman's uncanny, intuitive identification with everyday life. Reynolds, like many others, still calls Whitman "the greatest poetic innovator of nineteenth-century America," but he also demonstrates that the poet "was nurtured by a popular culture that carried the seeds of new thematic and stylistic rebelliousness," and that Whitman "moved from this appreciation to a literary performance that was at once scathingly subversive and individualistically reconstructive." But while Reynolds convincingly demonstrates Whitman's ties to reform literature (temperance pamphlets, for example) and other popular genres, he conceives of these ties unilaterally (literary influence only flows in one direction, from the popular to the more universal), because he is dedicated to preserving Whitman's status as a great American poet and high-cultural icon. Whitman may include popular culture, but popular culture does not include him.

Reynolds argues that the social survey attempted in some of the catalogs in the *Leaves* has its roots in sources like the dime novel, or the sensationalist literature of urban "mysteries," texts which purported to offer their readers exciting glimpses behind the facades of the official culture, where sordid sexual relationships were conducted, and crime was rampant. Many of the more daring scenes in Whitman's poetry are, according to Reynolds, analogous to similar scenes in the subversive, morally ambiguous literature of popular culture. The difference is that Whitman has taken such popular materials and given them "universal" value. Universality remains an important value for Reynolds, and he often reiterates the essential difference between "literary" texts and culturally significant, but ephemeral popular texts: "The distinguishing quality of the literary text is not radical subversiveness but unique suggestiveness and great reconstructive power" (10). This is a conservative argument, whether Reynolds acknowledges its conservatism or not (he doesn't), in that it substitutes reconstruction as a term of value in place of subversion (or its more political synonym, revolution). It is no surprise, then, that Beneath the American Renaissance preserves the established authors and rankings of canonical nineteenth-century American literature (Emerson, Thoreau, Hawthorne, Melville, Whitman, Dickinson). Reynolds's project is a recuperative exercise, which makes the classic American text's authority appear more deeply ingrained than ever. It emerges as *more* "universal" precisely to the *greater* extent to which it now can be seen to have refined popular representations in its vital literary core.

Reynolds does not take seriously his own characterization of popular culture as "subversive," if he imagines that Whitman can make use of its materials without their also subverting *Leaves of Grass*. His limited appreciation of the subversiveness of popular culture is especially odd, given his citation of Bakhtin's notion of "dialogism" in support of his case for Whitman's debt to popular sources. Reynolds writes: "I trust that we are leaving the period of hermetic close readings, based on the myth of textual autonomy, and are entering the era of reconstructive close readings, based on the reality of socioliterary dialogism" (564). He also writes that Whitman's poetry "is best understood as an arena for the confrontation of varied, sometimes contradictory cultural forces whose *creative fusion* is Whitman's poetic gift to a society he perceived as rotten and strife-ridden" (332, my emphasis). The metaphor of "fusion" is a favorite term of his argument, and Reynolds' use of it suggests that he believes American Renaissance writers to have created the sort of seamless verbal artifacts whose lack of contradiction is their most signal quality. The great American writers have, according to Reynolds, well-wrought the same materials which had been heedlessly and recklessly wrought by the popular culture of the time.

It appears, then, that in his reading of Whitman's work (as well as in the account he offers of the American Renaissance generally), Reynolds employs a double standard—which is *not* the same as a dialogic one—as a basic critical apparatus. On the one hand, the literature of reform and sensationalism which Whitman's poetry supposedly incorporates is described in terms of its social significance: it is a "social text" (7); on the other hand, *Leaves of Grass* is described in terms of its aesthetic significance: it is an "imaginative text" (7). The "social text" is then found wanting because it is not aesthetically polished ("imaginative"), while the "imaginative text" is judged to be superior because it is both aesthetically polished (i.e., it answers to the standard which it establishes), *and* it has the culturally plenary quality of the "social text," by virtue of its having engulfed the "social text" like a grouper swallowing an anchovy. This logic of the literary food chain informs the argument of *Beneath the American Renaissance*, where big fish like Whitman and Melville are portrayed snapping up cultural small fry and converting them, flesh and bone, into Art.

Readers familiar with Bakhtin will recognize that this valorization of "fusion" over subversion runs very much counter to the spirit of the dialogic. For Reynolds to avail himself of the concept of "dialogism" is misleading, and moreover, would seem to disable the argument he wants to make. Dialogism relies on a model of subversive speech as precisely that which *cannot* be contained, much less "reconstructed." To enlist Bakhtin's support in an argument for "literariness" as a quality possessed by only a few select texts is self-defeating. Bakhtin understands the modern literary universe to be radically unbounded, and he describes the virtual death of poetry—that most bound of literary forms—as a living genre.[2] Poetry, Bakhtin argues, survives only as a hybrid of the generically dominant novel, as a result of a process of formal devolution which he labels "novelization."

Bakhtin describes a pattern of omnivorous feeding and being fed upon operating between genres under the aegis of "the novel" reconceived as a mode of literary history (and not necessarily as one particular kind of text, "the novel" as we know it casually, as readers of books called "novels"). Reynolds ignores the fact that when Bakhtin offers his theories of dialogue and the novel, he is not thinking only of specific geniuses (like Rabelais or Dostoevsky or Cervantes), but of genres: Reynolds represents "dialogue" as something of which only great poets are capable, while for Bakhtin, the opposite is more the case. "Dialogue" is inherent in the materials of folk culture: folk materials, Bakhtin argues, do not appear in literature for the sake of having "literariness" conferred upon them: "Extraliterary genres (the everyday genres, for example) are incorporated into the novel not in order to 'ennoble' them, to 'literarize' them, but for the sake of their very extraliterariness, for the sake of their potential for introducing nonliterary language (or even dialects) into the novel" ("Discourse in the Novel" 411). A novelized *Leaves of Grass* therefore becomes *more* like its sources, not less.[3]

That it is "heteroglossic" or "dialogic," therefore, cannot be cited as one of the virtues of Whitman's work (or anyone else's) if one means thereby to suggest that his work is "major," in that it somehow rises above its cultural milieu, or "the mire of popular humor," as Reynolds calls it more than once (see *Beneath the American Renaissance* 513, 515). To put the same point another way: one has to be willing to surrender much of the status of *Leaves of Grass* as "poetry" in order to make it available for analysis based on a Bakhtinian concept of dialogue. That is, one has to discount or bracket the *Leaves'* fitful ambition to be a monologue of the sort Bakhtin argues is definitive of poetry as a genre: "a self-sufficient and closed authorial monologue, one that presumes only passive listeners beyond its own boundaries" ("Discourse" 274). Although there are instances in Whitman's poetry where he appears to yield to the forces of "novelization," or to engage in dialogue, as Reynolds has suggested, I want in the remainder of this essay to demonstrate how this appearance of literary and cultural latitude often proves to be a false one.

But first it will be necessary to say more about genre and the way in which Whitman and his contemporaries thought of it. For Whitman, poetry—especially lyric poetry, or "song," as he calls it—can (in theory, at least) squelch the protests of illogic made against it by rationality, by containing rationality as just one moment of its own ineluctable progress. Poetry can forego the philosophical complications of the dialectic: it can skip, or glide over, the middle term, the actually "dialectical" term, of antithesis. Whitman fancied himself a Hegelian; however, his poetry is *not* dialectical, because it leaps immediately to synthesis, to the great moment of *Aufhebung*—of inclusiveness.[4] This is one implication of those famous lines from "Song of Myself": "Do I contradict myself? / Very well then.... I contradict myself; / I am large.... I contain multitudes."[5] This transcendental quality may be essential to the generic character of poetry itself—it is certainly not uniquely a feature of *Leaves of Grass*. If, as Bakhtin suggests in *The Dialogic Imagination*, genre is "a zone and a field of valorized perception" and a "mode for representing the world" ("Epic and Novel" 28), then poetry is that mode of representation which most authoritatively valorizes its own perceptions (as "dream visions," "epiphanies," transcendental enlargements of the self, or whatever), and which is most dependent on the (alleged) unity of its own language: on the fit of this language with the world (its own world) which it designates (using what Bakhtin calls the "authoritative word"). Given the reliance of Whitman's poetry on a strategy of inclusion or containment, the tendency of multiple forms of otherness to recur in the subject matter of "Song of Myself" might be viewed as a challenge to the poet's authority, as an unwelcome manifestation of what Bakhtin terms "the realities of heteroglossia" ("Discourse" 270). And as it happens, the manifestation of heteroglossic reality in this poem does produce a crucial aesthetic problem: a crisis of genre.[6]

Many American writers of the mid-nineteenth century were faced with the same problem, and the situation—to judge from the frequency of their calls for a national literary rebirth—seemed to them a bleak one. They tried a variety of strategies for coping with it, and the result of their efforts was to produce a (supposedly) national literature characterized by generic hybrids (*Walden, Moby-Dick, The Scarlet Letter*, the *Leaves*), texts of the sort described by Bakhtin as containing mixtures of at least "two social languages within the limits of a single utterance" ("Discourse" 358). Ironically, American writers echoed the inchoate society of the country, about which many of them were, as we know, unhappy, in the inchoate formal character and heteroglot content of their books.[7]

Rather than viewing this literary hybridization as a peculiarly American
liability, however, I would like to view the inability of these texts to achieve
closure as illustrative of the process of novelization or heteroglossia itself,
and to regard Whitman's work as exemplary of the effects of that process on
the American literary imagination. I do not want to regard the apparent
openness and undecidability of Whitman's text, nor that of American
literature generally, as an especial virtue, either, as Reynolds and other critics
have done (Perry Miller, for example, who argued a literary version of the
frontier thesis). From a cosmopolitan point of view like Bakhtin's, the literary
woes of Whitman and his compatriots were foretold: far from representing a
break in or an exception to world literary history, they demonstrate its
continuity.[8] From this dialogic perspective, the encounter with everyday life
which is indisputably a feature of Whitman's work can be seen as part of a
historical process which dates back, according to Bakhtin, to the (other,
original) Renaissance, and which can be traced, as a minor cultural tendency,
to an even earlier period: "Familiarization of the world through laughter and
popular speech is an extremely important and indispensable step in making
possible free, scientifically knowable and artistically realistic creativity in
European civilization" ("Epic and Novel" 23), from the time of its birth in
classical Greek culture.

Most importantly, I would like to call attention not to Whitman's
embrace of this historical tendency, but to the ways in which he resists it: to
the ways in which his poetry insists on the continued defamiliarization of the
world by reasserting, in moments sometimes specifically and strategically
figured as crises of utterance, its lyric containment, in what Bakhtin terms "a
self-sufficient and closed authorial monologue" ("Discourse" 274).[9]
Consider the following lines from "Song of Myself" (I quote the passage at
length in order to illustrate the dynamic interplay of a variety of discourses
in Whitman's poetry):

> The suicide sprawls on the bloody floor of the bedroom.
> It is so.... I witnessed the corpse.... there the pistol had
>   fallen.
> The blab of the pave.... the tires of carts and sluff of boot-
>   soles and talk of the promenaders,
> The heavy omnibus, the driver with his interrogating thumb,
>   the clank of the shod horses on the granite floor,
> The carnival of sleighs, the clinking and shouted jokes and
>   pelts of snowballs;
> The hurrahs for popular favorites.... the futy of roused
>   mobs,

> The flap of the curtained litter—the sick man inside, borne to
>   the hospital,
> The meeting of enemies, the sudden oath, the blows and fall,
> The excited crowd—the policeman with his star quickly
>   working his passage to the center of the crowd;
> The impassive stones that receive and return so many echoes,
> The souls moving along.... are they invisible while the least
>   atom of the stones is visible?
> What groans of overfed or half-starved who fall on the flags
>   sunstruck or in fits,
> What exclamations of women taken suddenly, who hurry
>   home and give birth to babes,
> What living and buried speech is always vibrating here....
>   what howls restrained by decorum,
> Arrests of criminals, slights, adulterous offers made, accep-
>   tance, rejections with convex lips,
> I mind them or the resonance of them.... I come again and
>   again.
>
> (*Collected Poetry and Prose* 33–34)

In this passage, a crisis of utterance is obscured by unspoken changes of tack, which move the description from one level of experience to another, more general and ultimately more universal level. Whitman's writing in this and similar passages could be said to entail the unmaking or "decomposition" of other forms of discourse, and their immediate recomposition as lyric. The suicide—as Reynolds would have us recognize—is the sort of climactic narrative moment one might encounter in a popular nineteenth-century melodrama, or in sensational journalism. But what does this scene have to do with a "song" of "myself"? How does this evidence of generic hybridization, of "heteroglossia" and the "dialogic," relate to the poetic project announced in the title Whitman eventually gave his poem?[10]

The lines which describe the suicide suggest (momentarily) that a certain mystery is being put to us for solution, and the lines which follow are preceded by a break, a white space, in the text, as if to signify a gap in a narrative; but the gap also marks—or rather, masks—a change of tack and subject matter: the subsequent lines describing a busy urban scene do nothing to help us solve the mystery of the suicide. Rather, they halt whatever questions we may have about it on our lips; their intended function may be to deepen the mystery, and keep us in a state of literary arousal. Even if it does mark an end to this one life, the suicide figures not as a vital link in a given sequence of historical events, but as yet another moment in a generalized life, no more and no less meaningful than the discrete moments in the lines that immediately follow. The suicide scene must therefore be read as a "lyric," and not a narrative moment. It is an *image*, and not an "event." "Whitman's use of it is the reverse of dialogic: the image of the sprawling suicide is taken out of the context of daily life. It is not a means to a thorough exploration of that context; it is not an opening onto a wider world, but—appropriately, perhaps—an anticipation of the coming poetic closure, of that moment when the cruel world is bid farewell so that its "resonance" may be savored.

The long verse paragraph which follows the suicide results from a much more thorough gleaning of a particular context for striking imagery. It initially offers us only the briefest glimpses of the life of the street—of the "blab of the pave"—with no unifying perspective, but it gradually tends towards a fuller depiction of novelistic scenes: the sick man on his way to the hospital, the "meeting of enemies," and the policeman pushing his way through the crowd, all seem to be moving along paths which will converge in a commonly witnessed event. The interrogatories—or are they exclamations?—which arise in response to these scenes (e.g., "What groans of overfed or half-starved who fall on the flags sunstruck or in fits") invite precisely the sort of editorializing responses one might find in a more socially activist and fully "prosaic" (fully prosed) novel. Something by Dickens, for example, or—closer to home—*Uncle Tom's Cabin*. Whitman is exploiting sentimentalism similar to that exploited by authors like Dickens and Stowe: the suffering mothers, "taken suddenly," are meant to arouse not only our curiosity, but our sympathy, too. But his questions about these sufferers remain suspended in the lopsided space of an authorial monologue. Whitman does not try to answer them, nor does he really want his readers to: the questions are rhetorical, or "lyric." They are exclamations after all. The last line of the passage ("I mind them or the resonance of them.... I come again and again") could be read as Whitman's means of pulling away from the implications of the preceding lines: his "mind[ing]" of their "resonance" is a recognizably *poetic* gesture, made in immediate and obvious reaction to the narrative energies (insofar as they involve, or suggest, a chain of related events) and/or novelistic energies (insofar as they provoke sustained description and analysis of a social scene, and enrich the discursive mixture of his text), aroused by the rest of the catalog. Less obviously, it puts those more social and, indeed, political energies safely to rest in the "mind" or "mind[ing]" of a putatively single and singular individual. This rhetorical pattern is one Whitman relies on time and again in the course of his poetic career.

"Mind[ing]" is precisely the sort of thing that Reynolds praises in *Beneath the American Renaissance* as "fusion": we can now begin to evaluate the cultural implications of "fusion" as a term of value.[11] It is allied to a paradoxical kind of lyric quietism: Whitman's own term, "resonance," is a bit tame as a qualifier for groans, which grow faint—fail, that is to resound—even as it is applied to them. Minding their "resonance" is not the same thing, then, as *hearing* those groans. And if the bard can "come again and again," the street scene is reduced, even if at the same time it is glorified, to being (no more than) a spectacle of the "universal" experience of suffering—of which it serves here as an example. The historically specific street scene, taken out of its immediate context, is made to seem exemplary, and is thus revalued as an allegory.In the same way, all of the items Whitman catalogs become types, or lyric paradigms. What is figured in "Song of Myself" is not meant to be socially and historically specific; it is not meant to be a sample of experience, but an *example* (the "overfed or half-starved" are those who, in biblical terms, "you always have with you"). It therefore seems timeless, and—as Reynolds would have it—universal.

These lines from relatively early in the poem thus mark a crucial moment. The poet resorts to the catalogs as a way of stifling a discursive urge, an urge to describe and investigate and narrate, which the catalogs can satisfy because they are novelistic, fragmented narratives, packed with information gleaned from any number of different discourses: novels, newspapers, popular melodrama, geographies, histories (from the "remember'd print or narrative," as Whitman confesses in "Song of the Broad-Axe" [*Collected Poetry and Prose* 331]). Whitman's catalogs hint at the radically different kinds of texts that went into the making of *Leaves of Grass*, but are not themselves meant to be *like* those kinds of texts. In the process of (re)composition, a transformation of the dross is supposed to have taken place.

Stifling urges is, of course, one of the great themes of the *Leaves*. Think of the poetry's numerous representations of the act of masturbation: like masturbation, the catalogs offer a release, without involving the author in some possibly more complicated affair—be it discourse or intercourse. After enjoying this narrative release, Whitman can savor, or "mind" it: he can recollect, in relative tranquility, the social motion and emotion he has just witnessed. And he can try to rein in that motion and emotion by deploying the "unitary language" of poetry in its pursuit, language which, as Bakhtin argues, "is not something given ... but is always in essence posited...and at every moment of its linguistic life it is opposed to the realities of heteroglossia" ("Discourse" 270). And by opposing itself to heteroglossic realities, it is also always a gambit on behalf of a unitary culture—an affirmative or redemptive culture, whether that culture is actual or wholly imaginary.[12]

The heteroglossic is a vexed matter for Whitman. His catalogs allow him to embrace all kinds of things, but since the individual items in the catalogs always threaten to fall into logical relationships of identity and difference, and thus into forms of hierarchy and exclusion, he has to rely on an atomizing strategy: each item is almost always given only a single-line entry, and the interrelationships between items almost always go unremarked; until the poet asserts, in a subsequent passage, the lyrical meaning or "resonance" of all that has just passed before the reader's scrutiny—or, rather, before the bard's commanding eye. To put the point more abstractly, the catalogs unspool until, finally, the grammatical parataxis of the catalogs is discounted, by an assertion of their semantic or thematic hypotaxis, often figured as selfhood or one of its analogues (such as "union").[13]

The heteroglossic attracts Whitman for the same reason it attracted many of his literary contemporaries: because it offers a sure means of telling the tale of a particular time as well as of a definite place. He must, at the least, go through some of the motions of such telling—mimic it—if his poetry is to bear any markers of the distinctively "American." This necessity leads him to employ the compromise form of the catalogs, which substitute the synchronic form of the list (and *the* ... and *the* ...) for the diachronic form of narrative (and *then* ... and *then* ...). Whitman prefers the list to narrative, because the list has been cleansed of many of the vestiges of logical and causal connection. Lists, one might say, are more *transcendent* than narratives, more sublime, and less burdened by relations of difference and change (which is one reason why Emerson also uses the list in his essays). Lists read like inventories of the now, the immediate.

Sublimating the discursive urge by fragmenting the heteroglossic, and the subsequent savoring of those resonant fragments, are essential poetic maneuvers in "Song of Myself." The poem's pattern of alternating discursive and lyric passages might be said to be the result of Whitman's attempts to redact a much larger text (American history, for him always the master narrative), in order to make the single unified and unifying identity he claims is implicit in that larger text seem more plausible. This identity, however, remains purely theoretical and presumptive; it is *asserted* (rather than demonstrated) in the lyrical passages which try to counter the dissipating, centrifugal effects of the catalogs.

We have witnessed this supposition of union at work in "Song of Myself": in the long passage cited above, the sprawled suicide suggests an isolated life and a discrete personal history, one with a beginning, middle, and most dramatically, an end. This suggestion of the separate and the singular must then be countered by the picture of bustling street life which follows it, which happens all at once: street life goes on all the time, it has no discursive or narrative shape as such. It is, for Whitman, an image of vitality itself—and it is therefore fundamental. It does have discursive or narrative potential, however, if one begins to make distinctions, and recognize the connections, between the street, its denizens, and the events which occur there. If one begins to answer the rhetorical questions the poet asks as he presents these epiphenomenal scenes—if one begins to read "Song of Myself" in a less passive fashion—then relationships defined by difference begin to seem more significant (the "overfed" and the "half-starved" might not be so easily paired), political power begins to seem unequally distributed (the "policeman with his star" probably has more of it more immediately than does the "excited crowd"), and social contradictions begin to crystallize (the "hurrahs for popular favorites" and "the fury of roused mobs" might be products of class warfare). It is, at best, doubtful whether all these things can be reconciled by the poet. Whitman's attempts to "contain multitudes" might therefore be read as unwelcome mediation: as the intrusiveness of an author trying to master both his material, and his readers.

2: NARRATIVES

Telling history usually involves a narrative of some sort, and any instance of narrative in "Song of Myself" should be seen as historically fraught. Fraught, because narrative threatens to take the bard out of himself—both out of character as poet, and out of genre—and into history. Narrative also forces a recognition of differences—which it tends to proliferate—not so easily contained by assertions of unity. Narrative entails an understanding of history of an unwelcome sort: of history as process, rather than of history as containing form. It might make apparent the logical connections between the long lines of Whitman's poetry: relations of difference which might interfere with his inclusiveness, always dependent on the ostensible sameness of the items he catalogs.

The "blab of the pave" catalog in "Song of Myself" is immediately followed by ten instances of narrative, each resembling the two-line melodrama of the suicide, but unfolding more fully, over the course of two or three, to roughly a dozen or more lines. Each of these brief narratives is still fragmentary, however; and each etches more finely the figures of the stereotypes Whitman celebrates as essentially American.

Each has the appearance of particularity, but actually functions in general terms as an image, as the verbal equivalent of (say) a Currier & lves lithograph. The haying scene in particular functions this way, and it also represents a significant change of venue, from troubled urban streets to a familiar pastoral setting:

The big doors of the country-barn stand open and ready,
The dried grass of the harvest-time loads the slow-drawn
          wagon,
The clear light plays on the brown gray and green intertinged,
The armfuls are packed to the sagging mow:
I am there.... I help.... I came stretched atop of the load,
I felt its soft jolts.... one leg reclined on the other,
I jump from the crossbeams, and seize the clover and timothy,
And roll head over heels, and tangle my hair full of wisps.
                              (*Collected Poetry and Prose* 34)

This is a scene of simultaneous hay-making and safe-making: the poet is "there" to "help" what was work become play—to feel the "soft jolts" of the hay-wagon, and communicate his comprehension of the scene to us. It and the scenes which follow it (the western hunter camping with his dog; the Yankee clipper; the clamdiggers; the marriage of the trapper and Indian maiden; the runaway slave; the twenty-eight young men bathing; and brief vignettes of the butcher boy, the blacksmiths, and the negro wagoner), are really mere tableaux, and in keeping with Bakhtin's observation that poetry tends to be a monologue, none of the participants in these tableaux have a speaking role (I discount the voice of the poetic "I" or "persona," which in this section of the poem functions much like that of a narrator in a novel).

Taken all together, these tableaux make up an album of American life. Of course, if the main ambition of Whitman's poetry is to be lyrical, then the static, image-like quality of such scenes is generically determined. They must function as images, however full of movement and however discursive they at first appear, images which each encourage our understanding of a singular fact: their equivalence in democratic union. Whitman's point is that these little stories (if we can call them that) are really all the same, however much they sample different experiences, and however much they seem devoted to the experiences of various social and racial types. These stories achieve closure not syntagmatically, but paradigmatically: they begin as one form of discourse and end as another (they switch genres, from narrative to lyric, like a man changing boats in mid-stream). They are narrative "specimens," to use one of Whitman's favorite words, and like scientific specimens, only serve to confirm the ongoing identity and nature of the genus and species from which, and for the identification of which, they are taken. If they were not typical, they would have no lyric significance. This is tantamount to saying they are not really "stories" at all.

His use of such narratives reveals yet another way the bard has of creating poetry by trading between genres. In "Song of Myself" he sometimes represents himself as if he experienced history first-hand, as if he were the witness who reads events into the historical record for us: "I am the man.... I suffered.... I was there" (*Collected Poetry and Prose* 64). This eye-witness strategy entails an internalization of history as but one more aspect of the bard's multiplex sublime, an internalization which poets tend to effect magisterially, "as if no other language existed" (Bakhtin, "Discourse" 398). Whitman becomes all the names of history, particularly American history, and offers up what purport to be first-hand accounts of it: especially when, in the guise of a storyteller, he begins, in an extended and unusually continuous section of "Song of Myself," to tell us a number of stories from the pages of American history. A sea-battle, the clash of the *Serapis* and the *Bonhomme Richard*, receives perhaps the fullest treatment of any of the stories told in the poem.[14] Whitman takes several pages to relate it, and prefaces it with these remarks: "Did you read in the seabooks of the oldfashioned frigate-fight? / Did you learn who won by the light of the moon and stars? / Our foe was no skulk in his ship, I tell you, / His was the English pluck, and there is no tougher or truet, and never was; and never will be; / Along the lowered eve he came, horribly raking us". (*Collected Poetry and Prose* 67). This legendary narrative, which has an air of having already been told, of having made the journey from event to oral history to textual record ("Did you read?"), and back to oral history ("I tell you"), more than once, seems likely to be again a long-winded tale, as the poet strikes the pose of a garrulous old tar overcome by memory.[15] This posture serves to (mildly) ironize the story's telling from the beginning.

But more importantly, Whitman cannot let matters rest as they seem to many lines later, in a prosaic moment of narrative closure: "Toward twelve at night, there in the beams of the moon they surrendered to us" (*Collected Poetry and Prose* 69). Instead he "finishes" the story of the *Serapis* and the *Bonhomme Richard* by appending to it a lyric coda, a montage of gothic details from the battle's aftermath:

> Formless stacks of bodies and bodies by themselves.... dabs of
>   flesh upon the masts and spars,
> The cut of cordage and dangle of rigging....the slight shock
>   of the soothe of waves,
> Black and impassive guns, and litter of powder-parcels, and
>   the strong scent,
> Delicate sniffs of the seabreeze.... smells of sedgy grass and
>   fields by the shore ... death-messages given in charge to
>   survivors,
> The hiss of the surgeon's knife and the gnawing teeth of his saw,

The wheeze, the cluck, the swash of falling blood.... the
    short wild scream, the long dull tapering groan,
These so.... these irretrievable.

(Collected Poetry and Prose 69)

The anticlimax of the last line of this passage tempers the impression, the sense of painful reality, of bodily misery and death, so powerfully created by the immediately preceding lines. It is *intended* to do so. Like the oxymoronic "soothe of waves," it offsets whatever "slight shock" the passage gives us. Whitman ends, rather melodramatically, on a note of false protest: if his powers of representation are too weak for him to make a more emphatic judgment, if the best he can come up with is an ellipsis and the back-pedalling assertion that everything he has just retrieved is, after all, "irretrievable," then why does he tell it—and why does he deny his own success, having told it so well? He does not really mean that the story of the sea-battle is "irretrievable" in its details, but rather that he has no wish to go forward with the story, and perhaps draw some sort of conclusion as to its historical import or moral—which might have to do with conflict, with differences which cannot be resolved by assertions of a mysterious and unifying consensus. So Whitman adopts the ambivalent, more "poetic" pose of wistfulness. The last line of this passage works rhetorically to call attention to the writer's art, by ironically deprecating it, and it begins the reestablishment of the lyric mood: we are done with stories, they can tell us nothing of what really matters. The lyric coda adjusts the meaning of the first last line (which I identified above as a narrative moment: "Toward twelve at night, there in the beams of the moon they surrendered to us"), and it supplies the proper form of *poetic* closure.

    The telling of the story of the old sea-fight provokes a crisis of utterance, and engenders a momentarily unhappy, frustrated poetic consciousness. Whitman's ultimate elision of the battle story suggests that the bard must resist becoming the repository of memory for the nation, because there is more, and more important, work for him to do. Accordingly, "Song of Myself" continues as follows:

O Christ! My fit is mastering me!
What the rebel said gaily adjusting his throat to the rope
    noose,
What the savage at the stump, his eye-sockets empty, his
    mouth spiriting whoops and defiance,
What stills the traveler come to the vault at Mount Vernon,
What sobers the Brooklyn boy as he looks down the shores of

the Wallabout and remembers the prison ships,
What burnt the gums of the redcoat at Saratoga when he
    surrendered his brigades,
These become mine and me every one, and they are but little,
    I become as much more as I like.
(*Collected Poetry and Prose* 69–70)

When contemplating these images from American history, the poet can be sanguine about the threat they pose, not because he refuses the knowledge of them—after all, here they cause him to have a "fit"—but because history is only one more aspect of himself: "I become as much more as I like."[16] The poet—his self, his body, his language—functions as an inexhaustible and all-absorptive plenum. He—himself, his self—is the ultimate symbol in and of his own work. Although he tells us a little history now and then, it's just to show what he can do in that line of work, and not because history is truly important. It's an interesting imaginary diversion, only one of many layers of meaning: "they"—all the historic scenes he has recounted—"are but little." The utterances of others—"What the rebel said" or "What burnt the gums of the redcoat at Saratoga" (i.e., "I surrender")—are usurped by the poet ("these become mine"), and overwritten by an assertion of his own lyrical ability, of his own lyric personhood. Their dialogue is subsumed by his monologue.

    If the sea battle passage is a moment of crisis, one in which the poet encounters what Bakhtin would call the "stylistic limit" of his chosen genre, then it is no surprise that at this moment Whitman's language is in character with "the language of poetic genres" broadly speaking. In moments of crisis, according to Bakhtin, poetic language "becomes authoritarian, dogmatic and conservative, sealing itself off from the influence of extraliterary social dialects" ("Discourse" 287). The monological imagination—which I would argue Whitman's ultimately was—must refuse to record the words of others, even if those others excite its sympathy, in true dialogue, and will always enfold their words in and as its own. As Bakhtin writes, "heteroglossia (other socio-ideological languages) can be introduced into purely poetic genres, primarily in the speeches of characters. But in such a context it is objective. It appears, in essence, as a *thing*, it does not lie on the *same* plane with the real language of the work" ("Discourse" 287). It is "but little."

    What is remarkable about "Song of Myself" is the regularity and vigor with which it operates according to the genre rules Bakhtin elaborates, the alacrity with which it executes the tractical maneuver of representing the speech of others as not only embedded in its own speech, but as only meaningful when acknowledged as such by that speech. Encountering the heteroglossic, the poet intones lyric formulas, turning the words of others into "things." Whitman surrounds historical narratives like the one just examined above (or any heteroglossic discourse: it doesn't have to be a narrative) with the stabilizing mesentery of his own lyric tissue—at least, he *asserts* that he can do and has done that: "These become mine and me every one...I become as much more as I like."[17]

The translation of narrative moments into images, which then function as elements of a lyric whole, might be said to be constitutive of "literariness" in "Song of Myself." Each narrative, broken up in small pieces, and broken off from its culturally and historically specific context, is effectively defamiliarized by Whitman and comes to seem newly meaningful, perhaps even mythic. These images or mythemes are not open to chance, accident, and happenstance, and their significance is not debatable. We either accept them as Whitman offers them to us—as "poetry," that is—or we don't. We can refuse his fusion. Insofar, then, as genre can be thought of as a kind of contractual obligation (an understanding of genre basic to structuralism), accepting Whitman's poetry as such means looking the other way when it becomes too historical or heteroglossic for the fiction of its poetic unity to be maintained. That is, as good (in the sense of well-behaved) readers of Whitman's poetry, we must not question the transubstantiation of all kinds of material into poetic images.[18] Remarkably, in Whitman's poetry what Bakhtin calls the "canonization" ("Discourse" 398) of heteroglossic materials forms a part of the manifest content of the poem itself: his poetry tends to be *about* the "mind[ing]" of resonances, of meanings—about its own theory, and the categories it deploys—and does not merely rely on it as an unspoken fiction.

3: CONCLUSION: SIMILITUDE

In the 1855 Preface, Whitman makes it clear that he wants to do away with traditional literary devices, such as "rhyme or uniformity or abstract addresses to things," "melancholy complaints or good precepts," "gaggery and gilt," "ornaments and fluency," and handsome "measures and similes and sound" (*Collected Poetry and Prose* 11–12). But his rejection of literary tradition leaves him with an enormous problem: what is left for the poet to do, and what is left for the poet to do it with, once almost everything that has ever been understood as "poetic" has been discarded? Does "poetry" exist—*can* it do so—apart from the genre's signifying practices, its language games? In the wake of structuralism, post-structuralism, and deconstruction, we would say that the answer to this question must be "no." That, however, is not the answer Whitman would have given. This is: "The rhyme and uniformity of perfect poems show the free growth of metrical laws and bud from them as unerringly and loosely as lilacs or roses on a bush, and take shapes as compact as the shapes of chestnuts and oranges and melons and pears, and shed the perfume impalpable to form" (*Collected Poetry and Prose* II). The sort of structures ("rhyme," "uniformity," and so on) that literary theory has long understood to be in one way or another generative of literary effects, are taken by Whitman to be themselves the products of poetic "free growth." His "organicism" is of a very literal sort.

Whitman's belief that poetry was flower-like—a product of "free growth"—leads him to make some interesting remarks about other, less elevated genres. He sometimes argues against the novel, for example, because he associates it with the vulgar popular literature of his own day. In the 1855 Preface, he writes that "As the attributes of the poets of the kosmos concentre in the real body and the soul and in the pleasure of things they possess the superiority of genuineness over all fiction and romance" (*Collected Poetry and Prose* 18), and the word "romance" is meant to bear a particularly negative charge. This is especially true when he opposes "romance" to "history": "Great genius and the people of these states must never be demeaned to romances. As soon as histories are properly told there is no more need of romances" (*Collected Poetry and Prose* 19). Romance is wrong in Whitman's view because it is "unnatural"—i.e., untrue, or fictive, and exaggerated; and therefore, one assumes that to "properly" tell history would be to tell it in some more "natural" form. Given his beliefs about poetry, it follows that for Whitman the proper telling of history, should the poet chose to "tell" it, would also render history like poetry "impalpable to form"—but palpable, presumably, "to" something higher than form, whatever sublime something that might be. Poetically-told history thus would not really be "told" at all. It would be "sensed," or felt (perhaps even smelt, as Whitman's comparison of its effects to perfume would have it). Reading a poem would be an "aesthetic" experience in the root sense of the term. That is, it would— somehow—involve the body, just as Whitman always claimed. But does this putative embodiment provide anything more than a theoretical ground for Whitman's poetry? More importantly for the present discussion, is Whitman's body the same as the body celebrated by Bakhtin? No. Whitman's desire to be free from constraints leads him to reject literary tradition, but in terms so radical that, ironically, he has to reemploy a high aesthetic doctrine of the kind he began by militating against: one which ultimately rejects the folk and/or popular spirit he otherwise claims to love. He does not, after all, live up to his pledge in the 1855 Preface: "What I tell I tell for precisely what it is" (*Collected Poetry and Prose* 14). Instead, as he puts it in "Song of Myself," "Voices indecent" are in his poetry "clarified and transfigured" (*Collected Poetry and Prose* 50)—surely an assertion which ought to alert us to his less-than-complete sympathy with the raunchy, carnivalesque spirit Bakhtin identifies with the novel.

Whitman does not acknowledge the tension between the two ideals of telling something "for precisely what it is," and the transfiguration and clarification of indecent voices. He thinks that the two values can be fused into one standard, and it is his faith in "similitude"—the word is his own— that allows him to think so. The poet, he argues in the 1855 Preface, must be open to "the eternity which gives similitude to all periods and locations and processes and animate and inanimate forms, and which is the bond of time, and rises up from its inconceivable vagueness and infiniteness in the swimming shape of today" (*Collected Poetry and Prose* 23). Whitman opposes history ("all periods and locations and processes and animate and inanimate forms," as well as "the swimming shape of today"), to "eternity," where "similitude" ensures "the bond of time." However orphic this may sound, it suggests that his poetry is just as motivated by a distrust of heteroglot difference as by faith in it. What we might want to call "history" Whitman apparently regards as merely the content or stuff of history, which is bound by "similitude" (bound *symbolically*, that is) into that form of essential unity he calls "eternity." This symbolic bondage implies the mastery of its author and creator. How can the masterful poet produce anything other than a series of unrelated, particular statements, without the overarching rule of an imposed form, however disguised (symbolic) it may be? The proliferation of heteroglossic particulars always frustrates the inclusive impulse; something on the order of lyric "similitude" is needed to rein them all in.

The 1855 Preface speaks rather eloquently of the ways in which Whitman's understanding of human history, and his understanding of literary history, are linked. An awareness of this linkage helps us to mark the fluctuating line where Whitman's desire to utter a new poetic word, and his desire to have his utterance accepted as equal if not superior to other poetic words, especially those of the past, have become confused. On the one hand, he flaunts his distaste for tradition: "The poems distilled from other poems will probably pass away" (*Collected Poetry and Prose* 26). But on the other, Whitman (like his celebrants) wants the *Leaves* to have the same kind of cultural power and authority that once was invested in those "distilled," purely traditional poems. That is, he still wants to be understood as making the same kind of universally available and applicable utterance so long associated with the "great literature" of the past: "A great poem is for ages and ages in common and for all degrees and complexions and all departments and sects and for a woman as much as a man and a man as much as a woman"

(*Collected Poetry and Prose* 24). As his contradictory attitudes towards greatness and vulgarity would suggest, Whitman appeals to concepts of both high and low culture, and the result may be that his work never manages to be either one or the other, but is resolutely—if such a word can be used to describe a vacillator like Whitman—middlebrow.[19] In his work, the dialogue of high and low tends to collapse toward the middle. This collapse of dialogue is what comes to be regarded as the "fusion" of opposed discourses in the *Leaves*, that text's unique resolution of the dramatic tensions often encountered in the American literature of its time. The good gray terrain marked by this collapse once was enshrined as essentially Whitmanian. It may be that when Reynolds links "fusion" to the "universal" values espoused by American Renaissance writers, all he is really doing is describing the process by which these writers made the materials of popular culture— Indians, backwoodsmen, whalers, roughts—safe for contemporary polite readers, and future generations of college students.

A Bakhtinian reading should be conducted in a somewhat more skeptical spirit. From a Bakhtinian perspective, Whitman's presumed identity as a poet is one which allows him to speak the authoritative word: "The authoritative word demands that we acknowledge it, that we make it our own; it binds us, quite independent of any power it might have to persuade us internally; we encounter it with its authority already fused to it. The authoritative word ... is given (it sounds) in lofty spheres, not those of familiar contact. Its language is a special (as it were, hieratic) language. It can be profaned. It is akin to taboo, i.e., a name that must not be taken in vain" ("Discourse" 342). Following Bakhtin, the *Leaves* might be read as a compendium of authoritative words: not just the first-person pronoun, but "poetry" and "union" and all the other terms that define Whitman's "frame of acceptance," as Kenneth Burke called it, can be found there.[20] These terms make up a crucial vocabulary, the meaning of which is somewhat occult, or "akin to taboo." This vocabulary is, nonetheless, peculiarly enabling: witness the critical tradition's willingness to accept Whitman's supposed abrogation of genre rules by means of a vigorous assertion of such things as his own self, the country's nationhood and—ironically—the poetic character of his text.

It is curious that Whitman's readers have been mostly unwilling to recognize the implicit limits of his poetic vision. They have been more attuned to the all-inclusive, usually sweet-natured and "democratic" frame of acceptance than to the authoritative words which are its other aspect. Part of the reason for this lies in a basic confusion of terms. Just as the word "poetry" often does not refer to the genre but is applied willy-nilly as an affectionate label to texts we happen to like (a lot), so democratic as a political term (referring to a system of elected representation and open debate by means of which social and cultural differences are expressed) is often silently translated into "democratic" as a term of approbation applied to the egalitarian consensus or "fusion" sometimes celebrated in art. This translation of terms is particularly prevalent in the analysis of texts from the American Renaissance. And it seems to me that democratic fusion cannot serve as a critical yardstick in cases where it also served as the chief measure by which an author, and his culture, judged themselves: otherwise critics merely repeat the terms they propose to explain. The attempted rehabilitation of fusion as a critical concept—which I began this essay by describing—may be read as a latter-day, cultural version of the centrist politics to which Whitman, who sometimes addressed himself to "These States"—to the *many*, rather than the one—and a number of his contemporaries, believed themselves opposed. At the same time, it yields to the nationalism they also found so very tempting. In any case, whether one is the author or the reader of *Leaves of Grass*, fusion and the dialogic are incommensurable values.

Notes

1. *Beneath the American Renaissance; The Subversive Imagination in the Age of Emerson and Melville* (Cambridge, Mass.: Harvard University Press, 1989) 104.

2. Bakhtin argues that the historical and cultural dominance of the novel since the Renaissance (and even earlier) necessarily entails the withering away of poetry as a living, still evolving genre. For Bakhtin, poetry is "dead" precisely to the extent that the novel has "killed" it: "Studying other genres is analogous to studying dead languages; studying the novel, on the other hand, is like studying languages that are not only alive, but still young." From "Epic and Novel," *The Dialogic Imagination*, Michael Holquist, ed., Caryl Emerson and Michael Holquist, trans. (Austin: University of Texas Press, 1981) 3.

3. Not that I think that Whitman's poetry is fully "novelized." Rob Wilson, in a reading of Whitman's poem "One's-Self I Sing," which opens the final edition of *Leaves of Grass*, attempts to celebrate the poet's heteroglossic sensibility as Reynolds does, but with different values. He avoids the valorization of artistic unity: "Reeking of lexical impurity, of poetic and prosaic indiscrimination, Whitman showed that American poetry can be made from the here and now" ("Lexical Scapegoating: The Pure and Impure of American Poetry," *Poetics Today* 8, 1 [1987]: 61). The lines which

inspire this reading should be quoted here: "Of physiology from top to toe I sing,/Not physiognomy alone nor brain alone is worthy for the Muse, I say the Form complete is worthier far,/ The Female equally with the Male I sing." As Wilson's impressionistic language hints (language that seems typical of attempts to make use of Bakhtin in support of celebratory readings), his interpretation of the poem depends on an understanding of words like "physiology" and "toe" and "the Form complete" and "Female" as somehow "reeking of lexical impurity." It seems to me, however, that one could hardly ask for a better example of Whitman's abstract, high-minded approach to the heteroglossic, the dialogical, and the "carnivalesque" than "One's-Self I Sing."

4. Whitman's poetry *begins* at the stage of "symbolic merger," Kenneth Burke's term for thetorical transcendence, and an apposite label to apply to Whitman's version of *Aufhebung*, since "merge" is also one of his keywords. In fact, Burke had Whitman in mind when he wrote the entry for "symbolic mergers" in his "Dictionary of Pivotal Terms." See *Attitudes Toward History*, Third Edition (Berkeley: University of California Press, 1984) 328–29.

5. *Collected Poetry and Prose*, Justin Kaplan, ed. (New York: The Library of America, 1982) 87.

6. American writers in the first half of the nineteenth century often felt that the country's social life was too unformed for it to be available for literary representation. Martin Green has summarized this state of affairs as follows: "the genres (the code of the system of literature) which America inherited from England were not adapted to the imaginative material forced on her writers by her frontier experience.... That maladaptation was in part cultural; the new material was associated with cultural attitudes which were hostile to gentility, and so to 'literature-as-a-system.'...The imaginative experience that pressed upon the writers ... was in certain ways formless. That is, it existed only in minor forms—pungent dialectical anecdotes— forms outside the system, and hostile to it, in just the way the Indian tribes, and to some degree the frontiersmen, were outside the political and economic system" (*Dreams of Adventure, Deeds of Empire* [New York: Basic Books, 1979] 140).

7. There was, however, another approach to this crisis, which according to Larzer Ziff was advocated by a number of American intellectuals: "True democratic literature ... might not be belles lettres at all, but daily writings that grew from the activities of the republic: journalism, legal opinions, sermons, accounts of natural history. Literature ... would be the most vital things written by people engaged in the doings of the nation rather than in literary activity itself" (*Literary Democracy: The Cultural Declaration of Independence in America* [New York: Viking, 1981] 57).

8. Two recent studies have made this point very forcefully: William Spengemann writes that "the reigning theory of American literature as an independent, autochthonous, unique collection of writings with a history of its own appears to be little more than a political fiction, concocted in defiance of the literary facts" (*A Mirror for Americanists; Reflections on the Idea of American Literature* [Hanover, N.H.: University Press of New England, 1989] 132). Peter Carafiol argues that "the study of texts by Americans should dissolve the borders of what has been called American literature and leap beyond them to a reconsideration of literary history in general" (*The American Ideal; Literary History as a Worldly Activity* [New York and Oxford: Oxford University Press, 1991] 5–6). Both argue that attempts to define the ideal of "America" have hamstrung Americanists, and that the denial of the mutual cross-pollination of American with European and other literatures has outlived its political relevance.

9. My argument regarding the relationship of lyric and narrative in Whitman's poetry might be compared with that made by two other recent essays. In "Whitman and the Erotics of Life" (*American Literature* 65, 4 [December 1993]: 703–30), Onno Oerlemans reads the lyric passages in a poem like "The Sleepers" as moments in which the self resists discursive and, more importantly, ideological formulation, in the name of some sort of radical ambiguity and indeterminacy: "lyrical resistance and dissolution are both the means to and the virtual evidence of the actual functioning of individual autonomy" (710). The essay ends with the declaration that the "presence" lyric creates "can be explained neither by a semiotics nor an economics but by a desire for a contact and union which is fundamental" (727). Several objections can be made to this argument, which is diametrically opposed to my own. It ignores the centrality of the individual, autonomous self it celebrates to American ideology, a key strategy of which has always been to represent itself as non-ideological, and therefore unavailable to either semiotic or economic analysis; according to Oerlemans, the self which lyric both asserts and produces is one about which nothing substantive can be said, and yet that self is presumed to refigure everything it comes in contact with—so it appears that something *can* be said about it, after all; the essay draws a hard and fast distinction between Whitman's "political" prose and his poetry, even as it relies on the interweaving of what are obviously politically-inflected "narratives" (i.e., that of Washington's farewell to his men in "The Sleepers") with the more "lyric" strains of the verse—so that, while it contrives an argument to account for the supposedly apolitical character of the poetry's form, it cannot account for the manifestly political character of its content; finally, even though the essay is notable for its theoretical sophistication, it is also, at key moments, rather more

impressionistic, in a way that seems to me to recall the most traditional and celebratory modes of Whitman scholarship: "we feel the passion" of Whitman's verse, Oerlemans writes, and that "demonstrates at once the irreducibility of lyric" (726).

Karen Sánchez-Eppler, in "To Stand Between: A Political Perspective on Whitman's Poetics of Merger and Embodiment" (*ELH* 56 [1989]: 923–49), makes a case more like my own: she insists on the politically-charged character of the relationship between narrative and lyric in Whitman's verse (although she construes that relationship more narrowly than I do here, as having to do with race). And she emphasizes that "merger"—what I have been calling "inclusiveness"—"always occurs for Whitman in the now of lyric pronouncement" (934). It is this aspect of Whitman's poetry—that it is not so much lyrical as it is *about* being lyrical (it does not be, but means)—that I think Oerlemans fails to recognize, or at least is unwilling to admit.

One might also consult Quentin Anderson, "Whitman's New Man," in *Walt Whitman: Walt Whitman's Autograph Revision of the Analysis of* Leaves of Grass (New York: New York University Press, 1974) 22–23.

10. "Song of Myself" was not so-called in the early editions of the *Leaves*.

11. By invoking "fusion" as a value, Reynolds is in silent accord with not only the New Criticism, but with those writers who began the systematic study of American literature. For example, in one of the early efforts to describe American literature in general terms, Van Wyck Brooks wrote that "Whitman was himself a great vegetable of a man, all of a piece in roots, flavor, substantiality, and succulence, well-ripened in the common sunshine. In him the hitherto incompatible extremes of the American temperament were *fused*" (my emphasis). See *America's Coming-of-Age* (New York: Octagon, 1975, 1915) 112.

12. The term "affirmative" I borrow from Herbert Marcuse; see his essay on "The Affirmative Character of Culture," in *Negations: Essays in Critical Theory* (Boston: Beacon, 1968) 88–133. Leo Bersani's characterization of "redemptive" art seems to me to be directly applicable to Whitman's work, especially since Bersani offers it as part of a reading of nineteenth-century American literature generally: "A crucial assumption in the culture of redemption is that a certain type of repetition of experience in art repairs inherently damaged or valueless experience. Experience may be overwhelming, practically impossible to absorb, but it is assumed...that the work of art has the authority to master the presumed raw material of experience in a manner that uniquely gives value to, perhaps even redeems, that material.... The catastrophes of history matter much less if they are

somehow compensated for in art" (*The Culture of Redemption* [Cambridge: Harvard University Press, 1990] 1).

13. Whitman's stop-gap measures have been described by Rob Wilson in terms of the sublime: "the assumption abides that beneath the abyss of nature or disintegration of death, there is a 'well-join'd scheme' of unity which the disparate unity of the poem only reflects, or at best enacts. The sublime functions as a visionary compact or erotic glue by fusing the poetic ego to the massiveness and alienating power of the prairies or a broadway scene.... Each object gets used up by Whitmanic sublimation, absorbed into bliss-wrought unity of the self" (*American Sublime: The Genealogy of a Poetic Genre* [Madison: University of Wisconsin Press, 1991] 141–42). I would emphasize that the subliminal fusion Wilson describes is at best only putative.

14. Quentin Anderson's observation about this passage should be cited here: "It is impossible for Whitman to completely eclipse the idea that there have been events in the past. What he does do is to handle past events as exemplary, as instances of what I did, and hence of what I do. Events thus become aspects of myself—how I behaved when I was John Paul Jones—and the significance of event is thus somewhat awkwardly reduced to an aspect of my personal being" ("Whitman's New Man" 25).

15. In fact, Whitman is thought to have learned the story from at least two different sources: from his grandmother, and from an account—written by Captain Jones himself—which Whitman's own version of events rather closely follows. See Sculley Bradley and Harold Blodgett, eds., *Leaves of Grass* (New York: Norton, 1973) 68–69n.

16. John Engell has made a similar point about Whitman's concept of history: "By positing himself as a corporate body, composed somehow of the parts of the nation, he eliminates the need to record either a mythic, legendary, or actual national past, for his personal past substitutes." In "Walt and Sir Walter, or The Bard and The Bart.: Balladeers," *Walt Whitman Quarterly Review* 5,4 (Spring 1988): 7. Engell, however, sees this as a much more positive maneuver on Whitman's part than I do.

17. There is another sort of narrative—although it doesn't *seem* like one, which of course is precisely the point—to be found in *Leaves of Grass*. This kind of narrative takes the form of a catalog, but it is a catalog of categories—and not of things. This kind of catalog has only potential, or kinetic, narrative energy. It needs to be placed (by the reader) in some historically particular context; then, its categories can begin to organize their new context discursively and narratively. In order for this to happen, however, the reader—as Whitman so often insisted—must become the writer. For example, in "Song of the Answerer" he asserts that "The words

of the true poems give you more than poems, / They give you to form for yourself poems, religions, politics, war, peace, behavior, histories, essays, daily life, and everything else, / They balance ranks, colors, races, creeds, and the sexes" (*Collected Poetry and Prose* 318). This list of the categories which true poems "give"—a list which includes several other forms of discourse, such as history and the essay—is meant to demonstrate the all-encompassing quality of poetic understanding. And the ability of that understanding to make worlds is celebrated: poetry is a kind of how-to book. "You," if you are the reader of "true poems," can use the words Whitman provides: "you" can employ his paradigms. "You" can write—"form for yourself"—your own "poems [...] histories, essays." But this forming-for-oneself should not be confused with readerly participation, as full partner, in the act of composition: since "you" are following *his* instructions, the world "you" form will look suspiciously like Walt Whitman's (it will, for example, have phrenologists in it). Whitman's remarks to "you" are always addressed to a person sponsored by the authoritative "I" of the author. Such exchanges are not dialogue—certainly not in the Bakhtinian sense of the term. They are more like ventriloquism, with the reader playing the role of the dummy. Kerry Larson has examined in detail how Whitman's addresses to his reader "seek to establish the preexistent authority of a discourse"—i.e., his own—"that underlies all others." See *Whitman's Drama of Consensus* (Chicago: University of Chicago Press, 1988) 18.

18. Rob Wilson suggests of Whitman that "it seems mean-spirited to ponder this American free spirit in relation to *any* continuities of genre or language, no matter how mediating such conventions remain for the 'inner-speech' or 'intuition' of the most self-reliant self" (*American Sublime* 142–43). He is referring to Whitman's reliance on the stock terms of a certain romantic tradition of the sublime. He also argues, less temperately, that "Whitman became the American sublime that he imagined and saw inside the self and in the *genious loci*, and that remains a literary fact immune to ridicule or destruction" (145).

19. According to Lawrence Levine, it was Whitman and his contemporaries who helped to first define this disputed cultural register. See his *Highbrow/Lowbrow: The Emergence of Cultural Hierarchy in America* (Cambridge, Mass.: Harvard University Press, 1988).

20. "In Whitman we find, as a cluster: immortality, brotherhood, work, I, democracy, 'answering,' air-sweetness, life-in-death—and ... the Union (the corporate *reintegrating* symbol for his sympathetic *disintegration*), and Lincoln (the 'Captain' that is the Union's *personal* counterpart). The whole is Whitman's 'frame of acceptance'" (*Attitudes Toward History*, Third Edition [Berkeley: University of California Press, 1984] 18).

WORKS CITED AND ADDITIONAL BIBLIOGRAPHY

Anderson, Quentin. *The Imperial Self: An Essay in American Literary and Cultural History*. New York: Knopf, 1971.

———. "Whitman's New Man." In *Walt Whitman: Walt Whitman's Autograph Revision of the Analysis of* Leaves of Grass. New York: New York University Press, 1974. 11–52.

Arensberg. Mary, ed. *The American Sublime*. Albany: State University of New York Press, 1986.

Bakhtin, M. M. *The Dialogic Imagination*. Michael Holquist, ed. Caryl Emerson and Michael Holquist, trans. Austin: University of Texas Press, 1981.

———. *Rabelais and His World*. Hélène Iswolsky, trans. Bloomington: Indiana University Press, 1984.

———. *Speech Genres and Other Late Essays*. Caryl Emerson and Michael Holquist, eds. Vern W. McGee, trans. Austin: University of Texas Press, 1986.

Bersani, Leo. *The Culture of Redemption*. Cambridge: Harvard University Press, 1990.

Brooks, Van Wyck. *America's Coming-of-Age*. New York: Octagon, 1975, 1915.

Burke, Kenneth. *Attitudes Toward History*. Third Edition. Berkeley: University of California Press, 1984.

Carafiol, Peter. *The American Ideal: Literary History as a Worldly Activity*. New York and Oxford: Oxford University Press, 1991.

Engell, John. "Walt and Sir Walter, or The Bard and The Bart.: Balladeers." *Walt Whitman Quarterly Review* 5,4 (Spring 1988): 1–15.

Green, Martin. *Dreams of Adventure, Deeds of Empire*. New York: Basic Books, 1979.

Larson, Kerry C. *Whitman's Drama of Consensus*. Chicago: University of Chicago Press, 1988.

Levine, Lawrence. *Highbrow/Lowbrow: The Emergence of Cultural Hierarchy in America*. Cambridge: Harvard University Press, 1988.

Marcuse, Herbert. "The Affirmative Character of Culture." In *Negations: Essays in Critical Theory*. Jeremy J. Shapiro, trans. Boston: Beacon, 1968.

Oerlemans, Onno. "Whitman and the Erotics of Lyric." *American Literature* 65 (December 1993): 703–30.

Reynolds, David S. *Beneath the American Renaissance; The Subversive Imagination in the Age of Emerson and Melville*. Cambridge: Harvard University Press, 1989.

Sánchez-Eppler, Karen. "To Stand Between: A Political Perspective on Whitman's Poetics of Merger and Embodiment." *ELH* 56 (1989): 923–49.

Spengemann, William C. *A Mirror for Americanists; Reflections on the Idea of American Literature.* Hanover, N.H.: University Press of New England, 1989.

Whitman, Walt. *Collected Poetry and Prose.* Justin Kaplan, ed. New York: The Library of America, 1982.

———. *Leaves of Grass.* Sculley Bradley and Harold Blodgett, eds. New York: Norton, 1973.

Wilson, Rob. *American Sublime: The Genealogy of a Poetic Genre.* Madison: University of Wisconsin Press, 1991.

———. "Lexical Scapegoating: The Pure and Impure of American Poetry." *Poetics Today* 8.1 (1987): 45–63.

Ziff, Larzer. *Literary Democracy: The Cultural Declaration of Independence in America.* New York: Viking, 1981.

———. "Whitman and the Crowd." *Critical Inquiry* 10 (June 1984): 579–91.

W.C. HARRIS

Whitman's Leaves of Grass *and the Writing of a New American Bible*

"We too must write Bibles, to unite again the heavens and the earthly world."

—Emerson, *Representative Men*[1]

In 1857, between the second and third editions of *Leaves of Grass*, Whitman announced in a notebook his plan for *"The Great Construction* of the *New Bible"* (*NUPM* 1:353).[2] Like the calendrically referenced lectionary of the Elizabethan *Book of Common Prayer* (1558), the structure of this prospective Bible—"Three Hundred & Sixty Five" poems, one for each day of the year— would consist of internal textual divisions after which the life of the reader could be patterned.[3] Although Whitman says that the *"New Bible* ... ought to be read[y] in 1859," he makes only one other allusion in the 1850s to a neo-Biblical project: "'Leaves of Grass'—Bible of the New Religion."[4] Not surprisingly, critics have tended to minimize Whitman's reference to a *"New Bible"* as little more than a passing conceit, one of several ideas the poet considered as a symbol for the kind of cultural work he was endeavoring to do. The *least* dismissive accounts concede that if such a neo-Biblical intent manifests itself in any edition of *Leaves*, it would be the 1860 edition.[5] But if we weigh the force with which Whitman speaks of a New Bible as "the principal object—the main life work," and if we consider the fact that the mid-nineteenth century was to-date the most active period of sectarian

From *Walt Whitman Quarterly Review*, vol. 16, nos. 3/4 (Winter/Spring 1999). ©1999 by The University of Iowa.

splintering and Bible translation in American history, it seems that an important argument has been left unmade about the way in which the 1860 *Leaves* responds to demands that nineteenth-century Americans were making on the Bible, the work that sacred writing, in its received and newly invented forms, was being called to do (*NUPM* 1:353). As Emerson had insisted ten years earlier in *Representative Men*, "We too must write Bibles, to unite again the heavens and the earthly world."

A New Bible presents an alternative to the sacred but incomplete "covenant of the Republic ... sworn to by Washington ... with his hand upon the Bible," accomplishing what the Revolution had left incomplete.[6] If Whitman has memorably written that "[t]he United States themselves are essentially the greatest poem," it must not be forgotten that in the same preface (1855) he refers to that poem as "the great *psalm* of the republic," that is, as a sacred poem (*PW* 2:434, 437; emphasis added).[7] Recasting *Leaves* in 1860 as a New Bible allows Whitman to attack the problematic of the one and the many as the central cultural problem for America, not so much to revise the constitutional regime with a religious supplement as to replace it with a new order in which the political is no longer a category, or at least in which the function of the political has been subsumed by a formation both literary and theological in character, a text whose generic complexity implies a discourse of wider, more efficacious authority.

Critically, little has been said about a phenomenon of great interest to any investigation of the constitutional regime in American literature: the writing of a New Bible, the New American Bible. I refer not to one specific text, but to the mid-century deluge of private and institutionally sponsored translations and revisions of the received, Authorized (King James) Version. Idiosyncrasies of translation and redaction aside, these texts are all "new Bibles": foundational texts that constitute a protocol of relation divergent from, and meant to usurp the institutional status of, that of extant secular and/or religious documents. Within this context, the 1860 edition of *Leaves*, which is the next edition after the 1857 notebook entry planning "*the New Bible*," appears to be one such essay at an American Bible, a document intended to found a new, scripturally based social formation.

Understanding what Whitman means by a "*New Bible*" and what it means to read the 1860 *Leaves* as such requires some understanding of what the Bible itself meant both to Whitman and to American culture at large in the mid-nineteenth century. Many Americans turned to the Bible and to religion in the hopes of accomplishing the work at which secular texts and institutions were failing: the reconstruction of relations on an unmediated or egalitarian basis, either textual or sectarian. Yet the character of new religious sects and communities formed between 1830 and 1850 (including

Mormonism, Oneidan perfectionism, and Seventh-Day Adventism) must be differentiated from those which had gone before.[8] By the 1840s the de-authorization of the King James Version was almost a *fait accompli*: German-born Higher Criticism had discredited the Authorized Version's claims to historical accuracy, and the number of private translations was growing exponentially. The decades following the Second Great Awakening saw the decline of America's established or predominant religion (first Congregationalism, then Unitarianism) and the rise in prominence and membership of previously minor sects (Methodists, Baptists, and Disciples of Christ). Thus, while theological authority had come to seem, at least to Whitman, incompatible with the hierarchical and dogmatic character of institutions, it nonetheless appeared impossible to distribute identity without some structural or creedal basis. Paradoxically, the multiplication of sects (and thus of claims of a privileged relation to a transcendent term) which had drawn the status of the transcendent term into doubt *also* rendered its reconstruction more critical.

Redeeming the unrepresented may be Whitman's chief poetic and political objective. But that objective requires the redemption of something more dubious, problematic, and perhaps unattainable: theological authority. Whitman is fully aware of the various institutional causes in which theology has been enlisted, "the paraphernalia? of modern worship, [the] sects, churches, creeds, pews, sermons, [and] observances ... [that] have nothing to do with real religion" (*NUPM* 6:2091–2092). But just as the Disciples of Christ cast off ecclesiastical *doxa* in favor of *sola scriptura* ("the Bible alone"), so does Whitman reject institutional attempts to regulate the relation of the many to the one. This is not to say that mediation can be dispensed with: when the poet writes that "what passes as the authority of the Bible...[must] surely, surely go," his objection is not to mediation per se but rather to the restriction of the *right* to mediate to one text, the Authorized Version (*NUPM* 6:2091). Thus while theological authority should be disestablished, Whitman asserts just as strongly that it cannot exist outside *some* social or literary formation (a nation or a poem) that distributes it. "The people," he writes in the 1872 Preface,

> must begin to learn that religion, (like poetry,) is something far, far different from what they supposed. It is, indeed, too important to the power and perpetuity of the New World to be consign'd any longer to the churches, old or new, Catholic or Protestant—Saint this, or Saint that. It must be consign'd henceforth to democracy *en masse*, and to literature. It must enter into the poem of the nation. It must make the nation. (*PW* 2: 462–463)[9]

For Whitman poetry has the power to "make the nation." But the redemption of theological authority *without* mediation seems virtually impossible. When in the 1855 Preface Whitman declares categorically that "[t]here will soon be no more priests" to mediate the individual's relation to the divine, he immediately qualifies the revolutionary force of his words by adding, "A new order shall arise" and "take ... [the priests'] place": "they shall be the priests of man, and every man shall be his own priest. The churches built under their umbrage shall be the churches of men and women. Through the divinity of themselves shall the kosmos and the new breed of poets be interpreters of men and women and of all events and things."[10] The centrality of this paradox to Whitman's project—the mediation of non-restricted identity—is captured in his perhaps most well-known apothegm, from *Democratic Vistas*: "The priest departs, the divine literatus comes" (*PW* 2:365).[11]

The question, though, is whether sacerdotal functions can be assumed without the more negative consequences of institutionalization, whether a priesthood of men and women, no matter how inclusive its congregation, does not still constitute a hierarchy.[12] Whitman's answer may be paraphrased as "yes, but it cannot be helped." The advancement made by the 1860 *Leaves of Grass* is the realization that the mediatory structures necessary to the unification of disparates do not have to negate the value or scope of the new social identity being distributed. For Whitman, the new religion is to be an institution which is *not* an institution, meaning that it is not administered by an invested few, a class administering its own hierarchical distinction. Whitman expresses this paradox most succinctly in an 1857 notebook entry, "*Founding a new American / Religion* (? No Religion)," that is, a religion that is no religion, a rite that is practicable without being regulated (*NUPM* 6: 2046).[13] What Whitman attempts to forge with his New Bible is a protocol of relation that hovers between being an actualized and a purely theoretical state of affairs. Whitman may adopt an ambivalent stance toward formalization, rejecting all sectarian, doctrinal restrictions; still, the new housing of religion—whether nation-as-poem or poetry-as-Scripture—cannot escape its own creedal (and therefore mediatory) status. After looking more closely at the wider cultural project of the New Bible, I want to conclude by turning to "So Long!"—the last poem in the 1860 edition—as an experiment in the modeling of the commensurability of persons on the basis of *less* costly *in*commensurabilities: the sacrifice of immediacy, intranslatability, and silence for moments of mediation, translation, and a comprehensible social presence. "So Long!" suggests that free, open, unmediated relation is available, paradoxically, only *by way of* mediation, by disruption and fragmentation—only by admitting hierarchy as being on some level ineluctable, as that which *must* intrude upon any social or institutional reality.

Whitman was not the only American who found it necessary, either by revising the Authorized Version (the King James Version) or by writing an entirely new Bible, to produce an *American* Bible and so claim the United States, the New Israel, as the site upon which old covenants—Biblical as well as federal—would be fulfilled. The unprecedented formation of new religious sects between 1830 and 1850, most of which claimed an idiosyncratic understanding of Scripture *not* mediated by dogma, contributed significantly to the decentering of the Authorized Version and, consequently, to the democratization of the transcendental term. For those who chose to produce new Bibles, the greatest difficulty was distribution—both in the literal sense of distributing multiple copies of a uniform, foundational text and in the *symbolic* sense of translating, of making one text (whether the Authorized Version or not) speak to its many readers. In Whitman's hands, the ambiguous strategies of translation and distribution are the means for constructing a distributive model of social identity which is capable of evading the mediatory effect of institutions.

American Bible translation, revision, and distribution, all of which reached an unmatched peak in the mid-1800s, provided a concrete means of re-theorizing social order by creating a new community, the identity of which was mediated through a single (and often unique) document, so that the value of persons and the physical text itself transcended existing distinctions between states, races, classes, and sects. Before 1816, the year the American Bible Society (ABS) was founded in New York, the distribution of Bibles on a wide scale had been unknown. Any group distributing Bibles up to that point had done so on a local level and with limited means. As a national organization with corporate means, the ABS began to find it possible to realize what Peter Wosh refers to as the "fundamentally new idea" of "Christianiz[ing] the nation."[14] In just four years, the ABS printed and distributed 100,000 Bibles. Over the next four decades, as the Society sought to reach (or rather, create) a nationwide market, Bible recipients came to include immigrants, Confederate soldiers, and slaves. The sole criterion for admission to this new polity was the possession of a Bible. Equality was as available as a book; the resultant union, without limit—and, for once, without differentiation.[15]

A great part of the impetus for Bible distribution campaigns was the dramatic increase of interest in Bible *translation*. One cannot overemphasize how remarkable it was that, suddenly, so many people found it necessary, if not imperative, to make new translations of a text that had been accepted in one standard, authorized form—the King James Version (1611)—for over two hundred years. Furthermore, it was not just clerics and academics but lay believers who were calling for and executing new translations. What was being produced were not just scholarly, officially endorsed refinements of a master-text, or revisions meant to produce a more authentic and accurate translation. The trend was increasingly toward sectarian and idiosyncratic revisions and re-translations, emphatically private versions of a Bible believers came to see as that much more *their own* Bible.[16] The implications of this trend for social formation are obvious: total fragmentation; individual autonomy valued at the expense of the unity of not only the state but, very often, the sect that a new version was intended to found or establish. But, as a particularly striking episode in Bible translation history shows, translation, like distribution, is potentially as unifying as it is divisive.

In 1826 Alexander Campbell, who had founded the Disciples of Christ fifteen years earlier, published a version of the Bible intended to correct and update the language of the King James Version (KJV). One of the changes he made ignited a controversy that would last for over forty years. That change was the substitution, in the New Testament, of the word *immerse* for the word *baptize*. Campbell bases the alteration on the fact that the words *baptize* and *baptism*, which appear in the KJV, are not translations of the original Greek words, *baptizo* and *baptizein*, but rather transliterations. The source of what Campbell views as an error is the second-century Latin translation of the Septuagint, which transliterates *baptizo* into "baptize" instead of using the closest Latin equivalent (*immergere*, to immerse).[17] Linguistic accuracy aside, using "immersion" appealed to Campbell's nonsectarian instincts by avoiding any exclusive, denominational privilege "baptism" might be taken to lend to Baptists. In the next thirty years, at least eight English immersionist versions and foreign-language translations of the KJV followed suit, inciting both enthusiasm and outrage. In 1835 the ABS refused to print Bibles for Baptist missionaries in Calcutta who, faced with a language that lacked an equivalent for "baptize," had used the Bengali word for "immerse" rather than transliterate *baptizo*. Those within the ABS who had been outvoted on the matter, led by Spencer Cone and William Wyckoff, split off in 1836 to form the American and Foreign Bible Society (AFBS). Although formed by pro-immersionists, the AFBS soon became divided between those who favored the practice in foreign translations only and those who wanted to do so only in English. The latter faction, led again by Cone and Wyckoff, broke off in 1850 to start a third organization, the American Bible Union, which published the longawaited immersionist version (of the New Testament, at least) in 1862–1863. Matthew Conant's 107-page Appendix to his translation of Matthew demonstrates the length to which immersionists would go, the fervor that had brought them this far. Both immersionists and their opponents deeply appreciated the impact of single words: the implications of translation, the ability of textual changes to create or dissolve communities and societies.[18] Anti-immersionist Baptists claimed they rejected the practice because it was sectarian, but it seems clear that they themselves were acting out of sectarian interests.

What the immersionist controversy did for Whitman and his contemporaries was to intensify the problems facing any religious or social formation committed on the one hand to unity (to the idea of one God or one state) and on the other hand to equality (the acceptance of multiple interpretations of that God or state). One problem is that the distribution of identity on an unrestricted basis can be accomplished only through some form of mediation (a New Bible, in this case). In other words, the immediacy hoped for in a more open model of relation will always be qualified simply by being implemented, by the differences that bodies and texts inevitably bring with them.[19] The lesson Whitman might be said to have taken away from the tribulations of American Bible societies is the difficult yet important task of coming to terms with the exact nature of institutions. The great discovery of the 1860 *Leaves* is that the success of any prospective social formation in producing unity or distributing identity rests upon its ability to negotiate the inherently hierarchical character of representation itself. To overcome hierarchy, relation would somehow have to defy its own mediatory, static character. Alexander Campbell's sect, the Disciples of Christ, was initially dedicated to the merging of all Christian sects in a single, nondenominational form—dedicated, that is, to its own eradication. If the new American religion is to be anything like the new American social formation, that is, an institution that eschews hierarchy, then a model founded on self-refuting claims is ideal; its frangibility would render it capable of generating a structure which is not only open to but also capable of its own revision. In this way, Whitman's "new American Religion" evades stratification and restriction of access even as habits of relation are implemented and generalized; it is capable always of collapsing back onto itself, of re-initiating and refounding itself like the American Bible Society, thereby harnessing both the strength of an established structure and the openness of a praxis just being forged. The New Bible is the central element of Whitman's plan for a new religion, an entirely new theologically grounded institution that, with its own priesthood and sacred text, proposes, counterintuitively, to mediate *un*mediated discourse.

The means by which Whitman attempts to satisfy this paradoxical objective are also the terms by which he represents its constitutive tension. As in the immersionist controversy, the tension between unity and differentiation is played out in the inclusive and exclusive practices of religious communities—the former represented by *immersion*, or the dissolution of particulars into a nondifferentiated whole, and the latter by *baptism*, or the crystallization of one out of the many into a discrete body or sect. The immersionist impulse of *Leaves* is familiar from the heart-tongue kiss in "Song of Myself," Section 5. It is true that Whitman retains this impulse: "So Long!" (1860) contains similar moments of realized immediacy, or immersion, moments in which the obstacles to absolute unity (like bodies and institutions) are dissolved. But, by contrast with "Song," "So Long!" sets these moments in opposition to others in which the experience of oneness is mediated, translated, made legible and vocal so that it can be made available and can be distributed to the members of this New Bible's congregation. Translation and distribution, which served as much as they disrupted the objectives of Bible societies and sectarians, are deployed by Whitman as the ideal kind of mediation, a self-canceling form of hierarchy that builds a non-institutional, immediate unity that need not be spoken (the sub-vocal "hum" of "Song") on the disparities, the distances across which oneness must be translated, made available in writing to those who, not being one, do not already know it (*LG* 33). By concluding the 1860 edition with "So Long!," Whitman literally leaves us with the idea that it is only by the *sacrifice* of unity that unity can be actualized at all. By accepting translation *over against* immediacy, baptism over against immersion, and hierarchy over against equality, the poet of "So Long!" comes to understand that the latter term of each pair exists *only in relation to* the other, only within the whole that comprises them both.

As the last poem of the 1860 edition, as well as the next four editions, "So Long!" has the authority of being the last word. Yet it is not, perforce, a poem of "conclusion": "To conclude—I announce what comes after me, / The thought that must be promulged, that all I know at any time suffices for that time only—not subsequent time; / I announce greater offspring, orators, days, and then depart."[20] For the most part, this poem is a re-writing of organic death as symbolic life: ending as beginning, death as birth, disruption as continuity. Unlike the instant transformation of discourse and self achieved in Section 5 of "Song of Myself," the exchange of mediation for immanence is here neither certain nor instantaneous. The reward may not follow hard on the sacrifice, if it does at all. The sacrifice required may be ongoing. This time, shedding the difference of bodies does not render persons unequivocally accessible:

Dear friend, whoever you are, here, take this kiss,
I give it especially to you—Do not forget me,
I feel like one who has done his work—I progress on,

> The unknown sphere, more real than I dreamed, more direct, darts awakening rays
>   about me—*So long!*
> Remember my words—I may again return—I love you—I depart from materials,
> I am as one disembodied, triumphant, dead.[21]

"I am as one disembodied, triumphant, dead" implies that a disembodied Whitman will be present to each reader of *Leaves of Grass*, in the book itself. But his presence in the text is not assured; he speaks like an ascending Christ who promises no Paraclete or Comforter, or does so only equivocally: "Remember my words—I may again return—I love you—I depart from materials." The phrase "Death making me undying" describes a state of affairs in which an intelligible, mediated state has been traded for a less than or barely intelligible one, one that borders between the unmediated (the only register in which *meaning* can be made available to everyone) and the mediated (the only register in which *sense* can be made to *anyone*).

The most perplexing movement in this poem—and, in its occurrences here and elsewhere in Whitman's *oeuvre*, a common subject in the criticism[22]—is that by which Whitman is "disembodied, triumphant, dead" and yet *re*-embodied in the book before us. Although familiar to most readers of Whitman, the gesture is perhaps misunderstood. The lines "My songs cease—I abandon them, / From behind the screen where I hid, I advance personally" summon up that moment in "Song of Myself," Section 6, when the poet assures us with the image of interred bodies growing up from the graves into living grass that "there is really no death," that death makes no difference.[23] "So Long!" makes the more nuanced argument that death, in fact, makes *all* the difference, that, even though death takes much (it interrupts the familiar, transposing or translating it into a foreign tongue), the potential returns for persons and social formations are immense (it equalizes, it unites across difference).[24] When Whitman claims in "So Long!" to come out "[f]rom behind the screen," that disclosure has the same self-mitigating force as the claim to "advance personally" (or, as Whitman would later intensify the line, "advance personally *solely to you*" [*LG* 505, emphasis added]). Just as the poet *claims* to make the person immanent but must do so through textual mediation, so does the privileging of the reader who "solely" receives Whitman's "advance" undo itself by extending that privilege to anyone who reads this poem. Translation holds a no less complicated status, since what the poet makes available to each reader— "curious enveloped messages"—he does so "personally," in "whispers" that we must "ben[d] for" and decipher in our personal, non-linguistic vocabularies ("My songs cease"). Translation allows communication across difference, but, as a kind of death (as in "old age ... meet[s] its translation"), it entails the canceling out of the original text and the possible loss of meaning: "*So long!* / I announce a life that shall be copious, vehement, spiritual, bold, / I announce an old age that shall lightly and joyfully meet its translation."[25]

This brings us to what I take to be the import of "So Long!": *Translation is perhaps the only way we can be one.* As a species of mediation, translation risks error (either willful or unintentional); it involves fragmentation, the breaking down of a compositional whole, so that, as a collection of analogous fragments, the whole may eventually be transmitted. Yet translation only brackets the issue of incommensurability. The second-language version is always an approximation of the original text, and yet, unless we learn that second language, we must accept translation as being *more or less* commensurable to the original.[26] In the case of the unrestricted relation of persons, or the integration of the many into the one, we do not have the option of learning a second language. In unity, there is no language; in plurality, there are *too* many languages. We must parse out unity in so many moments of broken speech. Whitman has not said we will all understand, or that we will understand at once. When we do, however, the reward is substantial enough to keep us reading, to continue attempting to translate.

In opposition to the word "translation" in "So Long!" stands the word "immerged," for it is between these poles that Whitman suspends his "true theory of the youth, manhood, womanhood, of The States," his theorization of social formation and its potential for immanent change.[27] Although Whitman uses the word *immerge* instead of *immerse*, any substantive difference between these two words which come from the same Latin verb (*immergere*; past participle, *immersus*) seems negligible. For Whitman, immersion connotes absorption (cf. *LG* 43, line 299; and *LG* 166, line 10) and the erasure of the particularizing, sectarian marks that baptism confers in his lexicon (cf. *LG* 236, line 18; and *LG* 299, line 108). One meaning of "immersion" is "baptism," however, and it is on this connection, contested so fiercely among Bible societies, that Whitman plots the volatile course of social formation:

O how your fingers drowse me!
Your breath falls around me like dew—your pulse lulls the tympans of my ears,
I feel immerged from head to foot,
Delicious—enough.[28]

"[I]mmerged from head to foot" evokes its predecessor-image in "Song of Myself" ("[you] reach'd till you felt my beard, and reach'd till you held my feet" [*LG* 33]). The consummative moment of the earlier poem is simultaneously embraced and stayed, as the ambiguous "Delicious—enough" implies. Immediacy is at once "enough" and insufficient, because the message is immanent but its meaning is far from clear (or, on the other hand, because the meaning is immanent and the message capable of transmitting it, garbled or lost).

More than a fantasy about his posthumous reception and fame or a critique of the relation of the author's *corpus* (both his text and his person) to the market, "So Long!" presents us with an equality-based model of relation but can only do so by deferring complete fulfillment, translating some fraction of that equality into another, immediately inaccessible register. That is the difference which death reinstates, the mediation that unrestricted relation invokes, which it must invoke to stave off differentiation and the proliferation of hierarchy. Whitman presents us with a discourse that does not simply maintain itself over time by deferral and incommensurability but is sustained by its own interruption, its translation into registers that are never quite coincident.

The idea of translation brings us again to what must remain the central criterological question for a New Bible: what kind of Bible is it to be, compared with its predecessor texts? If the 1860 *Leaves* is to be regarded as one such New Bible, the question then becomes, How is Whitman's intent specifically neo-Biblical? As the beleaguered history of American Bible societies suggests (and as the title of Peter Wosh's study of the ABS emphasizes), "spreading the word" was the order of the day for poets like Whitman as well as for minister-scholars like Alexander Campbell, Spencer Cone, William Wyckoff, and Thomas Conant. The phrase *distributing the word* (by which I mean not just the logistics of doing so but the implications of having done so) serves to name a culturally active problematic in mid-nineteenth century America, the answer to which was sought by poets, ministers, and illuminists, through new books, sects, and religions. All of these individuals asked, How does one unite a community? How does one do so with one text, with a text that is individual for each yet possesses some consistent core for all? The New Bible is the salient model for the third edition of *Leaves* not simply because in 1857 Whitman writes that it is, but rather because in 1860 he takes this problematic to the extreme. Everyone's not having the same text—or having one that shifts between the legible and the inscrutable, between the "emblematic"[29] and the real—is the *fons et origo* of the self-refuting institution capable of its own continual re-theorization. Whitman's New Bible invokes an institution that is an non-hierarchical and unrestricted as relation ever *can* be because it is so *intermittently*.[30]

In "So Long!" Whitman himself is translated, as if he is the text. He is translated not into a language but rather into another representational space. As soon as he announces "an old age that shall lightly and joyfully meet its translation," he says, as if surprised, "It appears to me that I am dying."[31] Far from holding off his own translation as he had in the 1855 *Leaves* ("I too am untranslatable"), he greets translation as the movement into another tongue, another register, in which the gain cannot be communicated precisely but is known by the loss that accompanies it ("Song of Myself," *LG* 89). Since my interpretation of "So Long!" depends of the notion of "translation," which I connect to the various translations of the Bible, I should make it clear that my reading is not meant to elide the fact that the "translation" that "old age" meets in verse 14 *is* death, a translation of the self or consciousness from the material to the spiritual world. But, given the ways in which Whitman marks the 1860 edition as neo-Biblical (for instance, dividing the text into enumerated sentences, not sections or stanzas), I believe that "translation" should also be read as referring to a *linguistic* change. I do not regard these two senses of "translation" as interchangeable, nor does Whitman; but he *wants* to be able to do so. My reading draws attention to the way in which Whitman means to render books and bodies, if not interchangeable, then *communicable*, the way in which he regards words and selves as things that are, to common sense, not commensurable, yet whose very incommensurability demands an economy of exchange, a distributive logic, whose currency is grounded on frangibility, fragmentation, interruption—those breaks which are really what permits transmission, what allows something to come across. Any slippage in meaning, then, between the two kinds of "translation" is one upon which Whitman depends.[32]

The fact that this book before us is "no book, /...[but] a man" reinforces the sense in which translation is death *and* continuation, revelation ("From behind the screen where I hid, I advance") and obfuscation ("enveloped messages"; "immerged from head to foot"). "[D]ecease calls me forth"—both to us, the readers, and away from us, toward some unknown.[33] *Leaves of Grass* is still a book of poetry. We can decipher some of it; some parts remains obscure. But we are left to parse it on our own, in a dyadic congregation that links us, tenuously, to others working at the same text, if not with the same purpose. *Leaves* is part of the writing of the New Bible, not necessarily the final product itself. As Whitman wrote in the 1860 poem "Says" (a poem excluded from *Leaves* altogether after 1876), the "glory of These States [is] that they respectfully listen to propositions, reforms, fresh views and doctrines, from successions of men and women, / Each age with its own growth."[34] Only three years later, the war would offer Whitman the opportunity while nursing wounded and dying soldiers to practice such an economy, in which loss is accepted in lieu of a value-bearing gain to follow.

However, the increasingly unilateral investment of the post-war editions—in the transcendent soul alone, forsaking immanent materiality—suggests that Whitman either found that practice too demanding or found no such reward awaiting him in the Union's victory and its half-hearted Reconstruction.

The outlook, even so, is not as bleak as it may seem. Even though the Whitmanian lesson of personhood must be mediated if we are to receive it, the "mediums" specified in the 1860 *Leaves* are potentially numerous enough to cease being mediatory. As Whitman prophesies in "Chants Democratic" (1860), they are not only the priest-poets of America but also those they reach with their words, who become poets in their turn: "Strong and sweet shall their tongues be ... / Of them, and of their works, shall emerge divine conveyers, to convey gospels,/Characters, events, retrospections, shall be conveyed in gospels—Trees, animals, waters, shall be conveyed, / Death, the future, the invisible faith, shall all be conveyed."[35] The 1860 edition means, then, to spawn a literature ("divine conveyers," "gospels") that is also a distributive organization, the latter being as ephemeral as it is recurrent, as successful as it is delayed and indirect.

NOTES

I am grateful to Marsha Fausti, Ed Folsom, Allen Grossman, Judith Harris, Michael Moon, Geoffrey Sill, Larzer Ziff, and the *WWQR* readers for commenting on previous drafts of this essay and, through their questions and advice, contributing significantly to its development. I would also like to thank the organizers of *The Many Cultures of Walt Whitman* conference (Rutgers University-Camden, October 1998), at which I delivered an earlier version of this essay.

1. Ralph Waldo Emerson, *Representative Men*, Chapter 7 ("Goethe; or, the Writer"), in *Essays and Lectures*, ed. Joel Porte (New York: Library of America, 1983), 761. Writing new Bibles was not the fixation solely of Whitman or of sectarians and religious visionaries (see Lawrence Buell, *New England Literary Culture: From Revolution through Renaissance* [Cambridge: Cambridge University Press, 1986], 167–168). In Chapter 5 of *Representative Men* ("Shakespeare; or, the Poet"), Emerson writes that the "world still wants its poet-priest, a reconciler"; Chapter 7, from which my epigraph derives, ends with the following prescription: "The secret of genius is to suffer no fiction to exist for us; to realize all that we know; in the high refinement of modern life, in arts, in sciences, in books, in men, to exact good faith, reality, and a purpose; and first, last, midst, and without end, to honor every truth by

use" (*Essays and Lectures*, 726, 761). As an attempt to realize the unmediated discourse of "Song of Myself" on a larger textual and social scale, the 1860 *Leaves* seeks to "honor" the truth of the American project "by use," by rendering that truth in its avatars (social and political equality, religious immediacy) *usable* and practicable. Also to the point is Herwig Friedl's remark that *Leaves* "contains history in the attempts at *symbolic interpretation of the universal process* both as sacred or metaphysical and as profane history" ("Making It Cohere: Walt Whitman's Idea of History," *Amerikastudien* 28 (1983), 295–307; 299.

2. Walt Whitman, *Notebooks and Unpublished Prose Manuscripts*, ed. Edward Grier (New York University Press, 1984). All further references to the notebooks are marked *NUPM* and referenced by volume and page number.

3. In *Disseminating Whitman: Revision and Corporeality in* Leaves of Grass (Cambridge: Harvard University Press, 1991), Michael Moon adds that Whitman's choice of 365 as the number of poems in his New Bible is central to his dedication to "annularity, [that is, to] the making of a great ring or cycle of poems that would have the status of scriptural texts" (124). Thus the calendrical dimension of Whitman's *"New Bible"*—the stipulation of one poem for each day of the year—renders it both atavistic and non-traditional, suggesting that Whitman's Bible comes not only with an improved format but with a prior claim to legitimacy. Another Biblical or liturgical characteristic of the 1860 edition is the numbering not of lines or sections but of individual sentences. For instance, in the 1860 edition the originally undivided "Song of Myself" (which finally ended up in fifty-two sections) was divided into 372 sections, or more exactly 372 sentences, which contain anywhere from one to twenty lines. Furthermore, the marginal enumeration of stanzas in the third edition reads less as a literary effect than a reference aid of the kind found in modern Bibles, here designating the verses of Whitman's New Bible. Moon reminds us that the 1860 text's claim of priority ought also to be understood in relation to Whitman's own work, establishing "a kind of primacy for the third edition which he now wants to deny to the two previous editions, by belatedly deciding that the earlier editions were more tentative ('published ... on trial') and 'inchoate[]' projects than they had actually been" (125).

4. Whitman, *Notes and Fragments Left by Walt Whitman*, ed. Richard Maurice Bucke (London and Ontario: A. Talbot and Co., 1899), 55.

5. David Reynolds categorizes the *"New Bible"* as one of several ideas Whitman considered but never pursued while "floundering" for a "metaphor" to unite his book and characterize the kind of serious cultural work it was endeavoring to do (*Walt Whitman's America: A Cultural Biography*

[New York: Knopf, 1995], 368). Reynolds rightly argues that the final words of the 1857 notebook entry ("it ought to be read[y] in 1859") suggest that Whitman "expected the project would be done in two years. Presumably he expected to have completed by then 365 poems, largely of a religious or philosophical nature, to replace or complement the Bible. Although composing new 'Bibles' was not unusual in the era of *The Book of Mormon* and *The Great Harmonia*, it is surprising that Whitman would mention such a grandiose project and then drop it—unless the 1860 edition of *Leaves of Grass*, containing many new religious poems, can be seen as a kind of Bible" (367–368). Reynolds, however, fails to pursue the neo-Biblical argument, perhaps because even to him the evidence he cites for it—Whitman's enthusiastic review of *Harper's Illustrated Bible* (1846) and the decorative illustrations and ornate fonts of the 1860 *Leaves*—seems at best circumstantial. As I have already pointed out, *Leaves* bears a number of superficial Biblical characteristics, but it is possible to launch a much stronger argument for Whitman's neo-Biblical intention if we move beyond superficial similarities to affinities of motive and institutional intent.

Only a handful of critics have taken the neo-Biblical claim further than Reynolds. Michael Moon agrees that while Whitman seems by 1860 to have left off constructing a New Bible, "the scriptural ambitions he had first articulated for his project in 1857 account for some of the most significant differences between the 1860 *Leaves* and its two predecessor-editions" (124). Although, Moon admits, Whitman was "far from unique in cherishing scriptural ambitions for his writing," Whitman, unlike Harriet Beecher Stowe and Julia Ward Howe, did not seek to "tak[e] over such fundamental aspects of Judeo-Christian scriptural tradition as its pervasive soteriological or apocalyptic claims" (124n). My reading of the 1860 edition does not so much contest Moon's reading as it means to sharpen the terms and context of what Moon regards as Whitman's "attempt [ ] to launch a gospel of immanence grounded in the text's extensive interrogations of the natural and the real" (124n).

Along with Reynolds and Moon, Maria Anita Stefanelli is one of the few critics to deal substantively with the neo-Scriptural motive of Whitman's work (" ' Chants' as 'Psalms for a New Bible,'" *Utopia in the present tense: Walt Whitman and the language of the New World*, International Conference on Walt Whitman, University of Macerata, October 29–30, 1992 [Rome: Calano, 1994], 171–188). Her deManian reading of *chiasmus* in the "Children of Adam" poems and Psalms 4 and 23 makes the same general point as work by Karen Sanchez-Eppler ("To Stand Between: A Political Perspective on Whitman's Poetics of Merger and Embodiment," *ELH* 56 [1989], 923–949) and Mark Maslan ("Whitman and His Doubles: Division and Union in

Leaves of Grass and Its Critics," *American Literary History* 6 [1994], 119–139). Although Maslan's and Sánchez-Eppler's concerns are more strictly political and formal, my reading is consonant with theirs in contending that "division [as well as union] is a vital principle of Whitman's poetics," one that is "enabling rather than debilitating" (Maslan 136). (See also Herwig Friedl as to how Whitman's attempt to "make a meaningful [that is, a social, cosmic] whole" and yet "find symbols for a totality of change" ends up "creat[ing] the contradictions it sets out to overcome" [306].) Although Stefanelli takes as her starting point F. O. Matthiessen's claim that Whitman "seemed to think that he could gain universality by making his chants psalms for a new Bible," she fails to develop an explanation of what a new Bible might have meant to Whitman and to an audience for whom the founding of new sects and religions came to seem both the answer to the problem of unrestricted relation and no answer at all (Matthiessen, *American Renaissance: Art and Expression in the Age of Emerson and Whitman* [New York: Oxford University Press, 1941], 557).

6. Whitman, "The Eighteenth Presidency!" (1856), *Complete Poetry and Collected Prose*, ed. Justin Kaplan (New York: Library of America, 1982), 1307–1325; 1319. Whitman's relation to the founding documents is at once supplementary and foundational. He regards the Constitution as "a perfect and entire thing, and edifice put together," complete in itself, but also as something which "time only is great enough to give ... area," which can be "better understood from results, growths," supplements and revisions (1318). As a New Bible, *Leaves* implicitly eclipses the received Scriptures by accommodating present circumstances, by satisfying the need for a text that has an efficacious relation to the state, in a way the Authorized Version cannot (its authority having been bracketed by America's secular founding instruments). By addressing in this *new* Bible the originary site of state formation, *Leaves* professes a presence at the origins both of the state and of a transcendental, natural state (the site of relation not yet codified by either secular or theological institutions).

7. Whitman, "Preface, 1855, to First Issue of *Leaves of Grass*," *Prose Works 1892*, ed. Floyd Stovall, 2 vols. (New York: New York University Press, 1963–1964). All further references to this edition are marked *PW*.

8. American sects had certainly been formed before 1830, the most prominent being Ann Lee's Shakers (1774) and Alexander Campbell's Disciples of Christ (1811). But nothing could match the fervor with which new sects and new religions arose between 1830 and 1850: Mormonism (1830), Oneidan perfectionism (1838), Jehovah's Witnesses (1844), Seventh-Day Adventism (1844), and Harmonialism (1847)—not to mention a number of Protestant splinter-groups (among them, "Two-Seed" Baptism and

Universalism). I am stressing here what I perceive to be the missing subtext of the conventional history of the Bible and social reform in America during the first half of the nineteenth-century (a history recounted by Mark Noll, *A History of Christianity in the United States and Canada* [Grand Rapids: William B. Eerdmans, 1992]; and Timothy Smith, "Righteousness and Hope: Christian Holiness and the Millennial Vision in America, 1800–1900," *American Quarterly* 31 [Spring 1979], 22–45). Although the Bible may have adequately funded the state for many Americans, the mid-century welter of new religions and sects suggests that for an equally significant number the same was not true. In his farewell sermon, "The Lord's Supper," Emerson voiced his dissatisfaction in 1832 with established American religion (Congregationalism in his case) and its prescriptive, spiritually empty rituals (*Essays and Lectures*, 1129–1140). Joseph Smith broke away from his Universalist roots to found Mormonism in 1830. At the same time, evangelists and theologians like Charles Finney and William Ellery Channing were cutting denominational ties (with Presbyterianism and Congregationalism) in favor of revivals and new sects (for Channing, Unitarianism) that promised a relation to God unmediated by dogma or ecclesiasticism. Thus, although the term *post-theological crisis* may not refer necessarily to a uniform phenomenon, it seems to me the best term to describe the period of American religious life during which the "individualization of conscience" fostered by the Second Great Awakening (1795–1810) manifested itself not merely in idiosyncratic Biblical interpretations but in more ambitious projects for the re-grounding of American social formation on neo-Biblical or on literary bases (Nathan O. Hatch and Mark A. Noll, *The Bible in America: Essays in Cultural History* [New York: Oxford University Press, 1982], 66).

9. Whitman, "Preface, 1872, to 'As A Strong Bird on Pinions Free.'" Although written after what one might call Whitman's neo-Biblical period (1857–1865), the 1872 Preface is consistent, on this account at least, with notebook entries of the late 1850s and the 1860s (see *NUPM* 6:2061).

10. Whitman, *Leaves of Grass, Comprehensive Reader's Edition*, ed. Harold W. Blodgett and Sculley Bradley (1965), 729. All further references to this edition are marked *LG*. This passage is notable for the vacillation between "every man['s] ... be[ing] his own priest" and a select number of individuals (poets) fulfilling that function for them. Similarly, one of Whitman's notebook entries (dated 1857 or after) admits that as soon as the old churches are razed, a new one is immediately erected. It seems that even a religion "comprehensive enough to include all the Docttines & Sects" cannot be formed except as a sect, distinguished, if by nothing else, by its willingness to countenance what other sects will not: heterogeneity (*NUPM* 6:2046).

11. Although *Democratic Vistas* in its present form was not published until 1870 (falsely dated 1871), the essays from which Whitman composed this longer piece ("Democracy" and "Personalism") had already appeared in *Galaxy*, in 1867 and 1868 respectively.

12. A notebook entry from the 1860s instantiates this ambivalence between founding a more inclusive religious institution and the impossibility of doing so other than in a congregation, between persons, and therefore within a network of mediating differences: "religion ... [must] adjust itself to the ranges of real life and all men and women[.] That would be a religion of some account ... [namely, one with] reference ... to ... the people[.] The people! none excluded—not the ignorant, not roughs or laboring persons—even prostitutes.... This is what America is for—to justify this is what she means—If not she means nothing.... I will not be fooled with the facade of the few ... I say that a religion which from those vast ranges of life in the great cities, raises its house aloof, an exile—which, to them, enters not, and they enter not into it ... is no religion for These athletic and living States" (*NUPM* 6:2092–2093). Whitman may not be fooled by the "facade of the few," the structural gradations that admit only a select number into the visibility of a social formation, but, considering the analogy, neither is he fooled by the facade of the many—for the latter is still a facade. Any group, whether of the few or the many, must "raise its house"; and, since even a one-story house must have a floor, walls, and a roof, and blueprint must differentiate to this minimal degree.

13. Though the entry is undated, Grier concludes that "the date, from the paper, is 1857 or after" (*NUPM* 6:2046n).

14. Peter J. Wosh, *Spreading the Word: The Bible Business in Nineteenth-Century America* (Ithaca: Cornell University Press, 1994), 64.

15. It is true that in some aspects, the directors of the ABS, like the Federalists, demanded centralization: local Bible societies were expected, like states, to adopt constitutions modeled on that of the ABS. Nevertheless, the Society faced the same challeng as the Constitutional delegates: procuring unity without stifling the independence of the agents and auxiliaries through whom they were able to express unity. In terms of the structure of the ABS, hierarchy could extend only so far: realizing that their plan for national distribution could best be accomplished through paid agents and auxiliaries, the Society's directors depended on decentralized, semi-autonomous means for the instrumentation of a unified, centralized identity (the Christian nation). Peter Wosh's *Spreading the Word*, while primarily a history of the ABS, is probably the best account of Bible distribution in the period.

16. Rather than anomalies, the commercial success of *Harper's Illustrated Bible* (1846) and the impact of Joseph Smith's *Book of Mormon*

(1830) suggest the tremendous appeal that was becoming associated with having one's own distinct version of the Bible. Philip Barlow records it as a matter of fact that "the growing prestige of the Holy Book, as interpreted by oneself, reached its apex in the middle years of the nineteenth century." We can better gauge the height of that apex by noting that before the 1840s, new translations or revisions of the KJV were all but non-existent in America. Before the Revolution, only a handful of partial translations were made, typically Psalters; the only two *full* translations in the same period were into foreign languages (the 1663 Eliot Indian Bible and the 1743 German Saur Bible). The tide began to turn slowly with six new English versions and translations made between 1800 and 1830. The deluge began at that point and continued through the Civil War, averaging one new version or translation every two years. Through the 1820s, the focus had been on distributing copies of the Authorized Version rather than on making a new version on one's own authority. However, suddenly in the 1840s and 1850s, one finds almost as many translations of the Bible (either one or both Testaments) as there were individuals who were able, or thought themselves able, to make their own translation. A translator might not even have deemed knowledge of Hebrew or Greek necessary, relying merely on inspiration; many thought revision of the English KJV in itself was sufficient. In terms that reflect the centrality of the problematic of the one and the many to American consciousness, the attraction of private versions of the Bible derives from what one critic has called "an already strong reverence [in America] for unmediated scripture" (Philip L. Barlow, *Mormons and the Bible: The Place of the Latter-day Saints in American Religion* [New York: Oxford University Press, 1991], 7–8). Fuller accounts of the translation history are given by Harry M. Orlinsky and Robert G. Bratcher, *A History of Bible Translation in America and the North American Contribution* (Atlanta: Scholars Press, 1991), and Paris Marion Simms, *The Bible in America: Versions that Have Played Their Part in the Making of the Republic* (New York: Wilson-Erickson, 1936), an older but nonetheless authoritative work.

17. In the fourth century A.D., Jerome would follow the same practice in his Vulgate translation of the Septuagint. Given Campbell's passion for going back to the original text and recovering what he considered to be the original meaning, it is unsurprising that he, along with Barton Stone and his own father, Thomas, were founders of the Restoration Movement, an anti-denominational, anti-dogmatic group which included the Disciples of Christ and was dedicated to the purity of Christian text and tradition alike.

18. The disputes between Baptists and other sects in these Bible Societies, and among the Baptists themselves, present at least two notions of religious community (that is, of religiously-informed social formation): a

differentiated, sovereign sect (comparable to Whitman's "poetics of ... embodiment") or a non-sectarian whole (comparable to Whitman's "poetics of merger"); see Karen Sánchez-Eppler, "To Stand Between," 924. Details of the ABS's role in the immersionist controversy are available in Peter Wosh, *Spreading the Word*, 118–150; Roland H. Worth, Jr., *Bible Translations: A History through Source Documents* (Jefferson, NC: McFarland & Co., 1992), 152–160; and Orlinsky and Bratcher, *History of Bible Translation*, 48–86 *passim*.

19. Whitman's New Bible meant to unify disparates (disenfranchised persons) in a way that no institutionally sanctioned document like the Bible or the Constitution had, in a way that churches and governments *could* not, dependent as they are on the delegation of power and the reservation of identity—that is, on the hierarchical management of the representation of persons. But since the transformation of social structure was to occur through a text (*Leaves*), mediation could not be done away with entirely.

20. Whitman, *Leaves of Grass: Facsimile Edition of the 1860 Text*, ed. Roy Harvey Pearce (Ithaca: Cornell University Press, 1961), 452, 451. Following the practice of the 1860 edition, I have sometimes referred to lines from "So Long!" by the verse markings Whitman gave the poem in that particular text, the marginal numbers that set off each sentence of the poem, instead of the sections that characterize other editions of *Leaves*. The 1860 variants for "So Long!" are also available in Whitman, *Leaves of Grass: A Textual Variorum of the Printed Poems*, ed. Sculley Bradley, Harold W. Blodgett, Arthur Golden, and William White, 3 vols. (New York: New York University Press, 1980), 3: 452–458.

21. Whitman, *Leaves of Grass: Facsimile Edition of the 1860 Text*, 456. Whitman later underscored the idea of translation evoked in verse 14 ("I announce an old age that shall lightly and joyfully meet its translation" [454]) by adding the following between the third and fourth lines of the 1860 version: "I receive now again of my many translations, from my avataras ascending, while others doubtless await me" (*LG* 506).

22. Though often commented upon, the disembodiment/immediacy claim of Whitman's poetry is seldom gotten right, I think. Terry Mulcaire ("Publishing Intimacy in *Leaves of Grass*," *ELH* 60 [1993]: 471–501) gives a Marxist reading of the Whitmanian construction of the relation between book, body, poet, and public—a reading which, theoretical differences aside, insists as I do that *Leaves* does not simply offer moments of transcendence and immediacy but rather challenges us to comprehend what I have called the constitutive tension between union and disunion, between generality and particularity or the one and the many. In Mulcaire's terms (which owe much to Foucault), "[t]he cultural distinctions *Leaves* asks us to make, then, are not

between repression and alienation on the one hand and freedom and immediacy on the other but between different *linkages* of repression and alienation on the one hand and freedom and immediacy on the other" (495; emphasis added).

23. Whitman, *Leaves of Grass: Facsimile Edition of the 1860 Text*, 455; *LG* 34.

24. The other relevant moment also occurs in the 1860 edition. "Scented Herbage of My Breast" is often read a rejection of the "show of appearance," of the "[e]mblematic" meaning of the leaves of grass, which are "capricious" because rather than telling what they mean they "mask" the "real reality" they are meant to convey. Rather than a refutation of the signs that cannot be relied upon to "tell in [their] own way of the heart that is under" them, "Scented Herbage" marks a discovery which Whitman develops more fully in the later poem: namely, that "real reality" cannot be made immediate, that "death and love" "hide in these shifting forms of life, for reasons" (*LG* 113–115). One of those reasons, I would argue, is the necessarily mediated character of representation, the sacrifices in personhood that are required, paradoxically, to expand the category of person, to extend it in any one direction.

25. Whitman, *Leaves of Grass: Facsimile Edition of the 1860 Text*, 454. "Old age" was subsequently altered to "end," a word that better stresses the paradox of an end that is also a beginning in another register, a translation, and thus not an end, or a death, in its original register.

26. As W. V. Quine has noted, because no word has an exact foreign equivalent, "uniquely correct translations" do not exist (*The Oxford Companion to Philosophy*, ed. Ted Honderich [Oxford: Oxford University Press, 1995], 879).

27. Whitman, *Leaves of Grass: Facsimile Edition of the 1860 Text*, 454, 455, 453.

28. Ibid., 455.

29. Whitman, "Scented Herbage of My Breast," *LG* 114.

30. Focusing on the "Children of Adam" and "Calamus" clusters, Stefanelli argues that Whitman's "New Bible" is meant to counteract the Bible's vilification of sexuality and transgression: "Whitman reshapes the biblical pattern in order to people his poems with contemporary children of Adam who have interiorized their parents' experiences and live through them with a different attitude, thus transforming sin into a new consciousness of sexuality and nature. A centrifugal movement away from the Biblical text takes place in Whitman's poems, which is the counterpart of the centripetal forces supporting unity in Genesis" (173–174). I would argue, however, that rather than moving in strictly one direction (centrifugal, foundational), the 1860 *Leaves* moves in two contrary directions (centripetal

and centrifugal, supplementary and foundational), as intent on establishing itself as liturgy as it is refuting the authoritative and institutional status of liturgical texts.

31. Whitman, *Leaves of Grass: Facsimile Edition of the 1860 Text*, 454.

32. For examples of the slippage between the bodily and the linguistic in Whitman's use of "translate" and "translation," see "Song of Myself," Section 6: "I wish I could translate the hints about the dead young men and women" (*LG* 34); "Song of Myself," Section 21: "I am the poet of the Body and I am the poet of the Soul ... / The first I graft and increase upon myself, the latter I translate into a new tongue" (*LG* 48); and "Song of the Answerer": "He resolves all tongues into his own and bestows it upon men, and any man translates, and any man translates himself also" (*LG* 168).

33. Whitman, *Leaves of Grass: Facsimile Edition of the 1860 Text*, 455, 454.

34. Ibid., 419.

35. Whitman, "Chants Democratic," *Leaves of Grass: Facsimile Edition of the 1860 Text*, 189–190. In the 1867 edition, Whitman re-titled this poem "Mediums," the title it retains in *LG* 480–481.

MICHAEL D. SOWDER

Walt Whitman, The Apostle

Walt Whitman wrote in the midst of what I want to call an antebellum culture of conversion, a Christian culture of religious preaching and writing, which descended from the Second Great Awakening and sought the reformation of individual subjects through the reproduction of conversion experiences. The goal of these practices, as suggested by the *Christian Spectator* in 1847, was nothing less than "the complete moral regeneration of the world." Undoubtedly, Whitman wrote, to a significant degree, in opposition to this culture and to conventional religions of all kinds, famously declaring in his 1855 preface to *Leaves of Grass*, "There will soon be no more priests. Their work is done."[1] Horace Traubel reports how Whitman frequently asserted that "the day of the preacher is past.... 'I don't ... expect anything of the preachers.'"[2] But Whitman made such statements not as a nineteenth-century atheist but as a poet-prophet intending to assume the role of preacher and priest: "The priest departs, the divine literatus comes" (932). And as he declared his intention to "inaugurate a religion" and write "the new Bible" and "evangel-poem of comrades and of love," his new theology in the end replicated as many features of Christian and evangelical culture as it repudiated (179–180).[3] True, his new religion was hardly Christ-centered, and it promoted beliefs about the body, sexuality, democracy, equality, and human and social perfection that starkly opposed orthodox and

From *Walt Whitman Quarterly Review*, vol. 16, nos. 3/4 (Winter/Spring 1999). © 1999 by The University of Iowa.

liberal versions of Protestantism (though ideas like his did appear in some radical offshoots of the 1850s). Yet, in seeking to displace conventional religions, he appropriated and relied upon many of their cultural and rhetorical practices. This reliance resulted in what I find to be one of the most important, yet inadequately investigated, features of his poetry: its design to work like a preacherly performance and to produce conversions in his readers, affectively charged moments of religious experience by which reading subjects would be reborn into Whitman's image of a new American personality.[4] With rhetorical strategies borrowed from preachers, Whitman, like the evangelist, would produce conversions and thus redeem the nation.

Conversion seems at first an unlikely model to bring to a reading of Whitman's poetry because conversion always begins in an act of *negation*—a turning of the self away from the self and the sinful world. Whitman's poetry, in contrast, seems everywhere to affirm the self and the world, to ratify the notion that "men and women and all that concerns them are unspeakably perfect miracles" (1855 preface), that "there is in fact no evil" ("Starting from Paumanok"), and that "It is not chaos or death.... it is form and union and plan.... it is eternal life.... it is happiness" (1855 version of "Song of Myself") (16, 180, 87). His new religion is carved in relief against a Protestant culture that foregrounded sin, renunciation, and a rejection of the self and the world. Like a proto-Nietzschean, he denounces the evangelist's *contemptus mundi*. Rather than warn about the wages of sin, he goes to the riverbank, undresses, and admires himself, inviting us to admire him, too. Yet, even though affirmation seems the dominant tone of the poetry, appearing on every page, if not in every line, a certain burden of tension can be felt beneath those affirmations, resulting from the poetry's persistent desire to reform.

From his earliest stories and temperance novel, *Franklin Evans* (1842), to *Democratic Vistas* and the death-bed edition, Whitman's writing was impelled by reformist impulses. A desire to reform something is a desire to change it, to transform it, and to transform something, as we know from Hegel, is to *negate* it. Alexander Kojeve explains how in Hegel's view action achieves satisfaction only through negation, by the destruction or transformation of the desired object: "to satisfy hunger, for example, the food must be destroyed or, in any case, transformed."[5] And far from leaving the given as it is, "action destroys it; if not in its being, at least in its given form."[6] But negating action is not purely destructive, for if it destroys an objective reality, it creates in its place a "subjective reality": "The being that eats, for example, creates and preserves its own, by the 'transformation' of an alien reality into its own reality, by the 'assimilation,' the 'internalization' of a 'foreign,' 'external reality.'"[7] Kojeve's examples of negation as eating and devouring carry particular relevance for my reading of Whitman's poetry below. For now, I would simply note that the negating impulse is all the stronger in a desire to *reform*, for such a desire already presupposes a flaw, imperfection, or lack in the thing to be transformed. Some kind of imperfection, something in need of a healing reformation, something akin to sin seems to worm its way back into the poetry despite Whitman's best efforts to keep it out. Stated differently, the affirmations of the subjects *Leaves of Grass* celebrates—the self, the reader, and America—represent already redeemed versions of themselves, whose redeemed condition depends upon prior, unacknowledged negations. The poetry seeks less to affirm than to transform and convert, and the negation at the heart of conversion is the absent presence I want to illuminate.

Whitman's admiration for language and rhetoric that converts its readers and listeners can be seen clearly in two essays he wrote about religious preaching, essays that show the profound influence preaching had over him. In "Father Taylor (and Oratory)," an essay included in *November Boughs*, he reminisces fondly about hearing the religious preaching of the Methodist evangelist Edward Taylor (original for *Moby Dick's* Father Mapple) and compares Taylor's preaching to that of the radical Quaker preacher Elias Hicks: "Both had the same inner, apparently inexhaustible, fund of latent volcanic passion—the same tenderness, blended with a curious remorseless firmness, as of some surgeon operating on a belov'd patient" (1145). In this metaphorical operation, the listener does not direct his or her own spiritual healing (or interpretation of spiritual truth) but lies prostrate, as though etherized upon a table, unconscious beneath the minister-surgeon's rhetorical instruments. Somewhat surprisingly, violent figures appear frequently in Whitman's writings about oratory. In his essay on Hicks, America's other "essentially perfect orator," he again writes about preaching in terms of an overwhelming force, a "magnetic stream of natural eloquence, before which all minds and natures, all emotions [...] yielded entirely without exception [...] not argumentative or intellectual, but so penetrating" (1143, 1234). Although these essays appeared late in his life, his earliest manuscripts reveal similar preoccupations. Notes from the 1840s envision "the place of the orator ... [as] an agonistic arena. There he wrestles and contends with them—he suffers, sweats, undergoes his great toil and exstasy. Perhaps it is a greater battle than any fought for by contending forces on land and sea."[8] Later in the same manuscript he remarks how "[m]en witness the prodigies of oratory, when they are themselves the victims of its power."[9] And beginning a lecture tour in 1879, commemorating the death of Lincoln, he imagines himself going "up and down the land [...] seeking *whom I may devour*, with lectures, and reading of my own poems" (emphasis added).[10]

Whitman's musings in these essays about oratory have important implications for the poetry. It is well known that he dreamed of being an orator early in his career but abandoned the ambition, evidently upon realizing that he lacked the voice or talent for it. C. Carroll Hollis and others have demonstrated how his failure as an orator impelled him to attempt to reproduce in his "second-person poetry" the powerful effects he witnessed in oratory, and scholars as early as Thomas Harned have noted how lines from his early drafts for lectures were transferred unchanged into the poems.[11] But what the scholarship on Whitman and oratory, old and new, most frequently fails to emphasize is that the oratory Whitman admired and modeled was *religious* oratory. Taylor and Hicks, not Webster and Clay, met his ideal of the "essentially perfect orator," and the effects they sought to produce were conversions.[12]

The metaphors Whitman uses to describe their oratory—surgery, penetration, agon, war, victimization, and devouring—suggest a fascination with rhetoric that does not simply celebrate or affirm but overwhelms, conquers, and negates. The figure of a minister operating like a "good physician" draws upon a long tradition of Christian texts on preaching as good medicine, beginning at least with Augustine.[13] The image of Father Taylor as a surgeon "operating on a belov'd patient," moreover, incisively describes the kind of conversion-inducing sermons evangelists sought to produce, sermons that could generate a rebirth in their listeners by inscribing the Word upon their hearts. The benevolent violence of oratory suggested to Whitman the benevolent violence of surgery, which in turn evokes the benevolent violence of conversion, often described as an ecstatic rending of the subject, a slaying out of which a new self is born. At revivals and camp-meetings during the antebellum period—in the Second Great Awakening and its aftermath—sometimes hundreds fell prostrate on the ground, some in anguish, others in ecstasy, all under the spell of the minister's overpowering rhetoric. Describing the effects of one fiery sermon, a camp-meeting participant wrote: "In the midst of this Sermon the Spirit of God fell upon the Assembly with great Power, and rode forth with Majesty upon the Word of Truth. In a Minutes Time the People were seemingly as much affected as if a thousand Arrows had been shot in among them."[14] Charles Grandison Finney, one of the most famous of antebellum revivalists, remarked after one successful meeting: "If I had had a sword in my hand, I could not have cut them down ... as fast as they fell." Indeed, the metaphor of slaying and being slain is almost the *sin qua non* of such writings. And Whitman's image of his lectures and poems "devouring" his listeners similarly recalls the image common in conversion narratives of being "swallowed up in God."[15]

In this essay, I will focus on one element of Whitman's conversion-inducing poetry: the element of negation at work in the celebration of his own conversion, and how that element reappears in even the boldest affirmations in the poems. The central purpose of testifying about one's own conversion in the evangelical tradition is to inspire new conversions in others. Jonathan Edwards wrote that "There is no one thing I know of which God has made such a means of promoting his work among us, as the news of others' conversions."[16] Whitman's conversion is famously recounted and performed in Sections 4 and 5 of "Song of Myself." Section four initiates the event first by enumerating and then negating all the details of his ordinary, everyday life: "People I meet [...] The latest news [...] My dinner, dress, associates, looks, business, compliments, dues [...] / The sickness of one of my folks—or of myself.... or ill-doing or.... loss or lack of money.... or depressions or exaltations" (29–30). These, he says, "are not the Me myself" (30). The "Me myself," a redeemed figure, is, instead, something apart— "Apart from the pulling and hauling stands what I am" (30). With a pun on God's tautological theophany to Moses, this "what I am" hovers "amused, complacent, compassionating, idle, unitary," and "[l]ooks down" (30). The details that constituted an ordinary, everyday, historical life are negated and transformed into this God-like, gazing Self. And after this preparatory cleansing, the poem proceeds immediately into Section 5, the reenactment of the conversion scene proper. The fact that Section 5 is narrated in the past tense makes clear that the Self that is affirmed and celebrated in the present tense throughout the poem is an already redeemed Self. Interestingly, the scene begins with a statement of belief, "I *believe in* you, my soul," and then reenacts the benevolently violent overwhelming of the self by the Soul, drawing upon the same metaphorical vocabulary as his essays on preaching: the stunning, the emotional overwhelming, the prostration, cutting, penetration (here, with the surgical tongue), and devouring by what Whitman will later call the "fluid and *swallowing* soul" (30, 63, emphases added). The scene reenacts the conversion of an unregenerate self detailed in Section 4 of the poem—call him "Walter Whitman"—into "Walt Whitman, an American, one of the roughs, a kosmos" (50).

If, as I am asserting, these sections reveal an act of negation that underwrites the affirmations of the poem, then traces of that negating impulse ought to appear throughout the poem; and, indeed, they do. Let us look briefly at what is perhaps the most emphatic moment of affirmation in "Song of Myself"—its opening lines. Can we catch there the shadow of a negating turn? The brilliant, epiphanic tenor of the affirmation at the beginning of the poem results to a great extent from the way it has been prepared for by the 1855 preface. In the preface, we are told to be prepared for a momentous event—the coming of "the greatest poet," one who will be not only a great artist, but a vatic figure of divine power, a religious teacher who shall "indicate" for folks "the path between reality and their souls" (10). Something like Blake's depictions of the Deity and the apotheosized "what I am" of Section 4 appears in the preface's descriptions of this poet: "High up out of reach he stands turning a concentrated light ... he turns the pivot with his finger" (9). Indeed, the relationship the preface as a whole bears to the poem resembles the Biblical pattern of prophesy and fulfillment. Yet taken as prophesy, the preface speaks in a curious way about the future. Like most prophesy heralding the coming of a great figure, it speaks of this poet in the third-person. And as would be expected, it often uses future tenses and the subjunctive mood. But the predominant tense of the preface is the present tense—a kind of proleptic present that indicates that the coming of the greatest poet is so imminent that future tenses are inadequate to describe him.[17] For example, the first time the preface mentions the poet, it uses the predictive infinitive: "The American poets *are to enclose* old and new for America is the race of races. Of them a bard *is to be* commensurate with a people" (6–7, emphasis added).

But the language slips back into the simple present: "To him the other continents *arrive* as contributions ... he *gives* them reception for their sake and his own sake. His spirit *responds* to his country's spirit.... he *incarnates* its geography and natural life" (7, emphasis added), and the majority of the preface continues thereafter in this proleptic present, for, as the preface itself tells us, the greatest poet stands "where the future becomes present" (13). In the preface, then, we wait as on a threshold.

After this extended foretelling, the poem itself opens in a sudden shift of person, tense, and mood into the first-person, singular, simple present indicative, and in type twice as large as that of the preface the poet declares:

I CELEBRATE myself

With the future, subjunctive, and proleptic present cast aside, the "greatest poet" becomes "I" in a simple present of perfection, his prophesy fulfilled. The verb "celebrate" emphasizes the radical affirmation of the present. It signals the difference between Whitman's new religion and Christianity. This voice does not cower guiltily hoping for a better world, but celebrates a self and a world that is present—bodily, materially, now. A spear of grass then becomes a subject worthy of extended contemplation and the symbolic center of a poem of epic dimensions.

Yet even as we have stepped through the threshold of prophesy into the brilliance of presence, even here in the first line, startling in its exuberant affirmation, we find traces of another celebration, which constellate into a negative image recessed behind the positive. "Celebrate" has a deeply-layered etymology. In addition to the colloquial meaning of commemorating, as in celebrating a birthday, originally it meant "To perform publicly ... (a religious ceremony)," as in, to "celebrate ... the Mass," or, "to consecrate by religious rites" (*OED*). Religious rites and ceremonies frequently commemorate a completed event (a harvest, the return of a god), but often, and more importantly, they also perform ritual transformations and conversions. In the Catholic tradition, for example, a priest "celebrates" the Mass by converting bread into Christ's body, matter into spirit, flesh into Word. Similarly, when a minister "celebrates" a wedding, he or she transforms the status of two persons.[18] And one "celebrates" a contract by performing its contractual obligations—as, for example, by building a house—again pointing to actions that transform the world in accordance with an idea, here, a promise. "Celebrate," then, not only signifies commemorating but also transforming, completing, perfecting. And so when Whitman says, "I celebrate myself," he celebrates in the sense of publicly rejoicing in himself, again, the way one celebrates a birthday, but he also celebrates himself in the sense of ritually transforming a version of himself ("Walter Whitman") into something fulfilled, complete, redeemed: "Walt Whitman," our rough, American kosmos.

In the second line, however, the poem falls back away from the sense of a perfect present: "And what I assume, you shall assume." After having abandoned the preparation of the preface, having dispensed with traditional epic openings, those invocations and preparatory prayers, and begun the celebration in earnest with the arrival of the god-like poet himself, suddenly we hear a suggestion that the whole project may be ontologically at risk. The line suggests that the celebration will take place within a rhetoric of assumptions. "And what I assume, you shall assume" describes an as-yet-unrealized condition. Will we assume that "men and women and all that concerns them are unspeakable, perfect miracles," and that "there is in fact no evil"? Shuttled back outside of the doors of the celebration, we are back in the uncertain alleyways of the suppositional, the future, the proleptic. If the poem celebrates assumed identities or assumed realities, it does something other than simply affirm *what is*. "To assume" also means "to consume"—evoking again the devouring impulse of Whitman's "swallowing soul." And should we remember that "assumption" once signified a reception into heaven, foreshadowing the apotheosis of the self into "what I am" in Section 4? If the subjects of the poem—I, you, and America—will be subject to an assumption, we will be converted into more sublime conditions, another hint that our host is up to hierophantic play, planning not only to throw a party for the pleasure of making a joyful noise, but to perform the serious work of transformation—that is, conversion. Our minister-surgeon-poet comes not only to commend our good health, perhaps, but to perform some reconstructive surgery.

The third line also tends to keep us outside the doors of the celebration. In "For every atom belonging to me as good belongs to you" both "belonging" and "as good" fall just short of supporting the commemorative meaning of "celebrate," and reaffirm instead its transformative meanings. The poet might have said more definitively, though with inferior rhythm, "For every atom belongs to me and also belongs to you," but the participle, "belonging," keeps our possession just out of reach. It does not quite state what is. And the almost, but not quite, equalizing qualifier, "as good," falls just short of affirming an equality between the poet's and the reader's possession. "Every atom belonging to me as good belongs to you" again describes a condition just outside of present fact. So after the poem's spectacular opening, which abandoned prophesy and preparation for the affirmation and celebration of perfect presence, the poem as quickly retreats from this presence, as though that vision were too bright to gaze long upon. As he says later in "Song of Myself": A "touch...is about as much as I can stand" (55).

That the rhetoric of *Leaves of Grass* seeks to produce conversions in Whitman's readers he openly admits in the sly poem, "Whoever You Are Holding Me Now In Hand," from the *Calamus* sequence. There, he makes clear the negation at the heart of the celebration. Echoing Christ's admonition to his disciples, he warns that to follow him, "You would have to give up all else"; "the whole past theory of your life [...] would have to be abandon'd" (270). As conversion requires more than an assent to religious beliefs and rituals, demanding a fundamental unraveling of a narrative of identity, so Whitman's conversion requires the abandonment of "the whole past theory of your life." And once this self-abandonment is complete, the greatest poet, as the greatest lover, will intercede to fill the empty space opened by that self-negation to become your "sole and exclusive standard" (270) and engender in you the birth of a new American personality.

Notes

1. *Complete Poetry and Collected Prose*, ed. Justin Kaplan (New York: Library of America, 1982), 24. Subsequent references to this edition will appear by page number in parentheses in the text. Ellipses within brackets are mine.

2. *With Walt Whitman in Camden*, ed. Horace Traubel (Boston: Maynard, 1906), 1:120.

3. *Notebooks and Unpublished Prose Manuscripts*, ed. Edward F. Grier (New York: New York University Press, 1984), 1:352.

4. Whitman states in *Democratic Vistas* that "We must entirely recast the types of highest personality" (968).

5. Alexander Kojeve, *Introduction to the Reading of Hegel: Lectures on The Phenomenology of Spirit*, ed. Allan Bloom, trans. James H. Nichols, Jr. (New York: Basic Books, 1969), 4.

6. Kojeve, 4.

7. Kojeve, 4.

8. Quoted in Thomas B. Harned, "Walt Whitman and Oratory," *The Complete Writings of Walt Whitman*, ed. Richard M. Bueke et al. (New York: Putnam's Sons, 1902), 5:245.

9. Harned, 5:256.

10. *Prose Works 1892*, ed. Floyd Stovall (New York: New York University Press, 1963–1964), 2:682.

11. Kerry Larson, *Whitman's Drama of Consensus* (Chicago: University of Chicago Press, 1988), 7. My thinking on this topic began with and has been continually stimulated by the work of Kerry Larson. See also C. Carroll Hollis, *Language and Style in Leaves of Grass* (Baton Rouge: Louisiana State University Press, 1983), and Harned, 5:256.

12. As a Quaker, Hicks's views on redemption and sanctification were far different from the Methodist Father Taylor's. Hicks believed in a gradual awakening of the inner voice rather than in crisis conversions. Nevertheless, his memoir includes a description of his own dramatic conversion along with other examples of sudden religious experiences. His belief in the efficacy of preaching to produce individual transformations is apparent in his life-long intinerancy preaching throughout New England and the Middle Atlantic states. See Elias Hicks, *Journal of the Life and Religious Labours of Elias Hicks, written by himself* (New York, 1832); Bliss Forbush, *Elias Hicks: Quaker Liberal* (New York: Columbia University Press, 1956).

13. Stanley Fish traces the history of this metaphor in *Self-Consuming Artifacts: The Experience of Seventeenth-Century Literature* (Berkeley: University of California Press, 1972).

14. Quoted by Susan Juster, *Disorderly Women: Sexual Politics and Evangelicalism in Revolutionary New England* (Ithaca: Cornell University Press, 1994), 32.

15. Jonathan Edwards, *The Life of David Brainerd*, ed. Norman Pettit (New Haven: Yale University Press, 1985), 137–139. Containing an exemplary conversion narrative, Edwards's *Life of Brainerd* was republished numerous times as one of the most popular evangelical texts of the

antebellum period. See Joseph A. Conforti, *Jonathan Edwards, Religious Tradition and American Culture* (Chapel Hill: University of North Carolina Press, 1995): "[T]he canonization of Brainerd and the transformation of the *Life of Brainerd* into an American religious classic were yet additional aspects of the cultural work of the Second Great Awakening that included the revitalization of Edwards as a religious authority" (69).

16. Jonathan Edwards, "A Narrative of Surprising Conversions," *Select Works of Jonathan Edwards* (London: The Banner of Truth Trust, 1965), 1:39–40.

17. Without referring to it as an instance of prolepsis, Chaviva M. Hosek noticed something of this effect of the use of the present tense in the preface in "The Rhetoric of Whitman's 1855 *Preface to Leaves of Grass*," *Walt Whitman Review* 25 (1979), 163–173.

18. The popular, contemporary ritual of a wedding couple lighting a candle together and then extinguishing their individual candles achieves its emotional resonance as much or more from the act of extinguishing than the act of lighting, and thus emphasizes the negation inherent in the birth of the new.

BILL HARDWIG

Walt Whitman and the Epic Tradition: Political and Poetical Voices in "Song of Myself"

> What is America for?—To commemorate the old myths and the gods? To repeat the Mediterranean here?...—No;—(Nä-o-o) but to destroy all these from the purposes of the earth, and to erect a new earth in their place.
>
> —Whitman in the 1850s[1]

Walt Whitman's explicit dismissal of the mythology of the Greek and Roman Empires epitomizes his general suspicion of long-lived traditions—cultural, philosophical, or poetical. Whitman felt that if he were to redefine American notions of poetry and heroism, *Leaves of Grass* must, in his words, "take no illustrations from the ancients or classics."[2] He believed that poetry needed to be disruptive and revaluative—breaking away from past traditions rather than extending them. Although "Song of Myself" contains several obvious structural and thematic echoes of ancient epic poetry, Whitman employs these conventions in a disruptive manner in order to challenge the mythic authority of the epic tradition. Through his manipulation of epic conventions, Whitman forces a confrontation between "Song of Myself" and the "myths" of the epic tradition in order to question the ideological and political ramifications of ancient poetry and, I will argue, contemporary conservative political rhetoric.

Perhaps the tension between Whitman's use of the themes and

From *Walt Whitman Quarterly Review*, vol. 17, no. 4 (Spring 2000). © 2000 by The University of Iowa.

structure of epic poetry and his renunciation of the "myth" of classical tradition can be explained, in part, by examining the ancient epics that Whitman undermines in the context of his contemporary political and cultural milieu. Through an analysis of the thematic and formal parallels between epic poetry (Virgil's *Aeneid* will function illustratively here) and the political rhetoric of the mid-nineteenth century, we are able to understand why Whitman chooses to borrow conventions of epic rhetoric (such as the "high" epic voice, narrator, and catalogues), while rejecting the underlying functions of the genre as a whole. By implementing the rhetoric of the epic poem to elicit superficial comparisons between his poem and the epic genre, Whitman is able to interrogate the more deeply ingrained and implicit aspects of the epic's role in the shaping of cultural ideology. In short, Whitman seeks to expose the rhetorical artifice of epic narration—the ways in which epic poets manufacture consent—and in so doing, create an "anti-epic" that contests the establishment of conservative ideological consensus.[3]

One scholar of the epic, Suzanne Wofford, explains that the ideology in epic poetry contains "the entire set of unacknowledged assumptions and invisible interpretive solutions by which people understand and represent to themselves their relation to the world, and, similarly, the unexpressed presuppositions of logical requirements of an ethical or a political system."[4] It is these political and ideological systems, and their "unexpressed presuppositions" within epic poetry, that Whitman contests.

Although there is wide-ranging and proliferating critical commentary about Whitman's engagement with the epic genre, scholars still generally understand "Song of Myself" as a revision or extension of the epic mode.[5] Most notably, James E. Miller, Jr., has gracefully argued that Whitman revises the epic genre in "Song of Myself" and creates the first American "Lyric-Epic."[6] Miller regards Whitman as "an epic poet who will break all the rules for the epic, but insist on writing an epic anyway" (33). For him, there are several aspects of Whitman's poem that are at odds with his "epic intent," such as his lyric voice and his "indignation with reality" (47). He sees Whitman repeatedly "prodding himself, reminding himself of his epic role" (44).

Traditionally, epic poetry bolsters conservative ideologies by rendering mythic a society's political history, and in so doing, camouflaging its more tyrannical motives.[7] Epic poets do not purport to represent a particular political and historical faction of society; rather, they claim to relay the self-evident, universal, and destined truths of a nation. For example, in *The Aeneid*, Virgil declares that the story he tells is destined and already completed, that he merely has been called to sing its song:

> Be with me, Muse of all Desire, Erato,
> While I call up the kings, the early times,
> How matters stood in the old land of Latium
> . . .
> A greater history opens before my eyes,
> A greater task awaits me. (VII, 47–59)[8]

Seduced by the song, Virgil's audience is led to accept his ideological assertions (e.g., the validity of Roman colonization) without examining their contemporary implications or the poet's possible motives. When Virgil claims that the Romans are "incorporating" and "pacifying" weaker nations, the implications of this action can remain subordinate because they are pronounced under the rubric of a fated and justified Roman history. To question Virgil's defense of Roman colonization is to undermine the mythos supporting *The Aeneid*.

Like the genealogical catalogue in *The Book of Genesis*, which provides a certainty and historical continuity within the Judeo-Christian tradition, epic catalogues customarily serve to provide historical grounding and a sense of identity for the reader by symbolically connecting the past and the present. Through ideas of the organic harmony of the poem's ideology and a "destined" history, epic poetry symbolically connects the reader to the time of the events, making the reader feel invested in the moral and political messages of the poetry (McWilliams, 225). However, it does so while maintaining an "epic distance," which prevents any questioning of the ideological consequences of such a connection.[9] Although epics are created in specific historical contexts, the poets seek to efface the historical complexities and conflicts of these contexts from their poetry. The "distance" of classical epic poetry functions in a manner similar to the way that ideological systems operate in general: "An ideology," according to Sacvan Bercovitch, "arises out of historical circumstances, and then re-presents these, symbolically and conceptually, as though they were natural, universal, and right."[10]

For example, in *The Aeneid* Virgil creates the impression that he is portraying the distant past of Roman genealogy merely as historical context. However, by having the omniscient gods and nearly infallible heroes of his epic speak of Roman destiny and the inevitability of Roman triumph, he justifies Rome's subsequent imperialism. Because the events are locked in the unchangeable and distant past, they convey immutability and inevitability. Through this rhetorical ploy of creating a sense of historical destiny, Virgil is able to explain contemporary events through their relation to, and connection with, the past; by yoking contemporary actions to historical precedent, he gives modern Rome justification to follow the doctrine outlined in the epic past. In Book VI, Aeneas is in the underworld, listening to the shade of his father. Because he is a member of the underworld, Anchises is able to see the future and he foretells Aeneas's destiny:

> Roman, remember by your strength to rule
> Earth's peoples—for your arts are to be these:
> To pacify, to impose the rule of law,
> To spare the conquered, battle down the proud. (VI, 1151–1154)

In this brief prophecy, Anchises not only excuses Roman imperialism, he couches it in the terms of "pacifying" the barbarians; this becomes Aeneas's true "art." In this light, Rome's brutal conquest becomes an act of compassion and assistance. Clearly, Virgil included these details in part as an example of proper beneficent rule; Aeneas is to "spare the conquered." From this perspective, he can be contrasted with Turnus's "lust for steel" and "brute insanity in war" (VII, 634–635). Nonetheless, because this scene takes place in the "historical" past, the sanctity of that past (sanctified in part by the poem's epic distance) allows Virgil to promote without interrogation a specific political ideology of colonialism.

Even a schematic inspection of how Virgil's ideology informs his poem can reveal how he promulgates a monolithic and prescriptive view of Roman political history. It is important to realize that the ideological rhetoric in Virgil's poem often contains implied premises that can alter or contradict the surface values that the poem claims to exalt. For example, in Book XII, Virgil superficially claims to grant equality to everybody—both the conquerors and the conquered—in the new Latin empire:

> Let both nations, both unconquered, both
> Subject to equal laws, commit themselves
> To an eternal union.... (XII, 257–259)

However, Jupiter immediately undermines this equality and covertly establishes an unequivocal hierarchy of status and autonomy:

> ... Ausonion folk will keep
> Their fathers' language and their way of life,
> And, that being so, their name: The Teucrians
> Will mingle and be *submerged, incorporated.* (XII, 1131–1134, emphasis added)

As these lines illustrate, the implicit premise that a hierarchy is desired, if not necessary, lies beneath the stated ideals of nationhood and brotherhood. However, because Jupiter proclaims the incorporation of the colonized people as destined, Virgil and the reader have no cause to question such a policy. In fact, in many cases it is an epic's underlying premises that make the propagation of its ideological system viable.

I am not suggesting that Virgil's *Aeneid* functions in the same manner as all epics—that there is some universal epic formula. Yet there is much evidence suggesting that *The Aeneid* stood in the eighteenth- and nineteenth-century American literary imagination as The Epic, against which all other poetry was measured. For example, in his 1702 work, *Magnalia Christi Americana*, written to preserve New England's deteriorating sense of religious mission, Cotton Mather invoked (and slightly altered) Virgil's opening invocation in *The Aeneid*: "The reader will doubtless desire to know what it was that 'tot volvere casus / Insignes pietate viros, tot adire labores Impulerit.'" In the 1780s Samuel Low wrote that the Muse of Freedom would inspire his poetry, and added that a "new Virgil [will] grace this western shore." A 1784 commencement speech delivered at the University of Pennsylvania claimed that Americans would soon see a national poetry with "the correct majesty of Virgil." From 1807 to 1809, the *Monthly Anthology and Boston Review* published six articles on Virgil, in large part to prove that American poets were not capable of creating a "true" epic (cited in McWilliams, 18, 19). As the epigraph at the beginning of this essay illustrates, Whitman knew the mythological, Mediterranean epics as a standard commonly invoked to judge lengthy American poems. For Whitman the respect for these epics must be "destroyed."

Perhaps one way of understanding why Whitman so firmly distances himself from the epic tradition is to explore the specific political contingencies during the inception of "Song of Myself." In fact, Whitman's disdain for Virgil's poem may be related in part to the Whig party's frequent use of an epic-like rhetoric to defend their conservative ideology. Because the Whigs played such an important role in Whitman's conception of the political climate of the mid-to-late-1850s, it proves useful to examine their rhetoric at its most coherent (in the late-1830s and 1840s). While Whitman celebrated the unlimited possibilities of an unsettled American continent, the Whigs worried about constancy and tradition. When the Whigs voiced their disapproval of the Mexican War, it was because, as a risky attempt at brazen territorial extension, it threatened the stability of the American Union. A September 1845 article in the *American Whig Review* entitled "Will There Be

War with Mexico?" illustrates the Whigs distrust of expansionist policies: "Wars are fraught with crime, are dangerous to liberty, and necessarily tend to the subversion of those institutions upon which our political and social fabrics rest."[11] If the Whigs feared that the war threatened to subvert the institutions which support "our political and social fabrics," the Democrats saw it as an opportunity to secure "freedom" for the individual, a belief in which rapid and uninhibited expansion was an inevitable component. Major Wilson has labeled this difference as one between the Democrats' interest in a "quantitative expansion" through space, while the Whigs were concerned with a "qualitative development" through time. The Whigs looked for "internal improvements" and saw "external expansion" (such as the War with Mexico) as a threat to this internal stability.[12] Although Whitman's pacifist instincts ultimately caused him to question the violent results of the Mexican War, he initially supported the war with enthusiasm, as well as nearly every one of James Polk's expansionist policies.[13]

However, Whitman's political involvement certainly was not limited to the Mexican War. When he was writing the original version of "Song of Myself," he was very active (as a journalist, speaker, and occasional canvasser) in the political debate of the late 1840s and early 1850s.[14] As biographers of Whitman have pointed out, in these decades he heavily supported the Democratic party.[15] In fact, as early as the 1830s, Whitman held an apprenticeship with *The Patriot*, a Democratic newspaper which supported the Democratic workers against the Whig manufacturers. Later, while Whitman was in Queens Country, a Whig paper labeled him as a "well-known locofoco [radical democrat] of the town ... a champion of Democracy" (Erkkila, 14, 20).

Because Whitman's alliances and rivalries initially were divided so clearly along party lines, a brief look at general tenets of the Whig and Democratic parties will be useful. Although such distinctions inevitably are somewhat schematic and neglect conflicts within each party, they do provide a helpful context for Whitman's poetry. So, if the following outline seems to reduce the two parties to a simple binary, it does so in order to demonstrate the conflicting rhetoric of the period. While party politics are never cut and dry, the rhetoric surrounding these politics often are, and it was the Whigs' rhetoric, as much as any specific platform, to which Whitman objected. Whereas the Democrats claimed to be accepting of cultural and moral diversity as long as it supported their notions of personal freedom (in fact, it was a vital aspect of their myth of democratic independence), the Whigs invoked a culturally uniform society that "mut[ed] social conflict" (Howe, 20). In fact, much like Virgil, who justified the contemporary Roman Empire by mythically depicting its history, the Whigs spoke of the ultimate value of the past and, as upholders of conservative morality and stewardship by the educated elite, felt responsible for dictating what a culture should cherish and respect. As one historian of nineteenth-century America explains, an appropriate Whig leader "must not only defend the people's true interests but show the people where those interests lay" (Howe, 27).

In part because they presented themselves as social, political, and ethical guardians, the Whigs' ability to manufacture ideological consensus, as was the case with the epic poets, lay in the efficacy of certain rhetorical ploys.[16] By looking at *how* Whig politicians attempted to justify ideological systems (rather than looking at *what* values they specifically justified), we can see how the Whigs and Virgil use a rhetoric of unification in very similar ways. Both Virgil and members of the Whig party spoke in terms of a unified and harmonious cultural history; they frequently used metaphors and images that appealed to the audience's desire for stability and continuity without providing substantive explanations of their motivations. By speaking in terms of a mythic historical tradition (which they were merely continuing), the Whigs, like Virgil, invoked the sanctity and destiny of the past. By attaching the mythic history to the present situation, the Whig speakers were able to claim they were following precedent; consequently, they were not responsible for the present implications of their ideological policies. For example, by claiming that they wished to preserve the harmony of the American Union (both past and present), the Whigs were able to resist any movements of reform because they strayed away from national tradition. Notice how the author of "Our Country Maryland" in the 1845 *American Whig Review* dismisses the Democratic call for greater material equality: "Commend us to the spirit of the Past—the chivalric and thoughtful spirit, that prompted to wise counsel and valorous deeds—when worth was not gauged by the standards of wealth or fashion."[17]

None of these reform movements threatened the Whigs' reverence for past precedent more than the Women's Rights movement. Never did the conservative Whig politicians more assiduously call upon the harmony of the past and present than in their attempts to halt an increase in women's privileges. Like Virgil's Roman "nationhood," the Whigs' ideas of an organic harmony (one that informed the structure of society) contained a very specific and rigid, if unstated, hierarchy. In the 1848 article "'Woman's Rights'" in *The American Whig Review*, the unnamed author justifies the present sexual hierarchy and its attendant privileges by explaining it in terms of the Great Chain of Being. The article argues that since life has its root in the "sphere of nature" and woman was taken from man's side, any attempt to reverse, or alter, this hierarchy would be tampering with the organic harmony of the world: "With such natural and personal difference, the sexes are designated from the start to different spheres of life, and have widely different missions to fulfill in the social system."[18] While this argument is hardly original (and certainly not exclusive to the Whig party), the manner in which the author attempts to justify this assertion does illustrate the Whig tendency to use the myth of an organic harmony as a way of preserving "natural" and hierarchical values.

By claiming that any movement towards sexual equality would disrupt the fragile balance of the natural world, the author argues that women must forfeit their individual aspirations for the preservation of the whole: "This subordination of the single life to the general is of such vast consequence to the entire plan and structure of the moral world, that it must be secured by an invincible guaranty in the constitution of the world itself" (376). Invoking the "constitution" (both the political document and the natural coherence and interdependency of the world) is a favorite Whig rhetorical ploy, connoting a pre-ordained order. In this article, just as the Whigs called for a strong federal government rather than the autonomy of the individual states, the author champions the "subordination" of the "single life" to the "general." Therefore, advocates of Women's Rights are threatening the "entire plan" of the "moral world"—an exceptionally serious burden. Conveniently, it is the subjugated women who must make the sacrifice to preserve the Union; it is they who must accept the adverse consequences of a historical precedent of a fixed sexual hierarchy.

Whitman, on the other hand, strategically places women in the center of the pluralistic universe of "Song of Myself." Whitman's inclusion of women, and his emphasis upon gender equality seems to counter directly the Whigs' conception of gender roles: "A great poem is for ages and ages in common and for all degrees and complexions and all departments and sects and for a woman as much as a man and a man as much as a woman."[19] Unlike the Whigs, who claim historical precedent in their oppression of women, Whitman's democratic ideal confronts traditional sexual roles:

> I am the poet of the woman the same as a man,
> And I say it is as great to be a woman as to be a man,
> And I say there is nothing greater than the mother of men. (26)

Even the balanced phrasing of these lines contributes to the emphasis on equality. Although Whitman often depicts women in traditional spheres (as a mother or domestic recluse), he clearly intends to include women on equivalent terms in his revisionary moral universe. I am not claiming that Whitman does not present troubling images of women (as in his tendency to envision women as vessels that serve little purpose other than to contain and give birth to future generations—the "mother of men"), but his rhetoric of gender equality and his conscious attempt to place women prominently in his new America suggest a very different way to approach the world than does the Whig emphasis on tradition and constancy.

While the debate about the rights of women and sexual privilege was certainly volatile, slavery, as another matter of hierarchy and subjugation, was probably the most divisive ideological and political issue of the 1840s and 1850s. When Congressman David Wilmot suggested that slavery be forbidden in new states, the Union was instantly fractured. The turmoil and disagreement which this issue created threatened the stability of the nation. However, in his famous speech "The Constitution and the Union," delivered on March 7, 1850, the Whigs' premier orator Daniel Webster used images of unity and harmony to emphasize the Union's constancy and durability. Although the Whigs, as a party, were opposed to slavery in the new states, Webster saw the need to compromise.[20] Because, like most Whig politicians, Webster perceived the unity and harmony of the Union and its central government as one of the nation's most precious ideals, he felt he must take steps to preserve its fragile coherence. In this speech, Webster emphasizes the preservation of what is sacred and the need to rely on national tradition and precedent:

> Never did there devolve on any generation of men higher trusts than now devolve upon us, for the preservation of this Constitution and the harmony and peace of all who are designed to live under it. Let us make our generation one of the strongest and brightest links in that golden chain which is destined, I fondly believe, to grapple the people of all the States to this Constitution for ages to come.[21]

By claiming to desire the "preservation of the Constitution" and the "harmony and peace of all," Webster tacitly recommends the perpetuation of the status quo. Through the image of links in a destined chain, he promotes what he sees as the natural and systematic unity of conservative American politics. According to Webster, the "preservation" of the Union is inextricably bound to this inherent continuity and harmony. Whereas the Democrats often spoke in terms of the individual's "unalienable rights," the Whigs were more likely to invoke the citizen's "duty" (or, in Webster's case, "higher trusts") to the Union and, by association, the central government (Howe, 16). By speaking of one's duty to uphold the inherent harmony of conservative politics, Webster is able to paint any opposing political theory as unnatural or discordant and anarchical—as breaking the "golden chain" which "grapple[s]" the American people. Inevitably, this "golden chain" extends into the mythic past of American politics; the duty of "our generation" is merely to preserve the existing harmony. In this context, it is not surprising to learn that, whereas Whitman writes his anti-epic in contrast to Virgil's *Aeneid*, in his famous speech "The Bunker Hill Monument" Webster refers to the Roman epic favorably, linking the positive example of Anchises with the birth of the United States. He quotes Anchises without translation: "Totamque infusa per artus / Mens agitat molem, et magno se corpore miscet."[22]

Like Virgil, the Whigs tend to look to the past as a means of maintaining a conservative social order. By sanctifying the past, they can censure any Democratic claim for reform as "a perpetual revolution, cutting off the past from the present." In "The Future Policy of the Whigs," published in the April 1848 *American Whig Journal*, the author criticizes the Democrats for allowing the multitude "to govern the few by the many," a policy which keeps the individual in fear of the masses: "[The Whigs] regard the government as unchangeable except by a solemn decision of the nation in convention, the [Democrats] treat it as inferior in authority to the public opinion of the day."[23] Like epic poets, who generally espouse a conservative ideology that is resistant to drastic revision, the Whigs tended to attack any form of radical social change as chaotic and frivolous.

Whitman, by contrast, appropriates the epic voice to confidently dismantle these very stabilities, to disturb the accepted cultural continuity. Whereas the epic poet often relies upon the infallibility of the "high" epic voice in order to mute conflict and unify political and ideological sentiment, "Song of Myself" is filled with images of destruction and revolution that directly challenge the unifying metaphors of the "destined" epic poem, suggesting that "Song of Myself" is a radical reevaluation of conventional epic ideology. In the often-ignored catalogues of American experience (sections 10–23 in the 1881 version of the poem), Whitman's epic-like voice resounds with the prophetic self-assuredness that is generally associated with the classical poets.[24] However, whereas *The Aeneid* and "The Future Policy of the Whig Party" stress the continuity and unity of their ideological foundations, Whitman constantly emphasizes the breakdown of accepted values through metaphors of disintegration that point to his revaluative agenda:

> The butcher-boy puts off his killing-clothes, or sharpens his knife at the stall in the
>   market,
> I loiter enjoying his repartee and his shuffle and *breakdown*.

Blacksmiths with grimed and hairy chests environ the anvil
... there is a great heat in the fire. (20, emphasis added)

What Whitman enjoys, and finds instructive, is the process of the butcher's "breakdown," or disassembly, rather than his finished product. He presents the butcher's action as a perpetual dismantling that is not focused on the completion of the task. Similarly, what becomes valuable in the blacksmith's work is the moment of creation—not the result. Whitman focuses on the "great heat of the fire," which is capable of deformation and reformation. He stresses the potential for change rather than the specific results of such a process. Furthermore, by concentrating on the labor of the working class, Whitman is exalting the common laborer instead of the Whigs' educated elite.

    These conjoined images of destruction and creation, disintegration and potentiality, directly inform Whitman's political agenda and its influence on "Song of Myself." Indeed, Democratic political theory was often based on the rhetoric of constant change and restructuring at the hands of the younger generation and lower classes. A lucid example of the Democratic sentiment can be found in the article "Congress, the Presidency, and the Review," in the March 1852 *Democratic Review*: "Young America is the inheritor of their only principle, to throw aside hereditary servility, old-fogy fears or old-tory predilections, and live by their manhood, by mastering the necessities and wants of the time, and shaping their acts accordingly, utterly regardless of do-nothing precedent."[25] In this passage, the author stresses the notion of a fluid, and constantly evolving, political system which adapts to "the necessities" of the time, while scorning the ineffectual and stagnant "do-nothing" precedent.

    Like the radical Democrats that described themselves as defying "obsolete" models, Whitman yokes traditionally opposed images and impulses, thus challenging the relevance and authority of their definitions. Indeed, his destructive agenda disputes conventional demarcation and sentiment by reconciling the apparently unreconcilable: "Evil propels me, and reform of evil propels me" (28); "One side a balance and the antipodal side a balance" (28); "A word of the faith that never balks,/... Hurrah for positive science!" (28). However, this section of the poem that merges thesis and antithesis concludes with a resounding image of revolt: "Beat the gong of revolt, and stop with fugitives and them that plot and conspire" (29). Furthermore, unlike in the previous lines, there is no reversal or opposition to Whitman's identification with the revolters. By beating the "gong of revolt" and unifying his "heroic" narrator with the rebellious, Whitman is signaling his alliance with the revolutionary and disruptive factions of

American society. In this passage, Whitman challenges everything that is "organic," traditional, and customary, preferring instead to stop with "them that plot and conspire."

While Whitman and the Democrats generally felt that the potential for this type of revaluation was the only way to avoid the "do-nothing precedent" and insure a truly representative republic, the Whigs saw such a policy as the failure to heed governmental precedent: "Ultra Democratic doctrine indulges men in a perpetual revolution, cutting off the past from the present" ("The Future Policy of the Whigs," 330). In the Whigs' lexicon there was scarcely a more loathsome word than "revolution," which suggested an irresponsible pandering to fickle public sentiment.

Seemingly attacking directly the Whigs' suspicion of rapid social change, Whitman's poem is based on the value of revolution. Once again in the same catalogue, Whitman paints the rebelling masses in favorable terms, but it is important to note the sense of productive order (in this case the harvest) that follows his examples of revolution:

> The meeting of enemies, the sudden oath, the blows and fall,
> The excited crowd—the policeman with his star quickly working his passage to the
>   centre of the crowd;
> ...
> What living and buried speech is always vibrating here.... what howls restrained by
>   decorum,
> ...
> The big doors of the country-barn stand open and ready,
> The dried grass of the harvest-time loads the slow-drawn wagon.... (18)

Rather than conservative moral instruction, the "living and buried speech" becomes one of the vital aspects of American society; the restrained "howls" signify Whitman's belief that unvoiced sentiment lies just beneath public propriety. The nation's (and specifically Whitman's) task is to strip away "decorum," which is without a substantive foundation but remains essentially unquestioned. However, when the "excited crowd" (or as the Whigs might say, "unruly mob") ignores the policeman and "his star," they are defying more than mere "decorum;" they are revolting against conventional roles and traditional sites of authority. Seen in a larger political scope, this passage directly opposes the Whig's call for conservative morality and the subordination of local rights to the "superior" federal plan.

Whitman suggests that the key to a revolt against such "decorum" is the liberation of speech. This notion fits with Whitman's reverence for democratic ideals; indeed, unrestrained expression through speech, especially slang, is an essential facet of his idea of American individualism. The image of the harvest, ready but not yet begun, that directly follows his "excited crowd" signals the possibility of substantive change. In this instance, Whitman is clearly beginning another image when he speaks of the harvest time, but it is precisely how he chooses to juxtapose these apparently incongruous images that tells us so much about his revolutionary stance.

John McWilliams has pointed out that epic poetry often (if not inevitably) serves to reaffirm the social order and cultural values of the time. What seems to be a liberating and unifying document of cultural celebration, according to McWilliams, actually glosses over the diversity within a society: "Man's greatest medium for changing society's attitude, epic poetry, has repeatedly betrayed its promise. Instead of serving mankind, the epic has reclothed old barbarism in a new aristocratic dress" (56). Perhaps for this reason, McWilliams refuses to place Whitman's poem in the context of the American epic. Although he is perhaps overly critical of the epic genre, ignoring the formalized martial tradition of the poetry, McWilliams is correct in referring to Whitman's "anti-traditionalist" agenda. However, what he does not point out is that in "Song of Myself" Whitman is using the convention of the epic narrator for the very reason of its conservative, static, and distant nature. By juxtaposing seemingly incongruous images while employing the artifice of an unifying epic narrator, Whitman is able to manipulate the convention and partially remove the cloak of ideological infallibility from epic poetry.

In fact, in "Song of Myself," the narrator's resounding voice calls into question the official, monolithic nature of the epic by creating an indeterminate chaos, where traditional definitions and structures have little or no meaning. In the seemingly endless epic-like catalogues of the poem, Whitman hints at his ideological revaluation of American society. Unlike Whig ideology or Virgilian genealogy, there is certainly no Great Chain of Being or catalogue of heroic descendants in a dynastic succession in Whitman's revisionist poem; every person, every event is given equal attention, and nothing is excessively glorified or scorned. Aristocratic genealogy gives way to democratic, random lists. By juxtaposing conventionally disparate images and presenting them in equally weighted terms, Whitman presents what he understands as a revolutionary pluralistic ideal. In fact, every time a figure of established traditional valuation is introduced, the portrait is undermined with an immediate description of a person on the losing end of strict societal determinations: "The bride unrumples her white dress ... / The opium eater reclines with rigid head" (22). The "pure" bride is not kept cloistered in "Song of Myself;" rather, she is positioned adjacent to the semi-conscious drug user. Furthermore, the fact that she is "unrumpling" her dress questions whether such notions of purity and morality have significance in Whitman's cosmology. Whitman seems to be questioning fundamental aspects of cultural decorum, asking why and by whom these ideas of propriety have been created.

By bringing his poem into dialogue with the epic tradition through these epic-like catalogues, Whitman can simultaneously destabilize some of the ideological certainty of the epics and invent his own revaluative agenda that reexamines the most firmly established cultural definitions: "Patriarchs sit at supper with sons and grandsons and great grandsons around them, / In walls of abode [sic: adobie], in canvass tents, rest hunters and trappers after their day's sport" (23). In this passage Whitman inverts the word order of the second line in order to create a metaphorical melding of the patriarchs and the hunters. Upon an initial reading, the phrase "In walls of abode, in canvass tents" seems to be referring to the patriarch's environment, when in fact at least half of the phrase describes that of the hunters. Whitman not only constructs a sense of equality through the juxtaposition and poetic enjambment of aristocrats and lower class people, he also creates a referential instability, where traditional definitions and boundaries are disintegrating, even on the verbal level. In her biography of Whitman, Bettina Knapp isolates his revaluative agenda: "He was forever searching for ways to break down society's masks, its unshakable beliefs, its rigid thought processes, most frequently used by groups and individuals as defense mechanisms to protect them from the 'dangers' awaiting those who open their minds to untrodden paths."[26] As Knapp hints, hierarchies are created and maintained, in part, by "unshakable beliefs" which justify such an ordering and which often forbid any questioning of the existing order. Knapp uses these terms to describe Whitman's "shock techniques" that she believes allow him the "freedom and abandon he needed to reap the joys of earth" (87). This analysis seems to be too personal, ignoring Whitman's social and political agenda. Nonetheless, although she does not discuss the political milieu of Whitman's poem, Knapp implicitly identifies the Whigs' desire to maintain society's decorum, the "masks" that Whitman so ardently seeks to remove.

For Whitman, one of the surest ways to disrupt this cultural decorum in his poem is the constant variation of tone and diction. At times he is elegant and refined in his speech: "My own voice, orotund sweeping and final" (46). In these poetical moments, Whitman's narrator takes on a high and commanding tone that closely mimics conventional epic narrators. Then, often in the very next line, he becomes more sensual and imagistic— a man on the streets—mentioning that "washes and razors [are] for foofoos" (28). Through this use of slang and depiction of the everyday, Whitman calls attention to, and distances himself from, the artifice of epic poetry.[27] Indeed, Robert Scholnick points to the role of slang ("artlessness") in Whitman's revolt against the epic tradition: "Just as the 'rude' manners of the persona enable him to break with all social conventions in favor of an ostensibly original and authentic way of relating to others, so he adopts simplicity and artlessness to break with the conventions of his poetic predecessors."[28] Although Scholnick is dealing here with Whitman's revolution in a purely aesthetic sense, he does correctly identify Whitman's separation from his "poetic predecessors." By initially implicating his work with the legacy of epic poetry through his "orotund" voice, Whitman forces a clash between the rigidity and formality of epic poetry and what he believes to be the commonality and spontaneity of "Song of Myself." Scholnick limits this separation to an artist's "anxiety of influence," but Whitman's political involvement seems to suggest that the division between "Song of Myself" and the epic genre represents not only an artistic revaluation but a radical Democratic statement as well.

Whitman's oscillating tone may appear to be his attempt to retain poetic grandeur while simultaneously writing about "what is commonest and cheapest and nearest and easiest" (21), but actually the alternating of narrative voice points to the core of Whitman's destructive agenda. By depicting, and calling attention to, this stratification of language and subject matter, Whitman creates a symbolically democratic poem, where the awe-inspiring mingles with the wearisome; he believes that he is representing the myth of American diversity, multiplicity, and independence. In "Song of Myself," epic distance is not eliminated; the "distant" epic voice becomes intertwined with the basest, and most immediate, linguistic forms. As McWilliams states, "Whitman mixes levels of language in order brashly to assure us that Truth exists in every rank and order" (225). In fact, without Whitman's manipulation of the epic voice—without the sense of epic distance and sublimity through much of the poem—his "rude manners" and plebeian language would not have the revolutionary effect that they do. Whitman must first superficially construct an epic formality in order to reveal its deficiency.

While the Whigs promoted the continuity between the present and past, the Democrats were more inclined to question the validity of what they would call a coerced harmony. Indeed, the Democratic rhetoric of the time is filled with diatribes that cherish the value of the future *because of* its break from, and abandonment of, the past. In an article in the March 1852 *Democratic Review*, entitled "Congress, the Presidency and the Review," the author scorns the idea of relying on "connection" to past politicians (in this case, Jacksonian Democrats):

> Young America is *not* the offspring of old fogydom. Being wise in
> our generation, and being determined not to be burthened with
> more fathers than there is any need for, we declare that the young
> democracy, either in its principles or its actions, has no
> connection either in blood, policy, consanguinity, or look, with
> those antiquated, stiff-cravated personages, who have hitherto
> regarded themselves as the owners of the Democratic party. (203)

The writer stresses the obsolescence of past political "principals" or
"actions." In this quotation by a radical faction of the Democratic party, we
can see the "Young Americans" unhesitatingly optimistic view of the future.
By denying any relation whatsoever with their political predecessors, these
"young" democrats (like the young Jacksonian democrats before them, who
have since evolved into "antiquated, stiff-cravated personages") have spurned
past ideology for an undetermined future that is not governed by a "do-
nothing" precedent.

    Whitman similarly desires to wrench apart the continuity between past
ideological doctrine and present political practice. For Whitman, as for most
Democrats of the time, a society without rigid social constructs and
definitions is more apt to accommodate change and reevaluation.[29]
Throughout "Song of Myself," Whitman's narrator aligns himself with the
oppressed and suffering people in America. Although he thoroughly depicts
the privileged and aristocratic in the poem, he always identifies with those
who are under attack:

> The hounded slave that flags in the race and leans by the fence, blowing and covered
>   with sweat,
> The twinges that sting like needles his legs and neck,
> The murderous buckshot and the bullets,
> All these I feel or am.
> ...
> Agonies are one of my changes of garments;
> I do not ask the wounded person how he feels.... I myself become the wounded
>   person.... (39)

Whitman describes this pursuit in haunting detail and identifies with the
wounded slave. Although he has just claimed to "understand the large hearts
of heroes" (38), Whitman ultimately empathizes instead with the injured, the
dying, and the defeated. Rather than objectively reporting the slave's plight,
he becomes the slave: "I am the man.... I suffered.... I was there" (39). The
rhetoric of epic poems can manipulate the excitement of battle to downplay

the underlying controversial, and questionable, ideological import of the conflict. Whitman uses the suffering of the losers to undermine the foundation of such a claim.

Despite his apparent reliance on a Jacksonian exaltation of the "common man," Whitman does not believe he is displacing one ideology with a new ideology which will become generative of ossified cultural truths. Rather, he wishes to suspend certainty and absolute ideological doctrine and "loafe" in the resulting multiplicity. If we examine closely Whitman's statement in the 1855 preface that the expression of his poetry is "to be indirect and not direct or descriptive or epic" (iv), we can discern how it relates to his revolutionary and destructive agenda within "Song of Myself"—how he rebels against the very essence of Whig rhetoric. In many ways, this phrase provides a schematic outline of Whitman's agenda in "Song of Myself." The poem is to be "not direct or descriptive"—the message is not going to be excessively overt, and the poem is not going to fit snugly into predefined categories or national dogma. To do so would align his poem with the Whig rhetorical strategies he confronts. Instead, Whitman wishes that the diaphanous meaning of "Song of Myself" be revealed in multiple layers, contradictions, and conundrums that resist a monolithic and unified interpretation. Poetry, for Whitman, should remain "untranslatable" and represent the "indirect" potentiality of the unknown rather than "descriptive" doctrinal statements: "If [these thoughts] are not the riddle and the untying of the riddle they are nothing" (24). Indeed, in 1855 Whitman views ideological and political uncertainty as virtually synonymous with potentiality—the "chaos" of the future is a positive force.

In this way, for Whitman the lack of ideological certainty is not an unfortunate and terrifying result of his revolution; it becomes the guiding principle of his philosophy. In perhaps the crowning statement of "Song of Myself," he declares,

> Do I contradict myself?
> Very well then.... I contradict myself;
> I am large.... I contain multitudes. (55)

Rather than creating meaning through the buttressing of conservative myth and historical hierarchy (as do Virgil and the Whig politicians), Whitman's rhetoric finds purpose in the destruction of absolute meaning and ideological foundation.

Ironically, even though Whitman combats these unifying tendencies and exposes their rhetorical underpinnings, he appears to be blind to his own ideological framework and rhetorical ploys. Just as Virgil justifies the colonization of the Roman Empire, Whitman sees Manifest Destiny as the ideal manner to insure the American sense of individuality. In order to maintain the myth of unfettered individuality, there must be a vast expanse of potential territory to conquer or to escape to. That is to say, a community based on unrestricted individuality functions much more smoothly if there is sufficient area (such as the nineteenth-century Western frontier) to sustain a profusion of individual pursuits.

Virgil uses the myth of a destined imperialism to explain a cultural heritage. Whitman, in similar fashion, sees the unsettled continent as a sign of future freedom and potentiality. So while Whitman may identify with the wounded slave in a manner which exposes the epic poem's reliance on martial conquest and heroic battles, he also exalts the ship fight of John Paul Jones with the patriotic fervor of a zealous nationalist. Similarly, when he describes the Mexican War in his poem, Whitman always sides with the "heroic" American soldiers. In short, when it comes to the myth of Manifest Destiny, Whitman becomes staunchly nationalistic. Although Whitman's and Virgil's explanations of colonialism serve different political ends, both writers are trapped in their own ideological and nationalist assumptions which buttress their political and poetical beliefs.

Indeed, to our current sensibilities, Whitman's poem seems imbued with prescriptive ideological commentary. From the all-encompassing and almost didactic declaration that begins "Song of Myself" ("I celebrate myself, / And what I assume you shall assume") to the concluding lines which emphasize the enduring legacy of Whitman's message ("Missing me one place search another, / I stop some where waiting for you"), Whitman presents an almost imperialist ethos, one which devotedly, and at times unquestioningly, exalts the "Common Man." Certainly such a perspective is inextricably bound to the cultural dynamics of a firmly established mid-nineteenth century liberal ideology. However, as the lack of any punctuation at the conclusion of the poem suggests, Whitman seeks to underscore what he believes to be the unbridled and open-ended nature of his work. Certainly, we have seen that such "revolutionary" ideas are not somehow above, or removed from, ideological doctrine; nor does such an ideological framework preclude a work from being truly innovative or rebellious. Nonetheless, for Whitman ideology and cultural conservatism are insidiously linked. As Whitman confidently rejects "the old myths" of the classical epics, he unconsciously creates a new myth: a poem free of ideology.

Not surprisingly, Whitman's belief that he lacks a rigid ideological foundation seems fitting with the Democratic ideology of the pre-Civil War era. As Thomas Hietala discusses in his book on Manifest Destiny, the Democrats fervently defended laissez-faire economic practices and territorial expansion, not solely because of an overly ambitious confidence in the American future; rather, they perceived these tenets as prerequisites for "a society based upon individual acquisitiveness, geographical and social mobility, and a fluid class structure."[30] Ironically, the Democrats cherished this doctrine of rapid expansion, which proved to be one of the most tyrannical legacies of American history, because it helped to insure the liberation, decentralization, and freedom of American society, a future they saw as endangered by Whig conservatism.

In the November 1839 volume of *The Democratic Review*, John O'Sullivan, the founder of *The Review* and a staunch supporter of Manifest Destiny, states in his article "The Great Nation of Futurity" that "our national birth was the beginning of a new history, the formation and progress of an untried political system, which separates us from the past and connects us with the future only. We may confidently assume that our country is destined to be *the great nation of futurity*" [emphasis added].[31] Like O'Sullivan's "nation of futurity," Whitman's vision of the future is filled with a democratic optimism that leaves the past behind in order to invent the future. Indeed, in "Song of Myself" Whitman's celebration of an unregulated multiplicity seems intimately related to the Democratic criticism of the Whigs' reliance on the past and a traditional centralized government. Compare O'Sullivan's comment, "We have no interest in the scenes of antiquity, only as lessons of avoidance of nearly all their examples" (427) with "Song of Myself": "I do not know what is untried and afterward, / But I know it is sure and alive and sufficient" (49) and,

> Soft doctrine as steady help as stable doctrine,
> Thoughts and deeds of the present our rouse and early start.

> This minute that comes to me over the past decillions,
> There is no better than it and now. (28)

Because of an unabashed confidence in the present and future of American society, both O'Sullivan and Whitman seem to cherish their repudiation of historical precedent—valuing the "untried" over the firmly established. Furthermore, both writers use a rhetoric that suggests they are free from rigid ideological doctrine, when in fact they are deeply fixed in their own political and ideological sentiment. Certainly, this type of unconscious ideological sentiment—by virtue of its veiled existence—is among the most powerful of cultural determinants, influencing the manner in which a culture views itself; it is also one of the interpretive keys to Whitman's anti-epic, displaying his reliance on the Democratic trust in Manifest Destiny.

Although, as we have seen, Whitman relies heavily upon Democratic political doctrine, ultimately he does not wish to be confined by a prescriptive ideology—Democratic or Whig. As Betsy Erkkila has pointed out, in the late 1840s and early 1850s, Whitman became increasingly disgruntled with the fixity of the Democratic party, and party politics in general (47–58).[32] Certainly, by 1855 Whitman is not interested in simply writing a poem exalting the American Democratic party; rather, he envisions a metaphorical "union" that is not structured around rigid historical and nationalistic determinants.[33] Whitman's metaphorical union celebrates the multiplicity that often exists within, but is not exclusive to, the United States. In fact, he treasures its very lack of political and cultural homogeneity: "I am.../ One of the great nation, the nation of many nations—the smallest the same and the largest the same,/... Not merely of the New World but of Africa Europe or Asia" (23–24). Although the inclusiveness of these lines can be attributed in part to Whitman's all-encompassing "I," they seem to illustrate Whitman's belief that "Song of Myself" is not solely a poem about American Democratic ideology. It is interesting to note that these lines are eliminated in later editions when Whitman seeks to create a more traditional and national epic; by the time the Civil War ended, Africa, Europe, and Asia no longer fit into his poem of the New World.

Indeed, despite Whitman's obvious political and ideological bent, he firmly believes he is avoiding prescriptive doctrine. Even Democratic respect for plebeian labor and the working classes is too uncompromising for Whitman's revisionary cosmology. In an 1847 editorial, Whitman illustrates his repudiation of any anchored political affiliation and his exaltation of the "liberty" of the American individual:

> One of the favorite doctrines of leading Whigs teaches the intricacies and profundity of the science of government.... We have Democrats ... [who] assent to the same views.... Really, however, the principles that lie at the root of true government, are not hard of comprehension. The error lies in the desire after *management*, the great curse of our Legislation: every thing is to be regulated and made straight by force of statute. And all this while, evils are accumulating, in very consequence of excessive management. The true office of government, is simply to preserve the rights of each citizen from spoliation: when it attempts to go beyond this, it is intrusive and does more harm than good.[34]

Rather than defining what the future holds, Whitman would "loafe" in its very ineffability. To elucidate this idea, he chooses the metaphor of the open road: "I tread day and night such roads" (38). "Not I, not any one else can travel that road for you" (52). Although he focuses on the road, it is a road without a destination. The road is not a means to an end; it is the end in itself—the "perpetual journey." Although (as this endless road illustrates) Whitman consciously challenges the most deeply ingrained conservative ideological and political beliefs of his time, it would be wise to remember his own ideological investment. To refer to a cliché that invokes the era of Virgil's epic that Whitman so adamantly rejects, "All roads lead to Rome." Roads are routinely designed, constructed, and maintained by the prevailing empire in a manner which overtly benefits this empire. In this light, Whitman's "open road" (his indeterminate poem) can be seen, in part, as a visible sign of the American democratic empire.

NOTES

I would like to thank Robin Grey; without her countless readings of drafts and challenging comments this essay would not exist. Thanks also to George Hutchinson, whose suggestions and criticism helped with the genesis of this project.

1. Walt Whitman, *An American Primer*, ed. Horace Traubel (Boston: Small, Maynard, and Co., 1904), 32–33.

2. Cited in John McWilliams, *The American Epic: Transforming a Genre, 1770–1860* (Cambridge: Cambridge University Press, 1989), 222.

3. In the 1850s, Whitman's connections with the epic tradition would have been even more obvious than today. During this time, there was a great longing for the first great American epic poem. Many critics in the nineteenth century felt that American letters could never fully cut ties with the old world until a "successful" epic was written. As a consequence, there were numerous American works that were compared with the European epic poems, such as Timothy Dwight's "The Conquest of Canaan," Mason Locke Weems' "The Life of Washington," and Joel Barlow's "Columbiad." As "Song of Myself" gained popularity in the mid-nineteenth century, it was immediately discussed in relation to past European and American epics. See McWilliams, chapters 1 and 7.

4. Suzanne Wofford, *The Choice of Achilles: The Ideology of Figure in the Epic* (Stanford: Stanford University Press, 1992), 16.

5. For example, in 1951 Ferner Nuhn claimed that *"Leaves of Grass* belongs in the category of bardic or epic literature. It represents an Epos of modern democratic culture, expressed in an appropriate aesthetic form. The

particular culture which it presents is that of North America, but there runs through it a core of universal and permanent truth" (*"Leaves of Grass* Viewed as an Epic," *Arizona Quarterly* 7 [1951], 326.) Andrew Hudgins sees *Leaves* as an extension of the traditional epic with Whitman consciously trying to "connect" his work with the genre (*"Leaves of Grass* from the Perspective of Modern Epic Practice," *Midwest Quarterly* 23 [1982], 380–390). John McWilliams states that "Song of Myself" is a mix between a heroic and mock-heroic poem, but believes the poem is a "defiant rejection" of the epic tradition (224, 226). Charles Metzger writes that Whitman is revising the epic tradition by "concentrating heavily upon the wounded, the dead, the defeated" ("Walt Whitman's Philosophical Epic," *Walt Whitman Review* 15 [1969], 91–96). Roy Harvey Pearce discusses the structure of "Song of Myself" in the context of the epic genre: "If we only look at 'Song of Myself' as an exemplar of a further stage in the development of an American epic, we may see how it was necessary for the success of the poem that it be in no way externally or generically structured. In Whitman's conception, this new kind of poem was more a process than a form.... The new heroic poem, the specifically American Epic, is one of ordering, not of order; of creation, not confirmation; of revealing, not memorializing" (*The Continuity of American Poetry* [Middletown, CT: Wesleyan University Press, 1987], 73, 83). George Trail states that "Song of Myself" invokes the epic tradition in order to "provide a standard ground from which to deviate and upon which to embroider" ("Whitman's Spear of Summer Grass: Epic Invocations in 'Song of Myself,'" *Walt Whitman Review* 23 [September 1977], 120–125). Jeffrey Walker claims that "Whitman's position is not that of the ancient epic poet, who at least in theory could constitute himself as the mouthpiece of the culture to which and for which he spoke. Nor, for that matter, is Whitman's position exactly that of Northrop Frye's 'contrast epic' poet, who could excoriate (or view with ironic contempt) the sins of his society from an ethical perspective already recognized by that society as authoritative. The ethical perspectives to and for which Whitman's bard proposed to speak are in large measure antagonistic; the ethical center he proclaims is not, in fact, the center for the culture that surrounds him" (*Bardic Ethos and the American Epic Poet: Whitman, Pound, Crane, Williams, Olson* [Baton Rouge: Louisiana State University Press, 1989], 20).

6. James E. Miller, Jr., *The American Quest for a Supreme Fiction* (Chicago: University of Chicago Press, 1979), 33. See also Miller's *Leaves of Grass: America's Lyric-Epic of Self and Democracy* (New York: Twayne Publishers, 1992); *Song of Myself: Origin, Growth, Meaning* (New York: Dodd, Mead & Company, 1964); "Whitman's *Leaves* and the American 'Lyric-Epic'," *Poems in Their Place*, ed. Neil Fraistat (Chapel Hill: University of North Carolina Press, 1986), 287–307.

7. For a discussion of this concept, see Suzanne Wofford's introduction to *The Choice of Achilles*. There, Wofford discusses the ways in which ideology functions in Renaissance epic poetry. For examples of Whitman's attitude towards the ancient epics, see John McWilliams's chapter, "An Epic of Democracy?," in *The American Epic*.

8. I will be citing by line number Robert Fitzgerald's translation of *The Aeneid* (New York: Vintage Classics, 1990).

9. For the purposes of this essay, I am modifying Mikhail Bakhtin's notion of "epic distance." See Bakhtin's chapter "Epic and Novel" in *The Dialogic Imagination* (ed. Michael Holquist [Austin: University of Texas Press, 1981]). For Bakhtin, epic distance connotes an absolute temporal distance between the reader (and contemporary history) and the "epic world," in which the heroic past is a world of "bests" and "firsts." This distance is absolute and not transgressible and is only bridged by national tradition. Therefore, this distance creates, in epic, a finished product in which "there is no place ... for any openendedness, indecision, indeterminacy" (Bakhtin, 13–16). I am using this term in part to point to both the temporal and hierarchical remoteness that allows an epic poem to promote an ideological system without allowing the dissection and examination of the internal assumptions and presuppositions of that ideology.

10. Sacvan Bercovitch, "The Problem of Ideology in American Literary History," *Critical Inquiry*

12. (1986), 636.

11. Anonymous, "Will There Be War With Mexico?" *American Whig Review* (September 1845), 221–229.

12. Daniel Walker Howe, *The Political Culture of the American Whigs* (Chicago: University of Chicago Press, 1979), 21. Also see Major L. Wilson, *Space, Time, and Freedom: the Quest for Nationality and the Irrepressible Conflict* (Westport, CT: Greenwood Press, 1974).

13. Betsy Erkkila, *Whitman the Political Poet* (New York: Oxford University Press, 1985), 39–40.

14. See Erkkila, chapters 1 and 2. Also see Cleveland Rogers and John Black, eds., *The Gathering of the Forces* (New York: G. P. Putnam's Sons, 1920), a collection of Whitman's political essays and editorials. In these writings, Whitman consistently voices his support for the "true" Democrats and his disapproval of the Whigs's "doctrine of the science of government" (1:53).

15. See Richard Chase, *Walt Whitman Reconsidered* (New York: William Sloane Associates, 1955), chapters 2 and 3; Erkkila, chapters 3–5; and Bettina Knapp, *Walt Whitman* (New York: Continuum Press, 1993), chapter 1.

16. Namely, relying on the past models of a mythic and "destined" history and speaking in terms of an organic social harmony, both of which

depict implicit cultural hierarchies as foreordained, inevitable, universal, and/or natural.

17. Anonymous, "Our Country, Maryland," *American Whig Review* (March 1845), 277.

18. Anonymous, "Woman's Rights," *American Whig Review* (October 1848), 373.

19. Walt Whitman, *Leaves of Grass* (Brooklyn, New York: Fowler and Wells, 1855), 22.

20. See the introduction to Webster's speech "The Constitution and the Union, March 7, 1850" in the second volume of Webster's papers, cited in note 21. In this introduction, Charles Wiltse outlines the Whig resistance to Webster's compromise. Several Whigs believed that Webster had "sold out to the 'slave power' for the presidency" (513).

21. Daniel Webster, "The Constitution and the Union, March 7, 1850" *The Papers of Daniel Webster, Speeches and Formal Writings*, ed. Charles Wiltse (Hanover, England: University Press of England, 1988), 2:550.

22. Cited in McWilliams, 35.

23. Anonymous, "The Future Policy of the Whigs," *American Whig Review* (April 1848), 330.

24. The section numbers were added in the 1867 edition. "Song of Myself," of course, was untitled in 1855. These numbers, as well as other revisions, signal Whitman's evolution towards a more traditional poem.

25. Anonymous, "Congress, the Presidency, and the Review," *Democratic Review* (March 1852), 205.

26. Knapp, 87.

27. In fact, Whitman wrote an article titled "Slang in America" in which he stresses the importance of slang to "New World" poetry. By dismissing the "feudal institutes" of traditional poetic language, slang is "an attempt of common humanity to escape from bald literalism, and express itself illimitably" (Floyd Stovall, ed., *Prose Works 1892* [New York: New York University Press, 1963], 2:573).

28. Robert Scholnick, "'The Original Eye': Whitman, Schelling and the Return to Origins," *Walt Whitman Quarterly Review* 11 (Spring 1994), 189.

29. In the January 1853 *Democratic Review*, the unnamed author of the article "What is Democracy?" writes, "Democracy embodies ... great principles, among which the most important is that of Equality, with which Liberty is only another name for Aristocracy" (4). Equality, at least in a theoretical sense, implies a greater liberty in personal definition and social construction. For Whitman, democratic ideology protects his notion of radical individualism. He states, "Democracy has its foundations in the very

broadest notion of good to our fellow creatures and to our countrymen. It is based on the doctrine of equality in political rights and privileges; it overlooks the distinctions of rank and wealth; it comprehends in its protection all classes and conditions of society, nor allows that the refined and rich shall receive more consideration in its decrees than the poor and lowly born" (cited in Erkkila, 19).

30. Thomas Hietala, *Manifest Design* (Ithaca, NY: Cornell University Press, 1985), 256.

31. John O'Sullivan, "The Great Nation of Futurity," *Democratic Review* (November 1839), 426.

32. See chapter 3, "The Poet of Slaves and the Masters of Slaves," in Erkkila.

33. I am making a distinction here between American Democratic sentiment (which involves patriotic fervor and a specific national identity and pride) and Whitman's democratic ideal (which is founded on the very lack of a definite cultural ideology).

34. *The Gathering of the Forces*, 1:53–54.

Chronology

1789	Walter Whitman Sr., the poet's father, is born on July 14.
1795	Louisa Van Velsor, the poet's mother, is born on September 22.
1816	Walter Whitman Sr. and Louisa Van Velsor are married on June 8.
1818	Jesse Whitman, the poet's brother, is born on March 2.
1819	Born Walter Whitman, Jr. on May 31 in West Hills, Huntington, Long Island, the son of a Long Island farmer, Walter Whitman, Sr. and Louisa Van Velsor.
1821	Mary Elizabeth Whitman, the poet's sister, is born in February.
1823	Whitman family moves to Brooklyn during a building boom in May. Hannah Louis Whitman, the poet's sister, is born on November 28.
1825	Whitman enters public school in Brooklyn.
1827	Andrew Jackson Whitman, the poet's brother, is born on April 7.
1829	George Washington Whitman, the poet's brother, is born on November 28.
1830	Whitman leaves school in the summer and immediately goes to work as an office boy for a law firm, then for a doctor. At this time, he is already enamored of the romantic novels of Sir Walter Scott, one of the authors who was to give rise to his rich imagination.

1831	Whitman goes to work for the printing office of a newspaper, the *Long Island Patriot*, in Brooklyn, for which he also contributes some sentimental writing.
1832	In the fall, Whitman goes to work for the *Long Island Star* in Brooklyn.
1833	Thomas Jefferson Whitman, the poet's brother, is born on August 9.
1834	Whitman family returns to Long Island and Walt is now on his own. He is writing some conventional poems for one of Manhattan's best papers, the *Mirror*, and frequently crosses the ferry from Brooklyn to attend debating societies and the theater.
1835	In May, Whitman moves to New York City and works as a compositor, a journeyman printer. However, two major fires occur this year, seriously disrupting the printing industry. Edward Whitman, the poet's youngest brother is born.
1836	Whitman rejoins his family in Hempstead, Long Island and, for the next five years, he teaches intermittently at country and small-town schools where he takes a very innovative approach in the classroom but is nevertheless accused of being lazy by some of the farm families. Similarly, Walt resists conforming to country life and refuses to do farm work.
1838	In June, Whitman interrupts his teaching to start a newspaper of his own, the *Long Islander*. He has also become active in debating societies.
1840**	Early in the year Walt starts a series, "Sun-Down Papers from the Desk of a School-Master" for the *Long Island Democrat* and continues writing poems.
1841	Walt moves back to Manhattan and begins working at *New World*, a literary weekly founded by Benjamin Park and Dr. Rufus Griswold, both of whom are powerful in the world of literary politics. New World pirates certain British novels by such writers as Dickens, Marryat, Bulder and G.P.R. James. Whitman is simultaneously publishing stories in the *Democratic* Review, the foremost magazine of the Democratic party, joining ranks with such writers as Bryant, Whittier and Major D'Avezac.
1842	In March, Whitman becomes editor of the *New York Aurora*, a Manhattan daily, his editorial columns devoted to high democratic principles. Walt is charmed by the extremes of urban life, the violence of street gangs countered by Emerson's lectures and the accessibility of a

poet such as William Cullen Bryant. Whitman is eventually fired from the *Aurora*, once again being publicly charged with laziness and becomes the editor of the *New York Evening Tattler*. Late in the year, he publishes a temperance novel, *Franklin Evans or the Inebriate*, for the *New World*. For the next few years he works as a journalist, hack writer and minor politician.

1843	Whitman edits the *New York Statesman*.
1844	Whitman edits the *New York Democrat*.
1845	Returns to Brooklyn where he becomes a special contributor to the *Brooklyn Evening Star* where his assignment to Manhattan events includes musical and theatrical engagements.
1846	Walt assumes the editorship of the *Brooklyn Daily Eagle* where he works on most of the literary reviews of such authors as Carlyle, Emerson, Melville, Fuller, Sand and Goethe, to name a few. Like most Democrats, he also supports the Mexican War. At this time, he acquires the habit of a daily swim and shower at a bathhouse.
1848	At the beginning of the year, Walt is fired from the *Brooklyn Daily Eagle* because, like Bryant, he has become a Free-Soiler, opposed to the acquisition of more slave territory. Shortly thereafter, Whitman made a trip to New Orleans, his only extensive trip until much later in life when he goes out West. By the summer, Walt is back in New York writing poetry and, in August, serving as delegate to the Buffalo Free-Soil convention.
1851-52	During these few years, Walt has been influenced by his relationships with a group of Brooklyn artists. He simultaneously develops discrete groups of friends, the roughs and the artists, moving back and forth between them. Walt also becomes a "house builder," acting as a contractor and, at times, working as a carpenter.

The Whitman family returns to Brooklyn and Walt is now living with them once again. He tests their patience by refusing to adhere to a schedule of regular mealtimes, preferring to idle away his time strolling, writing in his room and reading at various libraries. He also undertakes a systematic plan of self-study, making frequent trips to the Egyptian Museum on Broadway where he spends a lot of time conversing with the proprietor. He also becomes a student of astronomy, attending lectures and reading contemporary books, much of which information |

forms the cosmic concepts in *Song of Myself*. Walt also forming distinct opinions about aesthetics and pantheism.

1853   Whitman demonstrates unique poetic ability in a little poem entitled "Pictures." At this point, he has given up newspaper work for carpentry.

1854   Walt gives up carpentry and focuses on his writing.

1855   In the beginning of July, *Leaves of Grass* goes on sale, the title page of which contains an engraving of a working man at leisure, shirt open at the neck, an image in stark contrast to the intense and complex poetry contained within. Having just read this new volume of poems, Ralph Waldo Emerson writes to Whitman congratulating him "at the beginning of a great career." And the prefatory essay to the *Leaves of Grass* is likewise as bold and daring, focusing on the sort of poet America required and the kind of poetry that America could expect from him.

Nevertheless, the publication of *Leaves of Grass* does not bring immediate success to Walt Whitman. As weeks pass, Whitman takes the audacious liberty of writing some reviews himself although they are published anonymously. Walt's father dies shortly after *Leaves of Grass* appears, and Walt is left responsible for supporting his mother and feeble-minded brother.

1856   Bronson, Alcott, Thoreau and others visit Whitman at his house in Brooklyn. In September, publishes the second edition of *Leaves of Grass*, some of the new poems reflect the nationalism of the election year. Among these poems is the "Sun-Down Poem," later renamed *Crossing Brooklyn Ferry*. The new edition flaunts Emerson's congratulatory letter and states Whitman's determination to establish a national identity for himself.

1857-59 Whitman's statements on the national crisis over slavery are published in the *Brooklyn Daily Times*. Whitman also working on a political, sexual and poetic program that he could use as a wandering lecturer, thereby satisfying his love of the open road and good camaraderie. Nevertheless, Whitman would only lecture locally. Writes another group of twelve poems, *Live Oak, with Moss*, which tells the story of his love for another man.

1860   Early in the year he receives an encouraging letter from the Boston publishing firm, Thayer & Eldridge. In May, Whitman publishes a third edition of *Leaves of Grass* which includes a cluster of twelve poems which focus on the amative love of a man for a woman, entitled *Enfans d'Adam*, and yet another cluster of forty-five poems about male love under the title *Calamus*. Emerson invites Whitman to Boston and tries to introduce him to such literary notables as Longfellow, Holmes and Lowell, all of whom objected.

1862   Whitman serves as a nurse to soldiers in Brooklyn hospitals. Just before Christmas, he goes to Washington to care for his wounded brother George and stayed on to help as many of the young soldiers as he could. Looking older than his age, he is a benign father figure to many of the young men on whom he bestows great sympathy and love.

1863   Whitman begins serves as a copyist n the army paymaster's office and serves as a nurse to soldiers in Washington hospitals. On December 3, Andrew Jackson Whitman dies.

1864   Whitman moves to Brooklyn.

1865   Publishes the *Drum-Taps* collection of war poems, which included "When Lilacs Last in the Dooryard Bloom'd" his masterpiece which followed Lincoln's assassination. Nevertheless, despite Whitman's patriotism and heroic efforts, when the new secretary at the Department of the Interior is given a newly revised version of *Leaves of Grass*, Whitman is fired for his explicit treatment of sexual themes.

1866   Whitman's devoted friend, William O'Connor, finds him a job in the attorney general's office, a position which he would hold for several years. O'Connor soon becomes a disciple, writing *The Good Gray Poet: A Vindication*, a book resembling hagiography as Whitman is identified with Jesus.

1867   *Enfans d'Adam*, renamed *Children of Adam*. Fourth edition of *Leaves of Grass* published.

1868   Early in the year, William Michael Rossetti publishes a British edition of *Leaves of Grass*, the effect of which created an audience of English admirers.

1870   Publishes *Democratic Vistas*, which looks to the future of democracy and democratic literature in America and *Passage to India*, both of which are dated 1871. Jesse Whitman dies.

1871   Meets Peter Doyle, a young streetcar driver and forms an emotional relationship with him. Publishes another edition of *Leaves of Grass*, which includes an assemblage of old and new poems in a new section entitled *Passage to India*. Fifth edition of *Leaves of Grass* published.

1872	Whitman publishes *As a Strong Bird on Pinions Free and Other Poems*.
1873	Early in 1873, Whitman's Washington years drew to a close following a gradual decline in his reputation as well as having suffered a paralytic stroke. His mother having died a few months later in May, Whitman returns to Camden, New Jersey to live temporarily with his brother George. His convalescence is a lonely experience and he is isolated from the intellectual stimulation of his friends and the emotional support of Peter Doyle.
1874	Government decides not to hold Whitman's job any longer, forcing him to become dependent upon sporadic publications in newspapers and magazines.
1876	Centennial edition of *Leaves of Grass* (a reissue of the 1871 edition) captures the attention of some English admirers and brings in funds from new subscribers. The Centennial edition also causes the American public to take notice that the invalid poet was achieving international acclaim from such writers as Alfred, Lord Tennyson, England's poet laureate. Whitman also publishes *Two Rivulets Including Democratic Vistas*, *Centennial Songs*, and *Passage to India* in January and *Memoranda During the War* in April.
1879	Whitman leaves on a trip to the West, traveling as far as Denver and returning home in January, 1880.
1880	During the summer, Whitman visits Richard Maurice Bucke, a physician and the superintendent of an insane asylum in London, Ontario.
1881	Sixth edition of *Leaves of Grass* published by the Boston firm of James R. Osgood & Co. Whitman lectures on Abraham Lincoln in Boston in April. In September and October, he visits Ralph Waldo Emerson in Concord.
1882	Boston district attorney threatens to prosecute the publication of *Leaves of Grass* on grounds of obscenity, and in April, Osgood withdraws it from sale. Sixth edition of *Leaves of Grass* is reprinted in Philadelphia. In October, publishes *Specimen Days & Collect*, mainly a personal account of one who experienced the great national events of his day while, at the same time, paying close attention to nature and his own well-being.
1883	Richard Maurice Bucke publishes his *Walt Whitman* during the summer.

1884	Whitman buys his own house on Mickle Street in Camden, New Jersey at the age of sixty-five, for the first time sleeping under his own roof.
1885	Whitman suffers a stroke in September.
1886	Seventh edition of *Leaves of Grass* is published in England.
1891-92	"Deathbed" edition of *Leaves of Grass*, which includes two new groups of poems, *Sands of Seventy* (from *November Boughs* published in 1888) and *Good-by My Fancy* (from the 1891 collection of that name).
1892	Whitman dies in Camden. In the spirit of living as he chose and dictating the terms of his ceremonial death, Whitman commissions a mausoleum, and even invites reporters and friends to spread the word about this monumental tribute to himself. Nevertheless, convinced that he is the victim of fraud, he is only able to pay for part of his monument, leaving his attorney, Thomas Harned, to pay for most of it out of his own pocket. A few weeks before Whitman's death, his physician, William Bucke, is relieved that the debt for this monument had finally been settled, stating that "[a]ll seems to be clearing off for the final scene which cannot now be much delayed."

Contributors

HAROLD BLOOM is Sterling Professor of the Humanities at Yale University and Henry W. and Albert A. Berg Professor of English at the New York University Graduate School. He is the author of over 20 books, including *Shelley's Mythmaking* (1959), *The Visionary Company* (1961), *Blake's Apocalypse* (1963), *Yeats* (1970), *A Map of Misreading* (1975), *Kabbalah and Criticism* (1975), *Agon: Toward a Theory of Revisionism* (1982), *The American Religion* (1992), *The Western Canon* (1994), and *Omens of Millennium: The Gnosis of Angels, Dreams, and Resurrection* (1996). *The Anxiety of Influence* (1973) sets forth Professor Bloom's provocative theory of the literary relationships between the great writers and their predecessors. His most recent books include *Shakespeare: The Invention of the Human*, a 1998 National Book Award finalist, and *How to Read and Why*, which was published in 2000. In 1999, Professor Bloom received the prestigious American Academy of Arts and Letters Gold Medal for Criticism.

ROBERT J. SCHOLNICK is a Professor of English at the College of William and Mary. He is the author of "'The Last Letter of All': Reese, Stedman, and Poetry in Late-Nineteenth-Century America" (1999) "'The Original Eye': Whitman, Schelling and the Return to Origins" (1994).

WILLIAM E. McMAHON has been a Professor in the Philosophy Department at the University of Akron, Ohio. He is the author of "Some Formal Aspects of Aristotelian Componential Semantics" (1990) and "Albert the Great on the Semantics of the Categories of Substance, Quantity and Quality" (1980).

ZONG-QI CAI is a Professor in the Asian Languages and Literature Department at the University of Illinois in Urbana. He is the author of "In Quest of Harmony: Plato and Confucius on Poetry" (1999) and "In Quest of Harmony: Plato and Confucius on Poetry" (1999).

MARK BAUERLEIN is Professor of English at Emory University in Atlanta, Georgia. He is the author of "Political Dreams, Economic Woes, and Inquiry in the Humanities" (2000) and "The Pragmatic Mind: Explorations in the Psychology of Belief" (1997).

HERBERT J. LEVINE has held teaching positions at Brandeis University and Franklin and Marshall College. He is the author of "Beyond Negation: Paradoxical Affirmation in Whitman's Third Edition" (1994).

MARK DeLANCEY is a Professor of English at Loyola University, Chicago. He is the author of "Interpreting Deconstruction: The Cause of Clarity" (1987) and "Some Cameroon Authors in the African Writers Series of Heinemann Educational Books, Ltd." (1976).

GAYLE L. SMITH is a Professor of English at Pennsylvania State University. She is the author of "Jewett, and the Meditative Sublime" (1999) and "The Word and the Thing: Moby-Dick and the Limits of Language" (1985).

WILLIAM BIRMINGHAM has taught humanities at the Touro College School of General Studies, New York City. He edited *Cross Currents: Exploring the Implications of Christianity for Our Times* (1989).

DANA PHILLIPS is a Professor of English at the University of Pennsylvania. He is the officer of "Is Nature Necessary" (1994) and "Nineteenth-Century Racial Thought and Whitman's 'Democratic Ethnology of the Future'" (1994).

W.C. HARRIS is completing a Ph.D. at The Johns Hopkins University. He is the author of "Edgar Allan Poe's "Eureka" and the Poetics of Constitution" (2000) and "Running 'Out of Bounds': The Search for Models of Bodily and Social Conduct in Francis Parkman's *The Oregon Trail*" (1997).

MICHAEL D. SOWDER is a Professor of English at the University of Evansville in Indiana. He is the author of "Walt Whitman, The Apostle" (1999).

BILL HARDWIG is the author of *A Rule of Thumb: Objectivity, Racial Classification and the Politics of Gender* (doctoral dissertation, 2001).

Bibliography

Allen, Gay Wilson. *The Solitary Singer: A Critical Biography of Walt Whitman*. New York: Macmillan, 1995: New York University Press, 1967.

———, ed. *Walt Whitman Abroad*: Critical Essays from Germany, Scandinavia, France Russia, Italy, Spain, Latin American, Israel, Japan and India. Syracuse, N.Y.: Syracuse University Press, 1955).

———, *Walt Whitman as Man, Poet and Legend*. With a Check List of Whitman Publications 1945-1960 by Evie Allison Allen. Carbondale, Ill.: Southern Illinois University Press, 1961.

Altieri, Charles. "Spectacular Antispectacle: Ecstasy and Nationality in Whitman and His Heirs. *American Literary History* 11, no. 1 (1999 Spring): 34-62.

Aspiz, Harold. *Walt Whitman and The Body Beautiful*. Urbana: University of Illinois Press, 1980.

Asselineau, Roger. *The Evolution of Walt Whitman: The Development of a Personality*. Cambridge, Mass.: Harvard University Press, 1960.

———, *The Evolution of Walt Whitman: The Creation of a Book*. Cambridge, Mass.: Harvard University press, 1962.

Bailey, John C. *Walt Whitman*. New York: Macmillan, 1926.

Bauerlein, Mark. "The Written Orator of 'Song of Myself': A Recent Trend in Whitman Criticism." *Walt Whitman Review* 3, no. 3 (Winter 1986): 1-14.

Bradley, Sculley. "The Fundamental Metrical Principle in Whitman's Poetry," *American Poetry* X (January 1939): 437-59.

Canby, Henry Seidel. *Walt Whitman, an American: A study in Biography*. Boston: Houghton Mifflin, 1943.

Chase, Richard. *Walt Whitman Reconsidered*. New York: William Sloan, 1955.

Clancy, Barbara M. "'If He Be Not Himself the Age Transfigured': The Poet, the 'Cultivating Class', and Whitman's 1855 'Song of Myself.'" *Walt Whitman Quarterly Review* 14, no. 1 (Summer 1996): 21-38.

Clifton, Joseph Furness. *Walt Whitman's Workshop*. Cambridge: Harvard University Press, 1928.

Cmiel, Kenneth. *Democratic Eloquence: The Fight over Popular Speech in Nineteenth Century America*. New York: Morrow, 1990.

Colwell, Anne. "'They'll Hear It': W.D. Snodgrass, Walt Whitman and the Construction of America." *Tuned and Under Tension: The Recent Poetry of W.D. Snodgrass*, Philip Raisor, ed. Newark: University of Delaware Press, 1998.

Daiches, David. "Walt Whitman as Innovator," *The Young Rebel in American Literature*, ed. Carl Bode. London: Heinemann, 1959.

————, "Walt Whitman: Impressionist Prophet," *Leaves of Grass One Hundred Years After*, ed. Milton Hindus, Palo Alto: Stanford University Press, 1955.

De Selincourt, Basil. *Walt Whitman: A Critical Study*. London: Martin Secker, 1914.

Dressman, Michael Rowan. "Walt Whitman's Plans for the Perfect Dictionary." Joel Myerson, ed., *Studies in the American Renaissance*. Boston: Twayne, 1979: 457-74.

Drinnon, Richard. *Facing West: The Metaphysics of Indian-Hating and Empire Building*. New York: Meridian, 1980.

Erkkila, Betsy and Jay Grossman, eds. *Breaking Bounds: Whitman and American Cultural Studies*. New York: Oxford University Press, 1996.

Faner, Robert D. *Walt Whitman and Opera*. Philadelphia: University of Pennsylvania Press, 1951.

Fauset, Hugh l'Anson. *Walt Whitman: Poet of Democracy*. London: Jonathan Cape, 1942.

Furness, Clifton Joseph. "Walt Whitman Looks at Boston," *New England Quarterly* 1 (1928): 353-70.

Folsom, Ed. *Walt Whitman's Native Representations*. New York: Cambridge University Press, 1994.

Fredrickson, Robert S. "Public Onanism: Whitman's Song of Himself." *Modern Language Quarterly* 46, no. 2 (1985): 143-60.

Gilbert, George. *Photography: The Early Years*. New York: Harper & Row, 1980.

Gravil, Richard. "'The Discharged Solider' and 'the Runaway Slave': Wordsworth and the Definition of Walt Whitman." *Symbiosis* 1, no. 1 (April 1997): 48-68.

Greenspan, Ezra, ed. *The Cambridge Companion to Walt Whitman*. Cambridge; New York: Cambridge University Press, 1995.

———. *Walt Whitman and the American Reader*. Cambridge; New York: Cambridge University Press, 1990.

Holloway, Emory. *Whitman: An Interpretation in Narrative*. New York: Knopf, 1926.

Jarrell, Randall. "Some Lines from Whitman," *Poetry and the Age*. New York: Knopf, 1953.

Kaplan, Justin. *Walt Whitman: A Life*. New York: Simon & Schuster, 1980.

Kummings, Donald D. and J.R. LeMaster, eds. *Walt Whitman: An Encyclopedia*. New York: Garland, 1998.

———, ed. *Approaches to Teaching Whitman's "Leaves of Grass."* New York: Modern Language Association of America, 1990.

Lewis, R. W. B., ed. *The Presence of Walt Whitman*. New York: Columbia University Press, 1962.

Loving, Jerome. *Walt Whitman: The Song of Himself*. Berkeley: University of California Press, 1999.

———. *Emerson, Whitman, and the American Muse*. Chapel Hill: University of North Carolina Press, 1982.

Middlebrook, Diane Wood. *Walt Whitman and Wallace Stevens*. Ithaca and London: Cornell University Press, 1974.

Miller, Edwin Haviland, ed. *The Artistic Legacy of Walt Whitman*. New York: New York University Press, 1970.

Miller, James E., Jr. *A Critical Guide to "Leaves of Grass."* Chicago: University of Chicago Press, 1957.

Orvell, Miles. *The Real Thing: Imitation and Authenticity in American Culture, 1880-1940*. Chapel Hill: University of North Carolina Press, 1989.

Pearce, Roy Harvey. *The Continuity of American Poetry*. Princeton: Princeton University Press, 1961.

Pollak, Georgiana. "The Relationship of Music to 'Leaves of Grass,'" *College English* XV (April 1954): 384-394.

Myerson, Joel. *Walt Whitman: a Descriptive Bibliography*. Pittsburgh: University of Pittsburgh Press, 1993.

Salska, Agnieszka. *Walt Whitman and Emily Dickinson: Poetry of the Central Consciousness*. Philadelphia: University of Pennsylvania Press, 1985.

Sarracino, Carmine. "Silence as Argument in 'Song of Myself.'" *Studies in Mystical Literature* 2 no. 1 (1982 January): 35-59.

Schmidgall, Gary. *Walt Whitman: A Gay Life*. New York: Dutton, 1997.

Spigelman, Julia. "Walt Whitman and Music," *South Atlantic Quarterly* XLI (April 1942): 167-76.

Stovall, Floyd. *The Foreground of Leaves of Grass*. Charlottesville: UP of Virginia, 1974.

Swayne, Mattie. "Whitman's Catalogue Rhetoric," *University of Texas Studies in English* XXI (1941): 162-78.

Thomas, M. Wynn. "'Song of Myself' and Possessive Individualism." *Delta* 16 (May 1983): 3-17.

Trachtenberg, Alan. *The Incorporation of America: Culture and Society in the Gilded Age*. New York: Hill, 1982.

Van Doren, Mark. "The Poet," in Walt Whitman: Man, Poet, Philosopher: Three Lectures ... Washington, D.C.: Library of Congress, 1955.

Wardrop, Daneen. "Whitman as Furtive Mother: The Supplementary Jouissance of the 'Ambushed Womb' in 'Song of Myself.'" *Texas Studies in Literature and Language* 40, no. 2 (Summer 1998): 142-57.

Ware, Lois. "Poetic Conventions in Leaves of Grass," *Studies in Philology* XXCI, (January 1929): 47-57.

Waskow, Howard J. *Whitman: Explorations in Form*. Chicago: University of Chicago Press, 1966.

Weathers, Willie T. "Whitman's Poetic Translations of His 1855 Preface," *American Literature* XIX (March 1947): 21-40.

Zitter, Emmy Stark. "Song of the Canon: Song of Solomon and 'Song of Myself.'" *Walt Whitman Review* 5, no. 2 (Fall 1887): 8-15.

Zweig, Paul. *Walt Whitman: The Making of the Poet*. New York: Basic Books, Inc., 1984.

Acknowledgments

"'The Password Primeval': Whitman's Use of Science in 'Song of Myself'" by Robert J. Scholnick. From *Studies in the American Renaissance* (1986). © 1986 by Robert T. Scholnick. Reprinted by permission.

"Grass and Its Mate in 'Song of Myself'" by William E. McMahon. From *South Atlantic Review* 51, no. 1 (January 1986): 41-55. © William E. McMahon. Reprinted by permission.

"Hegel's Phenomenological Dialectic and the Structure of Whitman's 'Song of Myself'" by Zong-qi Cai. From *CLIO*, vol. 16, no. 4 (Summer 1987). © 1988 by Henry Kozicki. Reprinted by permission.

"Whitman's Language of the Self" by Mark Bauerlein. From *American Imago*, vol. 44, no. 2 (Summer 1987). © 1988 by Mark Bauerlein. Reprinted by permission.

"Union and Disunion in 'Song of Myself'" by Herbert J. Levine. From *American Literature*, vol. 59, no. 4 (December 1987). © 1987 by Duke University Press. Reprinted by permission.

"'Song of Myself' as Whitman's American Bible" by Herbert J. Levine. From *Modern Language Quarterly*, vol. 48, no. 2 (June 1987). © 1987 by Duke University Press. Reprinted by permission.

"Texts, Interpretations, and Whitman's 'Song of Myself'" by Mark DeLancey. From *American Literature* 61, no. 3 (October 1989). © 1989 by the Duke University Press. Reprinted by permission.

"Reading 'Song of Myself': Assuming What Whitman Assumes" by Gayle L. Smith. From *American Transcendental Quarterly* vol. 6, no. 3 (September 1992). © 1992 University of Rhode Island, Kingston, RI.

Originally published in ATQ. Reprinted by permission of The University of Rhode Island.

"Whitman's Song of the Possible American Self" by William Birmingham. From *Cross Currents*, vol. 43, no. 3 (Fall 1993). © 1993 by the Association for Religion and Intellectual Life. Reprinted by permission.

"Whitman and Genre: The Dialogic in 'Song of Myself'" by Dana Phillips. From *Arizona Quarterly*, vol. 50, no. 3 (Autumn 1994). © 1994 by the Arizona Board of Regents. Reprinted by permission.

"Whitman's *Leaves of Grass* and the Writing of a New American Bible" by W.C. Harris. From *Walt Whitman Quarterly Review*, vol. 16, nos. 3/4 (Winter/Spring 1999). ©1999 by The University of Iowa. Reprinted by permission.

"Walt Whitman, The Apostle" by Michael D. Sowder. From *Walt Whitman Quarterly Review*, vol. 16, nos. 3/4 (Winter/Spring 1999). © 1999 by The University of Iowa. Reprinted by permission.

"Walt Whitman and the Epic Tradition: Political and Poetic Voices in 'Song of Myself'" by Bill Hardwig. From *Walt Whitman Quarterly Review*, vol. 17, no. 4 (Spring 2000). © 2000 by The University of Iowa. Reprinted by permission.

Index

on catalogs, 203-204

on celebrating himself and creation, 28

his childhood, 90-91

the common man, 272

on death, 231

as a Democrat, 260

and desire to be an orator, 248

on devine purpose, 59

on dialogue, 198

dualism, 65-66

on egalitaranism, 125

his egotistical style, 88

the Emersonian experience, 151-152

and equality, 27

on evolution in poetry, 14

his exploring the subconscious, 41

on his grammar, 163-166

the healing role of "Song of Myself", 105

identity in, 129

on Jesus, 131

on language and reality, 170

his law, 134

and lyric poetry, 199

on marriage of body and soul, 113

his materialism, 186-187

on meaning of the grass, 113

on the "me myself", 89

as model of the Union, 136

on his new Bible, 229

the new science, 46

his "open road", 275

on his poems after the war, 101

on preserving the Union, 106

his realized self, 183

on his relationship with the reader, 171-172

on sexual equality, 262

on his sexuality, 91

his similarities to Youmans, 16

on slavery, 106, 109

his speaking for all people, 107

the symbolic grass, 59-60

on theological authority, 225-226

his truth, 154-155

on his value of revolution, 266

the Wordsworthian experience, 151-152

Walt Whitman and the Body Beautiful, (Aspiz), 14

"Whoever You Are Holding Me Now In Hand", 252

Who Speaks in Whitman's Poems?, (Breitweiser), 95

Williams, William Carlos, 94

Wilmot, David
on slavery, 263

Wilmot Proviso (1847), 106

Wofford, Suzanne
on ideology in epic poetry, 256

Words, 163, 165-166
on language and reality, 170

Wordsworth, William, 153
and the past, 154-155
the soul, 151
on unity, 152

World's Progress, The (Putnam), 17

Wyckoff, William
formed the American and Foreign Bible Society, 228
as minister-scholar, 233

Yeats, 66

Youmans, Edward Livingston, 15, 20, 35
the brain, 42
his early life in New York, 16
on education, 40
on evolution, 21
as founder of *Popular Science Monthly*, 18
on health, 31
human sexuality, 36
on introducing Whitman to contemporary science, 51
as lyceum lecturer, 17